Reinterpreting the French Revolution

This book provides a synthesis of the most recent scholarly literature on the diplomatic, political, social, economic, and cultural history of eighteenth-century and revolutionary France. On the basis of that synthesis and current theoretical writing on major modern revolutions, Bailey Stone argues that the outbreak of the French Revolution, and the dramatic developments of the subsequent ten years, were attributable to the interacting pressures of international and domestic politics on those national leaders attempting to govern France and to modernize its institutions. The book furthermore contends that the revolution of 1789–99, reconceptualized in this fashion, needs to be placed in the larger contexts of "early modern" and "modern" French history and modern "progressive" sociopolitical revolutions. In staking out these positions, Stone offers a unique interpretation of the French Revolution, one that dissents from both the Marxist socioeconomic orthodoxy of earlier times and more recent "political-cultural" analyses.

Bailey Stone is a professor of history at the University of Houston. His previous books include *The Parlement of Paris, 1774–1789; The French Parlements and the Crisis of the Old Regime*; and *The Genesis of the French Revolution: A Global-Historical Interpretation.*

Reinterpreting the French Revolution

A global-historical perspective

BAILEY STONE

University of Houston

CAMBRIDGE
UNIVERSITY PRESS

CAMBRIDGE UNIVERSITY PRESS
Cambridge, New York, Melbourne, Madrid, Cape Town, Singapore, São Paulo

Cambridge University Press
The Edinburgh Building, Cambridge CB2 8RU, UK

Published in the United States of America by Cambridge University Press, New York

www.cambridge.org
Information on this title: www.cambridge.org/9780521811477

First published 2002

A catalogue record for this publication is available from the British Library

Library of Congress Cataloguing in Publication data
Stone, Bailey, 1946–
Reinterpreting the French Revolution: a global-historical perspective / Bailey Stone.
p.   cm.
Includes bibliographical references and index.
ISBN 0–521–81147–3 – ISBN 0–521–00999–5 (pbk.)
1. France – History – Revolution, 1789–1799 – Causes.   2. France – History – Revolution,
1789–1799 – Historiography.   3. World politics – To 1900.   I. Title.
DC138 .S77 2002   2002071509

ISBN 978-0-521-81147-7 hardback
ISBN 978-0-521-00999-7 paperback

Transferred to digital printing 2008

Contents

Acknowledgments

I wish first of all to acknowledge my indebtedness to all those individuals laboring in the trenches of old regime and French Revolutionary studies. They may or may not be able to endorse the analysis I put forth upon these pages; at the very least, however, I want them to realize how grateful I am to have been able to cite from such a rich literature in this field of historical scholarship.

I also acknowledge, in a more specific fashion, the encouragement and advice I have received from certain colleagues in the profession since taking up this project in 1993. I am in particular thinking here of Robert R. Palmer, Harold T. Parker, Dale Van Kley, Robert Darnton, Albert N. Hamscher, Hugh Ragsdale, Marie Donaghay, Marsha Frey, and Thomas E. Kaiser in the United States; and Jeremy Black, Colin Jones, and Robin Briggs in the United Kingdom. Probably I should mention others as well – including a number of specialists at recent meetings of the Society for French Historical Studies to whom I have explained some of my evolving ideas on the genesis, process, and ramifications of the French Revolution.

Recognition is due as well to the administration of the University of Houston and to my associates in the Department of History at UH. A Pratt Fellowship from the university enabled me to spend the fall 1993 semester embarking upon the reading required for this synthesis. A University of Houston Faculty Development Leave Grant subsequently made it possible for me to pursue my project unburdened by the usual academic responsibilities during the 1995–96 academic year. My colleagues in the History Department's research colloquium have at various times provided invaluable critical reactions to ideas destined to be elaborated in this book.

I am grateful as well to Frank Smith, Publishing Director for Social Sciences at Cambridge University Press in New York City, to his editorial associates, and to the anonymous readers of my manuscript for their roles in its acceptance and preparation for publication.

Finally – in connection with this project as with all my earlier projects – much is also owed to some very special people in the private precincts of my life. Again, as before: they know who they are.

Introduction

The Bicentennial of the French Revolution may have given rise to a flood of commemorative activities, but it has not left in its wake any scholarly consensus on the causation, development, and implications of that vast upheaval. To the contrary, historians barely finished with the pleasurable work of interring a Marxist view of the Revolution regnant in the first half of the twentieth century have turned their spades upon each other, all the while trying to establish their own explanations of cataclysmic events in the France of 1789–99. This book certainly does not expect to restore consensus in a field beset by such controversy, but it can at least hope to put forth some distinctive ideas on the subject. More specifically, it will contend that the Revolution broke out, and unfolded in the way it did, primarily because of competing international and domestic pressures on French governance in the late eighteenth century. By placing the revolutionary experience in such a broad spatial setting, as well as in the broadest possible temporal setting of modern world history, this book aims to present its case in genuinely "global-historical" terms.

Since this study is heavily indebted to the enormous historical and sociological literature on the revolutionary era, a few observations about the debate arising from that literature are first of all in order. We can then outline the argument that is to follow and spell out some of the capital assumptions undergirding that argument.

As intimated above, research and writing on the revolutionary period in France has long mirrored suppositions that were more or less Marxist in nature. Historians laboring in the long shadows cast by Jean Jaurès, Albert Mathiez, and Georges Lefebvre comfortably assumed that behind the collapse of the Bourbons' rule in the late eighteenth century loomed a struggle between an economically retrograde, "feudal" aristocracy and a progressive, "capitalist" bourgeoisie. The entrepreneurial interests, backed at critical junctures by urban artisans and shopkeepers and rural peasantry,

1

"won" the resultant contest for power in the tempestuous 1790s and would proceed to create nineteenth-century France in their own dynamic image. Thus, the dramatic seizure of political power in this revolutionary situation by profit-oriented bourgeois pointed to the even more fundamental phenomenon of structural *economic* change in French society.[1]

Paradoxically, the very success of this venerable thesis in provoking debate and innovative research has proven its undoing. Today there are few scholars on the various "cutting edges" of French Revolutionary studies who still subscribe to the socioeconomic orthodoxy of old.[2] They can report all too easily that there was no demonstrable correlation between economic and social roles in the *ancien régime*: noncapitalist "bourgeois" outnumbered capitalist bourgeois, and there were entrepreneurial as well as economically conservative nobles. They can point up the oversimplicity of the notion of sequential "class" insurgencies precipitating revolutionary change in France in 1788 and 1789. They can also show that the assemblies and committees of the decade of upheaval drew their personnel primarily from the staid worlds of bureaucracy and the law rather than from the adventurous marches of capitalism. And, perhaps most decisively, these revisionists can assure us that the economic ancien régime in France actually *outlasted* the sociopolitical old regime by a good half-century or more. In summation, there probably can be no cogent demonstration for France of systemic sociopolitical change grounded in transformative *economic* change.

So far, so good. Yet (predictably, perhaps) those who reject the old paradigm have found that it is one thing to participate in the demolition of an obsolete edifice and quite another to raise a durable structure in its place.

At this point, a broader question may first interpose itself: whether there is really any way to explain the Revolution convincingly *as one unified phenomenon*, from causes to consequences. Did Lefebvre and historians of similar persuasion err, not only in the specific sense of positing the centrality to the French Revolution of socioeconomics, but also in the more general sense of supposing that the gestation, process, and ultimate import of the Revolution are all explicable in the same terms? We will have to deal with this broader issue in due time. For the moment, however, we need to confine ourselves to asking what, specifically, the revisionist critics of the Marxist explanation of the events running from 1789 to the Bonapartist coup d'état of 1799 have been able to insert in its place.

---

1 The classic statement of this thesis, at least for American readers, remains Georges Lefebvre, *The Coming of the French Revolution*, trans. Robert R. Palmer (Princeton, N.J.: Princeton University Press, 1947).

2 For a very competent review of the literature on the specific question of the *causes* of the French Revolution, refer to the initial, historiographical section of William Doyle, *Origins of the French Revolution*, 3d ed. (New York: Oxford University Press, 1999).

The answer to this latter query seems to be: nothing fully adequate. Some contributors to the debate, while discarding the concept of an upheaval consecrating the triumph of capitalism, have tried to retain something of the social emphasis inevitably associated with that concept. Hence, Alfred Cobban, writing in 1964 and essentially turning the Marxist theory upon its head by accentuating the anticapitalist biases of the Revolution, held that "the revolutionary bourgeoisie was primarily the declining class of *officiers* and . . . lawyers and other professional men."[3] Such individuals, rather than commercial and industrial figures, dominated the bureaucracy and legislatures of the revolutionary years. Other authors – and here, revisionists like Denis Richet and Guy Chaussinand-Nogaret come most readily to mind – have contended that a vanguard of educated, landowning "notables" issuing from clergy, nobility, and Third Estate seized the helm of public affairs in 1789. Theirs was a *révolution des lumières*, a "revolution of enlightened notables," helped along, admittedly, by atrocious short-term economic conditions that furnished these respectable Frenchmen with daunting allies from society's plebeian ranks. Once the hurricane was over, these propertied notables would come fully and safely into their own.[4]

These arguments may have refined our understanding of social developments in the revolutionary era, but they have also proven problematic in their turn. Cobban's *officiers* seem upon closer examination to have been prospering for the most part, or at the very least holding their own, rather than "declining" on the eve of 1789. Moreover, they apparently made up a steadily *diminishing* proportion of active revolutionaries as the 1790s unfolded.[5] More seriously, perhaps, scholars have come increasingly to question the whole notion of elite solidarity in the advent and process of the Revolution. Richet himself had to allow that in the crucible of events defining 1789 the propertied *lumières* abruptly fell out over what he called the "problem of privilege" – that is, over what economic and social prerogatives to preserve, curtail, or abrogate altogether.[6] Other specialists, investigating the tumultuous years that followed, have conceded – ironically – that there are still good reasons to stress the continuing importance of social tensions

---

3 Alfred Cobban, *The Social Interpretation of the French Revolution* (Oxford: Oxford University Press, 1964), p. 67.
4 Refer to Denis Richet, "Autour des origines idéologiques lointaines de la Révolution française: Elites et despotisme," *Annales: E. S. C.* 24 (1969): 1–23; and Guy Chaussinand-Nogaret, *La Noblesse au XVIIIe siècle. De la féodalite aux lumières* (Paris: Hachette, 1976).
5 On the former point, see William Doyle, "The Price of Offices in Pre-Revolutionary France," *Historical Journal* 27 (1984): 831–60. He has recently returned to this and some related issues in *Venality: The Sale of Offices in Eighteenth-Century France* (New York: Oxford University Press, 1996). The latter point is made repeatedly by, among others, Lynn Hunt, in her provocative study *Politics, Culture, and Class in the French Revolution* (Berkeley: University of California Press, 1984).
6 Richet, "Autour des origines idéologiques," p. 23.

and conflict among the notables.[7] Indeed, a kind of "rediscovery" of conflictual social dynamics in the revolutionary era has figured prominently in the historiography of the last ten years.[8]

However, the most influential tendency among those historians who reject the socioeconomic orthodoxy of earlier days has been to develop and employ an explanatory perspective that concentrates on politics or (more accurately) "political culture" in revolutionary France.

The "rediscovery of politics" in this contentious field was foreshadowed as far back as 1967, when George V. Taylor declared roundly that what France had experienced during the years 1789–99 had in fact been "a political revolution with social consequences and not a social revolution with political consequences."[9] Before long, a number of historians were giving a truly novel twist to the meaning of "politics" in the French Revolution. In the late 1970s François Furet, probably the most influential of these scholars, emerged from a long-running vendetta with Marxists like Albert Soboul and Claude Mazauric to offer a political-ideological explanation of the maelstrom of 1789–99.[10] Furet asserted that new discourses of political legitimacy vied to fill the unforeseen and unprecedented vacuum left in public life by the collapse of the absolute monarchy. From 1789 through the climacteric of the Terror of 1793–94, this increasingly murderous competition of discourses, all proclaiming fealty to the newly sovereign "people," drove the Revolution leftward. For this brief, unforgettable period, ideology was independent of – and, indeed, constitutive of – sociopolitical reality; only after the overthrow of the Robespierrist dictatorship in Thermidor of Year II (July 1794) would "society" reassume its ordinary role as the primary determinant of historical evolution.

Furet's conceptualization of the unfolding of revolution in France has proven very influential – and, by the same token, very controversial. Specialists including Lynn Hunt, Keith Baker, and Emmet Kennedy have contributed enthusiastically to this endeavor to substitute political-cultural forces for the socioeconomic processes of the earlier historiographical school.[11] Moreover, the Bicentennial gave rise to a number of scholarly

---

7 As examples in point, consult Patrice Higonnet, *Class, Ideology, and the Rights of Nobles during the French Revolution* (Oxford: Clarendon Press, 1981); and David Andress, *French Society in Revolution, 1789–1799* (Manchester: Manchester University Press, 1999).

8 A point discussed in detail by (among others) Jack Censer, in "Social Twists and Linguistic Turns: Revolutionary Historiography a Decade after the Bicentennial," *French Historical Studies* 22 (Spring 1999): 139–67.

9 George V. Taylor, "Noncapitalist Wealth and the Origins of the French Revolution," *American Historical Review* 72 (1967), esp. 491–92.

10 François Furet, *Penser la Révolution française* (Paris: Gallimard, 1978). Translated into English by Elborg Forster as *Interpreting the French Revolution* (Cambridge: Cambridge University Press, 1981).

11 See Hunt, *Politics, Culture, and Class*, and, more recently, *The Family Romance of the French Revolution* (Berkeley: University of California Press, 1992); Keith M. Baker,

consortia and collaborative editorial projects through which Furet and like-minded colleagues reiterated their call for a cultural exegesis of revolutionary change in France.[12] True, not all proponents of the new approach endorse Furet's more extreme claims: for instance, they may balk at his contention that the Terror was fully implicit in the ideological "breakthrough" of 1789, and regard with some skepticism his postulation of ideology as an autonomous and constituting historical force up to 1794.[13] Still, they share with Furet the fundamental conviction that the Revolution was, as Lynn Hunt has put it, quintessentially "the moment in which politics was discovered as an enormously potent activity, as an agent for conscious change, as the mold for character, culture, and social relations."[14] And few would deny that they have a compelling and portentous story to tell: the story of how ordinary Frenchmen – and Frenchwomen – fashioned through rhetoric and ritual and raw human action a new identity for themselves in a world briefly and challengingly turned upside down.

We might go so far as to wonder whether we have here the makings of a new explanatory paradigm for the French Revolution. Such speculation, however, is probably premature. Indeed, quite apart from the schism in post-Marxist scholars' ranks over the issue of elite solidarity or discord in revolutionary France – an issue *not* resolved by forays into political-cultural analysis – there exists a potentially even more troublesome question. An institutional historian, Isser Woloch, broached this question in the midst of the Bicentennial euphoria. Woloch took Furet (and a number of his associates) to task for denying that circumstances shaped the revolution and, indeed, for maintaining that revolutionary exigencies could never "justify acts that were inexcusable by ordinary standards of liberal principle or morality."[15] At about the same time, another specialist, David Bien, raised much the same issue in an exchange with Furet himself.[16]

It was perfectly natural for Woloch and Bien to respond to Furet's ideologically driven schema of revolution by emphasizing the pressures of

Inventing the French Revolution (Cambridge: Cambridge University Press, 1990); and Emmet Kennedy, *A Cultural History of the French Revolution* (New Haven, Conn.: Yale University Press, 1989).

12 See, for example, François Furet and Mona Ozouf, eds., *A Critical Dictionary of the French Revolution*, trans. Arthur Goldhammer (Cambridge, Mass.: Harvard University Press, 1989), and Keith Baker et al., eds., *The French Revolution and the Creation of Modern Political Culture*, 4 vols. (Oxford: Pergamon Press, 1987–94).

13 On this point, see, most recently, Michael Scott Christofferson, "An Antitotalitarian History of the French Revolution: François Furet's *Penser la Révolution française* in the Intellectual Politics of the Late 1970s," *French Historical Studies* 22 (Fall 1999): 557–611.

14 Hunt, *Politics, Culture, and Class*, p. 236.

15 See Woloch's review article: "On the Latent Illiberalism of the French Revolution," *American Historical Review* 95 (1990): 1452–70.

16 Refer to the remarks by Woloch and Bien in "François Furet's Interpretation of the French Revolution," *French Historical Studies* 16 (1990): 777–802.

day-to-day circumstances on the revolutionary politicians. Both historians, after all, had been involved for some time in research on the armies of old regime and/or revolutionary France, and both had been sensitized by their research to the influence exerted upon French affairs by those uniquely urgent "circumstances" preceding and attending renewed European warfare in the 1790s.[17]

Then again, both Woloch and Bien could have easily enough cited the concern of earlier historians with larger geopolitical issues too often neglected in recent arguments between Marxists and their detractors. Indeed, a full century ago and more Albert Sorel was surveying the course of events in the 1789–99 period from a European diplomatic-military viewpoint.[18] True, those dominating the landscape of revolutionary historiography for the next half-century, while never losing sight of the great mobilization of French resources against foreign invasion in the 1790s, attributed the drastic sociopolitical changes of those years, in the most basic sense, to the progress of capitalism rather than to geopolitical exigency. Still, Sorel's notion of international affairs as being central to the Revolution has never disappeared entirely from the pertinent scholarly literature. The works of Robert R. Palmer signaled this in the years during and following World War II,[19] and so have syntheses authored in more recent times by Donald Sutherland and William Doyle.[20]

But perhaps the most forthright challenge to historians of both Marxist and post-Marxist vintage has come from the pen of a political sociologist, Theda Skocpol.[21] Writing ten years before the Bicentennial, Skocpol presented a comparative analysis of the French, Russian, and Chinese Revolutions that eschewed all "voluntarist" discussion of systemic changes in society, of "purposive, mass-based movements," of ideological trends, or of aspirations of those outside the conclaves of government. For Skocpol, analysis of the causes, process, and consequences of such great upheavals required a "structuralist" focus on the state, viewed as "a set of

17 See, for example: David Bien, "La Réaction aristocratique avant 1789: L'Example de l'armée," *Annales: E. S. C.* 29 (1974): 23–48 and 505–34, and "The Army in the French Enlightenment: Reform, Reaction, and Revolution," *Past and Present* 85 (1979): 68–98; and Isser Woloch, *The French Veteran from the Revolution to the Restoration* (Chapel Hill: University of North Carolina Press, 1979).

18 Albert Sorel, *L'Europe et la Révolution française*, 8 vols. (Paris: E. Plon, Nourrit et Cie, 1885–1904).

19 Robert R. Palmer, *Twelve Who Ruled: The Year of the Terror in the French Revolution* (Princeton, N.J.: Princeton University Press, 1941); and *The Age of the Democratic Revolution: A Political History of Europe and America*, 2 vols. (Princeton, N.J.: Princeton University Press, 1959–64).

20 See D. M. G. Sutherland, *France, 1789–1815: Revolution and Counterrevolution* (New York: Oxford University Press, 1986), and William Doyle, *The Oxford History of the French Revolution* (Oxford: Clarendon Press, 1989).

21 Theda Skocpol, *States and Social Revolutions: A Comparative Analysis of France, Russia, and China* (Cambridge: Cambridge University Press, 1979).

administrative, policing, and military organizations headed, and more or less well coordinated by, an executive authority." The state, Skocpol maintained, is "potentially autonomous from (though of course conditioned by) socioeconomic interests and structures," and at base is "geared to maintain control of home territories and populations and to undertake actual or potential military competition with other states in the international system." As applied to France, Skocpol's argument turned upon the efforts of the policymakers and administrators of 1789–99 to uphold their country's competitive status abroad through an unprecedentedly thorough utilization of human and material assets on the home front. For this analyst, accordingly, the cardinal bequest of the Revolution to future generations of French citizens was not (as it had always been for the Marxists) a modernized, more capitalist economy nor (as it was soon to become for the political-cultural school) a novel tradition of democratic republicanism, but rather a reconstructed state power equipped for the European and (increasingly) global struggles to come.

This attempt by a political sociologist to account for the cataclysm of 1789–99 within a context of international politics – though with reference as well to domestic forces of socioeconomic change in the countryside – has provoked a legion of criticisms in learned circles. The cultural historian William H. Sewell, Jr., has probably spoken for a very large number of his colleagues in faulting Skocpol for so rigorously shunning any consideration of cultural and ideological forces in the revolutionary process.[22] Lynn Hunt has commented upon the tautological, lock-step nature of Skocpol's model, in which the causes, process, and outcome of revolution are allegedly conflated in such a manner as to make it virtually impossible to appraise the events and personalities of this dramatic period in their own right.[23] Jack Goldstone, like Skocpol a sociologist, has argued for less of a focus upon the wages of (unsuccessful) military competition and more of a stress upon the destabilization of state and society supposedly induced by "the mounting population and inflationary pressures of the eighteenth century."[24] Critics have in addition complained that Skocpol's comparative schema, encompassing as it does revolutionary change in Russia and China as well as in France, overstates in the French case the revolutionary role of the peasantry and underestimates that of bourgeois and humble townspeople.

---

22 See William H. Sewell, Jr., "Ideologies and Social Revolutions: Reflections on the French Case," *Journal of Modern History* 57 (1985): 66–67, 84. But see, in the same issue, Skocpol's reply: "Cultural Idioms and Political Ideologies in the Revolutionary Reconstruction of State Power: A Rejoinder to Sewell," pp. 86–96.
23 See Hunt, *Politics, Culture, and Class,* esp. pp. 221–24.
24 Jack Goldstone, *Revolution and Rebellion in the Early Modern World* (Berkeley: University of California Press, 1991), pp. 208, 211, and 250. Goldstone's stress upon demographic and derivative economic factors is certainly original and stimulating; nonetheless, I think that he vastly overrates their significance.

What such strictures tell us at the very least is that this explanation of major social revolutions, like any similarly ambitious argument, can be challenged from many perspectives. But it is Hunt's and Sewell's reactions that have struck a particularly resonant chord among those toiling in the trenches of French Revolutionary research, since they raise two especially fundamental questions. First, can we unreservedly endorse Theda Skocpol's thesis that the origins, development, and results of this upheaval were essentially cut from the same cloth, and are therefore to be comprehended today in one set of explanatory terms? If this be true, the historian need not worry about playing up the discontinuities in the revolutionary experience, for they turn out to be less deserving of note than underlying historical continuities. Second, there is Skocpol's premise that a "structuralist" account of the maelstrom of 1789–99 hinging upon the interacting realities of statist competition abroad and statist "semiautonomy" at home has to prove more satisfactory than a "voluntarist" perspective keying upon the revolutionary roles of individual actors and/or social groups and/or ideologies. If this is accurate, the historian must concede that it was the French state, pursuing as a bureaucratic entity geostrategic and impersonal objectives, that instigated, carried out, and benefited from the Revolution, and not previously unempowered individuals or groups of individuals inspired by revolutionary ideology.

This latter assumption – that, for analytical purposes, the state can be reified as a historical "actor" imposing its "will" more or less independently upon society – has been especially challenged in the light of recent work in the field. Scholars usually departing from Furetian analyses of political culture have been blazing new paths in hitherto unexplored hinterlands of gender, linguistic analysis, and all that is currently subsumed under the rubric of the "new cultural history." In doing so, they have usefully suggested novel ways of conceptualizing the (French) state. It may yield rich dividends, Suzanne Desan has written, to view the state "more flexibly as a site of structured negotiation over power, resources, and relationships, rather than simply as a coercive entity separate from society." Such an approach, Desan and other sociocultural historians have maintained, would facilitate inquiries into the exceedingly complex relationships between revolutionary institutions and individuals, relationships mediated by the political culture of the period. The considerable ability of the state to structure social behavior and expectations would continue to be recognized even as governmental norms and procedures are portrayed as being themselves conditioned in part by developments within the revolutionary society at large.[25]

---

25 See Suzanne Desan, "What's after Political Culture? Recent French Revolutionary Historiography," *French Historical Studies* 23 (Winter 2000): 163–96.

Such theorizing may indeed provide a needed corrective to the Skocpolian tendency to reify the state – in this case, the French Revolutionary state. In a larger, historiographical sense, of course, observations like these also remind us that no explanatory paradigm currently dominates the field of revolutionary studies. What we seem to have, in the wake of the demise of the old socioeconomic argument, is a somewhat decentralized but no less fruitful dialogue between advocates of one or another brand of "social revisionism," on the one hand, and ever-multiplying proponents of "political-cultural" and "new-cultural" analysis, on the other.

Yet, at the risk of exposing myself to the slings and arrows of informed criticism in this contentious field, I would maintain that there is a way to enlist insights from both the "social revisionists" and the "political-cultural" analysts in the service of an explanation of the French Revolution hinging upon the roles of a carefully redefined French state. For it is certainly arguable that, if subtly conceived, that state can in fact still be seen as crucial to the onset, process, and various outcomes of the Revolution.

On the one hand, no reasonable specialist in this period can deny that the single most pressing reality that those governing or aspiring to govern France had to confront throughout this period was their country's centrality in the evolving European and extra-European struggle for survival, power, and prestige. This was as inescapable a reality for politicians in the radiant dawn of revolution as it had been for their most cynical predecessors in the ancien régime. We need not revert to Albert Sorel's excessively one-sided preoccupation with the international aspects of the Revolution to make this point. We can, however, note with some interest that the recent inquiries of T. C. W. Blanning into the historical forces and diplomatic calculations behind the French Revolutionary wars point in much the same direction.[26] In addition, we can join Blanning in avowing that the international concerns of France's leaders were a thread tying the entire revolutionary era to the years preceding it and the years following it. To a certain limited extent, then, the origins, process, and aftermath of the Revolution *were* cut from the same cloth.

On the other hand, just as no fair-minded observer can deny that the revolutionary leaders from start to finish were burdened with the legacies of past wars, the current needs of national defense, and anticipations of possible conflicts to come, so must that same hypothetical observer view the revolutionaries as caught up also in their own interests and expectations of domestic reform and as responding to every imaginable kind of pressure in French politics and society. Hence, it might be particularly advisable,

---

26 T. C. W. Blanning, *The Origins of the French Revolutionary Wars* (London: Longman, 1986), and, more recently, *The French Revolutionary Wars, 1787–1802* (New York: St. Martin's Press, 1996).

in reassessing the important foreign and domestic policies of the period and retracing the twists and turns of domestic politics, to underscore the complex ways in which those policies and politics, mediated continually by the political culture of the day, mirrored both European *and* uniquely French realities. This is, of course, another way of saying that the French state can only be an effective locus of analysis and vehicle of explanation if it is conceived simultaneously as an initiator of policy and events and as a focal point for political, ideological, and social struggle.

Essentially, what I am proposing to do in this study is to extend to the French Revolution a modified version of the perspective I employed in an earlier book to explain the anterior development, decline, and demise of the old regime.[27] The interpretation, as before, will be synthetic in nature, drawing from the best work in many fields of historiography. Yet it will also be "modified" along the lines indicated above: acknowledging the complexity of revolutionary politics and of state–citizen relationships in this period, it will continually revisit issues of political culture without abandoning a central concern with the roles of governance in France's public affairs. A brief exposition of the argument would seem at this point to be in order.

Chapter 1 will summarize developments in the old regime. It will first review the increasingly global outreach of French foreign policy after 1715 and suggest how, given changes in the European state system, that outreach was probably destined to fail. Next, it will examine the many ways in which the absolute Bourbon monarchy, insufficiently responsive to strategic realities abroad, also proved in the end to be insufficiently responsive to ever-evolving sociopolitical and ideological realities at home. Finally, it will maintain that the convergence of these statist failures lay behind the unprecedented politicization of the citizenry in the "prerevolution" of 1787–88 and ultimately brought about the government's financial collapse in the summer of 1788.

Chapter 2 will reexamine the process of France's descent into full-fledged revolution, from the government's definitive admission of bankruptcy in August 1788 to the removal of both king and self-proclaimed National Assembly from Versailles to Paris in the wake of the October Days of 1789. The argument will require an initial concentration upon the dangers faced by a paralyzed France in a Europe seemingly primed (as usual) for interstate warfare. The chapter will then turn to the domestic crisis of a government shaken by its revelation of bankruptcy and besieged by polarized social "notables" and popular insurgents. It will reappraise

27 Bailey Stone, *The Genesis of the French Revolution: A Global-Historical Interpretation* (New York: Cambridge University Press, 1994).

the differing prescriptions for reform offered by Finance Minister Jacques Necker and Louis XVI and then explain how the political initiative during these transitional months gradually shifted from the crown to the most progressive deputies in the National (Constituent) Assembly.

Chapter 3 will reassess the first attempt to stabilize the Revolution – at this juncture, upon the basis of a constitutional Bourbon monarchy – which lasted from October 1789 through the summer of 1791. Our general thesis will again call for an initial concentration upon the challenges confronting the French government in Europe and overseas. The focus then will shift to the domestic front. Chapter 3 at this point will discuss a number of the most significant institutional and social measures enacted by the Constituent Assembly. It will also query to what extent these reforms reflected the state's multifarious needs and to what extent they resulted from a "domestic" calculus of both "middle-class" interests and more broadly conceived humanitarian concerns. The concluding section of the chapter will deal with the continuing shift of political initiative from the crown and its conservative adherents to the most progressive constituent assemblymen.

Chapter 4 will reassess the "revolutionizing of the Revolution," an especially dramatic phase in the upheaval that commenced more or less with the first Legislative Assembly sessions in October 1791 and ended abruptly with the fall of the emergency Robespierrist dictatorship in Thermidor, Year II (July 1794). It will be even more imperative now to start with a reappraisal of the international situation, for the evolution of French policy and politics during this entire period took place against the constant backdrop of mounting European challenge to the revolutionary experiment. The next section of Chapter 4, like the analogous section in Chapter 3, will not only review the key domestic measures implemented by the revolutionaries but also reevaluate the roles played in the enactment of those policies by statist calculations on the one hand and by class-oriented and/or genuinely altruistic considerations on the other. The closing section of the chapter will revisit the theme of political radicalization, which during this stage of the Revolution played itself out in the factional struggles of the Legislative Assembly and National Convention, and in the horrific political and ideological climax of the Terror.

Chapter 5 will reexamine the second attempt by the French to achieve some degree of revolutionary stability, this time under the republican auspices of the Thermidorian Convention (1794–95) and Directory (1795–99). Analysis will have to bear first of all upon the gradual but momentous shift in French foreign policy from national defense to national aggrandizement, and upon the European reaction to this development. Chapter 5 will then reinterpret the institutional and social policies of the 1794–99 period in terms of the revolutionaries' commingled diplomatic and domestic concerns. It will conclude by returning one last time to the question of political evolution, which in this closing phase of the Revolution expressed itself primarily as a polarization and "militarization" of politics leading directly to the Bonapartist coup of November 1799.

A Conclusion, after briefly restating the central thesis of the study and summarizing the conclusions to be derived from it, will situate the entire revolutionary experience in a broader historical context, with reference to the *longue durée* of early modern, modern, and "contemporary" French (and world) history.

The argument, as outlined above, will "play" the French Revolution as tragedy – but tragedy with a certain ironic twist. At one level, it is easy to view the whole revolutionary experience as demonstrating the relentless durability of *expedience* – the expedience of "bourgeois" class interests, to be sure, but, equally, of French anxieties about and aspirations in Europe – and the ultimate fragility of more altruistic concerns. Whatever some historians may have written, the Revolution was *not* suddenly and fortuitously blown off course as the French turned to massive warfare during the 1790s.[28] In one fashion or another, war inhered in the Revolution from the start, and even before the start: in its causation as well as in its course and its aftermath. The sanguinary Terror of 1793–94 was, in hindsight, implicit not so much in the rhetoric and ideology of the times as in the paramount need of this proud nation to prevail, by whatever desperate means, in the sullied, scarred European world of the late eighteenth century. No faction of politicians could escape from this compelling reality, a reality that from one year to the next came to acquire precedence over all other realities. Whatever the revolutionaries might strive to do for their constituents (and, as we have already noted, our analytical approach obliges us to take account of those ameliorative efforts), they were forced in the end to tailor their dreams and their reforms to statist exigencies even more, perhaps, than to their sense of immediate "class" interest.

At a deeper level of perception, however, the sense of tragedy yields to irony – the irony in the fact that, to one extent or another, *all* persons in the new polity struggling to establish itself had a stake in the restoration of France's stature in the world, whether or not they were aware of this. It may be true that those on the fringes, or beyond the pale, of "civilized" and domiciled society were in fact as indifferent to the Revolution in general as their chronicler Richard Cobb has suggested in many studies.[29] Moreover,

28 An argument put forth by, among others, François Furet and Denis Richet in *The French Revolution*, trans. Stephen Hardman (New York: Macmillan, 1970), esp. chap. 5.
29 See, for example: Richard Cobb, *The Police and the People: French Popular Protest, 1789–1820* (New York: Oxford University Press, 1970); *Reactions to the French Revolution* (New York: Oxford University Press, 1972); and *Paris and Its Provinces, 1792–1802* (New York: Oxford University Press, 1975).

the Revolution insofar as it was a Parisian phenomenon undeniably violated at times the sensibilities (and the material interests) of those in the provinces.[30] Yet again, it is all too obvious that it categorically withheld its most meaningful opportunities, and many of its benefits, from women.[31] Still, even these unfortunates were shielded by the Revolution's military successes from the worst depredations of Europe's other armies (though, on occasion, they were harassed and oppressed by their own troops), and in some instances they genuinely profited from social and economic reforms enacted in this era. As for those adult males definitely sporting the new citizenship, they certainly stood to gain in more concrete ways from innovations that afforded them new civic options while associating them with an eventually triumphant patriotic "cause." The feuding revolutionary leaders, then, if compelled all too often to rob the Peter of socially beneficent expenditure to pay the Paul of military defense and aggrandizement, nevertheless were directly or indirectly serving the interests of Frenchmen (and, yes, politically unenfranchised Frenchwomen too) in *all* walks of life.

We might sound one final cautionary note in this connection. No matter how necessary it may be for our analytical purposes to separate the revolutionary leaders' governmental priorities from all the political and ideological and social issues they had constantly to engage, in the daily affairs of the Revolution these innumerable and conflicting matters could not be so easily sorted out. Still, we can assert in general terms that France's guiding spirits were striving to fashion and control critical foreign and domestic policies even as they themselves were borne upon the tide of clamorous events. And in this, as in much else, the years of upheaval testified both to the dogged continuities of French history and to the exhilarating novelties of revolutionary hopes and actions.

30 This has been pointed out in numerous excellent monographs on the Revolution in the provinces. For one of the most recent of these works, see Alan Forrest, *The Revolution in Provincial France: Aquitaine, 1789–1799* (New York: Oxford University Press, 1996). Our study will have to deal recurrently with the tensions between the capital and the provinces during the revolutionary era.

31 There is a steadily growing corpus of works on the roles of women in the revolutionary era. See, as examples in point: Olwen Hufton, *Women and the Limits of Citizenship in the French Revolution* (Toronto: University of Toronto Press, 1992); Sara Melzer and Leslie Rabine, eds., *Rebel Daughters: Women and the French Revolution* (New York: Oxford University Press, 1992); Shirley E. Roessler, *Out of the Shadows: Women and Politics in the French Revolution, 1789–1795* (New York: Peter Lang, 1996); and Dominique Godineau, *The Women of Paris and the French Revolution*, trans. Katherine Streip (Berkeley: University of California Press, 1998). Many other titles could be added to the list.

1

~~~~~~

The ancien régime: challenges not met, a dilemma not overcome

On 7 September 1782, French foreign minister Charles Gravier, comte de Vergennes, acknowledged in a letter to his eventual successor, Armand-Marc, comte de Montmorin, that England had "in its constitution and in the establishments which it has permitted her to form, resources which are lacking to us." Eight weeks later, the foreign minister again referred to English "advantages which our monarchical forms do not accord us."[1] It is striking that Vergennes, however loyal to his country's absolutist traditions, should nevertheless have ruminated so uneasily upon differences between the constitutional systems of the two rival powers. His reflections point to a basic discrepancy in the old France – that between the far-reaching objectives of its foreign policy and the national means actually marshaled to attain those objectives.

In retrospect, it is clear that those ruling France in the years before 1789 confronted a challenge that in time became an unmanageable dilemma. The challenge was to preserve French influence in an increasingly competitive system of West Eurasian states while at the same time maintaining fiscal, constitutional, and social stability at home. The dilemma was that the pursuit of what became an ever more ambitious foreign policy could not, in the end, be judged strategically realistic – or be squared with the sociopolitical tenets undergirding the ancien régime in France.

The statesmen/politicians of revolutionary France would find themselves similarly bedeviled by the interrelated complexities of foreign and domestic policy. But that is a matter for later chapters to address. For the time being, we shall concern ourselves with the prerevolutionary phase of the story. The following pages first recapitulate the historic drive of the old France toward security and greatness in (and beyond) Europe. The focus

---

1 Cited in Jonathan R. Dull, *The French Navy and American Independence: A Study of Arms and Diplomacy, 1774–1787* (Princeton, N.J.: Princeton University Press, 1978), pp. 304, 316–17.

then will shift to the ways in which the old regime state, in pursuing its goals abroad, became the primary catalyst for *domestic* changes that contravened its own legitimating sociopolitical principles. Finally, we shall reassess the "prerevolution" of 1787–88, seeing in it a convergence of deeply rooted diplomatic, constitutional, and social crises that would soon topple the old regime.

THE PROBLEMATIC DRIVE TOWARD GREATNESS IN THE OLD REGIME

The European state system in which absolutist France had to compete – and which it ever wished to dominate – was manifestly *not* designed for the weak. As Prussia's Frederick the Great put it, harshly but realistically: "the kingdom of heaven ... is won by gentleness; those of this world belong to force."[2] Perhaps more revealing from a French point of view were the remarks of René-Louis de Voyer, marquis d'Argenson. Although reputedly a "philosopher" in public office, d'Argenson could comment in 1739: "A state should always be at the ready, like a gentleman living among swashbucklers and quarrellers. Such are the nations of Europe, today more than ever; negotiations are only a continual struggle between men without principles, impudently aggressive and ever greedy."[3]

The French themselves had long been prominent contributors to this state of affairs. Preoccupied before 1648 with beating off the armies of the Austro-Spanish Habsburgs, they had subsequently assumed an increasingly aggressive European and extra-European role under the long-lived Louis XIV. The Sun King had developed over many years a national tradition meshing ambitions of a continental and mercantile/colonial nature. Moreover, he had stamped this national tradition with the imprimatur of his charismatic reign. If princelings all over Europe scrambled to emulate the *Grand Roi* by raising châteaux and gathering entourages and leading lives styled after his, is it any wonder that French statesmen found it natural in later years to assess their country's needs in terms at least as grandiose as those bequeathed to them by Louis XIV?

France's involvement in the two great mid-eighteenth-century wars witnessed starkly to these realities. The Sun King's ghost – the specter of his long adherence to a foreign policy implying warfare on both land and sea – continued to haunt Versailles.

The first of those conflicts, the War of the Austrian Succession (1740–48), was triggered by the death in 1740 of Holy Roman Emperor Charles VI

---

2 Cited in Rohan Butler, *Choiseul: Father and Son, Vol. 1: 1719–1754* (Oxford: Clarendon Press, 1980), p. 310.
3 Quoted in Derek McKay and H. M. Scott, *The Rise of the Great Powers 1648–1815* (London: Longman, 1983), p. 214.

and the lightning occupation toward the end of that year of Austrian Silesia by Prussia's Frederick the Great. Yet even before events boiled over on the Continent, Great Britain and Spain had drifted into war over tensions in the West Indies – and this was a war in which France was tempted early on to intervene. Louis XV's chief minister, Cardinal André Hercule de Fleury, would have preferred to keep France out of the continental struggle entirely and to bring all French strength to bear against the rival across the Channel.[4] Yet, tellingly, Fleury himself had helped to unleash the dogs of war on land, not only by clandestinely encouraging Bavarian demands on the Habsburgs in the 1730s, but also by appointing the young and bellicose comte de Belle-Isle to represent Versailles among the German states of the empire. Belle-Isle had been charged only with securing the election of a French candidate to the vacant imperial throne; but the count, "who knew that he spoke with the authority of public approval,"[5] exceeded his ministerial mandate by putting together in central Europe a coalition of states (including, eventually, France) that aimed at nothing less than the dismemberment of the Habsburg possessions. In the end, the French, proving true to their past, would try to have it both ways, warring simultaneously on land and sea.

And, just as predictably, many in France saw the strategic stalemate they extracted from involvement in the war of 1740–48 as inadequate. That the French and the British "switched partners" in the so-called Diplomatic Revolution of 1756, with France embracing the traditional continental adversary Austria and England establishing ties with Prussia, was less momentous than the fact that French foreign policy (unlike that of any other power) continued to portend major aggression in both the overseas and the continental arenas. In the midst of the Seven Years' War (1756–63), one diplomatic servant of Louis XV was to articulate to a colleague the philosophy underlying this policy. "The object of the politics of this crown," wrote François-Joachim de Pierre, cardinal de Bernis to Etienne-François, duc de Choiseul, in 1759, "has been and always will be to play in Europe the superior role which suits its seniority, its dignity, and its grandeur; to reduce every power which attempts to force itself above her, whether by trying to take away her possessions, or by arrogating to itself an unjust preeminence, or, finally, by seeking to take away . . . her influence and general credit in the affairs [of Europe]."[6] Inspired by such a canon, the French once

---

4 See Jeremy Black, "French Foreign Policy in the Age of Fleury Reassessed," *English Historical Review* 103 (1988): 359–84.

5 Arthur M. Wilson, *French Foreign Policy during the Administration of Cardinal Fleury, 1726–1743* (Cambridge, Mass.: Harvard University Press, 1936), p. 331.

6 Cited in Orville T. Murphy, *Charles Gravier, Comte de Vergennes: French Diplomacy in the Age of Revolution, 1719–1787* (Albany: State University of New York Press, 1982), p. 213.

again made war on both sea and land, striving to curb British expansion in North America, eject the British altogether from India, and drive London's vessels from the seas even as they abetted Austria's war of revenge against Frederician Prussia. That the duc de Choiseul, who took over Versailles's foreign policy in the midst of this conflict, should have conceived a spectacular scheme to end it to France's advantage by invading the British Isles, bespoke his country's current discomfiture as eloquently as it did the persistence of French ambitions. How often during the "Second Hundred Years' War" of 1689–1815 did the French, hopelessly overextended, dream of resurrecting their fading prospects by the deceptively simple means of a sudden thrust across the Channel!

Yet it was probably with Choiseul's tenure in the foreign ministry *after* the Seven Years' War that France's commitment to a world vision in strategic affairs became most unequivocal. The ink was scarcely dry on the Peace of Paris, registering genuinely disastrous French reverses, before Choiseul was once more at work weaving ambitious geopolitical designs – designs aimed primarily against the hated islanders across the Channel. "England," he declared in a memo of 1765 to Louis XV, "is the declared enemy of your power and of your state; she always will be.... Centuries will pass before you can make a durable peace with that country which aims at supremacy in the four quarters of the globe."[7]

Accordingly, Choiseul and his collaborators prepared for a resumption of war "in the four quarters of the globe."[8] They carried out sweeping army and naval reforms and urged their Spanish counterparts to do the same. They annexed the island of Corsica in 1768, thereby reinforcing France's strategic position in the western Mediterranean. Choiseul sent secret agents to the British colonists in America, whose rebellion against London he was one of the first to foresee. He also incited Hyder-Ali, an Indian prince, to rebel against British influence in the Eurasian subcontinent. He established even closer relations between Versailles and Madrid, and strengthened as best he could the traditionally pro-Bourbon monarchist faction in Sweden. In addition, Choiseul's ministry fortified several strategic islands in the Indian Ocean, upgraded the defenses of the Caribbean colonies, and sponsored settlers in Guyana on the South American mainland. In all of this, we should reiterate, the duke envisioned

---

7 Quoted in R. John Singh, *French Diplomacy in the Caribbean and the American Revolution* (Hicksville, N.Y.: Exposition Press, 1977), p. 35.
8 For additional sources on this subject, see: Roger Soltau, *The Duc de Choiseul* (Oxford: Blackwell, 1908); John Fraser Ramsey, *Anglo-French Relations 1763–1770: A Study of Choiseul's Foreign Policy* (Berkeley: University of California Press, 1936); and Thadd Hall, *France and the Eighteenth-Century Corsican Question* (New York: New York University Press, 1971). Eventually, interested readers may also want to consult the next volume in Rohan Butler's three-volume biography of Choiseul.

England as the cardinal antagonist of the future. Yet the sheer scope of the Choiseulist global vision is also indicated by the fact that it posited a grand interlocking of events in the overseas world, where British power was waxing, with tendencies in eastern Europe, menaced by Austria, Prussia, and, especially, Russia. Hence, when Choiseul exhorted Turkey after 1766 to make war on Russia, he did so both to challenge St. Petersburg directly and to put pressure on a British state viewed at Versailles as being far too friendly toward the Romanov colossus.

A British diplomatic historian has argued that, at the start of 1770, the French foreign minister saw only one more year of peace remaining to Louis XV and Britain's George III.[9] Whether or not this was true, the French and British undeniably came close to war in the course of that year over the Falkland question. For some time, Madrid and London had been contesting control over the Falkland Islands, whose location in the far South Atlantic made them a strategic gateway to the South Pacific and a vast region hitherto monopolized commercially by the Spanish. Bourbon Spain, not unreasonably, requested support on the issue from its Bourbon French confederate. Although there is much about the resultant diplomatic confrontation between London and Versailles – and the associated crisis within the French government – that remains obscure, what is certain is that a cabal of Choiseul's domestic enemies was able at this juncture to engineer his disgrace.[10]

However, Choiseul's fall from power really changed nothing. In corresponding with his Spanish cousin Charles III in the early 1770s, Louis XV repeatedly stressed the need for the two Bourbon governments to continue with naval rearmament as they looked forward eagerly to "making war against England," thereby retrieving the "honor" compromised in the most recent war. That, at the same time, France could also argue at London the case for intervening in eastern Europe against Russia underscored its commitment to a grandiose – if ultimately contradictory – foreign policy.[11] And this problematic commitment would continue to drive statesmen at Versailles in the reign of Louis XV's ill-starred successor.

That France's daunting "international mission" was not to be shirked was made retrospectively clear in a note that the new minister of foreign affairs, the comte de Vergennes, submitted to Louis XVI several years into his reign. "The deplorable Peace of 1763, the partition of Poland, and many other equally unhappy causes had profoundly undermined the

---

9 Ramsey, *Anglo-French Relations*, p. 163.

10 The second volume of Rohan Butler's projected three-volume study of Choiseul should throw valuable new light upon this minister's role in the Falkland crisis. But, for now, see William Doyle, "The Parlements of France and the Breakdown of the Old Regime, 1771–1788," *French Historical Studies* 6 (1970): 415–58.

11 Jeremy Black, *Natural and Necessary Enemies: Anglo-French Relations in the Eighteenth Century* (Athens: University of Georgia Press, 1987), esp. pp. 75–79.

consideration due the crown of France, which in earlier days, had been the object of terror and jealousy.... I confess, Sire, [that] all the arrogance and insults against which my heart revolted made me ... search for the means to change a situation so little compatible with the elevation of your soul and the grandeur of your power."[12] Not for nothing had Vergennes imbibed the philosophy of Choiseul; and not for nothing, it is equally obvious, had he been schooled in the remorseless ways of power politics through diplomatic service in Germany and at Constantinople and Stockholm. For if, on the one hand, the new foreign minister hotly resented the crushing defeat inflicted on French colonial and mercantile interests by London in the Seven Years' War, on the other hand he brooded over the spoliation of France's traditional Polish ally by the three East European powers and over the pressure exerted by Catherine the Great's Russia on those other redoubts of French influence to the east, Sweden and Ottoman Turkey. How, then, to retain for France a secure and prestigious role in Europe's competitive affairs?

Recent scholarship suggests strongly that the paradoxical and problematic key lay, for this statesman, in improved relations with the English. Such a reconciliation would in time allow for the diversion of French resources from the navy to the army. Even more important, cooperation between Versailles and London would greatly limit the ability of the other major continental countries to wage large-scale wars: having the armies but not the funds to engage in such hostilities, they could only draw the needed subsidies from France or England. The immediate problem Vergennes envisioned, however, was that Pitt's England was contemptuous of the French. Hence, France had first to "reduce England to a position of equality, ... to take from her a share of her strength, her monopoly of American trade and markets."[13] Vergennes, accordingly, came to project a two-stage relationship with the British. First, Versailles would work at humbling the "modern Carthage" by assisting the North American colonists in what looked very much like becoming a full-scale revolt against London. Subsequently, Great Britain might somehow be enlisted in a campaign to counterbalance the grasping, unscrupulous geopoliticians at Berlin, Vienna, and St. Petersburg. In discharging the first task, Vergennes, his sovereign,[14] and all their patriotic countrymen could indulge their prejudices against

---

12 Cited in Murphy, *Charles Gravier, Comte de Vergennes*, p. 217.
13 For this exposition of Vergennes's views, see Dull, *The French Navy*, esp. pp. 8–15. But also see Murphy, *Charles Gravier, Comte de Vergennes*, esp. pp. 211–21; Singh, *French Diplomacy in the Caribbean*, p. 148; and Jean-François Labourdette, "Vergennes ou la tentation du 'ministériat'," *Revue historique* 557 (1986): 89–90.
14 On Louis XVI's diplomatic philosophy, see Pierrette Girault de Coursac, *L'Education d'un roi. Louis XVI* (Paris: Gallimard, 1972), esp. 152, 168, 171–72; and Robert R. Crout, "In Search of a 'Just and Lasting Peace': The Treaty of 1783, Louis XVI, Vergennes, and the Regeneration of the Realm," *International History Review* 5 (1983): 364–98.

and revenge themselves upon the haughty English; in carrying out the second mission, they just might be able to restore that delicate equilibrium of European forces best calculated to maximize French security and influence.

For reasons explored in depth elsewhere,[15] Vergennes's imposing but complicated strategy – except insofar as it concerned the insurgency in North America – miscarried. Still, the few years intervening between the conclusion of that struggle and the final collapse of the ancien régime witnessed a reappearance of the old assertiveness in French foreign policy. This emerged most clearly in connection with the preparations for renewed maritime warfare coordinated by Naval Minister Charles-Eugène-Gabriel de La Croix, maréchal de Castries.[16] Castries, who had unavailingly called for transformation of the American War into a worldwide campaign against British colonial interests, acted after 1783 to build the navy back up to at least eighty ships of the line and to train it in offensive tactics on the high seas. He also expended enormous funds on stocking French arsenals with masts, hemp, and other war matériel. Most revealingly, perhaps, he tried to upgrade the seaworthiness of French naval forces – and probe for British weaknesses in the Far East – by sending one expedition after another around Africa into the Indian Ocean. British and French naval forces in fact clashed in waters off India during 1785. Also, Versailles acted the following year to shore up the finances of a local Indian prince, Tippoo Sahib, lately antagonistic to the British in the Mysore War.[17] But, if Castries's bellicosity was especially on display, contemporaries were just as quick to note the efforts of his counterparts in the war ministry to modernize that most venerable instrument of French geopolitics, the army. Those efforts would culminate on the very eve of revolution in a special council of war convened by Louis XVI.[18]

There seemed to be yet other harbingers of renewed French aggression in those years. Rumor had it that the French were planning facilities for no fewer than one hundred ships of the line at the artificial harbor under construction at Cherbourg. Did this augur an eventual strike across the Channel? Certainly Louis XVI, ordinarily untraveled, was willing to make a highly publicized inspection of the naval works at Cherbourg two years later. Then there was the formal alliance concluded between the French and the Dutch in November 1785. Since yet another French ally, Austria, held

---

15 See Stone, *The Genesis of the French Revolution*, pp. 119–29.
16 On Castries, see Murphy, *Charles Gravier, Comte de Vergennes*, p. 325; Labourdette, "Vergennes," pp. 91–92; and Dull, *The French Navy*, pp. 336–38.
17 On French activities in the Far East, see especially Blanning, *Origins*, pp. 47–51.
18 On this subject, refer to Bien, "La Réaction aristocratique avant 1789," pp. 23–48 and 505–34; and Samuel F. Scott, *The Response of the Royal Army to the French Revolution* (Oxford: Oxford University Press, 1978).

the intermediate Netherlands, did this presage a French strategic grip on both the Channel and North Sea coasts? Furthermore, there were the numerous indications, some of them already noted, of Versailles's scheming in the Far East. Since (as additional points in this connection) the French possessed the islands of Bourbon and Mauritius in the Indian Ocean, and since their Dutch allies held the even more crucial Cape of Good Hope at the southern tip of Africa and the superb harbor at Trincomalee on the northeastern side of Ceylon, just off India, were the British not justified in feeling their sea links with India to be vulnerable and perhaps imperiled? Under the circumstances, Prime Minister Pitt's gloss upon British–French trade talks was understandable: "Though in the commercial business I think there are reasons for believing the French may be sincere, I cannot listen without suspicion to their professions of political friendship."[19] In the twilight of his life, the comte de Vergennes found the entire thrust of a century of French hostility toward British overseas interests – hostility, ironically, given new life by his own North American policy! – to be militating against his dream of a future Anglo-French rapprochement.

Vergennes's death early in 1787 was symbolically appropriate, coming as it did at the start of an epochal political crisis to which his own foreign policy had so powerfully contributed. But there is a larger point to make here. Vergennes's policies – and, for that matter, those of all his eighteenth-century predecessors – were above all problematic because of their consistent failure to reckon adequately with the major changes in the European state system. That system had been transformed by the emergence on its outer flanks of Great Britain, Russia, and Prussia as major powers.

Britain's ability in the eighteenth century to carry out an international mission drawing general support from its affluent and articulate elites was rooted in the political revolutions of the preceding century. Those revolutions had beheaded one absolute Stuart monarch and chased another out of the land. It was particularly the second, or "Glorious," revolution of 1688 that proved decisive. It placed the profit-oriented agriculturalists of the peerage and gentry in a newly secure position of power. The English landlords, who wished to produce cereals and other crops for domestic and foreign markets and to purchase various colonial and domestically processed goods, plainly had much in common with English merchants whose livelihood consisted in the domestic and international exchange of such raw and finished commodities. Both groups perceived a compelling need for a diplomatic policy that ranked the acquisition and/or defense of colonies, trading posts, and commerce alongside dynastic and other purely

---

19 Blanning, *Origins*, p. 46. The foreign secretary, Carmarthen, "suspected that Vergennes was plotting a sinister plan to ruin England." Murphy, *Charles Gravier, Comte de Vergennes*, p. 436.

"political" considerations. Beginning in 1689, these interests were ideally situated, through their influence in the central and local organs of government, to urge such a policy on successive monarchs. William III may in his own mind have accorded a higher priority to humbling his detested foe Louis XIV than to fostering English commerce, and the Georgian kings seemed at times to be obsessed with the need to protect their Hanoverian homeland from predators one and all on the Continent. Nonetheless, the logic of British politics guaranteed that the country's foreign policy became almost as much a vehicle for upper- and middle-class economic interests as an expression of the general "patriotic" desire for British prominence in the world's affairs.[20]

Almost... but not quite. The bitter Anglo-French contest over colonies and commerce had for both powers a transcending geostrategic importance. England and France were competing above all for security and prestige, whether calculated in quantifiable terms of relative economic advantage or in terms of their constitutional systems, their religious and cultural values, or (most directly) their military and diplomatic establishments. Accordingly, both states saw the enormous and unparalleled wealth available through trade and colonization as decisively suited for power-political purposes. For the uniquely ambitious French, who coveted continental glory perhaps even more than maritime laurels, such largesse could fuel campaigns of conquest. For the fundamentally more defensive British, the danger was, as ever, that a power such as France, if dominant on the Continent, could destroy them, not only by denying them European markets for their trade, but also by cutting them off from the naval stores (timber, hemp, and so on) lacking which no more British ships could ply the seas. Hence, mercantile wealth signified for London a precious means whereby France's continental foes might be subsidized in wartime, thus contributing to the diffusion – and ultimate frustration – of the French war effort.

In this "Second Hundred Years' War" the British had over the French two interrelated and (as it turned out) insuperable advantages. First, as we have already noted, the islanders achieved an unparalleled harmonization of state and elite interests, of political and economic objectives. And this had crucial implications for government finances. The confirmation of the constitutional limits set upon the crown in the wake of the Glorious Revolution meant that state finance, previously considered royal in nature, came to be thought of as parliamentary instead. The mediation of private interests in Parliament engendered a sense of the public's interest that stamped the

---

20 On these issues, see John Brewer, *The Sinews of Power: War, Money and the English State, 1688–1783* (Cambridge, Mass.: Harvard University Press, 1990), pp. 21–22; and Black, *Natural and Necessary Enemies*, pp. 134–35.

revenue departments as out of bounds to private interests. Moreover, their budgetary duties forced the parliamentarians to face debt and deficit year after year.[21] And with Parliament ensconced at the center of political life in the kingdom, men with capital indirectly subsidized public policies by investing in the Bank of England, founded (significantly) just six years after James II fled British shores. The bank flourished, and by the mid-eighteenth century had assumed management of long- and short-term state debt. That interest rates declined throughout the century was ascribable to many factors, but surely one of them was confidence in a regime held consistently to account for its policies and procedures. It would prove exceedingly difficult for any controller-general of finances in absolutist France to borrow money on royal account at interest rates competitive with those across the Channel. Representative governance, then, paid fiscal dividends that over the long haul nonrepresentative governance, however "splendid," could not match.

The second great advantage possessed by the British derived from their insular geography. Protected as they were from the threat of sudden invasion by land that had long bedeviled their French opponents, they could afford to draw down their military defenses between wars and, most pertinently, focus their armament efforts in wartime upon their navy. This factor was pivotal. Whichever fleet could command the seas could control access to naval stores in the Baltic, to markets for exports, to sources of imports in Europe and the Levant, and to colonies and commercial entrepôts in the Americas, the Caribbean, Africa, and Asia. Moreover, such control of the seas would feed on itself, for it would deny to the losing side in this confrontation the long hours of experience on the high seas failing which no navy could establish competitive standards of seamanship, gunnery, and tactics. Hence the importance of the statistics Paul Kennedy has recently cited suggesting the relative sizes of the British and French fleets of this era. In 1689, Louis XIV's government could still boast 120 ships of the line as against the 100 of William and Mary. By 1739, however, the numbers were running 124 to 50 in London's favor; and in 1756, as yet another great war was getting under way, the figures were 105 for Great Britain and 70 for France.[22] Whereas, in Colbert's halcyon days, the French navy had generally overawed the combined fleets of England and the United Provinces, a century later France's fleet, even when augmented by that of Spain, could not equal the naval forces marshaled by London.

For Versailles, the nub of the problem lay in the contradictions inhering in the historic attempt to dominate both the oceans and the land.

---

21 J. F. Bosher, *French Finances, 1770–1795: From Business to Bureaucracy* (Cambridge: Cambridge University Press, 1970), pp. 22, 23–25.

22 Paul Kennedy, *The Rise and Fall of the Great Powers: Economic Change and Military Conflict from 1500 to 2000* (New York: Random House, 1987), p. 99.

Colbert and his successors, for all their industry in building up and maintaining this branch of the country's military service, kept the land-based naval administration (the *plume*) distinct from the seagoing officer corps (the *épée*). In doing so, they created and institutionalized disruptive tensions between administrators on the mainland, who had little knowledge of or sympathy for seafaring, and officers of the marine, who had no grasp of how overall naval strategy was to be synchronized with the kingdom's continental warfare. But the dilemma imposed upon the navy by the "amphibious" nature of French foreign policy was most outstandingly a financial dilemma. Research has revealed, with particular respect to the 1750s, that underfunding of the navy impeded organizational and administrative reforms, inhibited construction and repair of battleships and frigates, sapped morale in the arsenals and among the sailors, restricted opportunities for training in seamanship upon the high seas, and, in general, "severely limited long-term aspirations concerning naval power and effectively denied France fulfilment of the dream that she might one day be mistress of the seas."[23] Ultimately, however, such frustrations betokened an overextended strategic posture – a French dilemma from which the British would know how to profit.

These realities came home to dog the French in an especially sinister way during Vergennes's years in the foreign ministry. He involved his country, we have seen, in the American War (1778–83) in order, at least in part, to reverse the stinging verdict of the Seven Years' War. Yet, as the great naval victory of Rodney and Hood over de Grasse in the Battle of the Saints in April 1782 so dramatically revealed, the loss of its North American colonies had done nothing to shake Britain's fundamental superiority at sea. What was more, British naval prowess drew upon an economy whose postwar buoyancy not even optimistic French economic revisionism would attempt to deny. During 1784–89, exports of the British to their former American colonists (irony of ironies!) were already returning to 90 percent of the average yearly exports for 1769–74. Soon they would be forging ahead to unheard-of levels.[24] British dominance in European trade with the young American republic was especially crucial in light of its implications for the islanders' leap into industrialization. It has long been commonly accepted that the Americans, with their relatively high per capita incomes, large

23 James Pritchard, *Louis XV's Navy, 1748–1762: A Study of Organization and Administration* (Kingston, Ont.: McGill-Queen's University Press, 1987), pp. 207, 214. See also on this subject E. H. Jenkins, *A History of the French Navy* (Annapolis, Md.: Naval Institute Press, 1973), pp. 44, 108–9.

24 Dull, *The French Navy*, pp. 340–41. For some indications that the French economy in the eighteenth century was more competitive with that of Britain than has been thought, see John Shovlin, "The Cultural Politics of Luxury in Eighteenth-Century France," *French Historical Studies* 23 (2000): pp. 584–85.

aggregate wealth, and "middle class" traits, provided an ideal market for the cotton and wool textiles and ironware of everyday use fairly easily produced by the emerging, steam-driven technologies.[25] The British, furthermore, were matching or besting their rivals in other regions of the globe as well, including the Mediterranean, the Baltic – so crucial for its provisioning of naval stores to the cross-Channel powers – and even the Near East, hitherto dominated by the Franco-Turkish connection.[26] In addition, the British were apparently transporting around twice as many African slaves to the New World in the late 1780s as were the French, were penetrating the markets of Spain and its far-flung colonies, and were leading the way in exploiting the potentially rich markets of India and the Far East.[27] Indisputably, the French West Indies produced just about half of the Western world's sugar and coffee in the late 1780s, thereby securing for the metropolitan power much needed foreign exchange. Still, there was no demand in the French Caribbean islands for textiles and iron goods comparable to the desire for such mass-produced wares in the British-dominated markets of the United States. As a result, there was no colonial spur to industrialization in France (even assuming – counterfactually – a conjuncture of *domestic* forces favorable to the process there) comparable to the American stimulus to industrialization in England.[28]

Already by 1783, the volume of British trade worldwide was possibly as great as at any time before the American War. And over the years 1782–88 British merchant shipping seemingly more than doubled. The combined value of the islanders' exports and imports may have been increasing during the 1780s at a phenomenal annual rate of 4 to 5 percent. And the British share in overall global commerce must have been increasing – to the disadvantage, presumably, of France.[29] The uproar in France over the Anglo-French trade pact (the "Eden Treaty") of 1786 served to dramatize

---

25 H. J. Habakkuk, "Population, Commerce and Economic Ideas," in *The New Cambridge Modern History, Vol. 8: The American and French Revolutions, 1763–1793* (Cambridge: Cambridge University Press, 1968), pp. 40–45.

26 On these items, see Murphy, *Charles Gravier, Comte de Vergennes*, p. 430; Frank Fox, "Negotiating with the Russians: Ambassador Ségur's Mission to St. Petersbourg, 1784–1789," *French Historical Studies* 7 (1971): 52, 62; and François Crouzet, "Angleterre et France au XVIIIe siècle: Essai d'analyse comparée de deux croissances économiques," *Annales: E. S. C.* 21 (1966), esp. pp. 263–64.

27 On these points, see Crouzet, pp. 263–64; and Habakkuk, "Population, Commerce and Economic Ideas," pp. 40–45.

28 See Jean Tarrade, *Le Commerce colonial à la fin de l'ancien régime* (Paris: Presses Universitaires de France, 1972); and Robert Stein, *The French Sugar Business* (Baton Rouge: Louisiana State University Press, 1988).

29 On these points, see Kennedy, *Rise and Fall of the Great Powers*, p. 120; Habakkuk, "Population, Commerce and Economic Ideas," pp. 40–45; Dull, *The French Navy*, pp. 340–44; and Roger Price, *The Economic Modernisation of France (1730–1880)* (London: C. Helm, 1975), pp. 132–33.

the competitive disadvantages under which French merchants and industrialists had to labor. They prophesied sorrowfully that a reduction of duties on English hardware and textile imports would only damage the fledgling French industrial sector, and did not fail to berate their own government over the agreement. Similar controversies arose during these years over Franco-British commercial competition in the ports of the French West Indies and the Russian Baltic coast, and they, too, underscored the interrelated realities of the lagging commercial, agricultural, and industrial sectors in France.[30]

Inevitably, Britain's economic strength vis-à-vis France was translated into military strength. Pitt was able to have thirty-three additional ships of the line constructed between 1783 and 1790, thus raising the peacetime power of the British navy to new heights. By 1790, in fact, the ships of the line flying British colors would outnumber those of French provenance by 195 to 81.[31] "To be truly vulnerable," one specialist has written, "the Royal Navy would have had to be crippled by an especially heavy desertion rate or by a more protracted interruption of its supply of timber for hulls and masts than any opponent had yet managed to inflict upon it."[32] Realistically speaking, however, the chance that Versailles, even leagued with Madrid, could match London's forces upon the high seas was fading steadily in the 1780s.

And, just as the projection of British power increasingly foiled French ambitions at sea, so the enormous growth of Russian and Prussian power constrained and humiliated the French in the continental theater of politics. In the marches of eastern Europe as in the British Isles, the achievement of Great Power status rested upon a pragmatic self-restraint in foreign policy and an integration of governmental policy with domestic-elite values and aspirations that forever eluded ancien régime France.

Until Peter the Great's accession in the late seventeenth century, the Muscovite state, viewed in the west as semicivilized at best, had received most European influences only as filtered through Sweden, Poland, and Turkey. All this was fated to change, however, with the arrival on the scene of the amazingly "driven" Peter. The new tsar imposed upon his subjects the most updated techniques of maritime and continental warfare, of economic and bureaucratic organization – all borrowed from the West. Lacking in his empire the slow, organic evolution of society from below that had long characterized countries in the West, the tireless Peter sought through his own dynamic initiative to nullify in a brief span of years the other powers'

---

30 On these various trade issues in the 1780s, see Fox, "Negotiating with the Russians," p. 52; J. F. Bosher, *The Single Duty Project: A Study of the Movement for a French Customs Union in the Eighteenth Century* (London: Athlone, 1964), pp. 82–83; and Murphy, *Charles Gravier, Comte de Vergennes*, pp. 443–46.

31 Dull, *The French Navy*, pp. 340–44; and Kennedy, *Rise and Fall of the Great Powers*, p. 99.

32 Franklin L. Ford, *Europe 1780–1830* (New York: Holt, Rinehart and Winston, 1970), p. 63.

daunting lead in military and bureaucratic innovation.[33] Introducing his noted Table of Ranks in 1722, with its parallel ladders of promotion through military and civilian-bureaucratic ranks, this Romanov modernizer institutionalized compulsory state service for his serf-owning nobility. Under Peter, service to the government began at the age of fifteen and was for life. With little of the urbane clergy and educated middle class of Western societies to mobilize, how could the tsar have proceeded otherwise? It is true that several of Peter's successors found it politically expedient to lighten the burden of state-service requirements. Still, Russian historians insist that, even in the closing years of the eighteenth century, the nobles fulfilling military and/or civilian duties for the tsarist regime were no less characteristic of their class than had been Peter's nobles a century before.[34]

Thus did the Romanovs infuse Russian geopolitics with the skills and energy of the only elite in this crude, rural, and underdeveloped society. And one very tangible measure of their success in doing so was the explosive growth of this Eurasian state's military capacity. The Russian soldiery, it has been estimated, numbered only 170,000 as of 1690, but had increased to 220,000 by 1710, to 330,000 by 1756–60, and had stabilized at about 300,000 in 1789.[35] The Russians also conjured up a navy boasting as many as sixty-seven ships of the line by 1789; nevertheless, the tsarist state focused primarily on the possibilities inherent in land warfare. Although the Romanov land forces at this time could not vaunt the fearsome discipline or the strategic and tactical generalship of Prussia's army, they gradually gained esteem for their tenacity and bravery. "Experience has proved," one writer would even allege during the Seven Years' War, "that the Russian infantry is by far superior to any in Europe, in so much that I question whether it can be defeated by any other infantry whatever."[36] That the tsars also developed a diplomatic service whose personnel abroad compared favorably to diplomatic counterparts from all other states of the time further ensured that, in the eighteenth century, Russia's influence would soar in much of what Louis XIV had once pompously called "French Europe."[37]

But Russia would have to share the limelight of revolutionized east European geopolitics with Prussia. What Peter and his Romanov descendants did for Russia, Frederick William I and his son Frederick II ("the Great") did, over a much smaller area, for Hohenzollern Prussia.

33 Ludwig Dehio, *The Precarious Balance: Four Centuries of the European Power Struggle*, trans. Charles Fullman (New York: Knopf, 1982), pp. 94–96, 99–100.
34 Max Beloff, "Russia," in A. N. Goodwin, ed., *The European Nobility in the Eighteenth Century* (New York: Harper Torchbooks, 1967), pp. 175–76, 181, 189.
35 Kennedy, *Rise and Fall of the Great Powers*, p. 99.
36 Cited in M. S. Anderson, *Europe in the Eighteenth Century 1713–1783* (New York: Holt, Rinehart and Winston, 1961), p. 182.
37 Ibid., p. 153.

Careful analyses of the Prussian institutions of that era underscore how successfully the Hohenzollern monarchs integrated the country's landowning nobles, or Junkers, into the structures of state power. The crux of the matter seems to have been that the Prussian nobility received a novel and, in the end, ineffaceable sense of identity in the professional service echelons of this monarchy. These nobles served, in other words, as the indispensable army officers and administrators of the rising Prussian state. A symbiotic, triangular arrangement developed, involving the royal autocrat, those of his nobles serving for life or at least for many years in army officer ranks and top-level administrative posts, and those of his nobles dominating social and economic life on the village and county district level. Under Frederick II even more than under his father, the Junkers monopolized officer positions in the army and the more responsible and permanent posts in the civilian bureaucracy. At the same time, the local squirearchy tightened its grip upon the hapless peasantry and on most fiscal and policing activities.[38]

Moreover, in Prussia even more than in Russia, geostrategic vulnerability dictated a heavy reliance on the military. Indeed, for the Prussians, with their country cut out in morsels of land extending from the Rhineland in the west to the borders of Russia in the east, sheer survival more or less required a policy of calculated, preemptive aggression against neighboring states. Hence the devotion lavished by the Hohenzollern rulers on their army – on its discipline, its fighting morale, its commissariat, its equipment, and its strategic and tactical mobility. And, as these rulers forged their compromises with the Junker squirearchy, impressed Junker sons (and the ever-expendable peasantry) into military service and toughened the sinews of a war-making capacity, the Prussian army (like its Russian counterpart) exploded in size. It grew from barely 30,000 men in 1690 to nearly 200,000 by the time of the Seven Years' War and still counted about that many in its ranks in 1789.[39] True, Prussia lacked the Eurasian hugeness that endowed the tsarist regime with its vast swath of influence from the northern Baltic shores down to the troubled regions of the Balkans. Still, with its domestic resources harnessed tightly to its geopolitical will, Prussia became in this era a factor to be reckoned with – as the French would learn to their cost.

The addition of Romanov Russia and Hohenzollern Prussia to the system of competing European states led almost unavoidably to a waning of France's continental influence. The entire strategic calculus of Versailles, positing Austria as the principal and permanent antagonist in central Europe, and relying upon large eastern states like Sweden, Poland, and

38 Hans Rosenberg, *Bureaucracy, Aristocracy and Autocracy: The Prussian Experience, 1680–1815* (Cambridge, Mass.: Harvard University Press, 1958), p. 150.
39 Kennedy, *Rise and Fall of the Great Powers*, p. 99.

Turkey to counterbalance the Habsburgs, was rendered obsolete by developments at St. Petersburg and Berlin. And of course French difficulties on
land could only be aggravated by tendencies at sea, where in the long run
Britain was able to mobilize statist resources dwarfing those previously
deployed against the French by the Spanish and the Dutch.

The Russians never actually fought against the French in this period –
indeed, Versailles and St. Petersburg were both linked to Vienna in the
bloody campaigns of the Seven Years' War. Russia nonetheless undermined
France's influence in more insidious ways. It did so, for instance, by
encroaching relentlessly upon those three eastern outposts of French continental influence, Sweden, Poland, and Turkey. In 1763, the indomitable
and ruthless empress Catherine the Great imposed her own ex-lover
Stanislaus Poniatowski as king upon the Poles; nine years later, her state's
growing influence was reflected in the First Polish Partition, in which
Russia, Prussia, and Austria stripped away about 30 percent of Polish
territory.[40] The Russians also scored spectacular gains against Ottoman
Turkey during these years, extending their influence on the Black Sea and
its surrounding territories, striking into the Caucasus, and – even more
ominously – acquiring the right (behind a façade of concern for Orthodox
Christians at Constantinople) to interest themselves in Turkish domestic
affairs. Soon, Catherine and her Austrian counterpart would be meditating a partition of Ottoman holdings in the Balkans.[41] As for Sweden,
it experienced a French-supported coup that brought Gustavus III to
power in August 1772; but this drew from St. Petersburg threats of
Russian military intervention. Catherine was too profitably engaged at the
time in Polish and Turkish affairs to follow through on her threat, but she
continued in subsequent years to evince a disconcerting interest in Swedish
affairs.[42]

What was more, the growing influence of the Russians could no longer
be confined to regions adjacent to Romanov territories; it extended in the
1770s and 1780s to German affairs in the heart of Europe. Franco-Russian
mediation of an Austro-Prussian quarrel over the Bavarian succession pro-
cured for Russia "a formal *locus standi* in German affairs," and led the
French representative to the Diet of the Holy Roman Empire to com-
plain in December 1778, with considerable justice, that Catherine's state
now wielded the kind of influence in German politics previously enjoyed

40 On these developments, see, in particular, M. S. Anderson, "European Diplomatic Relations, 1763–90," in *The New Cambridge Modern History, Vol. 8: The American and French
   Revolutions 1763–1793* (Cambridge: Cambridge University Press, 1965), pp. 258–59, 262.
41 On these issues, consult Karl A. Roider, Jr., *Austria's Eastern Question 1700–1790*
   (Princeton, N.J.: Princeton University Press, 1982).
42 See, on Catherine's policies: Isabel de Madariaga, *Russia in the Age of Catherine the Great*
   (New Haven, Conn.: Yale University Press, 1981).

almost exclusively by France.[43] Indeed, the tsarina created a special department for German affairs in her foreign ministry and was eager at all times
to act as "honest" broker in German disputes.

This fundamental turn of events may have occasioned some anxiety at
Berlin, where Romanov arbitration in Prusso-Austrian altercations always
generated distrust; but at least Frederick II could derive satisfaction from
the drubbing his armies had administered to French forces in the Seven
Years' War. Louis XV's ministers, eager to chastise their erstwhile ally
Frederick for his frequent betrayal of French strategic interests in the
prior conflict over the Austrian Succession, had instead found their army
mortifyingly routed by a Prussian force half its size at Rossbach, on
5 November 1757. Historians would be hard-pressed to cite any single
event more emblematic of France's strategic decline in the eighteenth
century.[44] Certainly, military disasters such as that at Rossbach engendered
widespread anger and frustration in French ruling circles. "Never has there
been such a defective army," wrote the comte de Saint-Germain to a friend,
adding that "the first cannon-shot determined our rout and humiliation."[45]
In retrospect, the cardinal de Bernis would concur: "the troops were totally
undisciplined. Treachery and incompetence were the orders of the day.
Generals and nation were completely demoralised."[46]

Modern military specialists have generally endorsed these conclusions.[47]
The army, to begin with, was top-heavy, burdened with so many generals, it was often said, that they had to exercise their commissions in rota-
tion. Luxury softened the battle-readiness of some pampered generals and
officers of inferior rank. At the other extreme, however, were those officers
of the needy provincial nobility whose very survival in the army was jeopardized by late payment (or nonpayemnt) of wages from the government.
Quarreling and insubordination among the generals all too often found an
echo in the pillaging and general disorder of the soldiery on campaign. The
military efforts of the French often foundered on their failure to discard
the siege mentality of the past in favor of the much more aggressive, mobile
style of war adopted with devastating effect by the Prussians. Finally – and
we shall return to this point later on – conflicting visions of how the army
officer corps should be *socially* constituted had a detrimental impact on
morale in the ranks.

---

43 Anderson, *Europe in the Eighteenth Century*, pp. 191–92.
44 Blanning, *Origins of the French Revolutionary Wars*, p. 41.
45 Ibid.
46 Soltau, *Duc de Choiseul*, pp. 16–17.
47 For examples, see Lee Kennett, *The French Armies in the Seven Years' War* (Durham,
   N.C.: Duke University Press, 1967); Emile G. Léonard, *L'Armée et ses problèmes au
   XVIIIe siècle* (Paris: Plon, 1958); and André Corvisier, *Armies and Societies in Europe,
   1494–1789*, trans. Abigail T. Siddall (Bloomington: Indiana University Press, 1979).

Admittedly, all the other continental states (most notably Austria) experienced similar problems in their military establishments to one extent or another. Yet in one crucial respect the ills afflicting the French war effort stood out: they pointed up the insoluble dilemma of a power striving to uphold a decisive role both in Europe and on the seas. The intractable nature of this problem has emerged forcefully in scholarship stressing the fiscal restraints placed upon France's armies in the wars of the eighteenth century, much as it has come to dominate conclusions regarding the funding (or, more to the point, the habitual underfunding) of Louis XV's navy.[48] Just as its failure to concentrate adequately on the requirements of naval warfare hobbled France in its struggle against Britons so versed in maritime matters, so its failure to focus single-mindedly on the very different requirements of continental warfare inhibited France in its campaigns against a Prussian prince necessarily proficient in such warfare.

So the eighteenth-century French, aspiring to glory on both land and sea, stumbled in both competitive theaters. They could not help but be diminished in an international state system that was acquiring ever more global characteristics. And at the same time, in part because of their very effort to "keep up" with and master that outer world, those who were ruling France inadvertently sponsored – yet failed to "keep up" with – destabilizing changes at home.

SOCIOPOLITICAL CHANGE IN THE OLD REGIME

Long before French foreign policy assumed the "modern" attributes of global outreach, a political theorist named Louis Turquet de Mayerne had precociously invoked France's need for an Estates General wielding real legislative powers and for a renovated social elite of industrious, meritorious citizens.[49] His words have for us today an eerily prophetic ring. For, however much the warring rulers of the old regime might build up the apparatus of absolutism, they could not in the end help but undermine it both by provoking a debate over representative governance and by introducing a certain degree of change into the hierarchy of social orders.

That successive Bourbon kings elected to rule without consulting their subjects in regularly convened representative bodies, opting instead to develop, in piecemeal fashion, institutions of absolutism, was no doubt a logical reaction to the disorder of the sixteenth century's "religious" civil wars, and to the political instability that seemed to attend every royal minority.

48 Kennett, *French Armies*, pp. 138–39.
49 For a discussion of this political theorist's ideas, see Elizabeth Adams, "Seventeenth-Century Attitudes toward the French Estates General" (Ph.D. diss., University of West Virginia, 1976), pp. 170–87.

By the early eighteenth century the architects of absolutism apparently had their task well in hand.[50] France was a land effectively ruled by the standards of the day. Power at the center lay in the hands of the sovereign and varying combinations of ministers, "secretaries of state" heading up operative governmental departments, "councillors of state," and "masters of requests" transacting business and setting policy in the "committees" that were specific emanations for specific purposes of the king's Council. Decisions hammered out at Versailles were then applied in provincial France by intendants "commissioned from the Council," aided by their "subdelegates" and (in a somewhat uneasy collaboration) by military governors, provincial Estates, and municipal and village officeholders.

As a general phenomenon, we may thus acknowledge, absolutism responded first of all to historical developments *within* France. Yet, as the French state in the late seventeenth and eighteenth centuries both explored the possibilities and experienced some of the intrinsic limitations of absolutism, it did so increasingly as a result of its quest for security and preeminence in the larger European world.

It is clear, to start with, that under Louis XIV and Louis XV a frequent resort to war that transcended immediate domestic considerations led to a concentration of authority and prestige in the hands of ministers, intendants, and a host of financiers and minor administrators.

It is only to be expected that we should be able to attribute to the long personal reign of the former king especially important refinements in the structure and methods of absolutism – refinements that scholars have generally been able to correlate with international events. For example, though experts may still differ on precisely when prerogatives accumulated in the hands of the intendants, they agree in associating that process closely with France's growing involvement in war.[51] They see similar forces at work behind the rise to power of "fiscal functionaries" at Versailles. In general, Michel Antoine has written, each of the Sun King's wars "demanded...greater and greater resources, and the last one, that of the Spanish Succession, called for a genuine policy of national emergency." This ensured that "fiscal-administrative governance, and therefore statism in general" would emerge "in a chronology patterned after the chronology of warfare."[52]

Under Louis XV, the growing significance of the controller-general of finance witnessed to the increasingly symbiotic relationship between

---

50 See Pierre Goubert, *L'Ancien Régime*, 2 vols. (Paris: A. Colin, 1969–73); and Michel Antoine, *Le Conseil du Roi sous le règne de Louis XV* (Geneva: Droz, 1970).

51 See, for example, J. Russell Major, *Representative Government in Early Modern France* (New Haven, Conn.: Yale University Press, 1980), p. 668; and Bonney, *Political Change in France under Richelieu and Mazarin*, pp. 282–83 and 131–32.

52 Antoine, *Conseil du Roi*, pp. 76–77, 631.

war and absolutism. Indeed, Antoine has noted, "the War of the Austrian Succession and the Seven Years' War...[brought] to its apogee the preponderant authority of the bureau of the controller-general of finance."[53] It need hardly be added that this tendency continued right into the reign of Louis XVI, whose finance ministers, from Jacques Necker on, wrestling with the budgetary consequences of renewed war against Britain, would increasingly hold the fate of the regime in their hands.

There was, of course, a dampening message in all of this for royalty. In France, as in the other powers competing for security and prestige in eighteenth-century Europe, the purportedly "absolute" monarch was coming to play second fiddle to those impersonal administrative procedures that alone afforded him the money, men, and matériel required to support military campaigns. As Frederick the Great might have put it, the French king was becoming little more than the "first servant of the State." He must, in a real procedural sense, defer to his controller-general at Versailles, to his intendants and their subdelegates and all collectors and dispensers of royal moneys in the field, and to the innumerable, faceless administrators who assisted these agents of the crown at all levels. Even if we can agree that royal government in the final century of the old regime was at best "quasi-bureaucratic," that is, not yet fully bureaucratic in the modern sense, we are no less struck by the increasingly *depersonalized* nature of that government.[54]

However, if their waging of war on an unprecedented scale led the Bourbons to implement a certain kind of "administrative" absolutism, it also brought them up against the limits of that absolutism. Part of the problem, of course, was that the existence of privileged corps – craft guilds, syndicates of financiers, even peasant villages – under the panoply of absolutism made for networks of special interests that could deprive the crown of badly needed revenue in the long run. Plainly, the diversion of capital from agriculture, industry, and commerce to offices in guilds and high finance, and the economic conservatism of most peasants, only inhibited (taxable) economic development; at the same time, financiers battening upon the crown's fiscal operations had compelling reasons to oppose reforms in the royal fiscal administration.[55] But what ultimately underlay the

53 Ibid., p. 631.
54 Vivian R. Gruder, *The Royal Provincial Intendants: A Governing Elite in Eighteenth-Century France* (Ithaca, N.Y.: Cornell University Press, 1968), p. 208.
55 On these points, see, among many sources, the articles by Gail Bossenga, Liana Vardi, and Cissie Fairchilds in *French Historical Studies* 15 (1988): 688ff.; Hilton L. Root, *Peasants and King in Burgundy: Agrarian Foundations of French Absolutism* (Berkeley: University of California Press, 1987); Julian Dent, *Crisis in Finance: Crown, Financiers and Society in Seventeenth-Century France* (New York: St. Martin's, 1973), pp. 234–35; and Bosher, *French Finances*, passim.

crown's fiscal difficulties (at least among *domestic* factors) was its lack of accountability, and this stemmed from the kings' decision to rule in non-representative fashion. "Without a representative body," one specialist has observed, "French kings had the greatest difficulty in gathering support for their policies throughout the realm. In a sense the administrative apparatus that came slowly into being filled the vacuum which existed. But it was never a complete substitute."[56]

That, in fact, "it was never a complete substitute" was something the absolutists ruling France would themselves be forced to concede as their involvement in foreign affairs deepened. When, for instance, Louis XIV faced the prospect of defeat in the War of the Spanish Succession, he thought of seeking national support for his embattled government by addressing something like an Estates General. "I come to you," he said in a speech apparently drafted for such an event, "in order to ask your counsel and your aid in this meeting, which will assure our salvation. By our united efforts our enemies will know that we are not in the state they wish to have believed, and we can by means of the indispensable aid I ask of you oblige them to make a peace...honorable for us...."[57] At some point, this radical gesture, envisaged so incongruously by the exemplar of divine-right absolutism, was abandoned. Yet Louis still found it necessary to issue two extraordinary appeals for national support in the form of public letters, one to the French bishops and the other to the provincial governors. It is, moreover, telling that during subsequent peace talks the Sun King's negotiators were morbidly sensitive to allied propaganda concerning the Estates General. Such touchiness, it now seems, reflected the crown's fear that military defeat or a dictated peace could entail the destruction of Louis XIV's absolute monarchy.[58]

In the event, France and its enemies were able to achieve peace at Utrecht and Rastadt; and absolutism in France survived to fight another day. But a generation later, French ministers scouring the country for new sources of revenue with which to finance renewed warfare could not avoid reviving old constitutional questions, thus conjuring up once again the specter of the Estates General. They did so in part by levying a new tax called the *vingtième* on noble as well as common landowners. Lords who in many cases had already been helping impoverished peasant tenants pay their own "ignoble" tax (the so-called *taille*) would in future have to pay taxation assessed at 5 percent on their own lands. This turn

56 David Parker, *The Making of French Absolutism* (New York: St. Martin's Press, 1983), p. 146.
57 Cited in Joseph Klaits, *Printed Propaganda under Louis XIV. Absolute Monarchy and Public Opinion* (Princeton, N.J.: Princeton University Press, 1976), pp. 211–13.
58 Ibid., 267. See also, on this subject, Lionel Rothkrug, *Opposition to Louis XIV: The Political and Social Origins of the French Enlightenment* (Princeton, N.J.: Princeton University Press, 1965).

of events gave rise to a spate of antitax protests in the *parlements,* those royal courts of final appeal whose acknowledged right to approve or criticize royal acts made them lodestones of constitutional controversy throughout the eighteenth century.[59] The judges of these tribunals, being the king's "men," were expected to confine their remonstrances against royal edicts to protests relayed confidentially to Versailles; but as the *parlementaires* became increasingly embroiled in disputes with the crown in the 1750s and 1760s, "private" remonstrances increasingly gave way to published protests that were devoured by the reading public.

So law courts customarily devoted to upholding the writ of royalty set a precedent, dangerous to both the crown and themselves, of invoking the notion of "no taxation without representation." The Paris Parlement in remonstrances of 1763 (that year of Gallic diplomatic humiliation) insisted to Louis XV that "to levy a tax without consent" was "to do violence to the constitution of the French government" and – more to the point – to "injure...the rights of the Nation."[60] And what the Parisian jurists, restrained somewhat by a special working relationship with Versailles, did not altogether explicate, the more vociferous judges in the provinces did. "As long as there were Estates in France," the magistrates at Rouen recalled nostalgically, "the people...were familiar with the nature and extent of the government's needs....knowing [also] the nature and extent of their own resources, they could determine and regulate their tax contributions." Concluded the Normans: "The right of consent is the right of the Nation."[61] It was "crystal clear," stated Brittany's parlementaires unequivocally, that "in the common law of France the consent of the three orders...in the Assembly of the Estates-General is necessary for the establishment...of taxes."[62]

More of this was to follow, in a steadily escalating assault on the crown that eventually provoked, during 1770–74, an attempt at Versailles to govern without judicial interference in political affairs. But those who denounced Chancellor René-Nicolas-Charles Augustin de Maupeou's coup of 1770 against the parlements were in the end rescued by something less fortuitous than Louis XV's death in 1774. For, even prior to that event, the government was apparently moving toward a complete reversal of Chancellor Maupeou's policy. It seems, in other words, that extreme authoritarianism in France – meaning, chiefly, government without the moderating influence of institutions like the parlements – was viewed at

59 For an overview of the parlements, see Jean Egret, *Louis XV et l'opposition parlementaire, 1715–1774* (Paris: A. Colin, 1970).
60 Cited in Elie Carcassonne, *Montesquieu et le problème de la constitution française au XVIIIe siècle* (Paris: Presses Universitaires de France, 1927), p. 292.
61 Ibid., pp. 292–93.
62 Ibid., p. 294.

Versailles as unworkable. Therefore, Durand Echeverria's assertion that Louis XVI's dismissal of Maupeou in 1774 was "the inevitable liquidation of an exhausted expedient" essentially rings true.[63]

But, as the new king's government verged on yet another passage at arms with London, and was worried as well about developments in eastern Europe, it could not help but revisit constitutional issues. In early 1776 the Council debated whether or not to call the Estates General; that it chose not to do so did not necessarily mean that those in power were unaware of the benefits conferred on Britain by its parliamentary form of government. "The strong bond between citizens and the state," Finance Minister Jacques Necker was later to observe, "the influence of the nation on the government, the guarantee of civil liberty to the individual, the patriotic support which the people always give to their government in times of crisis, all contribute to making the English constitution unique in the world."[64] Because of his onerous fiscal responsibilities, Necker had somehow to find ways – short of British-style parliamentarianism – to bolster that confidence of taxpayers and bondholders in government failing which Vergennes would have no chance of achieving his geopolitical designs. Hence Necker's unflagging attempts in preambles to fiscal edicts, financial statements like the famous *Compte rendu* of 1781, and more general treatises to elucidate his reforms of the financial system, his curbing of courtiers' pensions and gratuities and landed proprietors' tax privileges, and his insistence that interest on state loans be paid out of a surplus in the "ordinary" or "fixed" finances of the crown.[65] Hence, also, his institution of provincial assemblies of landowners in the provinces of Berri and Haute-Guyenne – others were to follow elsewhere – to share with agents of the crown an array of tax-allocating and other administrative duties.[66]

Such initiatives, automatically, incurred the hostility of self-appointed champions of French absolutism and (in conjunction with other factors) brought about the disgrace of this resourceful finance minister in 1781. But Necker's fall from power could not spare a regime that was awash in geopolitically engendered debt from having eventually to seek a constitutional understanding with its own subjects. The Bourbons' engagements in the world beyond France had led them to adopt various refinements

63 Durand Echeverria, *The Maupeou Revolution: A Study in the History of Libertarianism, France, 1770–1774* (Baton Rouge: Louisiana State University Press, 1985), pp. 34, 122. This is also Egret's conclusion in *Louis XV et l'opposition parlementaire*, p. 228.

64 Cited in Robert D. Harris, *Necker: Reform Statesman of the Ancien Régime* (Berkeley: University of California Press, 1979), p. 121.

65 On these points, see also Harris, "Necker's Compte rendu of 1781: A Reconsideration," *Journal of Modern History* 42 (1970): 161–83; and Bosher, *French Finances*, passim.

66 See, on the provincial assemblies, Pierre Renouvin, *Les Assemblées provinçiales de 1787: Origines, développements, résultats* (Paris: A. Picard, 1921).

of fiscal-administrative absolutism; but the same policies forced them in the end to acknowledge, and finally to try to overcome, the constitutional flaws inherent in that absolutism.

Clearly, then, geostrategic and constitutional issues were ever more closely interrelated as the eighteenth century wore on. However, that those issues resonated as powerfully as they did was due to their *ideological* and *social* context. This involved, to begin with, an expanding public commentary upon issues of state. True, "public opinion" was an old phenomenon in France; still, as Keith Baker and others have been stressing for some time, it only arrived as a potent *political* force after midcentury.[67] "There is a philosophical wind blowing toward us from England in favor of free, anti-monarchical government," wrote the marquis d'Argenson. "All the orders of society are discontented together...a disturbance could turn into a revolt, and revolt into a total revolution."[68] "There has always been frivolous and inconsequential reasoning in France about the conduct of government," complained the eminent jurisconsult Pierre Gilbert de Voisins; "but today the very foundations of the constitution and the order of the State are placed in question."[69] Symptomatically, Jacob-Nicolas Moreau, a publicist and acolyte of royalism, urged the ministers in a memorandum of 1759 to take the offensive against the parlements and trumpet the virtues of monarchy in France.[70]

That the "mysteries of State" were being indiscreetly debated in public view owed something to broader trends in French society. The steady if not spectacular growth of the economy and related increase in population (most notably, of leisured bourgeois) must have found their reflection in a larger reading public (and in the associated rise of public opinion).[71] That public, in turn, was now encountering in Denis Diderot's *Encyclopédie* and a legion of less voluminous works the message of the philosophes. Under the aegis of "Enlightenment," if we may believe one of its most distinguished

---

67 Keith M. Baker, "On the Problem of the Ideological Origins of the French Revolution," in Dominick LaCapra and Steven L. Kaplan, eds., *Modern European Intellectual History* (Ithaca, N.Y.: Cornell University Press, 1982), pp. 216–17. On the linkage between "public opinion" and larger geopolitical issues, see Orville T. Murphy, *The Diplomatic Retreat of France and Public Opinion on the Eve of the French Revolution, 1783–1789* (Washington, D.C.: Catholic University of America Press, 1997).

68 Cited in Baker, "On the Problem of the Ideological Origins," pp. 208–9.

69 Cited in ibid., p. 213.

70 Ibid., pp. 214–15. See also, on Moreau, Keith M. Baker, *Inventing the French Revolution* (Cambridge: Cambridge University Press, 1990), pp. 59–85.

71 On these points, see C. E. Labrousse, *Esquisse du mouvement des prix et des revenus en France au XVIIIe siècle*, 2 vols. (Paris: Dalloz, 1933), and *La Crise de l'économie française à la fin de l'ancien régime et au début de la Révolution* (Paris: Presses Universitaires de France, 1940); and Jacques Dupâquier, *La Population française aux XVIIe et XVIIIe siècles* (Paris: Presses Universitaires de France, 1979).

students, educated individuals "started to assume . . . that politics must not be different from physics, from chemistry, or from the growing of wheat, that there should be no mysteries, no secrets, no *raisons d'Etat*, [and] that one had the right to observe, to discuss and to insist upon real and practical state reforms, just as if one were analyzing the composition of air or meditating upon the ripening of crops."[72] And certainly unheard-of numbers of nobles and bourgeois outside the precincts of government were in these years dabbling in "science," frequenting meetings of provincial academies and Masonic societies, patronizing reading clubs, and reviewing in salons and cafés the policies and rumored peccadilloes of the high and mighty at Versailles.[73] But more important, perhaps, the Enlightenment was sapping the "Establishment" from within. Chrétien Guillaume de Lamoignon de Malesherbes, in those days chief censor of the regime, made it possible for Diderot to bring out the first edition of the *Encyclopédie*, and protected the literary efforts of other social critics as well.[74] What was more, ministers like Jean Baptiste Machault d'Arnouville, Etienne de Silhouette, and Henri-Léonard-Jean-Baptiste Bertin, grappling with the kingdom's geopolitically induced fiscal problems, had to espouse "enlightened" values insofar as they were trying to rationalize administrative procedures and curb the tax exemptions and other privileges of regions, groups, and individuals. Their actions were perforce emulated (and their values endorsed) by the provincial intendants and their subdelegates.[75]

Moreover, the crown was challenged by men still fighting the battles of the past as well as by those struggling to define the issues of the future. Most notably, recent inquiries have shown how deeply embroiled the monarch and his parlementaires were in religious controversies over Jansenism and Gallicanism. Initially little more than a strain of thought stressing predestinarian and other austere tendencies within Catholicism, Jansenism in time became a focal point of constitutional debate in the old regime. The effort by both papacy and crown to suppress the Jansenists, whom they viewed as subversive, revived in some Frenchmen's eyes the old bugbear of an ultramontane attack upon the kingdom's historic "Gallican liberties."

72 Daniel Mornet, *Les Origines intellectuelles de la Révolution française 1715–1787* (Paris: A. Colin, 1933), pp. 473–75.
73 See, on these various activities, Daniel Roche, *Le Siècle des lumières en province: Académies et académiciens provinçiaux, 1680–1789* (Paris: Mouton, 1978); Dena Goodman, "Enlightenment Salons: The Convergence of Female and Philosophic Ambitions," *Eighteenth-Century Studies* 22 (1989): 329–50; and Alain Le Bihan, *Francs-Maçons et ateliers parisiens de la grande loge de France au XVIIIe siècle* (Paris: Bibliothèque Nationale, 1973).
74 Pierre Grosclaude, *Malesherbes, témoin et interprète de son temps* (Paris: Fischbacher, 1961).
75 See Marcel Marion, *Machault d'Arnouville* (Paris: Hachette, 1891); and Maurice Bordes, "Les Intendants éclairés de la fin de l'ancien régime," *Revue d'Histoire Economique et Sociale* 39 (1961): 57–83.

"Political" Jansenists in the Paris Parlement, longtime champions of those liberties, were, by the 1750s, calling for a monarchy in France that would be under parlementary and, ultimately, national tutelage even as it controlled – on the nation's behalf – a democratically structured "Gallican" Catholic Church. Since their ultramontane adversaries supported absolutism in both church and state, it was altogether predictable that some Gallican-Jansenist judges and lawyers would be tempted to appeal to "the nation" and even to invoke the Estates General explicitly in their increasingly radical discourse.[76]

Yet, in the coming years, the informed citizenry's attention would be inexorably drawn away from religious imbroglios (except, briefly, for that over the Jesuits' juridical status in the realm) and toward secular problems so perdurably inhering in the state's internationalist posture. Scholars may be right to descry traces of the old Jansenist ecclesiology in the parlementary rhetoric of those later decades; still, the judicial assault upon "ministerial despotism" that provoked the so-called Maupeou Revolution of 1770, and the Parisian and provincial judges' risky use of American antitax diatribes to combat Necker's augmentation of *vingtième* taxes a few years later, had to do chiefly with the mundane wages of war.[77] Moreover, the high judiciary's strictures against the alleged abuses of absolutism were echoed in a myriad of quarters. Barristers in the parlements, radicalized by their experience during the Maupeou crisis, and drawing on the legal briefs they could publish in uncensored form, were able to convert their tribunals into veritable forums for the discussion of religious, judicial, and social issues.[78] The *Encyclopédie*, as edited now by the press entrepreneur Charles-Joseph Panckoucke, continued to disseminate its message that "rational standards, when applied to contemporary institutions, would expose absurdity and iniquity everywhere."[79] A pamphlet literature, taking its cue from the antiministerial polemics of the early 1770s, dissected

---

76 Dale Van Kley, *The Damiens Affair and the Unraveling of the Ancien Régime, 1750–1770* (Princeton, N.J.: Princeton University Press, 1984), pp. 172–73; and Jeffrey W. Merrick, *The Desacralization of the French Monarchy in the Eighteenth Century* (Baton Rouge: Louisiana State University Press, 1990), esp. pp. 49–125.

77 On the latter controversy, refer to Bailey Stone, *The Parlement of Paris, 1774–1789* (Chapel Hill: University of North Carolina Press, 1981), pp. 77–82 and 96–100. On the persistence of Jansenism in the courts, see Van Kley, *The Religious Origins of the French Revolution: From Calvin to the Civil Constitution, 1560–1791* (New Haven, Conn.: Yale University Press, 1996).

78 David A. Bell, *Lawyers and Citizens: The Making of a Political Elite in Old Regime France* (Oxford: Oxford University Press, 1994), p. 207. See also Sarah Maza, *Private Lives and Public Affairs: The Causes Célèbres of Prerevolutionary France* (Berkeley: University of California Press, 1993).

79 Robert Darnton, *The Business of Enlightenment: A Publishing History of the Encyclopédie 1775–1800* (Cambridge, Mass.: Harvard University Press, 1979), pp. 539–40.

"social contract" concepts developed by writers like Jean-Jacques Rousseau and exalted the Estates General as embodying the popular will in France.[80] All the while, at a more visceral level, the *libelles* and *nouvelles à la main* that were pouring from the presses of Grub Street mocked the king for his sexual impotence and used causes célèbres like the "diamond necklace affair" to pillory decadence and despotism in high places.[81] Public opinion may have been deriving some of its influence in these years from serving – at least in some people's minds – as a replacement for a kingship whose sacral qualities they could no longer accept.

Paradoxically, the government contributed to the "contamination" of the political culture at home by pursuing its strategic goals abroad. Vergennes was warned by supporters in and out of the ministries that his espousal of anticolonialist insurgency in America, and in particular his subsidization of pro-American propaganda, could undermine his own country's absolutist credo.[82] And in fact there is some truth to the contention, articulated in many a textbook on the period, that French involvement in the American War became a Pandora's box out of which poured books and articles propounding all kinds of social and constitutional ideas inimical to monarchical absolutism.[83] The writings of Franklin, Paine, and Dickinson, the Declaration of Independence and Articles of Confederation, the constitutions and bills of rights of the various American states, and the resolutions and acts of the new American Congress were all widely reprinted and circulated in France. They could not, in the end, help but make all partisans of the ancien régime nervous – and this surely included Vergennes, already worried about the resonance of subversive ideas among the public. In 1782 and 1783, the foreign minister reportedly spent nearly as much time badgering British authorities to suppress a gutter press run by émigré French *libellistes* as he did sounding them out on diplomatic preliminaries to the Treaty of Paris![84] Vergennes's quandary was that, for geostrategic reasons we have already analyzed, he did not really feel that he could forego the attempt, however questionable, to turn the uprising

---

80 See Carcassonne, *Montesquieu*, pp. 553–54; Jeremy Popkin, "Pamphlet Journalism at the End of the Old Regime," *Eighteenth-Century Studies* 22 (1989): 363; and Roger Barny, *Prélude idéologique à la Révolution française: Le Rousseauisme avant 1789* (Paris: Les Belles Lettres, 1985).

81 Robert Darnton, *The Literary Underground of the Old Regime* (Cambridge, Mass.: Harvard University Press, 1982).

82 See Bernard Fay, *The Revolutionary Spirit in France and America*, trans. Ramon Guthrie (New York: Cooper Square, 1966); and Patrice Higonnet, *Sister Republics: The Origins of French and American Republicanism* (Cambridge, Mass.: Harvard University Press, 1988), passim.

83 Echeverria, *Mirage in the West: A History of the French Image of American Society to 1815* (Princeton, N.J.: Princeton University Press, 1956), p. 42.

84 Darnton, *Literary Underground*, p. 195.

in America to French purposes. Events were soon to show, however, that for the globally oriented government of France there could be no lasting alternative to a new constitutional compact with its own people.

That problem, moreover, was further complicated by the growing discrepancy between the crown's traditional vision of three "estates" – clergy, nobility, and Third Estate – and the much more dynamic reality of social evolution in France. And what was so ironic about this was the pivotal role played in social change by a state determined in theory to *resist* social change. It has been a commonplace since Voltaire's day to note that French absolutism in earlier times had lifted the curse of civil war from the land, thereby facilitating an increase in trade, manufactures, and the arts of peace as well as in governmental activities.[85] From this process of statist consolidation in France, several consequences followed. For one, a burgeoning governmental apparatus, having (at least temporarily) achieved law and order at home, was now able to take up an increasingly audacious mission abroad, which in turn meant a skyrocketing need for money and for professionals to perform the tasks of modern governance. For another, the very encouragement of "trade, manufactures, and the arts of peace" ensured that there would be a growing number of wealthy and ambitious bourgeois who could satisfy these statist needs (and their own social aspirations) by purchasing their way into the nobility – thereby altering over the long run the character of the social elite in France. In a nutshell, then, the crown did much to create the preconditions for sustained (and, in the end, destabilizing) social evolution and decided (for its own, largely geopolitical purposes) to cater to the needs and sensibilities of those who flourished in such circumstances.

Serving its own and its subjects' needs meant above all that the belligerent French state sold off vast numbers of titles of nobility and even huger numbers of offices conferring nobility or at least an enhanced social status. Louis XIV sold 500 noble titles by a single edict in March 1696, "and many hundreds more during the last 15 years of his reign."[86] His successors were less inclined toward this practice but could not entirely abandon it. At the same time, the traffic in offices boomed. J.-B. Colbert had estimated the number of venal posts at 45,780 in 1664; a government inquiry yielded a round figure of 51,000 in 1778. Both calculations, William Doyle has speculated, were "probably underestimates."[87] Of these posts in the eighteenth century, perhaps 3,700 could in theory ennoble the purchasers

---

85 C. B. A. Behrens, *Society, Government and the Enlightenment: The Experiences of Eighteenth-Century France and Prussia* (London: Thames and Hudson, 1985), pp. 55–56.
86 Ibid., pp. 49–50.
87 Doyle, "The Price of Offices in Pre-Revolutionary France," *Historical Journal* 27 (1984): 857, n. 181.

or their descendants; possibly two-thirds of them actually did so, going to ambitious Frenchmen still lacking their spurs of caste. How many people were thereby ennobled over the century? "One estimate is 6,500, another nearer 10,000. Multiplied by five for the families who inherited noble status from their newly ennobled heads, this gives a minimum total of 32,500 or a maximum of 50,000 new nobles during the eighteenth century – a major proportion of the whole order however it is calculated." If we note as well that at least 47,000 bourgeois families (meaning, by extension, several hundred thousand individuals) clambered up the ladder toward noble status via purchase of non-ennobling offices during the 1700s, we can begin to grasp the importance of officeholding for bourgeois infiltration into French society's elite ranks.[88]

There can be no doubt that, in its central and provincial administration, its financial apparatus, its judiciary, and its armed forces, the French government was driven by geostrategic and derivative fiscal necessity to encourage the assimilation of "new" civilian officeholding (or "robe") nobility to older military (or "sword") noblesse, and of wealthy bourgeoisie to recent "robe" nobility. In this sense, the crown was indeed an agent of social evolution – more specifically, of the metamorphosis of exclusive nobility into more inclusive "notability." Yet it is just as incontrovertible that there were limits in the old regime to this kind of social change.

Take, for instance, the case of the secretaries of state at Versailles. Although it is incontrovertible that distinctions still existed between the civilian and military branches of government personnel in Louis XIV's time, we know that the Sun King himself labored continually to reduce the "prestige differential" between the two branches. And indeed, at the level of secretaries of state this invidious differential had all but disappeared. In this purlieu of power men chosen from the robe nobility, recently risen from bourgeois ranks, were authorized to integrate with and become the equal of the highest nobles of the realm. As a result, their status was henceforward so high that they dominated the Second Estate. The eighteenth-century situation – in which even such commoners as Cardinal Guillaume Dubois and Jacques Necker could serve as secretaries of state – was, by virtue of this process, far removed from that of the seventeenth century.[89] Still, we may relevantly ask how many other cases of commoners acceding directly to such elevated responsibilities at Versailles could be cited by historians of the old regime. Granted, the balance between robe and sword within the ranks of high officialdom was shifting; yet upward mobility into those ranks was not exactly revolutionized.

88 For all these calculations, see Doyle, *Origins of the French Revolution*, pp. 119–20, 129–30.
89 J. François Bluche, "The Social Origins of the Secretaries of State under Louis XIV, 1661–1715," in Ragnhild Hatton, ed., *Louis XIV and Absolutism* (London: Macmillan, 1976), pp. 90, 95–96.

Research done on the eighteenth-century provincial intendants leads to similar conclusions. It would appear that, toward the end of the eighteenth century, a greater proportion of Louis XVI's intendants were new to the nobility and to the robe than had been the case with their predecessors under Louis XIV. As a matter of fact, Louis XVI's intendants were still busily engaged in making themselves "acceptable" in the highest ranks of the social hierarchy. Service to the king on his Council and in the provinces, therefore, may well have furnished increasing opportunities for social advancement in the twilight years of the ancien régime.[90] Moreover, the crown, assuming new domestic functions even as it pursued an ever more ambitious foreign policy, needed administrators with technical expertise in specific areas of domestic life – thus providing one more reason for recruiting into government the skills of those still engaged in the process of consolidating their status in society.[91] Yet, again, for the intendants struggling to manage provincial affairs as for the secretaries of state working at Versailles, the reality was that careers were not yet "open to talent" in any fully revolutionary sense.

In the ranks of the ever more indispensable financiers, too, a logical if somewhat less than revolutionary correlation between state service and social promotion manifested itself throughout the last century of the old regime. The Farmers-General, managers of the crown's indirect taxes, illustrated this correlation particularly well. As late as 1726, one investigator has noted, the membership of the "Company of General Farmers" was "a motley of financial speculators, stock jobbers, court favorites, and newly rich bureaucrats drawn from the upper echelons of the General Farms." Before Louis XV's reign was out, however, the Farmers-General were "usually men not only of wealth but of assured and cultivated manner," and their families now "interlaced at every level with the high nobility, the magistracy, and the clans which supplied the state with its chief administrators."[92] In other words, the Farmers-General, like other state financiers, had "arrived" socially. Yet here social evolution was, if anything, producing *more securely entrenched* nobles, not *newer* nobles. And for this the government would pay dearly. As John Bosher and others have repeatedly pointed out, royal fiscal woes were aggravated in the course of the eighteenth century by the crown's inability to extract unseemly profits from socially "well-connected" financiers (as it had in earlier times squeezed

90 Vivian R. Gruder, *The Royal Provincial Intendants: A Governing Elite in Eighteenth-Century France* (Ithaca, N.Y.: Cornell University Press, 1968), pp. 205–6.

91 Shelby T. McCloy, *Government Assistance in Eighteenth-Century France* (Durham, N.C.: Duke University Press, 1946).

92 G. T. Matthews, *The Royal General Farms in Eighteenth-Century France* (New York: Columbia University Press, 1958), pp. 238– 41. On this point, see also Yves Durand, *Finance et mécénat: Les Fermiers-Généraux au XVIIIe siècle* (Paris: Hachette, 1976), passim.

ill-gotten gains from less well-established "capitalists") in extrajudicial proceedings.[93]

The considerable, but ultimately limited, impact of state service was evident in the law courts as well. To be sure, the Bourbon kings had never really wielded a tight control over the personnel in the hierarchy of tribunals. The so-called sovereign courts at the apex of the judicial system – parlements, chambers of accounts, courts of *aides*, and so on – had long been self-recruiting bodies, and the ordinary workings of venality and heredity in office ensured that a similar situation prevailed also in the middle- and lower-echelon tribunals. On the one hand, this made for a degree of ongoing social evolution. Careful examination of the Paris and provincial parlements has revealed that the highly educated and technically skilled "robe" nobles, men who were often of fairly recent bourgeois provenance, achieved the same ascendancy in the higher courts as did their counterparts in the central and provincial administration. In these hugely influential courts, as in the king's Council and the provincial intendancies, the eighteenth century witnessed not so much an "aristocratic reaction" as a "professionalization" of elite Frenchmen.[94] Nonetheless, as a rule the parlements and other "sovereign courts" continued to be dominated by nobility of one stripe or another under Louis XV and his successor, and several of these institutions – most notoriously the parlement at Rennes – remained veritable citadels of the old sword. This could only guarantee heightened social frustrations – all the more in that the recruitment of literally thousands of ambitious and intelligent bourgeois into the "presidial," *bailliage*, and *sénéchaussée* courts at the intermediate level and into the provost and seigneurial tribunals at the lowest level of the judiciary served to diffuse professional and civic values – and, more to the point, expectations of promotion – among ever greater numbers in middle-class society.[95] In judicial as in administrative (and financial) ranks, then, service to the bellicose state contributed to (but could not, before 1789, complete) the modernization of elite French society.

But state service doubtless had its most divisive impact in the armed forces, those most immediate instruments of Bourbon geopolitics. Under the Sun King and his successor, duty as commissioned officers in the army imposed a formidable financial burden upon the men seemingly destined

93 Bosher, "*Chambres de justice* in the French Monarchy," in John Bosher, ed., *French Government and Society 1500–1850: Essays in Memory of Alfred Cobban* (London: Athlone Press, 1973), pp. 19–40.

94 The pertinent research is summarized in Bailey Stone, *The French Parlements and the Crisis of the Old Regime* (Chapel Hill: University of North Carolina Press, 1986), pp. 16–74.

95 See, on this point, Ralph Giesey, "State-Building in Early Modern France: The Role of Royal Officialdom," *Journal of Modern History* 55 (1983): 191–207.

for that role in the "society of orders": namely, the sons of the proud but penurious families of the provincial sword. As the novel geostrategic needs of the state had to take precedence over old-fashioned considerations of pedigree, France's monarchs, after having turned to the old provincial noblesse and to sons of old and moneyed court families as well, had again and again to avail themselves of the services of "new" nobles. The familial wealth of the last-named individuals, amassed from financial, administrative, and judicial service to the crown, and also from overseas trade and domestic industry, enabled them to purchase commissions and lead the increasingly luxurious style of life that seemed incumbent upon the king's officers. Moreover, the state had at times to reach out beyond even these circles to enlist into officer ranks out-and-out commoners whose wealth, obtained much as fortunes were obtained by nobles of recent vintage, accorded them preference in the army over the impecunious sons of the country noblesse. An additional factor favoring newer nobles and commoners was their ability to parlay personal wealth into the kind of formal education whose end result – an enhanced mental discipline and specialized, technical knowledge – was ever more in demand in military as in civilian state service.[96]

Such modernizing tendencies in recruitment, however, were bound to foment discord among military men. With the spectacular defeats suffered by French arms at Rossbach and elsewhere in midcentury, this discord erupted into a major debate within military circles – and, to some extent, within society as a whole – over how the French army's officer ranks should be composed and what values they should embody.[97] If we set aside the hopelessly anachronistic yearning of some commentators for an army commanded exclusively by the sons of the old provincial "sword," three schools of thought on this divisive issue stand out. First, reformist ministers like Choiseul and Saint-Germain and high-born essayists like Vauvenargues and the chevalier d'Arc advocated a kind of Prussian-style state-service military elite, rewarding its members (preferably but not necessarily issuing from the "sword") according to strictly defined criteria of military function and merit. Second, spokesmen for rich noble courtiers and bourgeois not unnaturally continued to chant the praises of venality in the commissioned ranks. Finally, there were those publicists (among them, Jean-Jacques Rousseau) who envisaged a citizen army, modeled along classical Greco-Roman or idealized modern Genevan lines, whose members, hailing from all walks of society, would share an intense emotional identification with the *patrie*.

96 On this subject, see, most recently, Jay M. Smith, *The Culture of Merit: Nobility, Royal Service, and the Making of Absolute Monarchy in France, 1600–1789* (Ann Arbor: University of Michigan Press, 1996).
97 See, in addition to Jay Smith's recent monograph, David D. Bien, "La Réaction aristocratique avant 1789: L'Example de l'armée," *Annales: E. S. C.* 29 (1974): 23–48, 505–34.

Of course, whether one argued for a meritocratic, a monetary, or a civic-republican criterion in visualizing the ideal French fighting force of the future, one was conceding the necessity, in the army as in other public institutions, to broaden the country's sociopolitical elite and modernize the constituent values of that elite. But it was perfectly natural for affronted reactionaries in various quarters to reject all such prescriptions. Admittedly, military reforms promulgated in the 1770s and early 1780s complicated the situation somewhat. Efforts to require at least four generations of nobility for commissioned officers (the notorious Ségur law of 22 May 1781), phase out venality, establish military schools for sons of the provincial noblesse, and cut back on prestigious ceremonial units and infantry companies alike tended as much to roil relations between wealthy court grandees and necessitous country squires, and between lords of ancient pedigree and upstart *anoblis*, as to foreshadow any "class warfare" between nobility and Third Estate. It remains no less true that, for most commoners, elevation into officers' ranks after 1781 was only attainable through the uncertain career of officer of fortune. The day would soon come when commoners' resentment over noble domination of the officer corps would boil over, resulting in (among other things) the purge of most noble officers. Those who replaced them would, for the most part, be *roturiers* whose simmering discontents had been largely ignored in the old regime.[98]

In the eighteenth-century navy as in the army, statist needs promoted a measure of social evolution without, however, bursting the chrysalis of the old society of orders. Whatever the ambivalence of social attitudes within France's fleet, it seems safe to conclude that its officer corps was undergoing major reform in the late ancien régime. In 1786 Castries did away with the *Gardes de la marine*, long seen as a root cause of arrogance and insubordination within the Grand Corps, and replaced them with *élèves-aspirants* and *volontaires* who, though drawn from elite society, were to be technically knowledgeable and beneficiaries of a new stress upon practical training at sea. Castries also suppressed the traditional intermediate officer grades, as well as the rank of *enseigne*, and created the new grade of "sublieutenant." These officers, recruited principally from the *volontaires*, might very well be commoners, could command small warships during hostilities, and were to be permanent members of the officer corps.

It is worthy of note that, in the navy as in the army, such reforms only ratified a situation already introduced by the imperious demands of war. "A large number of non-nobles did serve as naval officers throughout the eighteenth century," William Cormack has observed. "This was particularly true during the War of American Independence when the naval establishment was unable to provide sufficient officers for the expansion

98 Scott, *Response of the Royal Army*, pp. 30–31.

of France's maritime war effort. The fleet had to use a great number of auxiliary officers, most of whom came from the merchant service.... Many of these men distinguished themselves during the American War and a significant number became Revolutionary naval commanders."

Yet even if the prerevolutionary French navy was tending increasingly to select its officers on the basis of merit as well as privilege, this trend was by no means welcomed in all naval quarters; indeed, antagonisms continued to fester within the naval officer corps.[99] Another specialist on this topic, Norman Hampson, is even bleaker in his assessment: "The *Grand Corps*, like the army, was convinced that the aristocracy embodied specific military virtues that were neither expected nor demanded of the commoner.... Under pressure, they were prepared to admit commoners... but their intention was that the service should retain its predominantly aristocratic character, to which the newcomers would be assimilated."[100] In the armed forces, then, as in other state institutions, geopolitical and other pressures induced necessary – but not, in the end, sufficient – social change.

Venal officeholders whose numbers testified so eloquently to the French state's expanding financial and administrative needs also figured centrally in the elite of "notables" that was starting to emerge in communities all over the realm. Yet here again our most salient impression is one of social evolution that, up to 1789, could progress only so far and no farther.

The best scholarship on eighteenth-century urban elites indicates this time and again. At Orléans, for example, it is undeniably possible to find *officiers* and other respectable Frenchmen making up an "oligarchy" that was something other than the old noblesse. These oligarchs shared a certain way of life, and they tended to monopolize the urban administration. Yet, though such "notables" were destined to make up the ruling class in France once the revolutionary storm was spent, in the years before 1789 the privileges of the nobility remained a potent barrier within this elite, "dividing men whom so many other bonds united."[101] A like situation appears to have obtained at Dijon, Châlons-sur-Marne, Bordeaux, and twenty-nine other communities vaunting provincial academies. In these cities and towns, an economically and politically influential noblesse and a bourgeoisie of office, of administration, and of the liberal professions converged in a "society of elites" that prefigured in many ways the proprietary ruling class of nineteenth-century France. Still, these civic-minded nobles

99 William S. Cormack, *Revolution and Political Conflict in the French Navy, 1789–1794* (Cambridge: Cambridge University Press, 1995), pp. 35–48.
100 Norman Hampson, "The 'Comité de Marine' of the Constituent Assembly," *The Historical Journal* 2 (1959): 131.
101 Georges Lefebvre, "Urban Society in the Orléanais in the Late Eighteenth Century," *Past and Present* 19 (1961), 50–51.

and bourgeois never really challenged the "barrier of privilege" within their academic societies.[102] At prerevolutionary Lyons, it seems, a similar situation existed. In general terms, Lyonnais society may have witnessed the ascendancy of a modernized *notabilité*, in which bourgeois of various types were seeking a niche. On the other hand, relations between nobles and even the most affluent bourgeois, never very cordial, may have been growing even more distant as the Revolution approached.[103]

Whether, therefore, we look at state civilian and military institutions or at urban ruling elites in the ancien régime, we encounter realities more complex than those portrayed by either neo-Marxist theorists of "class" revolt or revisionists stressing "fusionist" social change. On the one hand, there is no blinking the fact that the old hierarchical values were being undermined in France. Of the many factors contributing to this process, one in particular stands out: the building of bourgeois fortunes in fields such as maritime trade (which, we note, was protected and even subsidized by the war-prone state), textiles and metallurgical ventures (stimulated chiefly by state military requirements), and – most strikingly – the lucrative business of state war finance. Private wealth thereby created continued to buy offices, *lettres d'anoblissement*, and landed estates, and so continued to pay off handsomely in terms of social advancement. This is really to say that the state's geopolitical and related financial needs, more than anything else, drove the process onward.

Where, then, did this leave those unrepentant conservatives in the first two orders who hoped somehow to "hold the line" against the menacing outriders of social change in the twilight of the ancien régime? Were there not Frenchmen of caste who despised newly ennobled or bourgeois aspirants to office in the parlements and the intendancies, in the army and navy, and in the cities and towns of the realm? Were there not Frenchmen of "race" who, in their thousands, looked out fearfully and disparagingly at the "century of Enlightenment" from their venerable but moldering châteaux in the custom-bound countryside? With these subjects, too, the government would have to reckon when it became irredeemably bankrupted by its policies pursued so arrogantly abroad.

This eventuality seemed to loom in 1787–88. The government was brought to the brink of collapse by the fiscal aftermath of war. Accordingly, it was also propelled to the threshold of an excruciating choice between sociopolitical ideals for which it had always stood and the more "modern" sociopolitical principles which it had – inadvertently? – done so much to advance.

---

102 Roche, *Siècle des lumières en province*, esp. pp. 255, 393–94.
103 Bill Edmonds, *Jacobinism and the Revolt of Lyon, 1789–1793* (Oxford: Clarendon Press, 1990), pp. 22–25.

A CONVERGENCE OF CRISES IN 1787–1788

In the very month (August 1786) that Finance Minister Charles Alexandre de Calonne submitted to Louis XVI a memorandum outlining fiscal and administrative reforms urgently needed in France, the death of Frederick the Great brought to power in Prussia a ruler, Frederick William II, who was ready to plunge his kingdom into reckless new adventures abroad. Meanwhile, Catherine II of Russia was persisting in an old endeavor to convince her Austrian ally, Joseph II, to join her in a partition of Turkey's European territories. The French "prerevolution" of the next two years was to unfold against a backdrop of war scares and actual armed conflict, underscoring once again the critical nexus between international and domestic affairs that has always haunted France's rulers.

The accession of a new Hohenzollern sovereign in Prussia was of immediate interest to Versailles because of French involvement in the troubled internal politics of the United Provinces. This engagement began, in part, as an offshoot of the endless Franco-British rivalry, but it was destined to become in addition an issue of high continental politics. The French, whose effort in the American War had been seconded by the Dutch, had committed themselves in November 1785 to a more formal alliance with the States General of the United Provinces. The leaders of that assembly, the Patriots, were able to seize power in 1787 from the pro-British "stadtholder" William V of the house of Orange. The British, for their part, fearing the possibility of French control of the Channel and North Sea coasts, wished to restore the stadtholder to power on terms that would destroy French influence at The Hague. Crucially, London was able in this instance to count on the strong arm of Prussia. The newly crowned Frederick William II, brother-in-law to none other than William V, had no desire to see his own sister, the princess of Orange, and her royal husband humiliated by the pro-French Patriot party in the United Provinces.

Under these circumstances, diplomatic observers augured – and in short order witnessed – the formation of an Anglo-Prussian coalition, and a military intervention to protect the Orangists. This in turn meant that France, to maintain its credibility with the Patriots – and in Europe generally – would have to follow through militarily on the strategic commitment made to the States General in 1785. But since, by 1787, "the French treasury was exhausted, and French domestic affairs were rapidly approaching chaos, warnings from Versailles that France would support the Patriots militarily, were interpreted as bluffs, as indeed they were."[104] In short order, events came to a head. The princess of Orange was stopped at Schoenhoven on the frontier of the province of Holland by a party of Patriots

---

104 Murphy, *Charles Gravier, comte de Vergennes*, p. 471. On the crisis in the United Provinces, see also Blanning, *Origins of the French Revolutionary Wars*, pp. 50–51.

on 28 June; her royal Prussian brother sent the duke of Brunswick with an army of twenty thousand men into the United Provinces six weeks later; Amsterdam capitulated on 12 October; and William V, reinstated essentially by an Anglo-Prussian stroke of power politics, repudiated the Franco-Dutch alliance of 1785. Thousands of angry Dutch Patriots fled into exile.

The French could do absolutely nothing for their Dutch republican protégés. Moreover, they had to watch from the sidelines, impotently, as a new diplomatic alliance arose from the ashes of their Dutch policy. An Anglo-Prussian convention was signed at the start of October; Anglo-Dutch and Prusso-Dutch compacts were concluded on 15 April 1788; and a formal defensive alliance was signed between London and Berlin on 13 August 1788. "A powerful Anglo-Prussian combination had now emerged as a factor in European affairs for the first time since 1761, and seemed likely to take a hand in the affairs of the Near East."[105]

That a new storm was brewing in that part of the world was largely attributable to the insatiable ambitions of Russia's Catherine the Great. Not content with having scored stunning gains at Turkey's expense around the Black Sea, from the Crimean Peninsula to Georgia in the western Caucasus, the Romanov tsarina endeavored to persuade Austria's Joseph II to join her in a new assault upon the Ottoman Porte. That Joseph, preoccupied anew with Prussian machinations within Germany, was hesitant to cross swords with the Turks in the Balkans did very little to relieve Russian pressure upon Constantinople. The Ottoman government, unable to rely on a traditional French ally that had deserted it twice in recent years, yet desirous of counteracting the threat from St. Petersburg, decided upon a desperate throw of the dice. It presented Catherine's government with an ultimatum demanding an immediate end to its meddling in the khanate of Georgia. When this ultimatum was rejected, Turkey declared war on its menacing neighbor in August 1787. Although the Russians were caught temporarily with poorly prepared armies in the field, and soon faced a new distraction in the form of a Swedish attack on their holdings in Finland, they did not remain long on the defensive. In fact, within two years the Russians, at last abetted by an Austrian push into the Balkans, would be resuming their historic drive against the Ottoman Porte, thereby threatening the European balance of power.

The French, erstwhile "arbiters of Europe," were manifestly as powerless to help their friends at Constantinople as they had been to aid the Dutch Patriots against London and Berlin. Vergennes admitted as much when, just a few weeks before his own death, he oversaw the conclusion of a commercial treaty between France and Russia. Although there were those

---

105 Anderson, "European Diplomatic Relations," pp. 274–76.

at Versailles who were tempted to speculate about gains that might accrue to France from some sort of Franco-Russian Near Eastern accommodation at Turkish expense, Vergennes himself most assuredly did not see the trade pact in that light. As one of the foreign minister's biographers has correctly pointed out, Vergennes considered the commercial agreement with Russia to be a means for increasing Louis XVI's leverage with Catherine in precisely such matters as attempting to moderate her ambitions against Constantinople, and not an instrument for facilitating the subversion or breakup of the Ottoman Empire. In other respects, however, the Franco-Russian commercial treaty of January 1787 "represented Louis XVI's recognition that Russia was now a permanent part of the European international system."[106] Just four decades before, the disdainful French had refused to allow Russian participation in the talks at Aix-la-Chapelle ending the War of the Austrian Succession; now, as war once again loomed (and, six months after Vergennes's death, broke out) in the contested Balkans, Versailles's inability to affect events there was an arresting indicator of how the power relationship between Bourbon France and Romanov Russia had changed.

Yet, although Russia's integration into European high politics was probably of more fundamental significance than that of Frederician and post-Frederician Prussia, it was Prussia's defeat of the Dutch Patriot forces in 1787 that most immediately jolted the French. The war minister, Ségur, seconded by the naval minister, Castries, urged the mobilization of twenty-five battalions under the command of Lieutenant General Rochambeau for possible action in defense of the Patriots; but Calonne's successor in the finance ministry, Etienne-Charles Loménie de Brienne, obsessed by the state's deepening financial crisis, vetoed this suggestion. Ségur and Castries thereupon resigned in disgust. The latter, notably, had "never ceased predicting resumption of the war with England after what he felt was the premature signing of the Treaty of Versailles in 1783."[107] He probably would have agreed with others in his class – Alexandre de Lameth, the baron de Bésenval, and the duc de Montmorency-Luxembourg, for example – that war in 1787 could have rallied army and people to the king and quenched the fires of domestic revolt. As it was, abandoning the Patriots served (in Montmorency-Luxembourg's words) to demonstrate "the inexperience, the weakness, and the incompetence" of Vergennes's successors, "prompting scorn for alliances with France and disgust with her conduct; she was the plaything of ... others."[108]

106 Murphy, *Charles Gravier, comte de Vergennes*, pp. 453–54. See also on these issues, Blanning, *Origins*, pp. 57–59; and Fox, "Negotiating with the Russians," pp. 70–71.
107 Jean Egret, *The French Prerevolution, 1787–1788*, trans. Wesley D. Camp (Chicago: University of Chicago Press, 1977), pp. 40–42.
108 Ibid., p. 41.

What made this derisive commentary even worse for the government was that it came on top of a withering critique of commercial policies which allegedly subordinated France's economic interests to those of the British. Radical men of letters, aggrieved merchants, and patriotic provincial parlementaires all lashed out at London and condemned their own leaders' impotence in connection with issues of trade in the West Indies, the Near East, and the Baltic. Moreover, we have already noted how the Anglo-French or "Eden" Treaty of 1786 multiplied the government's detractors.[109] But even more significantly, perhaps, a number of these observers drew revealing parallels between overseas and continental affairs, excoriating French statesmen who would immolate the interests of Dutch Patriots and Gallic entrepreneurs alike on the bloodstained altars of British and Prussian greed.

All of this could only ratchet up the pressure on a government already wrestling with the onerous costs of its global policies. Louis XVI might wistfully hope in April 1787 that his finance minister could curb expenses "without cutting the army or the navy." Loménie de Brienne himself might reassure Sweden's anxious ambassador to France in September of that year that his reforms would eventually permit France to "play the role that becomes her" in the world's affairs. And Keeper of the Seals Chrétien François Lamoignon might try to comfort the Paris Parlement just two months later with images of "a formidable navy, of the army regenerated . . . , of . . . a new port built on the Channel to insure the glory of the French flag."[110] But the realities confronting France were more accurately indicated by the Austrian ambassador, Mercy-Argenteau, in a comment upon Dutch developments confided to Vienna: "It is not credible that the Versailles ministry, in such straits, would risk getting involved in a war that would make bankruptcy inevitable."[111] And in 1788 matters would (if possible) only deteriorate further, as the new foreign minister, Montmorin, found himself compelled to desert both Sweden and Turkey in their struggle with avaricious Romanov Russia.

It is crucial to stress these facts, because only by doing so can we appreciate the sense of urgency motivating Calonne's and then Brienne's efforts to restore the crown's solvency. Despite their efforts, however, geopolitical, constitutional, and social issues became fused in such a way as ultimately to bring about the collapse of the ancien régime.

Actually, these matters were inextricably intertwined well before the "prerevolution" of 1787–88, as we have already seen. That this was the case explains why, by August 1786, Calonne was reduced to suggesting to

109 This commentary on trade issues is discussed by Frances Acomb in *Anglophobia in France, 1763–1789* (Durham, N.C.: Duke University Press, 1950), pp. 117–20.
110 Citations from Egret, *French Prerevolution*, pp. 32, 42, 107.
111 Ibid., p. 41. A letter of 15 September 1787.

Louis XVI the convocation of an Assembly of Notables to tackle the king-dom's mounting problems. Necker's strategy to manage the enormous cost of Vergennes's foreign policy had been allowed to lapse after 1781. Some in the government understood the need for strict accounting procedures, but the authorities were less sensitive to the equally pressing need to cut back venal officeholding in the financial administration and to curb concessions of special favors to parasitical figures at court and to privileged tax-paying nobles in the countryside. The result was predictable: the crown's care-fully nurtured – and publicized – ability to maintain a balance between "ordinary" income and "ordinary" expenditure, and thus pay the interest on its loans *out of a surplus in its ordinary income*, began to slip away. By 1786, Calonne found it impossible, whatever expedients he employed, to bridge an annual gap between fixed expenses and fixed income that – even in peacetime! – was inexorably passing beyond 100 million livres.[112]

What made this so serious a problem for the crown was its constitutional ramifications. Calonne was now discovering, tardily, that, failing the main-tenance of something like a Neckerite regime of fiscal-administrative aus-terity and accountability, globally competitive absolutism in France would have to risk consulting its own subjects on public issues. There was simply no other way to maintain the state's credibility in the financial markets both inside and outside the country; hence the finance minister's advice to Louis XVI in August 1786 to convene an Assembly of Notables. Such a forum, in which (according to Calonne) "it is the most important and enlightened magnates of the realm to whom the king is pleased to com-municate his views," would be less dangerous to royal authority than the dread Estates General, in which "it is the representatives of the nation who remonstrate, petition, and consent." Yet, given the power of public opinion, and the literate nation's "memory" of the Estates General meeting sporad-ically in earlier centuries, how likely was it that the consultative process initiated by the controller-general could have stopped with a summons to an Assembly of Notables?[113]

As it turned out, Calonne almost immediately became caught up in an uncontrollable dialectic of ministerial proposals and public response. The proposals themselves, first submitted to the Notables in February 1787, were provocative from the start insofar as they were designed to strengthen, not mitigate, the sway of bellicose absolutism in France. What might landed proprietors not fear from a "territorial subvention" (i.e., a land tax) whose yield and duration were as yet unlimited? What useful

112 On these points, see Eugene N. White, "Was There a Solution to the Ancien Régime's Financial Dilemma?" *Journal of Economic History* 49 (1989): 545–68; and Robert D. Harris, *Necker and the Revolution of 1789* (Lanham, Md.: University Press of America, 1986).
113 Cited in Egret, *French Prerevolution*, p. 4.

public purposes could provincial, district, and municipal assemblies serve if, in apportioning taxes fixed arbitrarily at Versailles, they would have to obey those minions of "ministerial despotism" the intendants? How could Frenchmen effectually resist the extended stamp tax of such a rejuvenated state? And why should they enthuse over the abolition of internal tolls and duties, the reduction of the various salt imposts, the liberation of the internal commerce in grain, and the conversion of the peasants' obligatory road work into cash payments, if such measures, by stimulating taxable agriculture and trade, merely refilled the coffers of the old absolutism?[114]

Calonne, attuned narrowly to that old absolutism, had failed to anticipate how quickly the Notables would perceive constitutional issues behind the government's reforms. He had also miscalculated on the more immediate question of the government's solvency. Inevitably, the Notables rejected his assertion that Necker's reported budgetary surplus of 1781 had now become a running deficit; just as inevitably, they demanded access to the state's financial accounts, and found their examination of those accounts, and of the controller-general's proposed reforms, to be radicalizing their thinking on all public questions. They may have assumed their duties initially as advisers to their monarch in a more or less traditional role; but with the passage of time they became little less than representatives of the nation, and their convocation little less than a legislature. Yet, when put to the ultimate test of deciding whether or not to endorse the crown's legislation, the Notables could only shuffle the awesome responsibility for this onto "other institutions, other instruments of the nation already established or to be called into existence."[115] And could there be much mystery in the final analysis as to what "institution" or "instrument" would be indicated? In fact, early on in the Notables' deliberations a distinguished jurist from Provence, Leblanc de Castillon, had declared that the Estates General would have to sanction any new taxes; and Lafayette was to issue a clarion call for the revival of the historic Estates on the eve of the Notables' dissolution. The warring Bourbon state could not, even now, lay the ghosts of venerable constitutional precedent.

It was equally powerless to prevent its argument with the Notables from being taken up by a "public opinion" to which both parties to the dispute then found themselves appealing. "A slight fever has gripped the country," wrote abbé Morellet to Britain's Lord Shelburne. "As soon as the public has seen the Notables... occupied with its interests, opinion has given them a power which they [otherwise] would not have had.... by reason of the confidence acquired they have become like the deputies of our old States

---

114 For details on Calonne's proposals, refer to ibid., chap. 1.
115 Gruder, "Paths to Political Consciousness: The Assembly of Notables of 1787 and the 'Pre-Revolution' in France," *French Historical Studies* 13 (1984): 348–50.

General."[116] And in fact the Notables' final referral of the pivotal question of taxation to either the parlements or the Estates General stemmed, at least in part, from their sensitivity to popular cartoons painting them as guileless geese about to be devoured by the ministers.

Yet the government, too, found itself courting the public. Calonne, in fact, precipitated his own disgrace in March by appealing over the heads of his adversaries to the literate citizenry with a vehement indictment of "privileges" and of all royal administration shrouded in "darkness." This was, understandably, too much for Louis XVI; yet, significantly, the king himself handed over to the Notables the fiscal accounts they had been demanding. Furthermore, the new steward of the crown's finances, Loménie de Brienne, chosen in a conciliatory gesture from among the Notables themselves, tried – though unavailingly – to satisfy his former colleagues by more carefully defining several of the government's mooted reforms and withdrawing others altogether.

The dismissal of the rebellious Notables shifted the venue of the debate to the Palais de Justice in Paris; but the dynamics of the debate were unchanged. Loménie de Brienne and the new Keeper of the Seals, Lamoignon, may have hoped to score in the tribunal of public opinion by offering some popular reforms, including the establishment of provincial assemblies that, one day, might supply some of the deputies to an Estates General. More immediately, however, enhanced tax revenues were needed to preserve the state's credibility in a fiercely competitive Europe; hence the ministers' submission of the stamp tax and "territorial subvention" to the Paris Parlement. But the parlementaires, loath to appear in the public's eyes any more amenable to ministerial desires than had the Notables, rejected both impositions in July and called defiantly for the Estates General.[117] They could well afford to, as they seem to have been riding what one historian has aptly called a "gigantic tidal wave of public opinion." Mercy-Argenteau, who in a season of impending crisis in the Balkans had every reason to be monitoring the domestic situation of Austria's nominal Bourbon ally, wrote to his home government about "the increasingly excited state of public opinion" in Paris. "Little by little," he noted fearfully, "the agitation is reaching all classes of society." He added, shrewdly: "It is this ferment which is giving the Parlement the power to persevere in its opposition."[118] The perspicacious Malesherbes said much the same thing, and more besides: "The Parlement of Paris is ... merely the echo of the Parisian public, and ... the Parisian public is the echo of the whole nation."[119] By August,

116 Cited in Harris, *Necker and the Revolution of 1789*, p. 134. On the public's political awakening, see also Carcassonne, *Montesquieu*, esp. pp. 554–57.
117 Egret, *French Prerevolution*, pp. 95–102.
118 Cited in Harris, *Necker and the Revolution of 1789*, p. 279.
119 Egret, *French Prerevolution*, p. 98.

Jean Egret has observed, "everyone was calling for the Estates General, and some daring journalists were already speculating about its potential composition...and about the task it would have to accomplish."[120] A pamphlet literature descanting boldly on constitutional issues was already flourishing.[121] In addition, the ministers, who had been compelled to banish the obstreperous Parisian judges to Troyes, and to exile Bordeaux's equally recalcitrant parlementaires to Libourne, were showered in late August and September with protests from law courts all over the realm voicing solidarity with the cashiered magistrates and augmenting the national chorus of demands for the Estates General.

Fearing in such a politicized atmosphere for the government's credit in the financial markets, let alone for his long-term reforms, Brienne had little choice but to bargain with a reinstated Paris Parlement. At a stormy judicial session on 19 November, the ministers promised the judges that the Estates would convene by 1792, but insisted at the same time upon immediate ratification of a series of loans designed, in combination with Brienne's administrative reforms, to restore the state's financial health. The ministers' attempt to secure passage of the first of these loans without permitting the customary judicial vote on the measure led the duc d'Orléans to denounce the proceedings to the king's face as illegal. Orléans was exiled for his temerity, and two of the more offensive magistrates were incarcerated. Over the next six months, relations between the crown and the parlement soured yet further, and by May 1788 the Parisian *and* provincial judges were sweepingly condemning the regime's "despotic" practices and invoking "fundamental laws" to circumscribe the crown's prerogatives.

The government struck back, endeavoring with its May Edicts to nullify the sovereign courts' political role, as well as to simplify royal justice at all levels, soften the rigors of criminal justice, and weaken or eliminate seigneurial tribunals and certain specialized courts.[122] Also, in these same hectic days, the finance minister and his associates were manfully laboring to renovate the military, reduce venality and streamline accounting procedures in the financial administration, invigorate agriculture and commerce, and grant a civil status to the country's Protestants. In addition, and as the initial fruit of their overhaul of royal finances, they unveiled the confidence-building capstone of all their efforts: a published budget for 1788. By such means, they hoped, the French government could carry on its ambitious international mission and realize a new legitimacy at home – and this without sacrificing absolutism altogether.

120 Ibid., p. 103.
121 See Ralph W. Greenlaw, "Pamphlet Literature in France during the Period of the Aristocratic Revolt (1787–1788)," *Journal of Modern History* 29 (1957): 353.
122 Egret, *French Prerevolution*, pp. 145–69, discusses those edicts and the controversy to which they gave rise.

Alas, it was not to be. The immediate problem here was the growing proportion of state income provided by short-term "anticipations" on projected future revenue. Ultimately, however, financial issues were caught up in larger constitutional questions. As Robert Harris has explained, "financiers who normally granted short-term credit in the form of anticipations... were unable to come forth with more money.... [they] were dependent upon the government's credit in order to raise that capital in the money markets."[123] But state credit, in turn, was collapsing because of Loménie de Brienne's inability to show clearly, in his 1788 budget, how ordinary revenues and expenditures would be balanced in the future. What was more, the government's future credit had also been linked by now with the eventual summoning of the Estates-General.

Due to this linkage of financial and constitutional issues, maintaining state credit required as a sine qua non public acceptance of the eleventh-hour measures enacted by Brienne and his collaborators. But that acceptance simply was not forthcoming. Even *before* the dramatic events of May, that attentive British observer Arthur Young was discovering among Parisians a general conviction that the "existing ministry" should "immediately call to its aid the Estates General." And Morellet, one of Brienne's most loyal adherents, informed him flatly: "We need some bar to the repetition of abuses: we need the Estates General or the equivalent. That is what people everywhere are saying."[124] It was hardly astonishing, therefore, that the government's coup against the refractory judiciary should have provoked widespread outrage in society. Celebrated literati like Target, Barnave, Bergasse, Condorcet, and Mirabeau, contributors to the *Gazette de Leyde*, the Gallican clergy, incensed notables assembled in Brittany and Béarn and Provence and Dauphiné, and even judges and barristers slated for new roles in a transformed judiciary – all joined in the antiministerial hue and cry. Ironically, the government only undercut its own position by subsidizing polemicists whose invocations of the "public interest," the "people," and the Estates General surely helped to prepare the way for abbé Siéyès and other revolutionary writers and politicians in the years to come.[125]

In such impossible circumstances, absolutism in France had to retreat – had, in the end, to sign its own death warrant. By early August the crown's irrevocable loss of credit, registered on the stock exchange, forced it to promise the Estates General for 1 May 1789 and to pledge to its creditors that the Estates would secure their investments. Not long after having thus

---

123 Harris, *Necker and the Revolution of 1789*, pp. 264–65. See also White, "Was There a Solution?" esp. p. 565.
124 Egret, *French Prerevolution*, p. 108.
125 See Stone, *Genesis of the French Revolution*, pp. 178–83, for a reassessment of the opposition to the ministry in 1788.

bound fiscal and constitutional issues together indissolubly in the eyes of the nation, Loménie de Brienne gave way to a resurgent Necker.[126]

Although these harried ministers had little occasion to note it, fundamental social tendencies reinforced financial and constitutional factors undermining the government's position in 1787–88. The warring crown's custom of selling offices to its subjects now rebounded upon it with lethal effect, for the resultant tensions within the elite and the multiplication of special corporate interests strengthened the opposition to badly needed measures of reform.

Polarization within the nobility during the "prerevolution" was especially noteworthy in the Assembly of Notables, the Paris Parlement, and the army, and produced some of the most reactionary opponents of state modernization. Admittedly, it is possible – up to a point, at least – to paint the Notables of 1787 and 1788 in reassuringly "progressive" colors. The Notables, after all, *were* "notables." As literate nobles and clergy, as administrators and magistrates and landowners and businessmen, they were the kind of Frenchmen who could reasonably expect to preside in a regenerated country over the "unenlightened" and laboring masses.[127] Yet, it has also been argued, such a group description is incomplete insofar as it leaves out of account those favored citizens wedded to privilege as the crucial "superintending" principle of society. Such Notables might disarmingly defend their fiscal prerogative of undertaxation relative to rural plebeians in *constitutional* terms as a "bulwark against despotism"; but, if pressed to the wall, they probably would have also championed that privilege, like all privileges, in *social* terms as well. That this was the stance of many (perhaps most?) of the Notables at their initial convocation early in 1787 could likely be inferred from their more explicit advocacy of noble privilege at their follow-up convocation a year and a half later.[128]

Social conservatism played a similar role in the Paris Parlement's protests of July–August 1787 against the ministry's financial edicts. The senior magistrates spared no effort to put their institution on record as unalterably opposed to a "territorial subvention" designed especially to tax wealthy nobles resident in rural France. The parlementaires especially hated the proposed new tax because it would force affluent proprietors – most of them, presumably, nobles like themselves – to compensate out of their

---

126 Egret, *French Prerevolution*, pp. 183–85.
127 Gruder, "Class and Politics in the Pre-Revolution: The Assembly of Notables of 1787," in E. Hinrichs et al., eds., *Vom Ancien Régime zur Französischen Révolution*, pp. 229–30. She has enlarged upon these ideas in "A Mutation in Elite Political Culture: The French Notables and the Defense of Property and Participation, 1787," *Journal of Modern History*, 56 (1984): 598–634.
128 Michael P. Fitzsimmons, "Privilege and the Polity in France, 1786–1791," *American Historical Review* 92 (1987): 274–75.

own pockets for whatever less wealthy landowners failed to pay in to government coffers. Hence, in the Parlement as in the Notables, resistance to financial reforms had undeniable social roots.[129]

In the army, too, the process of reform during the prerevolution stoked the fires of social reaction, thereby augmenting the opposition to the beleaguered government. The famous council of war convened in 1787–88 by Louis XVI promulgated useful reforms, modernizing tactics, reducing or altogether eliminating unneeded regiments, cutting back the excessive number of general officers, and improving conditions of military service. But the reforms, albeit urgently needed from a military point of view, exacerbated tensions and jealousies within the social hierarchy, pitting court aristocrats, provincial squires, newly created nobles, and ambitious, moneyed commoners against each other. "Witnesses all agree on the profound malaise produced in the army by the drastic treatment applied to it," Egret has commented. "It is easy to imagine, if difficult to measure, the disarray and exasperation produced among officers, especially older ones, by a reform that threw everything into confusion."[130] That the army (like the navy) was in addition demoralized on the eve of state bankruptcy by grossly inadequate funding was clearly not calculated to alleviate the anxieties and resentments of these highborn *militaires*.

But if reformers at Versailles and their agents in the provinces had to contend with the class prejudices and insecurities of traditionalist nobles, they may have faced an even more insurmountable challenge in the form of the innumerable privileged "corporations" in the kingdom. Obviously, the crown had the most to fear from those corps – for instance, the companies of financiers and the parlements – in which *esprit de caste* and *esprit de corps* intersected and proved mutually reinforcing. Just as the ministers could no longer launch extrajudicial inquests against "capitalists" who were no longer of the commonalty, so they found it difficult to overawe magistrates of impeccably noble lineage. But the dilemma went beyond even that. For how could Calonne or Loménie de Brienne or Lamoignon have possibly slain the hydra of parasitical corporate privilege that was suffocating the monarchy? It was truly the case that, as Rabaut Saint-Etienne had it, "one hears talk of nothing but rights, concessions, immunities, special agreements, privileges, prerogatives. Every town, every community, every province, every ecclesiastical or judicial body, has its interest to defend in this confusion.... A minister who wants to disentangle the wires does not know where to begin because as he touches them he makes the interest cry

129 See Stone, *Parlement of Paris*, pp. 161–63, for a discussion of the Parlement's stance on these issues.
130 Egret, *French Prerevolution*, pp. 47–54. For a detailed corroboration of Egret on this point, see Scott, *Response of the Royal Army*, pp. 27–33.

out to which they are attached."[131] The ministers striving in the late 1780s to "disentangle the wires," to enhance the efficiency of a state regarding itself still as the "arbiter of Europe," found that the proliferation of special corporate interests had deprived them of any rational basis on which to act.

But there was, ideologically speaking, yet another aspect to this. Some of the privileged corps were being tugged and pulled in opposing ideological directions during 1787 and 1788. If the parlements, for instance, were notorious strongholds of "aristocratic" reaction to the crown's meliorist legislation, they also won popular plaudits for their arraignment of "ministerial despotism" and (in some cases) for their idealistic renunciations of corporate rights and their stirring invocations of a renascent national interest.[132] But possibly just as significant (if not yet as methodically studied) were similar ideological tendencies in the lower echelons of French venal officialdom. Tentatively, it seems that some corporate bodies in these ranks were beginning to accustom their members to think in terms of legal rights – and statist threats posed to those rights. Hence, in their prescribed, humdrum activities such corps may have been, in a sense, seminars in modern notions of citizenship. In 1787–88, corporate forays into a universalistic discourse that played up the notions of popular consent to taxation, property rights, and above all else civic activism in all likelihood helped to erode the government's legitimacy while at the same time undermining the particularistic privileges of the corps themselves.[133]

It seems fair to conclude that, in 1787–88, Calonne and his successor Loménie de Brienne were both undone by a convergence of crises rooted deeply in expansionistic French absolutism – an absolutism that reflected and mediated sociocultural contention even as it initiated public policy. Just conceivably, a stronger economy in the 1770s and 1780s might have delayed the government's fiscal collapse by augmenting the tributes of noble and peasant taxpayers and by sustaining venal accountants' and bankers' short-term advances of capital to the crown. But, again, the chief conclusion to be derived from this chapter's analysis would seem to be that Louis XVI's ministers had to confront problems of a far more fundamental nature than whatever weaknesses might inhere in France's preindustrial economy.

Perhaps it would be best to close here with a few lines offering both retrospection and anticipation. In attempting to execute unprecedentedly ambitious policies abroad while simultaneously opting for absolutist principles and policies at home, France's rulers ensured that one day, against

131 Quoted in Behrens, *Ancien Régime*, p. 179.
132 This was most notably the case at Paris. See Stone, *French Parlements*, esp. chaps. 2 and 3.
133 Gail Bossenga, *The Politics of Privilege: Old Regime and Revolution at Lille* (Cambridge: Cambridge University Press, 1991), pp. 202–5.

a threatening backdrop of overextended foreign policy gone wrong, the crown would have to seek to "relegitimize" its finances (and therefore its policies) by accommodating its subjects' sociopolitical aspirations. But that would prove exceedingly difficult, since the French state's ongoing roles as an initiator of divisive constitutional and social change, and as a venue for debate over that change, would leave it exposed both to the nostalgic recriminations of sociopolitical conservatives and to the rapidly rising expectations of sociopolitical progressives. In such a condition of vulnerability abroad and at home, only a godlike combination of firmness and flexibility at Versailles could have enabled Louis XVI's government to raise a new structure of stability and glory upon the ruins of the past.

2

The descent into revolution: from August 1788 to October 1789

On 5 July 1788, the French government by decree invited "all Frenchmen, through provincial Estates or assemblies," to signify their opinions "on the appropriate rules to be followed" in the convocation of the Estates General. In August, the crown effectively acknowledged its own "temporary" insolvency but assured its creditors that the impending session of the Estates, now formally set for 1 May 1789 at Versailles, would permanently secure their investments. Yet, by October 1789, both king and Estates General (the latter now renamed the National "Constituent" Assembly) would be taking up new, Parisian quarters in the midst of a full-fledged revolution. Over the intervening period, dramatic events had transpired; most symbolically potent of them, for sure, was the Parisians' seizure of the Bastille on 14 July 1789.

This much is uncontested; but *why* events unfolded the way they did remains as controversial as ever. Georges Lefebvre, in what was for a long time the standard account of the coming of the Revolution, suggested that Louis XVI's government was determined on the eve of the July Days of 1789 to dissolve the increasingly rebellious Estates General, rely henceforth upon the support of the parlements, and "resign itself to bankruptcy."[1] Yet such a hypothesis, viewed from our global-historical perspective, seems wildly unrealistic. In late 1788 and 1789, *any* French king would very likely have been impaled on the horns of a dilemma recalling to us that which had faced Charles I of England and anticipating that which would confront Nicholas II of Russia. In each of these situations the sovereign was challenged both by history and by contemporary circumstances to uphold the integrity, and thus the financial viability, of his state; and yet doing so, in each case, required him to sanction domestic reforms subversive of his forebears' – and his own – public philosophy!

---

1 As cited in Lefebvre, *Coming of the French Revolution*, p. 91.

Cruel predicaments, to be sure; and, in the French case, this dilemma, recalling as well the challenge that the ancien régime had been unable in the end to meet, loomed in its initial revolutionary incarnation behind the events of August 1788–October 1789. After summarizing those events for the convenience of the reader, this chapter will analyze the onset of the French Revolution. It will start to do that by establishing the diplomatic and military backdrop to the historic drama of 1788–89. It will then reassess the failure of Louis XVI to make sociopolitical concessions that were probably crucial for the restoration of the French state's credibility (most imperatively, its international credibility) in the summer of 1789. Finally, it will show how that pivotal royal failure interacted with polarized elitist "sociopolitics" and with popular insurrection, thereby allowing the initiative in French policy-making to begin to pass from royal and ministerial hands into those of a revolutionary legislature.

PROLOGUE: NARRATIVE OF EVENTS

On 8 August 1788, the French government formally announced that the Estates General would meet at Versailles on 1 May 1789. This announcement was followed on 25 August by the resignation of Finance Minister Loménie de Brienne and his replacement by Jacques Necker. Necker confirmed the meeting of the Estates; he also restored the old judiciary. But the Paris Parlement's call (on 25 September) for Estates organized along traditional lines forced a hastily reconvened Assembly of Notables to consider this controversial question. When, however, the Notables themselves adopted a stubbornly traditional position on the Estates, and after the Princes of the Blood issued a fiercely reactionary commentary on public affairs, Necker brought about a royal intervention. But the king's decree (*Résultat du Conseil*) of 27 December only stoked the fires of controversy: although it called for twice as many Third Estate delegates as clerical or noble deputies to the impending national convocation, it failed to specify whether voting in that body would be "by order" or "by head." A war of pamphlets ensued, and sharpened already serious differences between adversaries and advocates of sociopolitical change.

In the early months of 1789, deputies to the Estates General were chosen, and grievance lists (*cahiers de doléances*) drafted, by electors at Paris and in the provinces. Once assembled at Versailles on 5 May, the Estates became swiftly bogged down in procedural disputes reflecting the deepening nationwide split between conservatives and "Patriots" or "Nationals." In the absence of effective royal/ministerial leadership, the Patriots decided to force a resolution of issues in June. On the seventeenth, progressive deputies induced the Third Estate to rename itself the National Assembly. On the nineteenth, a majority of clerical delegates voted to join the Third Estate in this endeavor. The next day, the members of the Assembly, excluded from their meeting place, swore a famous oath in a nearby tennis court not to disband before establishing a constitution for the country. At this point, Louis XVI once again intervened; but his rejection of fundamental sociopolitical change at the *séance royale* of 23 June only emboldened the Patriots to defy his will, and on the twenty-seventh the king felt constrained to order noble and clerical deputies to join the Third Estate in the newly designated National Assembly.

Louis, however, was not yet ready to yield to the progressive notables. In early July, troops were summoned to the environs of Versailles and the capital. Necker and several other reformist ministers were dismissed; their places were taken by individuals apparently supportive of a harder line on contentious social and constitutional issues. The popular response to this move (and to economic difficulties highlighted by the soaring price and localized scarcities of grain) was to seize the Parisian Bastille and the capital itself on 14 July. Once again, the king had no alternative but to back down: Necker and his disgraced colleagues were reinstated over the next few days. The Assembly was free to continue its work of national regeneration. Meanwhile, power in the provinces passed from the intendants and the old municipal elites to revolutionary National Guards and the progressive "notables" of cities, towns, and villages.

Even while savoring its triumph over the sovereign and his partisans, however, the National Assembly could never forget that it was legislating against a background of economic hard times and social unrest. Discontents festering in many rural regions since the spring broke out into insurrectionary movements over the summer as the strong hand of the government was removed. Rioting in the countryside reached an early peak in the "Great Fear" of late July and early August and continued to flare up here and there into the autumn. The Assemblymen at Paris were responding to this disorder, as well as acting out of altruism, when on the celebrated night of 4 August they "abolished" feudalism and much of the historic structure of French society.

The deputies, at the same time, had not yet vanquished royal and aristocratic opposition to their reforms. Louis XVI had not accepted the results of 4 August. He was only further alienated from the Assembly when it approved the text of a Declaration of the Rights of Man and the Citizen on 26 August and then, in the following weeks, voted down legislative bicameralism and accorded him merely a "suspensive" rather than an "absolute" veto over lawmaking. Already, militant politicians and journalists at Paris were talking of the need to install the king in his capital, where he (and the Court faction) could presumably be overawed by popular pressure.

A counterrevolutionary demonstration by the officers of a regiment recently summoned to Versailles provided the spark for a Parisian insurrection on 5–6 October. A riot of women over high bread prices quickly turned into a march of thousands of National Guardsmen and other Parisians to Versailles. The king tried to mollify these forces with belated sociopolitical concessions and a promise to ensure the provisioning of Paris, but in the end he had to accept his removal, and that of the Court, to the French capital. Since the National Assembly voted soon thereafter to follow its monarch, the "October Days" of 1789 had apparently secured revolutionary control of both the executive and legislative branches of the French government.

THE CRITICAL GEOPOLITICAL CONTEXT

In the caldron of diplomacy and war that was late-eighteenth-century Europe, those who closely monitored power politics were quick to take note of France's fall from greatness. "I hear much of French anger and of their plans for revenge," Lord Keith had observed complacently from England a few months before, "but I know that France has at this moment, a deadly fit of the gout, and is debilitated in her legs and arms."[2] The Prussian diplomat Hertzberg wrote tersely that "France has lost the alliance of Holland and the remnants of her prestige in Europe." Joseph II of Austria concurred. "This shows," he commented in a letter to his brother Leopold, "in how short a time so considerable a state . . . can lose credit, influence, vigor and power through the want of a capable leader and lack of order." And Catherine of Russia, so successful an aggrandizer of power herself, wrote contemptuously: "One cannot say that Louis XVI is flattered. Everything has been done to persuade him to accept guidance and to convince him that he understands nothing of his task." If the French were not going to bounce back from their decline, she continued, "then goodbye to the reputation acquired through two hundred years! And who will believe in people who have neither will, vigor, nor enterprise?"[3] These last reflections, coming as they did from one whose imperial predecessors had scarcely attracted notice at Versailles, drove home with particular force the collapse of France's international stature on the threshold of the revolutionary era.

What was more, the specific *timing* of the collapse – that is, its occurrence at the end of the 1780s – made it even more perilous (for France and, belike, for Europe as a whole) than it might have otherwise been. Since the close of the Seven Years' War, east European and west European

2 Cited in Jeremy Black, *British Foreign Policy in an Age of Revolutions, 1783–1793* (New York: Cambridge University Press, 1994), pp. 329–30.
3 Quotations are from Albert Sorel, *Europe and the French Revolution: The Political Traditions of the Old Regime*, trans. Alfred Cobban and J. W. Hunt (Garden City, N.Y.: Anchor Books, 1971), pp. 502–3.

diplomatic-military developments had tended to follow separate tracks. This state of affairs, however, proved to be temporary. Indeed, the outbreak of war between Russia and Turkey in the late 1780s touched off a sequence of events culminating in something not observed on the Continent for a generation: a crisis of European as opposed to merely regional dimensions.[4] Thus, the Anglo-Prussian defeat of the Dutch Patriots in 1787, however humiliating to the Patriots' backers at Versailles, was but an isolated squall heralding the approach of a tempest that could draw into its vortex all the powers of Europe. That France should be verging upon revolution in such a time of brewing continental troubles only lent additional urgency to its need to resynchronize its political and social systems, that is to say, its governmental and social-elitist values and ambitions. As we shall see, the politicization of French society that ensued during 1788–89 as a result of the country's converging geopolitical, constitutional, and social crises meant that growing numbers of people would come to acknowledge this critical nexus between foreign and domestic affairs. Catherine II's dismissal of the French as "people who have neither will, vigor, nor enterprise" would, as a result, stand revealed before very long as premature at best.

But the international challenge facing the French even as they concentrated most immediately upon their impending Estates General was formidable enough. Europe as a whole was becoming polarized between two potentially adversarial power blocs. On the one hand there was the combination, foreshadowed in October 1787 and formalized in August 1788, of Britain and Prussia. On the other hand there was the older alliance of Russia and Austria that finally bore full fruit in 1788 with Joseph II's decision to join Catherine the Great in a military assault on Ottoman Turkey. The Russo-Austrian collaboration threatened to destabilize the balance of power in eastern Europe radically. For that very reason (and because of the undiminished rivalry in Germany between Berlin and Vienna), there was a genuine chance that the British and Prussians might be drawn into war with St. Petersburg and Vienna over issues of geopolitics in the Near East.[5]

It was equally clear that France, habituated to seeing itself as the "arbiter of Europe," was utterly incapable of intervening on either side in this tense situation. Yet even if bankruptcy had not ruled out an active French role in the international politics of the day, could the statesmen at Versailles have gravitated happily toward either of the coalitions now existing on the Continent? On the one side, the British and Prussians had in alliance humbled the French twice since midcentury: that is, in 1757–63 and 1787. Now, Vergennes's successor, Armand-Marc, comte de Montmorin, held

4 Anderson, "European Diplomatic Relations, 1763–90," p. 274.
5 For a classic account of all this, see Sorel, *Europe and the French Revolution*, esp. pp. 502–5, 514–17.

steadfastly to the French tradition of distrust toward London and Berlin. The new foreign minister, to begin with, found it impossible not to suspect the eternal opponent across the Channel of scheming for the further reduction of French influence. "This government is jealous of us and hates us," Montmorin wrote on 8 February 1789; "if we are friendly with them they will want to dominate us; if we resist their desires they will not scruple to betray us. . . ." At the same time, the foreign minister was no less wary of Prussia's machinations.[6] Yet, on the other side, why should France hasten to endorse the actions taken in the Balkans by its nominal ally Austria in league with voracious Russia? It is true that Montmorin's colleague Saint-Priest later claimed in his memoirs that he, the foreign minister, and all the other members of the Council save for Necker had in early 1789 advocated Versailles's adherence to a "quadruple alliance" bringing together France, Austria, Russia, and Spain.[7] Such a diplomatic gambit by Versailles undoubtedly would have been one way of spiting the British and Prussian authors of the French humiliations of 1757–63 and 1787. In addition, it would have well served the purposes of those diplomatists, *militaires*, *gens de lettres*, and merchants in France who still dreamed of a vastly expanded sphere of French influence in the eastern Mediterranean. Still, adoption of such a policy at Versailles could not have been squared with the traditional French commitment to the security of Turkey, and it would have redounded chiefly to the advantage of the already dangerously successful Catherine of Russia.

Therefore, even a powerful, self-confident France in 1788–89 would have found it impossible – as it always had – to achieve predominance in Europe. This was all the more certain given the global-historical realities looming behind the Anglo-Prussian and Russo-Austrian alliances of the day. More than ever before, Great Britain and Russia were attuned to extra-European worlds wholly beyond the ken of their feuding German confederates, Prussia and Austria – and now largely beyond the reach of the crippled French as well.

There can be little doubt in retrospect that, by the late 1780s, Britain was consolidating its position as the most potent naval state in the world, prepared as no other country could be to project its power across the globe. Reflecting this unique status were the Britons' establishment of a colony in Australia in 1788 and their unremitting challenge to Spain's presence on the Pacific side of the New World. Moreover, London's success in the recent Dutch crisis had done much to preclude any French challenge to its imperial position.[8] Of course, British success in affairs abroad also spoke volumes

6 Ibid., pp. 514–15.
7 Robert Harris discusses this diplomatic option in *Necker and the Revolution of 1789*, pp. 304–6.
8 Black, *British Foreign Policy*, p. 536.

about fundamental economic and sociopolitical strengths at home. Indeed, against the background of a booming economy and growing bullion reserves in the Bank of England, and benefiting naturally from his country's securely rooted tradition of accountable governance, Pitt was at this time enacting fiscal and administrative reforms that would pay immeasurable dividends in the next round of European warfare. As Hawkesbury could smugly put it: "the revolutions that have lately happened in the government of France afford a very flattering contrast to the stability and prosperity of our administration."[9]

At the other end of Europe, Catherine's state enjoyed a similarly enviable situation. If, on the one hand, Russia lacked the insularity that spared the British the nightmare of a lightning invasion by land, on the other hand its Eurasian hugeness allowed it to play Berlin and Vienna off against each other, and its sheer distance from the West would for the foreseeable future insulate it somewhat from any destabilizing consequences of renewed Anglo-French conflict. Furthermore, just as London was occupying itself at this time with Australia, Spanish-held territories and markets on the "Pacific Rim," and other concerns far removed from Europe, so St. Petersburg was as immersed in its dealings with Persia and China as it was in its machinations in central and eastern Europe.

For France, then, any taking of diplomatic sides in 1788–89 would have entailed, even more than previously, a challenge to state power generated within but also far beyond the confines of west-central Europe. In point of fact, however, Versailles could not even think of attempting the impossible, as it had so often essayed it in the past. The king, the queen, and Necker realized only too well that governmental insolvency precluded for the time being any kind of French assertiveness in foreign affairs. Apart from the possibility that an alliance between France and Russia could impede rather than facilitate any French effort to mediate between Austria and Turkey, Marie-Antoinette repeatedly reminded her compatriot Mercy-Argenteau, it would require new expenditures on the French side and consequently give to the impending Estates General an excellent excuse to trespass on the king's domain of foreign policy.[10] As for Necker: Mercy-Argenteau reported somewhat simplistically and unfairly to Joseph II in April 1789 that the director-general of finances could see "only the financial problems to which he subordinates all else."[11]

It is certainly true that Necker, backed in this instance by the royal couple, prevailed in conciliar debates over militants like Saint-Priest, who held in 1789 (much as Nicholas II's advisers would hold, more successfully if not more wisely, in 1914) that resorting to warfare abroad might bank the

9 Ibid., pp. 135–36.
10 Harris, *Necker and the Revolution of 1789*, pp. 304–6.
11 Ibid.

rising fires of sociopolitical insurgency at home.[12] The Genevan therefore was able to block what otherwise would likely have become a costly new French involvement in the Byzantine alliance politics of the Continent. This did not at all signify, however, that Necker, as the guiding spirit of the moment at Versailles, was oblivious to resplendent French diplomatic tradition, or to the implications of stability and prosperity at home for the pursuit of security and prestige abroad. The conciliar decree (*Résultat du Conseil*) of 27 December 1788 is best known to historians for its attempt to arbitrate the dispute within the kingdom over procedural matters relating to the approaching assembly of the Estates; but it is noteworthy that the director-general in obtaining it was mindful, too, of larger issues. "If there is established in Your Majesty's finances an immutable order," the decree sanguinely prophesied, "if confidence soars, as one may hope, if all the forces of this great kingdom ... become vitalized, Your Majesty will enjoy in his external relations an ascendancy which adheres much more to real and well-ordered power than to an authority that is irregular."[13]

Less than five months later, in his eagerly awaited address of 5 May 1789 to the Estates General of the realm, the Genevan returned to this fundamental theme. "You will not forget that the financial needs of the government are not separate from your own," Necker somberly reminded his audience. Indeed, he continued, they were "one and the same," since "expenditures for defense, [and] for policing the kingdom, treating the creditors of the government justly, rewarding truly meritorious service, and the needs of maintaining the dignity of the foremost throne in Europe ... concern the nation as much as the monarch." Louis XVI's finance minister went on to declare that modern warfare could not be financed solely out of "ordinary" revenue; that loans would again be required should France reenter the lists of combat; and that, as a result, the financial integrity of the crown remained a matter of national security and honor.[14]

Like Calonne, Loménie de Brienne, and Lamoignon before him in the turmoil of the "prerevolution," so now Necker in the opening months of the Revolution itself was calling for and indeed bravely auguring the convalescence of France at home and abroad. Yet all his exhortations and assurances could not mask the embarrassing reality of French impotence in 1789. At the very least, France's nullity in continental affairs ruled out any credible mediatory role for Louis XVI's government in matters pitting Britain and Prussia against Russia and Austria.[15] Moreover, by treating so timorously with Russia over its envisaged quadruple alliance and then

---

12 Ibid., p. 305. Saint-Priest, for one, was explicit on this point in his later memoirs and recalled as well that he had advanced the same argument eighteen months earlier in connection with the Dutch crisis.
13 Quoted in ibid., pp. 330–31.
14 Cited in ibid., pp. 421–23.
15 Anderson, "European Diplomatic Relations," p. 275.

lamely rejecting the concept, Versailles only excited disdain in the courts of Europe. "By our rapprochement with Russia we have embittered the league (England, Prussia, Holland), [as well as] Poland, Sweden, and Turkey," wrote French ambassador Louis-Philippe, comte de Ségur, disconsolately from St. Petersburg on 22 May 1789. "By not signing the alliance," he went on, "we have given the two imperial courts a grievance. Thus we have got out of the alliance all the kicks and none of the halfpence. This is what our domestic troubles have brought us to." Ségur went so far as to raise the possibility of a reconciliation between London and Berlin, on the one hand, and St. Petersburg, on the other, that could "completely overthrow" French influence at Catherine's court even as it spelled a new defeat for Versailles's Turkish client.[16] And indeed, Ségur's anxiety on this last point may not have been in all respects unfounded: Austria's ever-vigilant Mercy-Argenteau had expressed a similar concern in his correspondence with Vienna just four months earlier.[17] Still, the outstanding fact here was not so much the diplomatic uncertainties attending the Near Eastern crisis as the total inability of the onetime "arbiter of Europe" to have anything effective to say about it.

Those holding the diplomatic and military portfolios at Versailles – Montmorin, Saint-Priest, Puységur, and La Luzerne – must have tasted especially bitter frustration as events now unfolded rapidly in eastern Europe. In the spring of 1789, Joseph II's forces, rebounding from setbacks of the preceding year, once more seized the offensive, sweeping through Turkish-held Serbia; by that autumn they would be in Belgrade. Sweden's audacious attack on Russia's northwestern flank soon fizzled out, due as much to mutiny in Gustav III's army and to general discontent within his kingdom as to Denmark's sudden strike against Sweden. Meanwhile, Catherine's gifted general Suvorov led a relentless Russian offensive against the Turks in eastern Romania. Sweden, abandoned by its onetime confederate France in 1789, would consider itself fortunate to be able to make peace with Russia upon a status quo ante basis in 1790; Turkey would be compelled to cede its Black Sea territories down to the Dniester River to the Romanov colossus; and Poland would feel more vulnerable than ever to its rapacious neighbors.

Clear winners, clear losers, and countries somewhere in between emerged from the fog and din of these dramatic developments. M. S. Anderson has accurately commented that "Russia . . . had shown a greater capacity for territorial expansion than any other European state and was now the greatest power on the continent." Austria, although deserted by France in its duel with Prussia, had gained at least temporarily at the expense

16 As quoted in Sorel, *Europe and the French Revolution*, p. 517.
17 See Harris, *Necker and the Revolution of 1789*, pp. 305–6.

of Turkey (also abandoned by France) and might look to consolidate its security in the always perilous reaches of eastern Europe through participation in a new division of Poland – yet another polity for which Versailles could do nothing more. Prussia still had its pact with London, was ever casting about restlessly for new friends on the Continent, and was not about to be outdistanced by either St. Petersburg or Vienna in demanding new territorial concessions from the embattled Poles. The British, fearful as always in 1788–89 of being dragged into the predatory power politics of central and eastern Europe, could hope to mitigate their continental anxieties by continuing to move ahead into industrialization and by solidifying their commercial links with the vast and inviting world beyond Europe. As for the French, they struck most observers as being destined for many years to relative inconsequence in international affairs.[18]

Were the French in fact to be left behind by the abhorred "modern Carthage" in the competition for the limitless resources of the extra-European world? And (in part as a result of *that* failure) would they have to acquiesce without a murmur in the unchecked shift of power on the Continent from a French-dominated west toward a "Slavic-Teutonic" east? Necker made it abundantly clear in the *Résultat du Conseil* of 27 December 1788, and in his address to the Estates General on 5 May 1789, that he was as alive as any of his colleagues to the worrying implications for French foreign policy of the sociopolitical crisis at home. External affairs challenged the director-general as urgently in 1788 and 1789 as they had ten years before. But the evolution of *internal* affairs since the heady days of France's intervention in British North America just as plainly complicated the situation faced by the French government. As responsibilities in all areas of public policy came gradually to be shared by broader circles of politicized citizens, would this undercut ministerial efforts to revive the war-making capabilities of France, or could Necker and his associates reasonably draw some encouragement from the patriotic sentiments of an awakening general public?

The issue was at all times in doubt, given the dynamic political and social factors now in play; what could not be questioned was the strength of that patriotism as full-fledged revolution set in. The recent emphasis in French Revolutionary historiography on political-cultural analysis has brought to light some intriguing evidence of a literate nation engaged in the process of recovering its historical identity even as Louis XVI's advisers lurched desperately from one financial expedient to another. For instance, of 230 political pamphlets published between February 1787 and

18 Anderson, "European Diplomatic Relations," p. 278. See also Ford, *Europe 1780–1830*, pp. 73–74, for corroboration of all these points.

March 1789 and subsequently analyzed, more than 50 percent invoked events in French history as so many arguments for asserting the current rights of the "national" community. Also, the authors of these treatises, as if to certify their "nationalist" credentials, were willing to mention English, Dutch, or Swiss constitutional precedents only insofar as they could then brand those precedents as inapplicable to France, given the country's unique traits and historical experience. Moreover, these publicists were determined to "make the history of France begin with the Franks." No longer would it be acceptable, as it had been for commentators like the abbé Dubos earlier in the century, to glorify the supposed link between the imperial tradition of ancient Rome and the unbridled sovereignty of later French kings. The "nation," sustained by claims of legitimacy harkening back to "Frankish" freedoms rather than to "Roman" servitude, would now reign in partnership with a king whose powers would henceforth be limited by the laws.[19]

And from a "nation" liberated as never before could emanate "nationalism" – a point elaborated in older studies as well as in scholarship keying recently upon political-cultural exegeses. It is true that the nationalism inspiring the French at the commencement of their revolution was not very strident. One of the first statistical analyses of the *cahiers de doléances* of 1789 yielded the cautious conclusion that the *patrie* of most French citizens at that time, however much it might celebrate the solidarity of king and nation and sanctify Jansenism and other national traditions, was tempered by "cosmopolitanism" and by a "peaceful and unaggressive spirit."[20] Yet how long could this emancipated national consciousness retain its cosmopolitan and pacific qualities in the seething crucible of continental and extracontinental politics? It turns out that those *cahiers de doléances* drawn up in northern and northeastern communities and jurisdictions likeliest to come to blows with France's customary foes, Britain and Austria, in time of renewed war most insistently demanded such reforms as nationalization of the army, universal liability for military service, increase of the navy, and state control of the making of war and peace. Such petitions, insisting that France uphold its historic honor and prestige, demanded (in the manner of radical essayists of the ancien régime) that, at the outbreak of war, the Estates General be forthwith summoned. In other words, war in the future was to be a national, not merely a dynastic enterprise. Finally, several *cahiers* quite candidly alleged the superiority of French institutions or looked upon France as the preeminent power in all Europe, or even of the entire world, and added that such a country must naturally be "an example

19 Furet, *Interpreting the French Revolution*, pp. 33–36.
20 Beatrice Hyslop, *French Nationalism in 1789 According to the General Cahiers* (New York: Octagon, 1968), pp. 194–95.

to the world." This "messianic psychology" only too plainly foreshadowed the chauvinistic oratory of the Legislative Assembly of 1791–92 and, beyond that, the bellicose mentality of 1793–94.[21]

What was more, a "messianic psychology" was already discernible in such institutions as the army and the soon-to-be National Constituent Assembly. Of course it is hardly astounding that this should have been the case with the military. Those Frenchmen who wielded authority in the army, whether of noble or common extraction, thought of themselves as professionals in the métier of war, trained to take up the cudgels against the perdurable Austrian foe – or to exact a sweet revenge against Prussia.[22] No matter how divisive status considerations may have been within army officer ranks in 1788–89, the stinging memory of Rossbach and other combat fiascos tended to forge within those ranks a countervailing patriotic consensus.

More intriguing were the sentiments of the neophyte representatives who transformed the Estates General into the National (Constituent) Assembly during the summer of 1789. It is true, of course, that the members of this body were little inclined at the time to hurl anathemas at the crowned heads of Europe. They had more pressing problems on their hands, including the drafting of a constitution for France. Still, it is worthy of note that the Assemblymen betrayed their underlying patriotism even as they went about this irenic task. "They have so much national vanity," observed a Swiss publicist of these legislators, "so much pretension, that they will prefer all kinds of stupidities of their own choice to the results of British experience."[23] During the constitutional debates, Robespierre declared that "the representatives of the French nation, knowing how to give their country a constitution worthy of her and of the wisdom of this century, were not delegated to copy servilely an institution [i.e., the English constitution] born in times of ignorance, of necessity, and of the strife of opposing factions." Camille Desmoulins brazenly predicted: "We shall go beyond these English, who are so proud of their constitution and who mocked at our servitude."[24] And Alexandre de Lameth queried amazedly: "Well! Do we not have the precious advantage over England of being able to assemble all the parts of our Constitution at the same time?" Even Jean-Joseph Mounier, marked for his Anglophile opinions, conceded defensively that it was in the power of France "to have a Constitution superior to that

21 Ibid., pp. 124–25, 172–73.
22 Jean-Paul Bertaud, *The Army of the French Revolution: From Citizen-Soldiers to Instrument of Power*, trans. R. R. Palmer (Princeton, N.J.: Princeton University Press, 1988), p. 21.
23 Cited in Frances Acomb, *Anglophobia in France, 1763–1789* (Durham, N.C.: Duke University Press, 1950), pp. 120–21.
24 Cited in ibid., p. 121.

of England."[25] Such rodomontade in the National Assembly, like much of the rhetoric in the anonymous pamphlets and official *cahiers de doléances* of the early Revolution, heralded "a spirit that would joyfully assume the mission of carrying that Revolution to other nations as well, by force of arms."[26]

True, not all of these politicians gave themselves over to disparaging constitutional arrangements across the Channel. Some of the more far-sighted among their number, including Mirabeau and Talleyrand, were concerned, like Vergennes before them, about the need to preserve an equilibrium of geostrategic forces in Europe, and seem accordingly to have been willing to solicit British aid in counteracting Russian, Prussian, and Austrian depredations to the east. This does not mean that such individuals were unstintingly pro-English. Surely Mirabeau was not – and yet at the same time he apparently concluded that the configuration of forces on the Continent was driving the English and his countrymen together. Indeed, in striking anticipation of diplomatic ideas that Talleyrand himself would relay to London just three years later, Mirabeau in 1789 optimistically broached the possibility of an Anglo-French collaboration in Spanish American markets that would reconfirm ties of friendship already rooted (he assumed) in the "Eden Treaty" of 1786 and in shared fears of St. Petersburg, Berlin, and Vienna.[27]

Whether such ruminations were any more realistic in 1789 than they had been in Vergennes's time may, however, be doubted. It is hard to see how even the most creative statesmanship could at this point have fashioned an Anglo-French pact warding off colonial and maritime rivalry between the two powers. All the more was this true in view of the English and French naval buildups undertaken during the Dutch imbroglio.[28] In any case, few of Mirabeau's and Talleyrand's compeers in the National Assembly drew such sophisticated distinctions between Great Britain, on the one hand, and the three east European autocracies, on the other. For most of these men, an unquestioned pride in country went hand in hand with an inveterate distrust of *all* foreign states. For precisely this reason, the Assemblymen striving to fashion a new France could not escape the misgivings and fears that derived then, as they would derive throughout the revolutionary era, from the turbulent international context of their efforts.

Today it is easy enough for us to perceive, through the eyes of Périsse-Duluc, a deputy from Lyon to the self-proclaimed Constituent Assembly,

25 Lameth and Mounier are cited in Egret, *La Révolution des notables: Mounier et les Monarchiens* (Paris: A. Colin, 1950), p. 149. My translation.
26 Acomb, *Anglophobia in France*, p. 123.
27 On the diplomatic thinking of Mirabeau and Talleyrand at this time, see Sorel, *Europe and the French Revolution*, pp. 311–12.
28 Black, *British Foreign Policy*, pp. 161–62.

how that international context could be translated into the nagging anxiety of one intelligent and articulate bourgeois. As June ended and July began, Périsse-Duluc got wind of alarming rumors that the king's reactionary younger brother, the comte d'Artois, would flee the country and solicit aid from foreign monarchs should his efforts to throttle reforms prove unavailing. And what could have been more natural? Was not Louis XVI brother-in-law both to the Habsburg emperor at Vienna and to the king of Naples? Furthermore, was he not cousin to Charles IV of Spain, and were not his two brothers, Provence and Artois, married to daughters of the king of Sardinia? Why, then, should such foreign princes *not* invade France at the sinister behest of Artois? Such a scenario seemed all the more believable to Périsse-Duluc in that he remembered having explicitly foreseen, before the first session of the Estates General, that France's aristocracy might follow the example of the Dutch counterrevolutionaries in 1787. They, needless to recall, had invited the Prussians in to secure a victory over their own compatriots! With memories of what had transpired in the United Provinces still unpleasantly fresh in Patriot minds, it would have been surprising if a reasonably well-informed bourgeois such as Périsse-Duluc had not found a number of his fellow delegates in the Third Estate sharing his fears and suspicions in that tense and eventful summer.[29] The latest inquiries into the Constituent Assembly, admittedly, suggest that most of the deputies did not subscribe this early in the Revolution to any notion of a conspiracy being hatched against the public weal.[30] Still, the "exposed" situation of France in battle-scarred Europe likely made it easier for some of these men to entertain such an idea.

Furthermore, elitist Frenchmen in the Constituent Assembly were often exposed to anxieties and paranoia in society's popular ranks. For the humbler classes, mistrust and outright fear of the world beyond France – and folk memories of how French kings had repeatedly raised troops to combat that world – interacted with and magnified a veritable complex of economic, social, and political concerns in the course of 1789. It was all too easy for artisans, urban laborers, and peasants, prey to the wildest of rumors even in the best of times, to believe in 1789 that selfish aristocratic reactionaries favored the hoarding of food in order to annihilate the Third Estate and, for similar reasons, were delighted to see the harvest being pillaged or the crops cut down before they were ripe. Even more to the point, those laboring subjects who viewed the "aristocrats" as

29 Lefebvre, *Coming of the French Revolution*, pp. 100–101.
30 See, in particular, Timothy Tackett, "Conspiracy Obsession in a Time of Revolution: French Elites and the Origins of the Terror, 1789–1792," *American Historical Review* 105 (2000): 691–713.

disposed to resort to arms naturally expected them to recruit followers among vagrants and vagabonds, just as the kings' recruiting officers filled their quotas from such sources. Furthermore, since it was widely expected that the aristocrats would call on foreign troops, was it not equally natural to believe that they would also draw on "brigands" from adjacent countries? It was this assumed and unholy collusion between highborn Frenchmen and foreigners of all social backgrounds that diffused anxiety about so-called brigands throughout the kingdom, endowing it thereby with major social and political significance. Townspeople and countryfolk reacted fearfully and at times violently to stories about the emigration of nobles, the movements of brigands, and the diabolical preparations of the British, Spanish, Piedmontese, and other foreigners to invade France.[31]

It is also important to note that, at times, the incendiary passions of the populace reflected international pressures in ways that were much more indirect, and hence much less obvious. For example, popular hearsay in 1788–89 frequently ascribed the widespread suffering occasioned by the industrial recession to the commercial treaty recently concluded with the nefarious English. Although subsequent scholarship has not unconditionally confirmed that contention, it *has* seen the recession as aggravated by the dislocation of markets for French goods in eastern Europe, and this latter phenomenon resulted directly from the military strife involving Russia, Austria, Turkey, and Sweden.

There were, in sum, a number of ways in which the old nexus between external and internal affairs reincarnated itself as part and parcel of the revolutionary process in France from the very beginning. The king and his closest advisers could not help but deplore the country's unabated decline among the European powers. It is difficult to see how they could have failed in the long run to assign a high priority to the task of reinforcing the security and (beyond that) restoring the traditional greatness of France in the world at large. What was more, a determination in the ministries to remain true to this international mission could – *under the right circumstances* – command powerful support among citizens in all walks of life motivated (in part) by pride in France and mistrust of foreigners. But "under the right circumstances" meant in the first place a monarch psychologically capable of accepting an ongoing process of sociopolitical reform at home that would accommodate the aspirations of progressive Frenchmen in the upper and middle classes. How, then, Louis XVI would position himself on fundamental constitutional and social questions unavoidably posed in 1789 would be critical.

---

31 Lefebvre, *Coming of the French Revolution*, pp. 108–9, 146. On all these points, see also, by the same author, *The Great Fear of 1789: Rural Panic in Revolutionary France*, trans. Joan White (New York: Pantheon, 1973).

THE FAILURE OF THE KING TO COMPROMISE

There can be no doubt that the process of change in France in and after 1789 would have been markedly different – among other things, probably, less violent – had Louis XVI been able to relinquish unequivocally his commitment to the old ways of absolutism and social privilege. Yet such speculation is as profitless in connection with this monarch as like conjecture would be in the cases of England's Charles I and Russia's Nicholas II. The entire course of events from August 1788 to October 1789 revealed that this sovereign, like his counterparts in the other revolutions, simply could not bend to the degree required by evolving geopolitical and sociopolitical realities. Some of the kingdom's brightest luminaries tried to convince Louis XVI that basic sociopolitical reform was inescapable and that he, as king, would in fact be a prime beneficiary of that reform; and Necker, the minister who for the moment attracted most patriotic and progressive hopes, certainly argued and acted in the same sense. But Louis, confirmed in his conservative sociopolitical leanings at pivotal moments during 1789 by reactionaries in the country's splintering social elite, would not adequately heed the voices counseling compromise. He thereby helped unfailingly to radicalize the situation within the realm.

In the late months of 1788, some of France's most thoughtful citizens, moved by their fidelity to and concern for the royalist cause, spoke out on the pressing need for the crown to sponsor domestic reform. The retired chancellor, Maupeou, wrote to Louis XVI that the nation lacked integrative principles that could focus its latent loyalties. "Hence ... the eternal condemnation [of the government] ... which is nearly always absurd ... [and] the continual tendency towards the fragmentation of desires which if united would make for the strength and prosperity of the monarchy. The people, almost everywhere left to itself, sees in the government only the force which restrains and represses it."[32] Even more to the point was a memorandum forwarded to the king from another minister in retirement, Malesherbes, as soon as the Estates General became the object of serious discussion in the conclaves of power. Malesherbes, in language recapitulated by the barrister Pierre-Louis Lacretelle, exhorted Louis to convene a new kind of national consultative body. "Seize people's imagination with an institution that will surprise them and please them, that the nation will approve and in which it can more easily prevail." A sovereign at the close of the eighteenth century, insisted Malesherbes, should be summoning "the proprietors of a great nation renewed by its civilization," not convoking the "three Orders" of the fourteenth century. A constitution, he went on, should "correspond to the best ideas produced and tested by discussion." And the erstwhile minister enjoined his king: "Create the constitution of your century; take

32 Quoted in Behrens, *Society, Government and the Enlightenment*, p. 164.

your place in it, and do not fear to found it on the rights of the people."[33] Wise counsel, this – and, it seems, very similar to confidential advice that Mirabeau was at a later point to tender to the king.

And many were the publicists who argued in a like vein for a natural compatibility of royal and popular interests. Proclaimed Lanjuinais: "The king is the supreme motor, the repository of executive power. He gives the laws, consented to by the nation, the seal of public authority. He is the necessary support of the people, the foundation stone of our social edifice." Averred Lacretelle: "The august monarchy fits our physical situation and our moral nature. Our aims and principles do not tend to weaken it; we wish only to regulate it in order to strengthen it." And Servan riposted sarcastically against those *privilégiés* resolved to stand between Louis XVI and the citizenry: "There now exists in France a sedition of about 20 million subjects of all ages and sexes, who ask only to unite with their king against two or three hundred magistrates, a few hundred great lords, the sacred little legion of bishops, and fellow-plotters who, in the name of the 1614 convocation [of the Estates General], would reduce the people to an extremity."[34]

Such individuals, eager to see the crown rejuvenated through a constitutional process (a process that "respectable" citizens presumably would control) pinned most of their hopes on the Genevan financier reinstalled at Versailles in August 1788. And there is every indication that Necker, whatever his faults and miscalculations, labored honestly to fulfill their expectations. The resultant tension between a minister striving to renovate and thus preserve the monarchy and a sovereign passively resisting those efforts constituted one of the dominant themes in this period of transition from prerevolution to revolution in France.

From the very start of his second ministry, Necker perceived as clearly as did the Maupeous, Malesherbes, and Mirabeaus the crying need of France for a new "constitution" – in the broadest sense, for a reintegration of public purposes and private talents and aspirations. He argued, then, all the more insistently that the crown, having already tied its legitimacy explicitly to the convocation of the Estates General, must now proceed with that assemblage and must try to make of it the "single great enterprise ... that would ensure public regeneration." The kingdom, contended the director-general of finances, had had its fill of "continual vicissitudes in the fundamental principles of government." Without question, it longed for "a proper and durable balance finally established between incomes and expenses, cautious use of credit, sensible distribution of taxes, a general plan of public charity, an enlightened system of legislation, and above

33 Cited in Egret, *French Prerevolution*, p. 188.
34 For these citations, see ibid., pp. 196–97 and 210.

all, a constitutional guarantee of civil liberty and political liberty."[35] But Necker also knew all too well that the selfsame "kingdom" was composed of a plethora of political and social interests that would have to yield ground on some very specific issues were France to attain these objectives. "Throughout his second ministry," Robert Harris has plausibly argued, "Necker's role was that of mediator, attempting to find the right compromise that would be not only acceptable but just to all sides, and reasonable in the light of the circumstances."[36]

Thus, after the deliberations in the reconvened Assembly of Notables in the late autumn of 1788 drove a wedge between progressives and conservatives over the composition and procedures of the approaching Estates General, the director-general announced in his *Résultat du Conseil* of 27 December several governmental decisions intended to heal the divisions over this imminent convocation.[37] For instance, deputies of the Third Estate were to be as numerous as all clerical and noble representatives taken together. Such a measure, in addition to pleasing all progressive spectators in the throng of public opinion, would guarantee the presence in the assembly of men of affairs who could offer the government much valuable advice on economic and administrative matters. Again, voters would be able to deputize to the assembly at Versailles Frenchmen hailing from any of the three orders, and not solely individuals from their own Estates. Necker hoped that this concession would be particularly efficacious in fostering a spirit of national solidarity among the delegates and their constituents.

It is true that the Genevan in other respects accepted the recommendations from the "second" Assembly of Notables, in the process disappointing many of his progressive supporters. Most notoriously, Necker stated that, in the impending convocation as in its predecessor of 1614, deliberation and voting would be "by order" rather than "by head" unless the king and the three orders should in unanimity decide otherwise. Yet Necker manifestly hoped that if the three orders should reach deadlock on any concrete issue or issues they might agree to meet in common to resolve their differences. Furthermore, and of far greater significance, the director-general used the *Résultat du Conseil* to proclaim in so many words the "abdication of Louis XVI as an absolute monarch." According to the controversial *Résultat*, the king had informed his ministers that he would never levy another imposition without the Estate General's sanction; that he would consult with the upcoming assemblage about its periodicity in the future; that he would ask for its advice on how to ensure henceforth a competent management of public finances; and that

35 Cited in ibid., p. 189.
36 Harris, *Necker and the Revolution of 1789*, p. 325.
37 For a recent and detailed analysis of the *Résultat du Conseil*, see ibid., pp. 323–33.

he would invite the Estates to debate such questions as the freedom of the press, the use of *lettres de cachet*, and the publicizing of the government's ordinances.

At this point, it seems, Necker deemed financial issues to be the main obstacle to consensus among the three orders. "It will never enter the minds of the Third Estate," the director-general confidently prognosticated, "to seek to diminish the prerogatives, either seignorial or honorific, of the first two orders, or their property, or their persons. There is no Frenchman who does not recognize that these prerogatives are as respectable a property right as any other, that several are intimately linked to the essence of a monarchy."[38] Such an assessment, however, was in the end to prove overly sanguine: conservatives and progressives in the course of the following year would be falling out over a daunting array of social issues. Moreover, even Robert Harris, a biographer strongly sympathetic toward Necker, has conceded that the Genevan underestimated the constitutional difficulties attending the creation of a durable balance between the executive powers to be retained by the crown and the legislative role to be acquired by the new national assembly. Thus Necker, however sincerely he intended through promulgation of the conciliar decree of 27 December 1788 to overcome discord within the emerging body politic of the realm, failed to anticipate the intractability of both social and constitutional questions.

The director-general nonetheless pursued his policy of domestic conciliation in addressing the opening session of the Estates General on 5 May 1789. Seemingly with his noble listeners in mind, he urged that "those distinctions which pit citizens in opposition to one another because of status or birth" be subordinated, at least for the time being, to the public welfare. "We do not ask you to forget them entirely; they even make up the social order, they form that chain so necessary for the regulation of society. But these rival considerations must be suspended for a time, and their sharpness mitigated, to be returned to only after a long period has been spent working in common for the general interest."[39] Necker, it appears, was looking for accommodations on social and constitutional issues to be reached in France as he believed they had been achieved on the other side of the Channel. Indeed, Harris has suggested that the king's principal minister was angling for the establishment in France of a constitution somewhat like that of the British. Presumably this would have allotted a significant executive role to the monarch even while providing for a periodically elected and convened legislature of two chambers. However, the upper legislative chamber would have amounted to something more than the British House of Lords, and would just as obviously have been more than a citadel of France's "privileged orders." The king would have chosen

38 Quoted in ibid., p. 328.
39 Cited in ibid., p. 426.

its members from a pool of citizens who, whatever their origins in French society, had served the *patrie* with distinction.[40] Yet from what we know today about the Anglophobia that was never altogether absent from the Constituent Assembly – Anglophobia that, Necker himself states, the king shared as well in 1789 – a constitutional settlement drawing even to this limited extent upon British experience was unlikely to find many adherents in France.[41]

There is still considerable debate among scholars over the foresight and forcefulness of Necker's stewardship of public affairs during these critical months. Virtually no one today would deny that the director-general succeeded at least temporarily in reviving the royal finances. Yet some specialists have faulted him for holding unrealistic expectations of the Estates General and thus for leaving the nation without adequate direction on the fundamental problems it had to confront.[42] Again, we have seen even a largely sympathetic biographer like Robert Harris conceding the Genevan's oversimplification of the issues involved in constitutional change in France. Finally, there are those who have suspected Necker of trying to turn the schism between the conservatives and progressives to the king's, or to his own, benefit.[43]

There may be some truth to all these strictures. Necker at least might have tried to act more decisively than he did at certain points – for example, by prescribing the vote by head for the Estates in the *Résultat du Conseil*, by sponsoring candidates for that assembly, and by laying out an elaborate program of reforms during the electoral campaign in the spring of 1789. He was certainly bombarded by friendly counsel to all those effects. It is also rather strange that a minister as familiar as Necker was with the ambiguities of constitutional questions in this country should have exuded such optimism regarding the allocation and delimitation of executive and legislative powers in the governing arrangements of the future. Finally, if (as we know) the authorities in the summer of 1788 had unabashedly sought to foment discord among their critics as part of their effort to delay the convocation of the Estates General, was not Necker, at least in theory, just as capable of resorting to divisive tactics the following spring?

Still, whatever justice may adhere to such criticisms, they may in a very real sense be beside the point. For in the final analysis Necker, like any other minister of Bourbon France, had to defer to his royal master; and

---

40 Ibid., pp. 434–35.
41 Necker's characterization of Louis XVI's distrust of all institutions British is cited by Egret, *Necker: Ministre de Louis XVI, 1776–1790* (Paris: Champion, 1975), p. 323. See also, on the same subject, ibid., p. 351.
42 See, for example, Doyle, *Origins of the French Revolution*, pp. 139, 150.
43 Consult, for instance, Fitzsimmons, "Privilege and the Polity in France," pp. 278–79, regarding the crown's issuance in January 1789 of regulations for the convening of the Estates General.

there is simply no evidence that Louis XVI was at bottom prepared to concede what it was probably necessary for him to concede on the cogent sociopolitical issues of the day.

To be sure, the king and queen seem to have been sufficiently angered by aristocratic opposition to the reforms of Brienne and Lamoignon in the summer of 1788 to have rallied to the Genevan at the summer's end. The king may have "welcomed" Necker back into the conclaves of power at Versailles with palpable reluctance, but both he and Marie-Antoinette could perceive that Necker's enemies had also been Loménie de Brienne's detractors. They also knew that only this reputed master of financial wizardry could now lure French and foreign funds back to the thoroughly discredited "arbiter of Europe." Hence, the Genevan, at least for the time being, and above all for geopolitical reasons, was empowered once more in France.

However, when push came to shove, what did this reinstatement actually amount to? As Louis XVI's most recent biographer has had to admit, the king in the wake of the *Résultat du Conseil* seemed utterly unprepared to think in terms of trying to influence the elections to the Estates General by such concrete means as backing suitable candidates or overseeing the drafting of model *cahiers de doléances*. To all those trying to fathom the government's intentions at this critical juncture, Louis remained obstinately unapproachable and silent. "Silence was now not just to questions but on questions."[44] Thus, to criticize Necker for failing to seize the political initiative in late 1788 and early 1789 is, in the end, to ponder the failings of the man he served.

Come the stalemate in the Estates General in June 1789, however, the king had, finally, to divulge his deepest convictions. Georges Lefebvre rightly observed that Louis XVI's exposition of those reforms he deemed acceptable for France at the *séance royale* staged in the Assembly on 23 June "is of the utmost interest because it shows clearly what was at stake, not only in the following weeks but in the whole Revolution."[45] Whether, however, the monarch was as "willing to become a constitutional monarch" as Lefebvre claimed he was, and hence betrayed inflexibility only on *social* questions, is less certain. We can most fully elucidate this matter by contrasting Necker's ideas on reform, submitted to the royal Council on 19 June, with those articulated by the king at the royal session four days later.

Necker was assuredly not at this moment of truth calling for an unconditional surrender by the crown on all substantive points raised in recent days

---

44 John Hardman, *Louis XVI* (New Haven, Conn.: Yale University Press, 1993), p. 145.
45 Lefebvre, *Coming of the French Revolution*, p. 87.

by reformist Assemblymen and publicists.[46] He would, for instance, have had the king insist that the future legislature be bicameral, require royal sanction for all its acts, and acknowledge royal retention of the "plenitude of executive power." The finance minister suggested, moreover, that the public be barred from the Assembly's deliberations and urged that the honorific privileges of the nobility be declared sacrosanct. Yet in other respects the Genevan called for a fundamental break with the past. The king would command that the bickering delegates of the three orders reassemble and vote in common, that is, by head, on all questions of "general interest." These would include "the financial measures, taxes and loans, and accountability." No more would the king ask that the "privileged orders" surrender their financial prerogatives; he would summarily abrogate them himself. "Also, and the most significant clause, the deliberations on the new constitution would be done in the common assembly and the vote taken by head." Necker also would have had the king satisfy many of the most salient demands in the Third Estate's *cahiers*. Thus, Louis XVI should admit qualified commoners to all civilian and military employments, abolish the tax (*franc fief*) on plebeian owners of fiefs, and make it possible for peasants to redeem the feudal payments they owed to their seigneurs. In addition, Necker wanted the king to recognize each individual's rights to security and property, freedom of assembly and of the press, and in fact "all the rights later appearing in the Charter of 1814."

Had the French sovereign announced these changes to the self-proclaimed National Assembly on 23 June 1789, and stood by them thereafter, the whole course of the Revolution might have been different. But, inevitably, he was lobbied by the queen, by his brothers, and by conservative ministers and courtiers – all of them to one degree or another caught up in the politics of polarization within the country's social elite – to follow what probably was in any case his own inclination and reject Necker's ideas. Indeed, Louis's message to the Assemblymen on 23 June diverged markedly from that formulated by his director-general of finances.

At that fateful session, the king commanded the deputies of the "Estates General" (as he continued to call this body) to retire to their respective chambers. They were to deliberate and vote *by order* on all questions save those for which the unanimous consent of the three estates and the monarch secured discussion and suffrage in common and by head. Accordingly, everything – the form of the constitution, the structure of society, even the fiscal immunities of the clergy and nobility – was effectively to be held

---

46 For this discussion of Necker's and the king's ideas on reform in June 1789, see Harris, *Necker and the Revolution of 1789*, esp. pp. 506–7 and 514–18; Hardman, *Louis XVI*, pp. 149–53; and Munro Price, "The 'Ministry of the Hundred Hours': A Reappraisal," *French History* 4 (1990): 317–39. Direct quotes unless otherwise noted are from Harris.

hostage by the members of the first two orders. True, Louis did repeat his "exhortation" of 5 May that the three orders come together "for this session of the States-General only" to discuss matters of public interest. But he expressly designated as off-limits to deliberation and suffrage in common some of the most pivotal issues: "the feudal and seigneurial rights of the fief-owners, the economic and honorific privileges of the first two orders, all matters concerning religion and ecclesiastical organization," and, perhaps most sweepingly of all, "the future organization of the States-General, in other words, the Constitution."

In light of these remarks, prescribing as they did restrictions upon meaningful change in this war-prone realm, it simply was not enough for Louis XVI to announce grandly that the "Estates General" would henceforth be convened periodically; that it would supervise and control the finances of the crown and discharge many administrative duties; and that he, as king, would grant all the basic rights and liberties invoked in the *cahiers*. It would have been truly astounding had the representatives of the Third Estate not regarded the implementation of such a program as likely to curtail drastically their public roles in the new France. The king's parting threat – to send the deputies home if they should prove recalcitrant and then take upon his own shoulders the task of regenerating the country – only added fuel to fires of legislative rebellion that, in alliance with the blaze of popular rage in city and countryside, would soon incinerate the sociopolitical institutions of the old France.

It is telling that even the most sympathetic scholarly interpretations of Louis XVI's stance at the *séance royale* of 23 June 1789 have portrayed it as inadequate to the times. The king's most recent biographer, though stoutly contending that the royal address differed more in its emphases than in its substance from what Necker would have had Louis say, has still allowed that those changes in "emphasis" were in the circumstances fatal. In fact, if this account is correct, the king wanted to hedge even further against disruptive reforms by requiring a two-thirds majority even to carry motions discussed and voted on by all delegates in common sessions of the Estates.[47] Louis XVI has fared no better at the hands of those revisionists who focus narrowly on the issues of the *séance royale*. At best, they see the program set forth on 23 June as a compromise between the position of the king and queen, on the one hand, and that of Louis XVI's youngest brother, the comte d'Artois, on the other. But this, unhappily, is not saying much for the reformist cause! Artois emerges on the pages of revisionist historians, as on those of most earlier scholars, as the most inflexible paladin of ancien régime absolutism and privilege in the crisis of 1789. His actions prevented Louis XVI and Marie-Antoinette from adopting bolder measures toward

47 Hardman, *Louis XVI*, p. 153.

conciliating the Third Estate, concede such revisionists, and thus helped to deepen the sociopolitical crisis. In the end, the "glimmerings of accommodation" offered by the king to the deputies at the *séance royale* "were not enough to satisfy the third estate."[48]

Another way to point up the inadequacy of the royal position on 23 June 1789 – and at the same time highlight the connections between geopolitical, constitutional, and social issues – is to focus for a moment on the practical and crucial question of access to military employment. When Necker spoke out on behalf of the concept of meritocracy in the Council on 19 June, he was immediately assailed by his more conservative colleagues. In particular, the war minister Puységur bitterly protested "against any measure by which the king's hands should be tied in the appointment of army officers, and the king, much disturbed by this possibility, blamed Necker for having even thought of it."[49] Here we have both a constitutional question of *power* – should the executive continue to monopolize control of the kingdom's armed forces? – and a social question of *defining that kingdom's power elite* – should all Frenchmen qualified to serve their country in its positions of public responsibility be permitted to do so irrespective of their social origins? As we have seen, Louis XVI, at the behest of conservatives of Council, Court, and countryside, chose to go against his finance minister's advice, answering the former query in the affirmative and the latter query in the negative. In doing so, he was unwisely seeking to swim against the current of sociopolitical evolution in France. But the controversy over appointments to the army in 1789 also draws our attention again to the old issue transcending domestic matters: the connection between the foreign and internal policies of the French state. The controversy reminds us that behind the origins and process of the French Revolution lay the imperative need of France to harness its people's aspirations, wealth, and talents to its statist requirements – meaning, in the first instance, its geostrategic statist requirements.

Over the next four months Louis XVI would be coerced on no fewer than three occasions to retreat publicly from the position he had staked out at the *séance royale* of 23 June. He retreated immediately after the *séance* itself in order to hold onto the services of Necker, who was riotously championed by the populace of Paris and Versailles; and of course he abandoned the field again after the July and October Days. In connection with the July crisis, it has been argued that the Council never really had the stomach to impose a solution by military means, and that even Necker's short-lived and conservative successor Breteuil would have preferred, for personal and policy related reasons, to negotiate a settlement of outstanding issues with

48 Price, "The 'Ministry of the Hundred Hours,'" esp. pp. 322–27.
49 As reported by Lefebvre, *Coming of the French Revolution*, pp. 83–84.

the aroused parliamentary leaders of the Third Estate.[50] In a similar spirit, it has been suggested that some Third Republic historians were too ready to assume the existence of a dark conspiracy of Court reactionaries lurking behind the October Days.[51] Such revisionism may be well founded. But it has nothing really new to say about the crucial issue – namely, the attitude of Louis XVI. Although this sovereign, in 1789, neither raised the banner of civil war in the provinces in imitation of Charles I nor ordered his troops to mow down his countrymen in unknowing prefigurement of Nicholas II, he does appear to have rejected, in the sullen depths of his conscience, the momentous sociopolitical changes that the year brought to France.

For example, Louis XVI reacted to the decrees pushed through the Constituent Assembly on the tumultuous night of 4 August, decrees that curtailed seigneurial and particularist privileges in the kingdom, by writing to the archbishop of Arles: "I will never consent to the spoliation of my clergy or of my nobility. I will not sanction decrees by which they are despoiled."[52] And he condemned all the concessions wrung from him over the summer in a statement sent surreptitiously to his Spanish cousin, Charles IV, soon after the October Days had forced the royal family's removal to Paris. "I owe it to myself, to my children, to my family and to my entire dynasty," the statement read in part, "not to . . . let the royal dignity, confirmed in my dynasty by the passage of centuries, become debased in my hands." Louis informed his regal cousin that he had selected him, as head of the "second branch" of the House of Bourbon, "to receive my solemn protest against all the acts contrary to my royal authority extracted from me by force since 15 July of this year, and, at the same time, to witness my determination to fulfill the promises I made in my pronouncement of 23 June."[53] This was the catechism of someone schooled since childhood to believe in the divinity of his rule and of the old society of estates and *privilège*. Louis was never to deviate from this philosophy. His persistent refusal to do so was one of the factors that in 1789 and subsequent years led respectable Frenchmen who favored the recovery of Gallic power abroad and progressive reformism at home to endorse a degree of revolutionary violence that they otherwise would never have tolerated.

To refer in this connection to "respectable Frenchmen" is to introduce this chapter's final task: to place the critical policy differences between Necker and the king in 1788–89 in a broader political and social context. It is evident that the two men, in disagreeing over substantive issues, were in part responding to, and in part helped to further, the process of polarization

---

50 Price, "The 'Ministry of the Hundred Hours,'" esp. p. 336.
51 See Harris, *Necker and the Revolution of 1789*, passim.
52 Cited in Lefebvre, *Coming of the French Revolution*, p. 185.
53 Cited in Egret, *Necker*, p. 372. My translation.

within the country's aroused elite of leisured Frenchmen – clerics, lay nobles, and bourgeois. Just as plainly, the readiness of French "elitists" to fall out over fundamental constitutional and social issues encouraged humbler souls of town and country to add their raucous voices to the national debate over the kingdom's regeneration. All of these social dynamics were inevitably reflected in the politics of the new legislative body toward which the management of public affairs began to gravitate before the end of 1789.

THE POLITICS OF POLARIZATION: TOWARD THE OCTOBER DAYS

Historians today generally agree that it took the elections to the Estates General in the spring of 1789 and subsequent events to transform the tensions long festering in elite French society into revolutionary and counterrevolutionary politics and to incite broad-based popular insurrection as well. Yet the former of these social developments, at least, was foreshadowed in the preceding autumn and winter, when clerics, nobles, and bourgeois were forced by the imminence of the Estates General to begin crystallizing their sociopolitical philosophies.

The authorities from July 1788 on cleared the way for a truly national discussion of public issues by granting broad freedom to the press, liberating all or most booksellers and pamphleteers who had recently been incarcerated for disseminating antiministerial writings, and tolerating "clubs," "societies," and other associations in the capital and elsewhere. The various clubs and societies, once given free rein, took it upon themselves to publish the tracts of the abbé Siéyès and other Parisian luminaries of the "Patriot" Party. They also corresponded with "Patriot" societies and individuals in the provinces and helped to circulate works by such provincial notables as Rabaut Saint-Etienne, Albisson, and the comte d'Antraigues, all from Languedoc; Jean-Joseph Mounier and Lenoir-Laroche from Dauphiné; Brittany's Volney; and Servan from Provence.[54]

Prominent among these activist organizations was the Society of Thirty. Some of its members, courtiers of the old aristocracy, embraced sociopolitical change because they had lost out in the competition for government posts and patronage to families of the provincial squirearchy; others, whether issuing from the military noblesse, the judicial nobility, or the bourgeoisie, acted out of genuine idealism.[55] In any case, from such clubs,

---

54 Egret, *French Prerevolution*, p. 193.
55 On the Society of Thirty, see especially Daniel L. Wick, *A Conspiracy of Well-Intentioned Men: The Society of Thirty and the French Revolution* (New York: Garland, 1987).

and from the outpouring of pamphlet literature associated with them, emerged the challenge of the National or Patriot party to the status quo in France at the end of 1788.

Addressing constitutional questions, some in this faction – including Huguet de Sémonville, the prince de Beauvau, and Jean-Nicolas Démeunier – looked hopefully to regular Estates General and rejuvenated provincial Estates to rescue the kingdom from the yoke of "despotism." Others, such as Mounier and Rabaut Saint-Etienne, spoke of adopting the English constitution. The most audacious among them, like Siéyès, located the nation's sovereignty squarely and without appeal in a hypothetical unicameral legislature.[56]

But constitutional issues could not be aired without invoking social issues as well. Declared Mirabeau: "War on privileges and privileged, that is my motto. Privileges are useful against kings but detestable against nations, and ours will never have a public spirit until delivered from them." Exhorted Target: "Provinces, cities, courts, companies, Orders – oppose the king with your privileges, but strike them [down] before France assembled." And A.-J.-J. Cérutti pierced to the heart of the matter as the Patriot faction perceived it:

It is said that the people are conspiring on all sides against the nobility, the clergy, and the magistracy. Here is the conspiracy: excluded from brilliant careers in the army, they are allowed only to die there. Excluded from high dignities in the church, they are allowed only to work there. Excluded from important positions in the courts, they are allowed only to plead there. Excluded from the legal share of legislative authority in the Estates General, they will be allowed only to pay there.

It does not seem that, at this (relatively early) point, most Patriots were specifically advocating the abolition of the old schema of orders, either within the impending Estates General or within society as a whole. But they most certainly were arguing for a France in which social rank would reflect merit rather than genealogy; and double representation for the Third Estate and voting by head in the approaching convocation were in their minds prerequisites to that end. "The fate of the nation is at stake," warned Target. "With such great issues every uncertainty is a danger; every worry, a torment; every truth, a duty."[57]

Crucially, too, support for modernizing the Estates General's makeup and procedures and for the whole notion of meritocracy in society was now welling up from the grass roots. "The nobility's privileges are truly properties, all the more respected because we are not excluded from them

56 Refer again to Egret, *French Prerevolution*, p. 194. On abbé Siéyès in particular, see William H. Sewell, Jr., *A Rhetoric of Bourgeois Revolution: The Abbé Sieyès and What Is the Third Estate?* (Durham, N.C.: Duke University Press, 1994).
57 Quotations are from Egret, *French Prerevolution*, pp. 195–96.

but may acquire them," proclaimed the barristers of the Burgundian town of Nuits. "Why should anyone suppose we would think of destroying the seeds of emulation, the lodestar of our labors?" At Rouen in Normandy, bourgeois in huge numbers signed a petition to the king clamoring for deliberation in common in the Estates. In Provence, nineteen communities and nine parishes drafted petitions demanding doubling of the Third. By 30 December, one *nouvelliste*, generally well informed, could report that "the number of demands from Provinces, Cities, Communities, and Corporations for the doubling of the Third Estate is immense, and some put it at more than 800 without reckoning those arriving here daily from all quarters."[58] Needless to add, many of these manifestoes called as well for voting "by head" in the Estates and for "careers open to talent" in French society. Yet, again, a cautionary remark is indicated. "Most advocates of the Third Estate," Michael Fitzsimmons has noted, "were simply seeking a role coequal to that of the other two orders in the management of the state.... Indeed, all over France the Third Estate made clear how modest and limited its goals were and how favorably disposed it was to the maintenance of social distinctions."[59]

Even this, however, was too much in late 1788 for those elitists committed to the unqualified survival of the old regime. Spearheading the defense of the old France was the Parlement of Paris, which reacted to the Patriots' clamor for sociopolitical change on 25 September by counseling that the Estates be modeled in composition and procedures upon the convocation of 1614. The judges, in other words, raised the specter of a national assembly that, with equal contingents representing the three orders and with voting on all issues by estate rather than by head, would effectively stifle all meaningful reform. Though a case certainly can be made for discerning in this pronouncement a vestige of the Parlement's Jansenism and Gallicanism,[60] it probably constituted more than anything else a conservative reflex against a perceived threat of destabilizing change. This was the interpretation of the Parlement's action offered later by two of the magistrates who had attended the tribunal's session of 25 September.[61] The parlementaires wished, however quixotically, to preserve the balance of sociopolitical forces characterizing the France they

---

58 Ibid., esp. pp. 206–43.
59 Michael P. Fitzsimmons, *The Remaking of France: The National Assembly, the Constitution of 1791 and the Reorganization of the French Polity, 1789–1791* (New York: Cambridge University Press, 1994), pp. 28–30.
60 See Van Kley, "The Estates General as Ecumenical Council: The Constitutionalism of Corporate Consensus and the *Parlement*'s Ruling of September 25, 1788," *Journal of Modern History* 61 (March 1989): 1–52.
61 These testimonies (by Louis François de Paule Lefevre d'Ormesson and Guy Marie Sallier) are discussed in Stone, *French Parlements*, pp. 102–3.

had always known, and saw an Estates General functioning in 1789 as its predecessor supposedly had in 1614–15 as instrumental toward that end.

From 6 November to 12 December a similar message issued from the "second" Assembly of Notables, called by Necker to advise him on the composition and procedures of the Estates. Only one of the Assembly's six committees, that chaired by the king's brother the comte de Provence, endorsed a doubling of the Third (and that by the threadbare margin of 13 to 12). The Notables even more overwhelmingly rejected the notion of suffrage by head. They would concede to the National party financial equality and nothing else. What was more, they went on the offensive against their progressive foes. The crusty and reactionary prince de Conti inveighed against "scandalous writings spreading disorder and dissension throughout the realm," and in the closing days of the Assembly the Princes of the Blood presented a manifesto to Louis XVI restating the Notables' opposition to all changes other than those relating to taxation. "Prejudices, pretentions, caution, habit, all appear to be so deep rooted in most heads," disconsolately observed one of the outvoted liberal Notables on 10 November, "that I have no illusion that the simplest logic could ever penetrate there."[62]

Even when the Paris Parlement attempted in a decree of 5 December to restore its popularity, shattered by its earlier invocation of the 1614 Estates General, it stood adamantly by its guns insofar as suffrage by order in the national convocation was concerned. Moreover, J.-J. Duval d'Eprémesnil, author of this latest parlementary pronunciamento, candidly restated his unflagging support for "the just prerogatives of the Nobility and the Clergy" in a pamphlet he had published on 7 December.[63] Soon Duval d'Eprémesnil would be splitting with his erstwhile liberal allies on the "Committee of Thirty" and establishing a conservative "Committee of One Hundred," which, Timothy Tackett has suggested, "probably had a far greater influence on the nobility of France than the Committee of Thirty." That nobility, acting in Brittany, Franche-Comté, Provence, Burgundy, and wherever else it could make use of institutions such as parlements or provincial Estates to make its voice heard, found common cause with Parisian reactionaries in opposing the renovation of French institutions. As Tackett has observed, many of the soon-to-be deputies to the Estates General unavoidably had in such circumstances "a keen sense of ... political polarization over stakes that were extremely high."[64]

62 See Egret, *French Prerevolution*, pp. 199–202, on the subject of the "second" Assembly of Notables.

63 On the parlementary decree of 5 December 1788 and its aftermath, refer again to Stone, *French Parlements*, pp. 104–6.

64 Timothy Tackett, *Becoming a Revolutionary: The Deputies of the French National Assembly and the Emergence of a Revolutionary Culture (1789–1790)* (Princeton, N.J.:

It was against this backdrop of deepening division between advocates and opponents of political and social change in France that the hard-pressed Necker promulgated his conciliatory *Résultat du Conseil* on 27 December 1788 and soon thereafter set forth electoral procedures for the national convocation. Yet it was likely beyond the abilities of any individual to reverse the process of polarization within the elitist ranks of society. "Aristocratic" initiatives taken against "subversive" innovation in Paris and in the provinces only provoked counteractions and counter-rhetoric in Patriot quarters. In Provence, the Third Estate boycotted the sessions of the provincial Estates. In Brittany, where "the class conflict degenerated into civil war," law students championing the reformist cause besieged their adversaries in the hall of the Breton Estates. Rabaut Saint-Etienne, throwing his recent call for British-style bicameralism to the winds, now demanded a unicameral legislature and voting by head. Abbé Siéyès, in his celebrated tract *What Is the Third Estate?*, poured cold scorn upon the aristocracy. And Mirabeau, excluded by class snobbism from the Provençal Estates, lionized Marius in print "less . . . for having vanquished the Cimbrians than for having exterminated the order of nobility in Rome."[65]

Of course, none of this goes to show that compromise between conservatives and progressives would have been impossible at this time – had only the former been willing to concede the entrance of affluent and aspiring commoners into the purlieus of power and status in France. The assemblies of 1788 in Dauphiné, at Vizille and Romans, had shown that deliberation in common and voting by head on substantive issues could be squared with the traditional hierarchy of orders; and the evidence suggests that for some time to come the political moderation exhibited in Dauphiné would hold more attraction for France than the extremism of the Bretons.[66] Indeed, analysis of the *cahiers de doléances* has revealed a widespread desire among the electors to the Estates General in early 1789 to proceed on a traditional basis. Many *cahiers*, it turns out, regarded the division of the French nation into three estates as fundamental to the French "constitution." Few of these writs of grievance actually condemned the hierarchy of orders as such, but were more concerned to equalize conditions *among* the three estates.[67] It seems that even concentrating exclusively on the petitions of

Princeton University Press, 1996), p. 94. See pp. 90–94 for a discussion of the aristocratic side in this growing polarization of attitudes.

65 Lefebvre, *Coming of the French Revolution*, pp. 60–62.
66 Tackett, *Becoming a Revolutionary*, p. 85. On the politics of Dauphiné in 1788, see Egret, *La Révolution des notables: Mounier et les monarchiens* (Paris: Armand Colin, 1950); and Robert H. Griffiths, *Le Centre perdu: Malouet et les "monarchiens" dans la Révolution française* (Grenoble: Presses Universitaires de Grenoble, 1988).
67 Beatrice Hyslop, *French Nationalism in 1789 According to the General Cahiers* (New York: Octagon Books, 1968), p. 83.

the Third Estate does not enable the historian to find examples (at least outside of Paris) of commoners viewing the foundation of "national sovereignty" as requiring the destruction of the hierarchy of estates. And even those commoners who in their *cahiers* called the impending Estates General a "national assembly" implied that each of the three orders should follow custom by selecting its own deputies to that assembly.[68]

Yet these selfsame analyses make it equally clear that the Third Estate (and progressives in the clergy and nobility as well) viewed a substantial broadening of access to status and power in France as essential. In nearly 36 percent of the general *cahiers*, one can find the "civic" principle of enno-blement for service prevailing over the "mercenary" principle of ennoble-ment by purchase. To express such a preference may not have amounted to a forthright assault upon hereditary nobility; still, its implementation would in time transform the French aristocracy into an elite of public servants, an elite to which all could aspire.[69] Yet we know that this was *not* what most nobles were hankering for when, in their *cahiers*, they railed against purchase of nobility and advanced their more exclusionary conception of a state-serving elite. The majority of them, obdurately wedded to the past on this question as on so many others, were therefore bound to see voting by order in the approaching convocation at Versailles as a crucial bridle on change in the kingdom.

Even the most prominent anti-Marxist "social revisionists" in the field, however eager they have been to unearth in the *cahiers* evidence of a fusion of nobles and bourgeois on the threshold of the Revolution, have had to concede a real difference between the noble and the Third Estate *cahiers de doléances* on a number of important issues. One of these scholars, for instance, acknowledged a general insistence among commoners on voting by head, whereas, in contrast, he could find only a small proportion of the nobles' petitions pronouncing unambiguously for such an arrangement.[70] Another revisionist, concentrating more narrowly upon the *cahiers* of the Second Estate, arrived at similar conclusions regarding the nobility.[71] At the same time, passing beyond this immediate procedural issue, the latter historian admitted in a more general vein that only a "radical fringe" of noble *cahiers* accepted "the access of all, without distinction of birth and status, to public and military employments, [and] the suppression of dis-tinctions and formalities humiliating for the Third Estate."[72] Again, both of these revisionists documented a significant divergence between noble and

68 George V. Taylor, "Revolutionary and Nonrevolutionary Content in the *Cahiers* of 1789: An Interim Report," *French Historical Studies* 7 (1972): 494.

69 Hyslop, *French Nationalism in 1789*, p. 88.

70 Roger Chartier, "Cultures, lumières, doléances: Les Cahiers de 1789," *Revue d'histoire moderne et contemporaine* 28 (1981): esp. 90–91.

71 Chaussinand-Nogaret, *La Noblesse au XVIIIe siècle*, p. 190.

72 Ibid., p. 219.

bourgeois grievance lists on the subjects of seigneurial dues and seigneurial justice.

Significantly, this last point (like all the others, for that matter) has been substantiated by sociological inquiries unrelated to the academic wars of Marxists and revisionists. Those investigations have confirmed the revisionists' finding that a considerable number of noble *cahiers* were less enthusiastic about the idea of abrogating seigneurial rights than were the writs of grievance drafted by commoners. Third Estate *cahiers de doléances* typically left the door open for the possibility that peasants still saddled with the obligation of paying seigneurial dues could redeem them altogether.[73] It seems, then, that the electors' writs of grievance, although testifying to a rudimentary consensus among urban and rural elitists on a variety of constitutional and administrative issues, also betrayed the continuing potential divisiveness of privilege, and especially *social* privilege, in the politics of the "natural rulers" of the realm.[74]

The electoral process itself increased the likelihood that this latent divisiveness would become actual discord. Those contests within the Second Estate, it has been frequently noted, generally played into the hands of nobles unlikely to meet aspiring bourgeois halfway on contentious social issues. Only those with full and transmissible noble status (and hence not *anoblis*) had been admitted into the electoral assemblies in the first place. Not surprisingly, therefore, these contests were something of a triumph for those in the Second Estate who hailed from the provinces, often lacking in wealth and previously inactive in public affairs but now bent upon using this serendipitous opportunity to wrest the role of speaking for noble interests from the more progressive members of their order.[75] And, if one may judge from what some of these deputies-designate of the Second Estate were saying in speeches published at the time, noble apprehension over demands being voiced by the Third Estate, and opposition to those demands, were increasingly common. "One cannot but be impressed by the extent to which all of the noble orators either felt that their positions were directly threatened by the Third or sensed that many of their peers were experiencing such threats."[76]

In analogous fashion, the electoral process within the Third Estate ensured that the untitled laity would enjoy an aggressive advocacy in the debates of the Estates General. Those who were conspicuous in city and

---

73 John Markoff, "Violence, Emancipation, and Democracy: The Countryside and the French Revolution," *American Historical Review* 100 (1995): 364–65. For a fuller discussion of these and related issues, see Markoff, *The Abolition of Feudalism: Peasants, Lords, and Legislators in the French Revolution* (University Park, Pa.: Pennsylvania State University Press, 1996).

74 See again, on this point, Fitzsimmons, "Privilege and the Polity in France," esp. pp. 279–80.

75 Doyle, *Origins of the French Revolution*, pp. 152–54.

76 Tackett, *Becoming a Revolutionary*, p. 115.

bailliage meetings had already assisted in drawing up *cahiers* of parishes and urban corps, and at each stage of deliberation they probably gained a clearer sense of their order's interests, greater skill in promoting them, and a more finely attuned sense of public issues as they were likely to affect all three estates. The Third Estate delegates at Versailles thus "had been schooled in a series of revolutionary seminars." They had been chosen logically enough, on the basis of abilities locally demonstrated, to articulate their order's interests on a national stage. The Estates General consequently acquired from these elections held within Third Estate precincts what one historian has called "the sifted and seasoned nucleus of a national revolutionary elite."[77]

In the meantime, the electoral assemblies of the clergy were bitterly divided from the start. They testified to the culmination of years – even decades – of struggle between parish clergy seeking a more equitable distribution of power, status, and wealth within the Church, and blue-blooded ecclesiastics defending the existing hierarchical system. The clerical assemblages in the spring of 1789 were thus plagued constantly by rancorous exchanges between the two opposing factions, and on occasion by open splits causing one of the contending parties to walk out.[78] That the First Estate was so deeply fissured along ideological lines could only heighten the chances for strife in the Estates General over the months to come.

It was in these circumstances, not very auspicious from the government's point of view, that Jacques Necker resumed the mediating role he had earlier assumed in promulgating the *Résultat du Conseil*. Yet, as is common knowledge today, the bottom fell out of the director-general's plans from the start of the national convocation at Versailles. Necker, obsessed as ever by a fiscal emergency grounded primarily in the relentless pressures of international politics, had hoped that each of the orders would verify its members' credentials and constitute itself as a deliberative body with all due speed; that the first two orders would then renounce their financial privileges; and that the three estates would then decide quickly on which substantive issues they could deliberate in common and vote by head. What actually happened, of course, was markedly different. The nobility certainly proceeded straightaway to validate its delegates' credentials, but in doing so it rejected the Third Estate's call for verification of credentials in common. The clergy, split internally over this question, failed to take any such resolute action; and the Third Estate, for its own reasons, flatly refused to constitute itself as a separate body. Activists on both sides correctly descried behind this immediate dispute the ultimate question of how much

---

77 Taylor, "Revolutionary and Nonrevolutionary Content," p. 500.
78 Tackett, *Becoming a Revolutionary*, p. 97. See also Ruth F. Necheles, "The Curés in the Estates General of 1789," *Journal of Modern History* 46 (1974): 425–44.

change was likely to come to France. The conservatives understandably feared that conceding the principle of validation of credentials in common would be to open the floodgates to plenary sessions of the Estates voting by head on all questions; the progressives (Patriots) just as predictably feared to set what might become an unbreakable precedent for deliberating and voting by order on public issues. Thus, deadlock set in – and with deadlock, during May, June, and early July the extremists in both ideological camps could only harden their positions.[79]

Yet we can see, with the benefit of hindsight, that sooner or later the leaders of the Third Estate were likely to force the question. They knew that Lafayette and other reformist deputies in the Second Estate and the majority of parish priests in the first order were keen to break ranks and join them; they sensed that the ever more potent force of public opinion was on their side; and, paramount fact, they knew that the crown's bankruptcy in an ever-competitive Europe held public affairs at their mercy. Hence, the assurance with which one of their number, Ménard, could upbraid the nobility "for a stubbornness that could expose France to the greatest danger."[80] And hence, their momentous decision on 17 June, by a lopsided vote, to adopt the revolutionary title "National Assembly" and declare "that it is in the power of this assembly, and this assembly alone, to represent the general will." The self-styled National Assembly promptly took it upon itself to authorize royal taxes (lacking which sanction, it stated, those imposts would be "illegal"). It also announced on 17 June that it would examine and consolidate the nation's debt and review the question of popular subsistence. Then, three days later, all the deputies in the chamber save one swore the famous Tennis Court Oath that they would not disband before having drafted a constitution for the new France. And on 23 June, the day of Louis XVI's fateful *séance royale*, the delegates of the Patriot party endorsed Mirabeau's defiant motion threatening with the charge of *lèse-nation* anyone who should lay hands on a National Assemblyman.[81]

The king, constrained for the time being to keep Necker from resigning and taking with him the government's credibility in the financial markets, commanded his ideological brethren in the first two Estates to join the rebellious commoners. But, although grudgingly obedient to this royal summons, the conservatives left no doubt as to the constancy of their

79 See Harris, *Necker and the Revolution of 1789*, pp. 445–96. Also helpful on this period is Fitzsimmons, "Privilege and the Polity in France," esp. pp. 279–81; and Tackett, *Becoming a Revolutionary*, esp. chaps 4–6.
80 Tackett, *Becoming a Revolutionary*, p. 144.
81 See Harris, *Necker and the Revolution of 1789*, pp. 486–89, 509–10, and 519–20. See also, on the constitutional debates in the Assembly during this period, Baker, *Inventing the French Revolution*, esp. pp. 252–305.

attitudes. On 25 June, the unrepentant majority in the second order vowed in a letter to the monarch "that the Nobility would continue to insist on the right, granted by the king himself at the Royal Session, to ... exist as a separate order and to have its own assembly for deliberations and voting on matters that concerned the Nobility." Two days later, the Cardinal de La Rochefoucauld set off an uproar in the Assembly by informing the deputies that the clergy, though acquiescing in the king's order to join in common deliberations on questions of urgent national interest, nonetheless reserved its "right, according to constitutional laws of the monarchy, to assemble and to vote separately." Early in July, traditionalists in the Second Estate passed a resolution reaffirming their stance on the special privileges of the nobility.[82]

In mid-July, the deepening schism in "respectable" society played a pivotal role in precipitating the July Days. When the king attempted to overthrow the reformists in the ministries and legislature, he was undeniably drawing encouragement from individuals at Court and in the Assembly whose conservative philosophy, however irreconcilable with continuing French prominence in global affairs, largely dovetailed with his own. But Louis XVI not only underrated on this occasion the mettle of progressive "notables"; he also reckoned inadequately with the muscle power of the working masses. This last fact requires that we reassess the intervention of artisans, shopkeepers, and wage earners in the contentious elitist sociopolitics of July 1789.

Whether France was actually in the throes of a full-blown economic "crisis" at the end of the 1780s, as Ernest Labrousse and those following in his wake long contended, has become debatable in the light of recent economic research. Yet, whatever the import of this revisionism, it hardly leaves us with the impression of favorable economic conditions for Frenchmen and Frenchwomen of humble social station in 1789.[83] Absorbed even in relatively good economic times by the task of keeping themselves and their dependents alive from one day to the next, Louis XVI's laboring subjects had now to reckon with the high prices and scarcity of grain resulting either from a poor harvest in the preceding summer or from manipulations of the grain supply attending the political uncertainties of 1789. Moreover,

82 Harris, *Necker and the Revolution of 1789*, pp. 536, 539–40.
83 See, for examples of this revisionist thrust, Robert Aldrich, "Late-Comer or Early-Starter? New Views on French Economic History," *Journal of European Economic History* 16 (1987): 89–100; David Weir, "Les Crises économiques de la Révolution française," *Annales: E. S. C.* 46 (1991): pp. 917–47; George Grantham, "The French Cliometric Revolution: A Survey of Cliometric Contributions to French Economic History," *European Review of Economic History* 1 (1997): 353–405; and, most recently, Philip T. Hoffman and Jean-Laurent Rosenthal, "New Work in French Economic History," *French Historical Studies* 23 (2000): 439–53. On the other hand, for what follows immediately here, see Doyle, *Origins of the French Revolution*, pp. 159–60.

with more individuals than ever vying for lands in a century characterized by population growth, the agricultural rents that plebeian folk had to pay frequently rose – and this at a time when the same demographic pressures sometimes meant that the wages earned by humble cultivators as supplemental income lagged behind the prices they had to pay for additional foodstuffs. And how many countryfolk in these years could have owned enough land to profit from rising agricultural prices, let alone from rising agricultural rents?

More to the point, perhaps (in helping to explain the rioting at Paris and elsewhere in July 1789), was the relationship between these multiplying difficulties in the countryside and those in the cities and villages of the realm. The fact that agriculture still lorded it over manufacture in this typically "premodern" economy meant that hardship in the former sector all but guaranteed tribulations in the latter. Recent swings between good and bad harvests had especially serious repercussions in textiles, which accounted for 50 percent of French industrial production and ranked only after food as an item in popular consumption. The wildly varying fortunes in textiles reflecting fluctuations in demand had a devastating impact in weaving towns such as Nîmes, Lyon, Rouen, and Amiens. Weavers were likely to find themselves out of work just when the price of bread was already rising beyond their means. As if this were not enough, the scarcity of hay and other fodder crops in recent years had restricted the supply of flax and hemp to workers in a variety of textiles; and the silk harvest had completely failed in 1787. Whether the Anglo-French Commercial Pact of 1786 actually aggravated the crisis by permitting English woolens and cottons to compete in France with the textiles of Rouen, Lyon, and Amiens is still debated; yet this agreement most surely did nothing to alleviate the woes of French spinners and weavers, and they naturally saw the treaty in the worst possible light.[84]

In any case, the grain crisis of 1789, whether natural or man-made (or, perhaps, a little of both), ate into the subsistence margin of many peasants; it also wreaked havoc upon textiles and other industries whose commodities could no longer be purchased by both townspeople and rural folk forced to spend their funds on ever more expensive food. This development led in turn to widespread unemployment in the industrial sector, so that through most of 1789 the difficulties in the urban and rural areas

---

84 Doyle, *Origins of the French Revolution*, pp. 160–61. On this matter, see also these articles by Marie M. Donaghay: "Textiles and the Anglo-French Commercial Treaty of 1786," *Textile History* 13 (1982): 205–24; "The Exchange of Products of the Soil and Industrial Goods in the Anglo-French Commercial Treaty of 1786," *Journal of European Economic History* 19 (1990): 377–401; and "The French Debate on the 'Free Trade' Treaty of 1786," *Fra spazio e tempo: Studi in onore di Luigi de Rosa* (Naples: E.S.I., 1995), pp. 327–39. I am indebted to Professor Donaghay for these references.

were mutually reinforcing. The bitterly cold winter of 1788–89 and subsequent spring floods may have aggravated these problems by impeding
the milling of grain and the transport within France of fuels, foodstuffs,
and other essential commodities.[85]

It is not surprising, then, that by 1789 the king's laboring subjects should
have been caught up (even more than they usually were) in the toils of dire
need. The price of bread at Paris, on the rise ever since the preceding August,
passed fourteen *sous* for the four-pound loaf by the spring of 1789 and at
times was absorbing as much as 88 percent of the average worker's salary.
In the provinces, the towns and peasant communities, traumatized by the
fear of famine, fought to preserve local stores of grain; riots erupted in mar-
ketplaces, and millers and bakers were assaulted; and grain was often seized
on the roads. The most serious disturbances before the events of the summer occurred in March and April in Flanders, Provence, Franche-Comté,
Dauphiné, Languedoc, and Guienne. At Versailles, Necker, bedeviled by
the subsistence crisis as well as by the sociopolitical impasse, had to spend
the straitened government's precious currency and credit to import grain,
subsidize merchants at Paris and elsewhere, establish workshops for the
unemployed and hungry in the capital, and pay troops supervising the
transport of grain through the countryside. Government and people alike
were adversely affected by the grain crisis.[86]

These economic difficulties alone would have furnished ample incentive
for the craftsmen, shopkeepers, and laborers of Paris and other communities to intervene in the constitutional and social wrangles of their betters.
Yet other forces were also inclining them in that direction. Some of those
forces, intriguingly, were elitist and ideological in origin. Competing elements within the dominant classes at Paris took to appealing to the populace
during the "Prerevolution" with published and verbal attacks against each
other and with shrill antiministerial invocations of liberty and social justice.
The skilled workers and shopkeepers whom history would soon know as
the *sans-culottes* developed early on the habit of championing one courtier
faction against another, one institution (such as the Paris Parlement) against
another (such as the government itself), and so by 1789 were already
psychologically prepared to break into the arena of politics.[87]

Hence, as all the world knows today, news of the king's dismissal of
Necker and several other ministers in the second week of July 1789 ignited
a popular insurrection at Paris whose climactic event, the seizure of the
Bastille on the fourteenth, ensured (at least for the time being) the triumph

85 Doyle, *Origins of the French Revolution*, pp. 160–67.
86 On Necker's handling of the subsistence crisis in his second ministry, see Harris, *Necker
   and the Revolution of 1789*, esp. pp. 273–74 and 544–59.
87 See George Rudé, *The Crowd in the French Revolution* (New York: Oxford University
   Press, 1959); and *Paris and London in the Eighteenth Century* (New York: Viking, 1973).

of progressive elitists over reactionary elitists in the sociopolitics of the realm. Rather than telling yet again the gripping story of what happened in Paris and in the other communities of the realm, we need to account in broad analytical terms for the municipal upheavals of 1789 and evaluate their significance in helping to launch France irreversibly upon its momentous revolutionary adventure.

The municipal revolution in the summer of 1789, it is crucial to remember, *was* a nationwide phenomenon, more dangerous to the authorities than an uprising confined to Paris would have been. We know today that at least twenty of the thirty communities in the kingdom vaunting populations of twenty thousand or more saw the formation of revolutionary committees during the latter half of July, to be followed by six additional towns in August. To be sure, Grenoble and Lille claimed such impromptu institutions for just a few days in July, while Toulouse and Clermont-Ferrand never had them at all. Yet, even though a few municipal administrations rode out the period essentially unaltered, most of them witnessed major changes of one kind or another during the summer of 1789.[88] They did so because urgent political and economic issues, though we know them best in connection with the pivotal insurrection at Paris, were truly national in character.

Four factors, it has been argued, were especially influential in determining the extent of change in a given municipality: the structure of its economy and society; the recent politics of its ruling elite; the problems it experienced in the economic crisis; and the closeness of its ties with other towns. Of these four variables, the first was the most important; yet all four tended to work together to limit the political options available in each town. Major change was least likely in administrative centers whose ruling elites had either stood up to the crown or opened their ranks in 1787–88, in which prices did not continue to climb throughout 1789, and that were not in close contact with centers of revolutionary agitation. On the other hand, revolution was *most* likely in manufacturing, military, and naval communities. Committees particularly claimed power "where ruling elites had refused to open their ranks, especially during the meetings to elect deputies to the Estates General; where prices rose steeply in 1789 (the north); and where the local leaders of the revolution had close contacts with other revolutionary centers." In a somewhat special category were commercial and (notably) port towns that displayed ambivalent political leanings in 1789. Their committees seldom took complete control unless they faced ruling elite intransigence. They often enjoyed optimum access to sources of foreign grain and so avoided the steepest price rises afflicting

---

88 Consult Lynn Hunt, "Committees and Communes: Local Politics and National Revolution in 1789," *Comparative Studies in Society and History* 18 (1976): 324.

interior communities. And even though their merchants profited from connections with counterparts within and outside France, the leaders of such towns were much less subject to the revolutionary influences emanating from Rennes, Dijon, or even Paris, than were the leaders of the smaller hinterland towns.[89]

Because of its unique status, Paris did not in all respects fulfill the criteria for revolutionary upheaval adduced on these pages. Nonetheless, it is easy to see why the capital, with its politicized judges, *officiers*, and men of letters, its inflexible governing elite, its huge subsistence problems, and its exposure to the rumors (and eventual reality) of counterrevolutionary measures coordinated at nearby Versailles, should have exploded in July. It is, furthermore, easy to understand why so many other cities and villages across France, which *did* more or less satisfy these revolutionary requirements, should also have revolted. And the brawn in most of these uprisings was provided by small shopkeepers, artisans, journeymen, and unskilled toilers, some of whom had participated in the spring in the politicizing tasks of electing deputies to the Estates General and drafting protests to the king, and all of whom must have harbored throughout 1789 fears of starvation, aristocratic plots, and foreign invasion.[90]

With the kingdom's teeming capital lost to its king, then, and with other cities and towns, like Paris, setting up insurrectionary committees, forming citizen militias, and obeying only such orders from the National Assembly as sorted with their own local political and economic concerns, power during July–August 1789 began to slip from its old moorings. It began to shift, in other words, from Louis XVI to Necker, from ministers and intendants to Assemblymen, from conservatives to progressives inside the Assembly – and even, to some extent, from the Assembly itself to local municipalities. But this historic transference of power only affected the majority of Frenchmen and Frenchwomen in meaningful fashion with the advent of the peasant upheaval in high summer.

At Versailles, as we have seen, the king remained, even in the wake of his reverse in July, fundamentally opposed to the agenda of the victorious Patriots. But for the latter as well as for their conservative foes, the tendency toward social disorder in both urban and rural France in the wake of the July Days posed a genuine dilemma. True, the progressives in the National Assembly were determined to maintain their recent gains. On 14 July the Assembly declared that the king's ministers would be held criminally liable for any actions contravening legislative decrees or the nation's rights. Moreover, the deputies ringingly reaffirmed their proclamations of 17, 20,

89 Ibid., pp. 327, 328–29.
90 On the elections to the Estates General, refer to the papers by François Furet and Ran Halévi in Baker, ed., *Political Culture of the Old Regime*. On the beliefs of the townspeople in 1789, see Lefebvre, *Coming of the French Revolution*, esp. chap. 6.

and 23 June; set about drafting a declaration of rights and a constitution; and on 21 July ratified Siéyès's assertion that "all public powers without exception are an emanation of the general will, all come from the people, that is to say, the Nation."[91] On the very next day, however, the sudden lynching in Paris of two royal officials, Foullon de Doué and his son-in-law, Bertier de Sauvigny, accused of involvement in schemes to hoard grain, reminded the delegates of the atrocities to which at least some of "the people" could be driven. Yet even more ominously, in July and early August the Assemblymen were deluged with letters sent in from provincial France, painting an alarming picture of towns and villages menaced by aristocratic plotters and "brigands" and appealing for governmental assistance against such social malefactors.[92] Disorder, in other words, was spreading through provincial and rural France, and was about to ascend to one of its revolutionary climaxes in the peasant "chain-reaction" panic known to history as the Great Fear.

Any attempt to explain the upheaval of the French peasantry in the summer of 1789 must reckon with long-term, structural factors as well as with the immediate economic difficulties we have already discussed. A structural analysis might well begin with the observation that peasant revolts like those of 1789 inhered naturally in an agrarian social structure characteristic of France (and of western regions of a yet to be united Germany) in eighteenth-century Europe. Despite sundry constraints imposed by the seigneurial regime, French peasants controlled usage of much more of the arable land than did the increasingly enserfed peasantry of eastern Europe or the dispossessed lower classes of rural England. What is more, France's peasant communities, which had been shaped through long centuries of struggle for administrative autonomy and economic security, had by the eighteenth century emerged as formidable competitors with their lords for local agrarian rights and influence. It is noteworthy that the government played a central role in this process – as it did in so much else in French history. As it penetrated into each locality, the statist administration gradually pushed the seigneur aside, leaving him as only the "first subject of the parish," wielding little more than judicial powers over a peasantry subject to the authority of no one but the intendant and his subdelegate. The village assemblies consequently could still function, and frequently did, as forums for the discussion of local affairs by all heads of families; but they did so under the umbrella of state absolutism.[93]

It is possible to take this "structuralist" approach to the gestation of peasant revolution in 1789 even further. One could argue that it was the

91 Harris, *Necker and the Revolution of 1789*, pp. 576, 601.
92 Tackett, *Becoming a Revolutionary*, p. 169.
93 Skocpol, *States and Social Revolutions*, pp. 118–21.

emergence of a bureaucratic state in France and the integration of the village into that state which gave the peasant community a robust self-image and the confidence to challenge its seigneur as it had never challenged him before. Displaying this new confidence rather than responding to any novel "class" demands on the part of its lord, the rural village tapped the burgeoning talents of the legal profession to launch a withering critique not only of specific seigneurial rights but, indeed, of the historical and moral legitimacy of seigneurial authority itself.[94] Whether one chiefly emphasizes here the paternalistic role of the absolutist state or the (limited) autonomy of peasant communities, the psychological readiness of the peasantry to perform an active role in the politics of 1789 seems as evident as does that of the Parisians and of French townsfolk in general.

So structural as well as economic realities lay behind the peasant upheaval of July–August 1789. But their impact was reinforced enormously by the electoral campaign in the spring of 1789; for this campaign enabled every man aged twenty-five or older and paying any amount of taxes to participate in a village assembly convened both to elect representatives to the *bailliage* assembly and to draw up a *cahier de doléances*. In effect, every one of these villages was being invited by Louis XVI to meditate collectively upon its outstanding grievances. This concession must have heightened the possibilities for rebellion on the part of peasants who were already predisposed toward revolt for the reasons already discussed. Insurgency in the countryside began to break out at this time, well in advance of the uprising at Paris; and quite often it targeted not only the immediate evil of "hoarded" stores of grain and bread but also the tithes, feudal rights, and feudal records of the seigneurial system as such. Even at this early date, such outbreaks were widespread, occurring in Anjou, Dauphiné, the Paris region, Picardy, Hainault, and the Midi.[95] Still, only in the summer did this phenomenon became nationwide in scope, culminating in the "Great Fear" of late July and early August.[96] Cultivators became obsessed by fears that "brigands" in the pay of foreigners (or of French aristocrats) would cut down the crops ripening in their fields,

94 See Hilton Root, "Challenging the Seigneurie: Community and Contention on the Eve of the French Revolution," *Journal of Modern History* 57 (December 1985): 652–81. This interpretation receives additional support in Jones, *Peasantry in the French Revolution*, passim; and in John Markoff, "Peasant Grievances and Peasant Insurrection: France in 1789," *Journal of Modern History* 62 (1990): 445–76.

95 Skocpol, *States and Social Revolutions*, pp. 122–23. The very widespread incidence of these outbreaks well in advance of the summer's "Great Fear" has also been stressed by Jones, *Peasantry in the French Revolution*, esp. pp. 60–62. Georges Lefebvre had also made the point earlier.

96 The classic study of this fascinating subject remains Georges Lefebvre, *The Great Fear of 1789: Rural Panic in Revolutionary France*, trans. Joan White (New York: Pantheon, 1973).

torch their barns, and mutilate their livestock. As a result, they banded together defensively and then proceeded to attack the manors of their lords.

Clearly, the insurrection in the countryside, as a *national* development, was initially made possible by, but then reacted back upon, the municipal revolution. As early as the spring, it now appears, the peasants' *cahiers* had revealed intriguing signs of "proto-citizenship," that is, of at least a rudimentary appreciation of national issues such as government finances and elitist contention over projected reforms.[97] And now, peasant soldiers, allowed to return to their home provinces to assist in harvesting the crops, were disseminating there the news of revolt in cities and towns across the realm. In doing so, they only generalized the kingdom's sense of disorder and insecurity.

What, then, were the men of the National Assembly to do? It is not so astonishing that the Patriots should have hesitated to employ armed force to crush the rural insurrection. They may have flirted with the notion of using militias or calling upon units of the royal army to protect property rights in the countryside; yet to do so, they were well aware, might play into reactionary hands. Most Patriots were unprepared to run this risk. Significantly, only in a few localities did militia units act against the peasants.[98] Progressive notables, some of whom believed that foreigners and "native" aristocrats were plotting against the new France they were trying to create, and who had just received in the July Days unnerving evidence of the king's enduring hostility to their endeavors, could hardly have afforded at this point to turn against their rural plebeian supporters.

There is also some question as to whether much of a "military option" would have been available to the Assembly even if it *had* been inclined toward repression of popular protest in the summer of 1789. After all, the authorities had already shown themselves unwilling or unable to employ the regular army against the revolutionaries at Paris. This, at least in part, reflected back upon the military's difficulties in the ancien régime. The crown may have foreclosed upon the ability of *any* faction to use the army for disciplinary purposes in 1789 by implementing in 1787–88 reforms that (as we have seen) exacerbated existing tensions within that institution. Court aristocrats, provincial nobles, *anoblis*, and affluent commoners feuded among themselves – and vented their frustrations and anger at times upon the government itself. As Samuel Scott has observed, the crown's policy "contributed to the deterioration of morale within the Royal Army, especially among officers." The polarization within the broader strata of

97 See Markoff, "Peasants Protest: The Claims of Lord, Church and State in the *Cahiers de Doléances* of 1789," *Comparative Studies in Society and History* 32 (1990): 452–53.
98 Skocpol, *States and Social Revolutions*, p. 124.

elite society in 1788–89 must have compounded this problem insofar as it drove "notable" officers within the army even further apart. Yet "what ultimately incapacitated the army and led directly to the collapse of both royal and noble authority," Scott has also noted, "was the break-down of the discipline exercised by officers over their men. This failure arose primarily from the conditions of military life, particularly the relationship between soldiers and officers."[99]

On more than one occasion during 1788 and early 1789, officers hesi-tated to order their troops into action against rioters, or the troops them-selves proved reluctant to march against their own countrymen. Such failures on the part of the army in a number of areas troubled by unrest pointed in some measure to the lack of empathy between noble officers and soldiers of humble background. When, in addition, we recall that officers and soldiers alike wore themselves out policing the countryside in a time of subsistence crisis, and were often underpaid and hungry themselves, it becomes even easier to account for the diminishing reliability of the army as an instrument of social control in 1788–89.[100]

Later, in the unsettled aftermath of the October Days, a new appreci-ation of the importance for social order of a reliable army might come to the legislators. In the meantime, the most perspicacious Patriots may have drawn comfort from realizing that the king himself could hardly have used military coercion – even assuming its momentary efficacy – to solve the bedrock geopolitical and sociopolitical problems that had bankrupted his government in the first place. Necker's warnings against any such employ-ment of the army – and the sage misgivings of Louis XVI himself on the subject – only underscored the fact that the situation in France had by now evolved far beyond the point at which a military coup could conceivably have served any positive long-term design.[101]

The Patriots in the National Assembly attempted to defuse the rural crisis in their own fashion. In the storied session of the night of 4 August, they stampeded their colleagues into curbing if not entirely abandoning the old system of seigneurial servitudes, dues, and justice. They also altered much else on that memorable occasion. They formally abrogated the tax exemptions of the first two orders and decreed that taxes were henceforth to be levied on all classes in a uniform manner. They jettisoned the entire system of venal officeholding as well as the separate status of the

99 Scott, *Response of the Royal Army to the French Revolution*, pp. 27–33.
100 On the army's problems in 1788–89, refer also to Bertaud, *The Army of the French Revolution*, esp. pp. 22–29.
101 For some very thoughtful observations on the role (and political options) of Louis XVI during the July and October Days, consult Harris, *Necker and the Revolution of 1789*, pp. 577–78 and 691–93.

pays d'états. Patriot prelates abandoned their tithes. Moreover, the Assembly affirmed the crucial principle of "careers open to talent." All in all, the system of privilege which had so long underpinned the ancien régime was dealt an effective if not yet final blow by the National Assembly on that dramatic night.[102]

However, as the full significance of what had been wrought on 4 August sank in, and with unrest in town and countryside continuing largely because of the persistence of economic difficulties, the old tensions between progressives and conservatives surfaced once again. The outrage among the latter over the reforms of 4 August appeared in one noble Assemblyman's confidential denunciation of "a revolution which in fact destroys nobility and fiefs, deprives 500,000 families of their property and prepares France for fetters which we are amazed to see borne by Orientals." As late as 10 August, the marquis de Thiboutot, delegate from Caux, tried to defend in the Assembly "the special law of fiefs and the honorific prerogatives of manorial lords." He also asserted his order's timeless right to "the distinctions that characterized it."[103] As August wore on, moreover, religious issues – the suppression of tithing without compensation, for example, and proposals for the nationalization of church property and for other ecclesiastical changes – seem to have helped crystallize opposition to the Patriots in a number of quarters.[104]

Yet what most alarmed the Patriots in August and September was the attempt by Jean-Joseph Mounier and some of his Anglophile or "Monarchist" friends, advocating like Necker a British-style variety of constitutionalism, to fashion a coalition of moderate and reactionary deputies against changes they could all consider too precipitate and radical. It is true that, in the event, the Patriots need not have worried unduly about the obstructive potential of such a grouping on the right. As Jean Egret accurately observed, the "majority of the Nobility and high Clergy ... felt nothing but hatred and contempt for these Monarchists," whose slightest stirrings of political moderation they stigmatized as betraying the good old ways of the past.[105] The progressive deputies unsurprisingly profited from this split within their opponents' ranks to defeat, early in September, attempts to grant the aristocracy an upper chamber in the future legislature and to give the king an absolute veto. On the eighth, bicameralism went down to crushing defeat by a vote of 849 to 89; and just three days later, by a margin

---

102 Ibid., pp. 627–28.
103 Lefebvre, *Coming of the French Revolution*, pp. 165, 156–57.
104 See Tackett, *Becoming a Revolutionary*, pp. 176–95; and, by the same author, "Nobles and Third Estate in the Revolutionary Dynamic of the National Assembly, 1789–1790," *American Historical Review* 94 (1989): 271–301.
105 Egret, *La Révolution des notables*, pp. 227–28, 126.

of 673 to 325, a "suspensive" rather than an absolute veto was accorded the monarch.[106]

Still, the Patriots in the Assembly felt no less under siege during these weeks preceding the October Days. They were uneasily aware of the depth of reactionary sentiment that drove so many secular nobles and high ecclesiastics to sabotage the Monarchists' efforts to secure a bicameral legislature. They sensed that such deputies, hailing in most cases from the relatively impoverished and "unenlightened" countryside, detested both the notion of an upper legislative chamber dominated by cosmopolitan notables like Mounier and the alternative – a unicameral deliberative body controlled by progressive nobles and commoners. They also could see in a "suspensive" veto a constitutional power every bit as suited to the crown's purposes as would be an "absolute" veto. And they were hardly likely to be reassured by Mounier's election as president of the Assembly on 28 September.[107]

One of their number, Lombard, wrote home that "our party is absolutely in the minority." His colleague L.-P. Lofficiel was convinced that, failing the support of about forty clerics and a hundred or so liberal nobles, "we would certainly be defeated on every vote." The celebrated deputy from Anjou, Volney, saw the Assembly as so divided, so menaced by aristocratic machinations, that it needed to be dissolved immediately and replaced by a new body whose membership, excluding most clerics and nobles, would more faithfully mirror the composition of French society. At one point the delegation from Brittany, already famed for its radicalism, considered walking out of the Assembly for good.[108] And on the very eve of the October Days, Barnave despairingly informed an unknown correspondent that "almost all of the governing part of the Nation," having become "our enemy and the enemy of liberty," was poised to restore the old order and accord it "the means to annihilate us, almost without combat."[109] Such fears were only too plainly deepened by Patriot memories of the events of July, and sustained as well by the king's continuing refusal to sanction the Assembly's revolutionary legislation.

Thus, the polarizing tendencies at work within the Assembly and within the elitist ranks of society at large before the July Days were also in play on the eve of the October Days. What is more, that polarization interacted in October (as it had in July) with the popular unrest stemming from the subsistence crisis. As a consequence, the Patriots in the Constituent

106 These are Egret's figures, in *Necker*, pp. 353, 357. For corroboration of these figures, and
    some additional details, see Tackett, *Becoming a Revolutionary*, pp. 192–95.
107 Tackett, *Becoming a Revolutionary*, p. 195.
108 Tackett, "Nobles and Third Estate," p. 289.
109 Cited in Egret, *Révolution des notables*, p. 168.

Assembly and their confederates at Paris and in the provinces remained under popular pressure (had they needed it) to defend the Revolution as it had developed up to that point. Here, then, was yet another calculation behind the Parisian insurrection of early October that removed both the sovereign and a politically strengthened legislature to Paris.

After every conscientious effort has been made to reassess the converging forces driving France into revolution in 1788–89, we must still acknowledge as ultimately crucial the discrepancy between the crown's grandiose international mission and the civic resources it was able to mobilize to sustain that mission. Louis XVI was sufficiently alive to his geopolitical responsibilities to grant Necker a free hand in convoking the Estates General in 1789; yet, in the end, he could not bring himself to accept the reforms that, by fully integrating his "respectable" subjects into public affairs, would have enabled his government to resume the unending French quest for security and greatness. He was encouraged in his predisposition to uphold his forebears' and his own principles by the queen, his brothers, the courtiers, and all those high clerics and lay nobles in the Assembly and throughout the kingdom driven ever farther to the right by the prospect of basic sociopolitical change. Sadly, one specialist's attempt to characterize Louis XVI as "liberal to some extent, almost won over to the revolutionary cause" must yield to another scholar's less flattering description of the king at this moment of truth as "either feebly submissive . . . or deviously reactionary."[110] But the Patriots within and outside the Assembly, driven to the left by their fear of counterrevolution, and riding the perilous tide of popular anxieties and revolt, began gradually to take control of public affairs in the course of the summer and early autumn.

Georges Lefebvre argued that the October Days marked the end of the "coming of the French Revolution" and the start of a long-term revolutionary process. Most later historians have endorsed this contention. "Nothing could disguise the fact that political authority had shifted decisively," D. M. G. Sutherland has written. "Unlike July when Parisians' actions had been essentially defensive, the October Days represented the first . . . occasion when direct Parisian intervention decisively affected national politics."[111] Only now, Colin Lucas has observed, did the "crowd" invade "both seats of national government – the royal palace and the Assembly – rather than merely the seat of municipal government." Only now did it secure the king's person "as a permanent, political solution to

110 Citations from John Bosher, *The French Revolution* (New York: Norton, 1988), p. 148; and Simon Schama, *Citizens: A Chronicle of the French Revolution* (New York: Knopf, 1989), p. 419.
111 Sutherland, *France 1789–1815*, p. 85.

a perennial problem rather than a temporary solution."[112] Yet how lasting a solution to a "perennial problem" would the king's forcible removal to Paris turn out to be? As they endeavored over the next two years to regenerate their country, France's revolutionaries would be repeatedly reminded of the precariousness of their partnership with Louis XVI. And even more important, with Great Britain asserting itself as always in the overseas world, and with Russia, Prussia, and Austria projecting their power in old and new ways on the Continent, the French would have to remain equally obsessed with the "perennial problem" posed for them by the interaction of global and domestic affairs.

112 Lucas, "The Crowd and Politics between *Ancien Régime* and Revolution in France," *Journal of Modern History* 60 (1988): pp. 448–49. Yet another historian viewing the October Days as a turning point is Egret, in *Necker*, p. 377. Admittedly, Doyle, in his *Origins of the French Revolution*, prefers to break the story off with the events of early August.

3

The first attempt to stabilize the Revolution: from 1789 to 1791

Timothy Tackett has observed that the impact of the October Days on the structure and dynamics of politics within the National Constituent Assembly was "considerably less than is sometimes suggested by historians." The Assembly, in an attempt to stabilize the political situation, prudently limited the number of passports issued to nervous deputies wishing to leave the country, and over the ensuing weeks legislative attendance recovered to the levels of early August.[1] It is always useful to stress underlying continuities of any kind holding for these early months of the Revolution, as historians are so frequently inclined to do just the opposite. Indeed, when they seek to characterize developments in 1789, they dwell with predictable relish on the dramatic emergence in France of national representative politics, or proclaim a major "breakthrough" of discourses of popular sovereignty and conclude that nothing for the French could ever be the same again.

There is, of course, something to be said for such a conclusion. Yet there may be grounds for arguing, with respect to 1789 and indeed with regard to the entire phase of revolution dominated by the Constituent Assembly, that continuities mattered as much as discontinuities. After summarizing events in this period, Chapter 3 will reassess the European high politics of 1789–91 and the initial harbingers of a French resurgence in the face of old and new international challenges. It will then take up some of the basic institutional reforms enacted by the Constituent Assembly and present them from a global-historical viewpoint as responding as much to old-fashioned state security needs as to newfangled expectations of citizens caught up in revolution. Finally, this chapter will track the changes in the balance of political forces within the Constituent Assembly and show how they principally benefited those policymakers and activists (at Paris and elsewhere) who were most determined both to uphold French influence abroad and to pursue a revolutionary agenda at home.

1 Tackett, *Becoming a Revolutionary*, pp. 199, 202–3.

109

PROLOGUE: NARRATIVE OF EVENTS

Over the roughly two years of its existence, the Constituent Assembly passed a barrage of reforms. Some of these measures were of such obvious utility to the nation that they aroused relatively little opposition. Thus, the Assembly created a uniform administrative system of departments, districts, cantons, and communes. It rolled all internal tolls on commerce back to the national borders, standardized weights and measures, overhauled the judiciary, and began the process of codifying French law.

In other areas of public policy, however, the deputies could not help but foment new controversies. By selling off church properties, suppressing "useless" religious orders, and enacting (and then requiring clerical adherence to) a Civil Constitution of the Clergy, the Assembly antagonized both Gallican Church and papacy. By depriving nobles of their seigneurial justice, tax privileges, and monopoly of employments in the armed forces, and then abolishing hereditary nobility itself, the Assemblymen multiplied their enemies in the erstwhile Second Estate. On the other hand, by establishing a divisive distinction between "active" and "passive" citizens, legitimizing the heaviest seigneurial dues owed by peasants to their former lords, allowing grain prices to rise, closing down public workshops, and banning all unionizing, the deputies alienated legions of plebeian Frenchmen and Frenchwomen.

In these circumstances, the role of the king would palpably be critical. Louis XVI dutifully attended the first annual celebration of Bastille Day (*fête de la fédération*) on 14 July 1790. However, three months later he began to sanction secret overtures to foreign courts that could in time lead to military intervention against the Revolution. Papal pronouncements of March–April 1791 condemning not only the Civil Constitution of the Clergy but also the founding principles of the Revolution itself only reinforced royal reservations about the course of events in France. In addition, Louis was coming under mounting pressure from his wife and brothers (and from émigrés already congregating in foreign parts) to repudiate the Revolution.

Hence, the royal family's abortive attempt, on 20 June 1791, to flee the country. Five days later, upon his forced return to Paris, the king was "suspended" from his functions by an Assembly that was now confronting an unanticipated constitutional dilemma. Although the deputies and the Court cobbled together a compromise of sorts (on 15 July), reinstating Louis pending his acceptance of the almost completed constitution, the "Flight to Varennes" had aroused political passions in French society at large. Indeed, the Jacobin Club at Paris, until now home to many of the revolution's most illustrious Patriots, split over the question of the monarch's fate: the conservative majority of its membership withdrew to form their own ("Feuillant") association. Meanwhile, the sponsorship by the ultraradical Cordelier Club of a petition implicitly calling for a republic provoked a "massacre" of Parisians by National Guards on the *Champ de Mars* (17 July). A new line had been drawn – in blood – between Lafayette, Bailly, the "Feuillants," and other notables still desirous of preserving the crown, on the one hand, and the more radical revolutionaries – Jacobins, Cordeliers, and so on – on the other.

True, Louis XVI formally accepted the completed Constitution of 1791 on 13 September and was formally reinstated in his regal duties. On the thirtieth, the Constituent Assembly dissolved, thus making way in orderly fashion for the newly elected Legislative Assembly. But prospects for a fruitful collaboration between the executive and legislative branches of government were clouded at best. A counterrevolutionary manifesto left by the king at the Tuileries Palace on 20 June 1791 had betrayed his real feelings about the upheaval in his kingdom. Meanwhile, politicians and activists on the Left seemed to find new reasons daily for rejecting all thoughts of compromise with those on the Right. And overshadowing everything else were signs of deteriorating relations between revolutionary France and the other European powers.

THE INTERNATIONAL SITUATION:
CHALLENGE AND RESPONSE

Any review of European geopolitics in this period conjures up the same hard realities that France had been facing for decades: a predatory Russia responsive to the desires of Catherine the Great; a restless Hohenzollern Prussia contending with a somewhat less aggressive Habsburg Austria for influence in central Europe; and a Great Britain opportunistically moving into markets on the Continent and acquiring colonies overseas. The French had, somehow, to acknowledge and respond to these forces – and actually found ways to do so on occasion, even in the midst of their prodigious labors of domestic reconstruction.

The resumption in 1787 of the historic Russian drive against Turkey had initially assumed defensive colors: Constantinople had, after all, preemptively declared war against St. Petersburg. The Russian effort was at first hampered by drought and harvest failure, inadequate military preparations, Swedish military incursions into the northwestern reaches of Catherine's empire, and, perhaps most significantly, the possibility of Prussian and British intervention on behalf of the Turks. In the end, however, all of these factors together could not counterbalance the inherent strengths of the Romanov state's position. Indeed, the last of these potentially inhibiting factors – that is, the possibility of a coordinated Prusso-British strike against the Russians – was never very likely to become a reality. Astute observers found it easy to differentiate between diplomatic viewpoints at London and Berlin. Pitt's government had only reluctantly entered into the alliance of 1788 and saw it primarily as a hedge against instability in Europe; at the same time, few British statesmen appeared yet to be greatly concerned about the fate of the Turks. Prussia, in contrast, saw the alliance as a means toward important territorial gains. But proposals made by Frederick William II's government for cessions of land by Turkey to Austria, by Austria to Poland, and by Poland to Prussia failed to enthuse the British. The two "allies" in addition differed sharply over whether or not to support the secession of the southern Netherlands – modern-day Belgium – from the Habsburg dominions. In summary, from the start of Europe's latest diplomatic crisis, Pitt's government and the Hohenzollern authorities were at clear cross-purposes.[2]

This is essentially why Prussian negotiations undertaken with both Turkey and Poland in the course of 1790 have, in retrospect, an air of unreality. However it might indulge in saber rattling against Vienna and St. Petersburg and pledge aid to the Turks and Poles, Prussia was not about to intervene single-handedly (that is to say, in this instance, without London's support) in the parlous affairs of eastern Europe. Even at this relatively early date, the most farsighted observers could suspect that Berlin, unaided by a British "ally" championing the current balance of forces on the Continent, might in time turn toward either Russia or Austria (or to both together) and against Warsaw and Constantinople in its quest for territorial acquisitions.

But that was still several years in the future. In the meantime, the gradual but inexorable shift of fortunes in the Russo-Turkish War against Constantinople forced Pitt's government to reassess the situation to the east. British diplomatic intervention at Berlin and Vienna, coupled with the quixotic wish of Austria's Leopold II to stabilize central Europe through a resolution of Austro-Prussian differences, led to the signing on 27 July 1790 of the Convention of Reichenbach. Under terms of this pact between the two Germanic powers, Austria agreed to make peace with Turkey through the offices of Britain, Prussia, and the United Provinces. By separate arrangement, Constantinople acquiesced in a minor surrender of frontier lands to Vienna – a concession that, along with the larger Convention itself, would presumably enable the Turks to husband their remaining resources for the struggle with Russia.[3]

---

2 M. S. Anderson, "European Diplomatic Relations, 1763–90," pp. 276–77.
3 On the Convention of Reichenbach, see in particular Karl A. Roider, Jr., *Austria's Eastern Question 1700–1790* (Princeton, N.J.: Princeton University Press, 1982), pp. 188–89; and Anderson, "European Diplomatic Relations," pp. 277–78.

The British, too, obsessed as ever by the need to maintain a strategic balance on the Continent, and temporarily reassured by the paralysis of affairs within France, concentrated increasingly upon the crisis in eastern Europe. But they faced in Catherine's state a more resourceful power than Leopold II's Austria. By the end of 1790 the Russians had overrun the Danubian principalities and seized Ismail, the key Turkish fortress at the mouth of the Danube on the Black Sea. By the time the Peace of Jassy had formally ended this latest conflict between St. Petersburg and Constantinople in January 1792, Russia's southwestern frontier had advanced another one hundred miles or more, to the Dniester River. Pitt's government had (in T. C. W. Blanning's words) marched "to the very brink of war" with Catherine in March 1791, but in the end it had backed down and allowed the tsarina carte blanche in her dealings with the Turks. For this there were many reasons: "divisions in the cabinet, opposition in Parliament, the deft manipulation of public opinion by the Russian ambassador Count Vorontsov, the problems involved in bringing military and/or naval pressure to bear on inaccessible Russia, and ... the indomitable will of the Tsarina."[4]

In the final analysis, it was probably above all Russia's Eurasian hugeness and its standing as the "flanking power" at the opposite end of Europe from Britain that enabled it to defy the other major powers and impose peace on the Ottoman Empire on its own terms. And as if to drive home the diplomatic implications of its auspicious geographical situation, Russia in 1791–92 was already turning from its triumphs over the Turks to the alluring possibilities of a renewed intervention in Polish affairs. The Poles, who were striving desperately to modernize their political, military, and social institutions, had enjoyed a temporary respite from the pressures generated by Russian expansionism only because of the Russo-Turkish War.[5] Now that Catherine II had settled her account with Constantinople, she could attempt to revive the old Austro-Prussian rivalry in central Europe, as well as profit from a more novel obsession at London, Berlin, and Vienna with revolution in France, to reassert her will at Warsaw.

Thus the growth of Russian power in eastern Europe, directly affecting three long-standing outposts of French influence, Turkey, Poland, and Sweden, marked the early 1790s as surely as it had characterized preceding decades. In times very soon to come, a France expanding first under revolutionary and then under Napoleonic auspices would unavoidably collide with the Romanov colossus. In the early years of the Revolution, however, the new statesmen at Paris had primarily to deal (at least in continental matters) with the policymakers at Berlin and Vienna.

4 Blanning, *The Origins of the French Revolutionary Wars*, p. 59.
5 Ibid., pp. 59–60.

We have already seen that the Prussia of Frederick William II was restless and acquisitive, ever seeking potential victims amid the political uncertainties of the Continent. In the course of 1790–91, the Prussian monarch was induced by considerations discussed earlier to discard Foreign Minister Hertzberg's complicated scheme of territorial exchanges involving the major states of central and eastern Europe as well as to abandon any rash idea of war with either Russia or Austria. As time wore on, and as the political situation within France deteriorated, aggressive instincts at Berlin were increasingly directed toward the west. On 27 August 1791 Prussia joined Austria in declaring, at Pillnitz, that Louis XVI's situation merited the concerted attention of all the sovereigns of Europe. It was perhaps significant that Frederick William II was accompanied only by military officials to Pillnitz and gave a more sympathetic hearing to French émigrés foregathered there than did Leopold. Moreover, the Prussian king would soon be dispatching a senior general to Vienna to expedite preparations for a coordinated attack against the French.[6]

Austria's sentiments toward the French were a good deal more ambivalent than those of the Prussians. For this there were a number of reasons. The most basic of them become apparent if we emphasize Vienna's geostrategic vulnerabilities in the eighteenth century. The Habsburgs had long realized that Russia's persistent drive toward the Black Sea, the Balkans, and Constantinople could eventually bring about an Austro-Russian confrontation that would pose as great a threat to the security of the Habsburg dominions as that presented by the Turks in the preceding century. But how could Vienna contest Russian expansionism in southeastern Europe without forfeiting tsarist support in its campaign to check its enemies to the west and north?[7] Because the Austrians, unlike the Russians, had real or potential adversaries on all sides, they had to formulate their policies in the early 1790s (including their policy toward revolutionary France) with extreme caution. Any action taken in concert with Prussia against Paris had to reckon, not only with the highly volatile situation in France, but also with the easily renewable rivalry between Vienna and Berlin in central Europe, and with the unavoidable Austro-Russian tensions in the Balkans.

There were other complicating factors at work as well. As has often been noted, concerns about revolutionary ideology as a source of domestic subversion weighed much more heavily at Vienna than at Berlin. The Prussians had little to fear from this quarter, facing only traditional and easily isolated peasant uprisings in hinterland regions like Silesia. Even Prussia's western

6 See ibid., pp. 85–86, for an analysis of the Prussian stance on these matters in 1790–91.
7 Roider, *Austria's Eastern Question*, pp. 194–95. See also, on Austria's strategic dilemma throughout the eighteenth century, Paul W. Schroeder, *The Transformation of European Politics 1763–1848* (Oxford: Oxford University Press, 1994), passim.

territories, adjacent to France, offered no evidence of the impact of revolutionary propaganda. Habsburg policymakers, on the other hand, were severely tested by events in 1789–90, when Belgium had seceded, Galicia and Hungary had threatened to follow suit, and many other Habsburg territories had been restive. Furthermore, Leopold II's reassertion of Austrian rule in Belgium at the end of 1790 gave notice that retaining this possession was – and would remain – a higher priority for him than it had been for his brother Joseph II. But this meant that, as Paris was sheltering a swarm of Belgian refugees who zealously anticipated a crusade to liberate their country, Leopold had to be commensurately more sensitive to the threat emanating from France.[8]

Finally, of course, there was the fact of the emperor's kinship with France's embattled royal couple. "During the course of the summer of 1791," one historian has aptly observed, "Leopold's policy oscillated between a fraternal instinct to help his sister and a rational assessment of Austrian *raison d'état*." The news from France that the emperor's royal brother-in-law had formally accepted his subjects' new constitution on 13 September was a great source of relief to Leopold and his chief adviser, Kaunitz. Of course, they were only too cognizant of the fact that Louis XVI had on this occasion acted under duress and insincerely; still, they seem to have been hoping for the establishment in France of a constitutional monarchy that could bank the fires of revolutionary enthusiasm without acquiring the ability to challenge Habsburg interests in the Low Countries, Germany, or Italy. Yet this was, from the start, a forlorn expectation: the men feverishly engaged in remaking France were not likely to accept for long a reduced French role in continental affairs. The implications of this last fact were daunting: "a strong France and a strong Austria," it has been observed, "could not coexist amicably, no matter what their formal relationship might be."[9]

It was clear, then, that France faced in the early stages of its revolution, as it had faced through much of the eighteenth century, a continental situation replete with challenges to its sense of national mission. It became speedily obvious as well that Great Britain would continue to compete unabatedly with its French rival in a world of markets and colonies that included – but ultimately transcended – battle-scarred Europe.

The British during these years made striking advances along a road paved with enticing expectations of global empire. Nowhere was this more the case than in the zone – virtually half the planet – of the "Pacific rim." Historians of international relations have underscored the importance to the politics of this period of the contest for influence in the Pacific region.

8 Blanning, *Origins of the French Revolutionary Wars*, pp. 85–86.
9 Ibid., pp. 88–89.

They have, in doing so, chronicled the enormous strides taken by the British in this connection.[10] In the southwestern reaches of this enormous theater, the British acquired Lord Howe Island in 1788 and, three years later, Pitt Island and the Chatham Islands. Captains Bligh, Lever, Gilbert, and Marshall discovered and charted insular lands; Lieutenant John Shortland sailed along Guadalcanal and San Cristobal in 1789; and the Vancouver expedition explored a stretch of the coast of New Zealand, discovered the Chathams, and charted the Snares.[11] Meanwhile, on the other side of the Pacific, the imprisonment of three British merchantmen by Spanish authorities in May 1789 at Nootka Sound, situated on the west coast of Vancouver Island, essentially resulted from "a collision between the relentless surge of British commercial expansion and the traditional Spanish claim to a monopoly of trade and settlement on the Pacific coast."[12] Here, of course, was another story long familiar to those versed in issues of European and global competition.

Of even greater moment, however, was the fact that the upshot of the Nootka Sound incident – a Spanish capitulation to Pitt's ministry on most relevant points by October 1790 – signified a larger humiliation of France, just as surely as had Madrid's retreat over the Falkland Islands less than two decades before. Once more the Spanish had looked to their Bourbon confederate for support in the face of British naval and commercial expansionism – and once again, the French had failed to assert themselves. London's victory over Madrid reflected both a "very successful naval mobilisation, which was a measure of Britain's recovery from the Anglo-Bourbon struggle of 1778–83, and the diplomatic situation. Britain's allies had stood by her, conspicuously so in the case of the Dutch fleet, while Spain had been unable to obtain reliable assistance."[13] As has often been pointed out, ties between the Bourbon allies were now being strained not only by geopolitical considerations – that is, Spanish perceptions of French strategic weakness – but also by ideology – that is, Spanish fears of revolutionary subversion emanating from the other side of the Pyrenees. And all this was happening in the disheartening light of renewed British assertiveness upon the high seas.

In his careful reappraisal of the impact of the Nootka Sound incident upon Anglo-French relations, H. V. Evans has emphasized the undiminished wariness of George III's government toward Paris. Speaking off-the-record to a colleague, William Pitt voiced his hope that a letter he had sent to a British diplomat, Hugh Elliot, "steers quite clear of anything like *cringing* to France, which I agree with you ought to be avoided *even* in the present

10 Jeremy Black, *British Foreign Policy in an Age of Revolutions, 1783–1793* (New York: Cambridge University Press, 1994), p. 252.
11 Ibid., pp. 252–54.
12 Blanning, *Origins of the French Revolutionary Wars*, pp. 61–62.
13 Black, *British Foreign Policy*, p. 252.

moment of their weakness, and certainly in all others." It was quite easy for the prime minister's ghost writer, James Burges, to portray him as saying: "We have felt too strongly the immense advantage to be derived by this country from such a state of anarchy and weakness as France is at present plunged in, to be so mad as to interfere in any measure which may...tend to put France into the situation where...she [would have] the power to injure us."[14] Evans has noted that Pitt's stance toward Paris throughout this period remained "one of expediency." Nootka Sound was, for him, but one milepost along Britain's road toward ever greater incursions into American markets and the vast fisheries of the Pacific. He might condescend, along the way, to "befriend" the powerless French "in anticipation of breaking the Family Compact," but not at the cost of a rapprochement that could even faintly imply parity between London and Paris.[15]

The stunning decline of French influence that loomed behind Spanish difficulties in the Americas and in Pacific waters manifested itself elsewhere as well. In the West Indies, revolution broke out in the French colonies, pitting slaves against masters. A leading sector of French overseas commerce was thus jeopardized. In the Middle East, Jeremy Black has remarked, "Jezzar Ahmed Pasha, the governor of Palestine, felt able to expel the French merchants who enjoyed a monopoly of Palestine's external sea trade at the end of 1790, only inviting them back in 1791 on his own terms."[16] Such were the diplomatic ramifications, in this strategic region, of growing Russian (and British) influence and of attenuated French support for Turkey. Meanwhile, in the Far East, the intensifying commitment of British brains, enterprise, and brawn to India and to trade in the fabulous markets of the Moluccas and other islands was not at all counterbalanced by d'Entrecasteaux's expedition of reconnaissance in 1791. In this theater as elsewhere, "the energy that had characterized French activity in the mid-1780s was not maintained, and this activity was cut short by the Revolutionary Wars."[17]

It was clear, then, that as the European state system moved into the 1790s, no Brave New World of revolutionary idealism was going to quench its competitive fires. What was more, the French, if initially immersed in their great project of domestic reconstruction, would in time be reengaging themselves in this competitive system, and with a vengeance.

Indeed, from the very beginning, as a phalanx of historians have attested, the revolutionaries heralded such a turn of events by appealing to an international audience. Whether they were anathematizing the "feudal regime" on 4–5 August 1789, enacting the famous Declaration of the Rights of Man

14 Citations from H. V. Evans, "The Nootka Sound Controversy in Anglo-French Diplomacy – 1790," *Journal of Modern History*, 46 (1974): 638–39.
15 Ibid., p. 638.
16 Black, *British Foreign Policy*, p. 533.
17 Ibid., p. 254.

and Citizen several weeks later, or issuing some other pronunciamento, the Constituent Assemblymen were in effect notifying their European contemporaries of what was soon to come. They drew all the more encouragement to do so from political émigrés in Paris representing virtually every oppressed national or ethnic group in Europe – and beyond. Victims of Geneva's aristocratic counterrevolution of 1762 rubbed elbows with more recent refugees from the Low Countries, and these and other foreigners edited their own news sheets, operated their own clubs, and adopted the heady discourse of "national liberation." Their incredible diversity was spotlighted on 19 June 1790, when an applauding Constituent Assembly received a delegation including Arabs, Chaldeans, Prussians, Poles, English, Swiss, Germans, Dutch, Swedes, Italians, Spaniards, Americans, Indians, Syrians, Brabanters, Liègeois, Avignonnais, Genevans, Sardinians, Grisons, and Sicilians![18] With such aggrieved patriots shouting slogans from the galleries, and undoubtedly lobbying for their causes in less public venues as well, is it any wonder that the men who were attempting to remake France found themselves distracted from the very start by foreign affairs?

Even when they were not, perhaps, aware of doing so, the Assemblymen raised issues of European import. The curtailment of "feudalism" in early August 1789, we have seen, was directed primarily at a domestic audience of insurrectionary peasants; but it also contravened prerogatives long conceded to various princes of central Europe's Holy Roman Empire. The Treaty of Westphalia in 1648 had confirmed the French crown's hold on the former imperial province of Alsace; yet it had also promised that the ex-rulers in Alsace would forever enjoy title to certain "feudal" rights. But now, in 1789, did not the "sovereign" National Assembly have the right to break a royal treaty concluded in the benighted past and abrogate those vestiges of feudalism in Alsace?[19] Moreover, what implications would popular sovereignty, once embraced by the Assembly, hold for future treaties negotiated between France and other European polities, and for the continental balance of power in general? To raise such questions could be immensely subversive in a Europe whose wars and dynastic successions had, at one and the same time, brought peoples of different languages, customs, and traditions together in entities called "states" and yet kept such peoples artificially divided by internationally recognized boundaries.[20] The "sovereignty of the people," once accepted as gospel in revolutionary France, could be exported all over Europe as "national self-determination" and might subvert all existing public order within – and among – states.

These potentially explosive principles, invoked in connection with the situation in Alsace, also motivated the Constituent Assemblymen to annex

18 Blanning, *Origins of the French Revolutionary Wars*, pp. 73–74.
19 Ibid., pp. 74–75.
20 Jacques Godechot, *France and the Atlantic Revolution of the Eighteenth Century, 1770–1799*, trans. Herbert H. Rowen (New York: Free Press, 1965), pp. 147–49.

Avignon and the Comtat-Venaissin, two papal territories enclosed within France. In June 1790, subjects in both enclaves rose up against the papal authorities and clamored for unification with revolutionary France. In both cases, tellingly, the question of how sovereignty was to be legitimized was debated at Paris, and this led to a sanctioning of self-determination as the controlling principle of rightful sovereignty. It took some time before this radical idea was fully spelled out and accepted, but the Assembly finally approved the annexation of Avignon and the Comtat-Venaissin in September 1791. Austria's Mercy-Argenteau warned that by resolving the issue in this manner the revolutionaries had "declared war on all other governments."[21] We can assume that Austria's ambassador was similarly afflicted when rebels in Savoy (a province of the king of Sardinia) and in several parts of the Austrian Netherlands cited the notion of popular self-determination as justification for their demand to be united to France.[22]

Yet there are good reasons for divining behind all of these territorial controversies something even more fundamental than a clash between old regime diplomatic legalism and revolutionary ideology. It is striking that those governing France both before and during the Revolution shared something of vital import with many of the kings, dukes, margraves, and other rulers within the Holy Roman Empire: namely, *the desire to consolidate secular state power*. Administrative and juridical reforms implemented by both Calonne and his immediate successor, Loménie de Brienne, during the Prerevolution as part of their eleventh-hour efforts to salvage Bourbon absolutism in France had already infringed upon the rights of the German princes in Alsace and accordingly elicited reactions of outrage from the latter. In this sense, what the Constituent Assembly did in 1789 and thereafter represented but a continuation of traditional policy in France. Especially revealing in this connection was the manner in which the revolutionaries handled the status of Avignon. Taking care to base their claim to this papal enclave on historical precedent quite as much as on ideology (i.e., the "right to self-determination"), the Assemblymen happily cited a decree issued by – of all institutions! – the Parlement of Aix asserting French rights to Avignon. We can see that what such a controversy erupting early in the Revolution betokened was "not so much a conflict between historical rights and national sovereignty as a conflict between historical rights and *state* sovereignty." Indeed, how many of the German princes must have ached to follow the French example of abolishing all outside pretentions to jurisdiction![23] For here, again, was the larger point: Europe in the eighteenth century was witnessing, on the local level, a consolidation of secular state power. Could it have been otherwise, given (among other factors)

21 Blanning, *Origins of the French Revolutionary Wars*, pp. 74–75.
22 Godechot, *France in the Eighteenth Century*, pp. 147–49.
23 Blanning, *Origins of the French Revolutionary Wars*, pp. 76–78.

the pressures exerted on the leaders of great and lesser states by military competition?

In analyzing French attitudes toward the outside world during 1789–91, therefore, we must take into account traditional patriotic sentiment and statist ambition as much as novel revolutionary ideology. That these forces would in fact turn out to be mutually reinforcing became apparent early on in the revolutionary process, most obviously in regard to those time-honored enemies of France, Britain and Austria.

Even before the end of the dramatic month of July 1789, the British ambassador to France, the duke of Dorset, was reporting French suspicions that British money was being doled out to foment public disorder. Dorset claimed as well that he and his countrymen risked physical harm as they circulated among the public.[24] Rumors about British vessels hovering with wicked intent off the coast of Brittany and about British logistical support for incursions by foreigners into southern France reinforced anti-British sentiments in the capital.[25] Within the Constituent Assembly, most deputies were exhibiting their customary ambivalence toward London: was Britain "perfidious Albion" or the cradle of constitutional liberty? In reality, given the age-old rivalry between the two countries, and in particular the aggressiveness with which George III's government pursued what it regarded as its European and global economic interests, it is somewhat surprising that any vestiges of eighteenth-century "Anglomania" could have survived at all among the French politicians. Nonetheless, over the long run, a revolutionary regime seeing French national interests as everlastingly threatened by those across the Channel was bound to be tempted to revive the embers of war and, perhaps, to give any new struggle against London an unprecedentedly virulent character. Moreover, the fact that the British government was *representative* in nature would make it all the easier for statesmen at Paris to transfer their compatriots' hostility from Pitt's ministry to the British people as a whole. A war of people against people seemed already a realistic possibility in the not-too-distant future.[26]

Well before this actually happened, a foreign-policy debate in the National Assembly gave ample warning of the Anglophobia lurking just beneath the deceptively placid surface of French politics. On 14 May 1790 the deputies were informed of a precautionary mobilization of fourteen ships of the line ordered by Louis XVI in response to British naval deployments and Spanish requests for assistance stemming from the Nootka Sound incident. The ensuing deliberation in the Assembly was punctuated

24 Ibid., p. 131.
25 On these rumors, see (among other sources) Lefebvre, *The Coming of the French Revolution*, pp. 118, 127.
26 Norman Hampson, *Prelude to Terror: The Constituent Assembly and the Failure of Consensus, 1789–1791* (New York: Blackwell, 1988), p. 129.

by outbursts of bellicose rhetoric and by more reasoned but no less somber statements concerning Franco-British relations. Among the former was the declaration by the baron de Menou, eliciting repeated applause from his audience, that the French would know how to react in the event that Britain on this occasion was in the wrong and refused to make amends: "We shall demonstrate the courage and the power of a nation which is truly free; we shall proceed to attack England in England itself!" Among the more thoughtful pronouncements was that tendered by Pierre-Victor Malouet, erstwhile diplomat and naval administrator. Even a cursory review of history, Malouet affirmed, led unfailingly to the conclusion that free peoples were, if anything, even more zealous to wage aggressive wars than were despotic regimes.[27] Precisely the same commentary came at another juncture in this debate from Mirabeau, perhaps the most percipient and prophetic of all Assemblymen. "Mirabeau," noted Albert Sorel, "saw clearly; he dissipated the mists, tore aside the veils and for an instant revealed to an unbelieving Assembly that strange and fatal future which the Revolution bore within itself.... He showed that free peoples were more eager for war and democracies were more enslaved by their passions than the most absolute despots." In the event of war, Mirabeau warned, the revolutionaries, borne upon the tide of their own heady expectations, would inflame rather than becalm the masses and push the country headlong into new and uncharted waters of international adventurism.[28] Only Mirabeau's sudden death in April of the following year prevented him from witnessing the melancholy fulfillment of his prophesy.

It is true that on 22 May 1790 the National Assembly solemnly declared: "the French nation renounces the undertaking of any war with a view to making conquests, and ... will never use its power against the liberty of any other people."[29] Yet this statement was but one article in a constitutional "compromise" on the conduct of French foreign policy which, admittedly, left Louis XVI in control of day-to-day management of that policy but reserved for the legislators the major decisions of war and peace.[30] As if to signify their resolution to take a more active role in this crucial domain of policy-making once time permitted, the Assemblymen insisted upon doubling the number of warships to be mobilized on this

---

27 Citations from Blanning, *The French Revolutionary Wars, 1787–1802* (London: Arnold, 1996), pp. 48–49.
28 Cited in Albert Sorel, *L'Europe et la Révolution Française*, 8 vols. (Paris: E. Plon, Nourrit et Cie, 1885–1904), 2:88–89.
29 Cited by Blanning, *The French Revolution in Germany* (New York: Oxford University Press, 1983), p. 59.
30 See also, on this subject, Barry M. Rothaus, "The Emergence of Legislative Control over Foreign Policy in the Constituent Assembly, 1789–91" (Ph.D. diss., University of Wisconsin, 1968).

occasion. Subsequently, they would increase this number by yet another 50 percent.[31]

H. V. Evans has argued plausibly that, at least for the time being, the balance of political forces within the new legislature militated against a resumption of Franco-British hostilities. At bottom, most of the delegates distrusted and would always distrust their haughty cross-Channel neighbors; still, they had little use for what they regarded as a superannuated and reactionary alliance with the Bourbon government of Spain. The strongest advocates of the Family Compact within the Assembly were naturally the royalists, but it was precisely the royalists whose influence was most palpably on the wane in this second year of the Revolution. Thus, the Family Compact, if still a major issue in May, excited little controversy six months later. Nevertheless, the Patriots, ever more influential in the Assembly, were not about to abandon their prejudices against the English. Lafayette, for example, could never be convinced that Britain did not covet revenge for France's role in the American Revolution and always saw London's armaments as aimed chiefly against the French. And the "hero of two worlds" was but one of the Assembly's incorrigible Anglophobes.[32] Moreover, the very dialectics of constitutional debate worked to the advantage of such individuals. As time went by and as the center of gravity in the Constituent Assembly shifted toward the Left, the old admiration for British constitutional arrangements tended gradually to give way to an understandable annoyance at the constant references to British practices by those in the Center and on the Right. This could only serve to revive an animus against France's insular rival that had at most been repressed.[33] In the end, the Patriots were likely to remember Malouet's assertion in May 1790 that "France needed her colonies, Spain her alliances and British ambitions were liable to endanger both."[34]

But if the French gave notice to the world in May 1790 (and thereafter) that their revolution was doing nothing to diminish their historic antipathy toward the British, they were almost as quick to own up to their undying Austrophobia. An incident in July 1790 underscored this powerfully. The legislature received the news that Vienna had requested permission for a detachment of Austrian soldiers to traverse French territory on their way to restoring "order" in Belgium. The revolutionaries, already mistrustful of the Austrians due to long historical memories, and energized further by wild rumors circulating daily about Marie-Antoinette and an "Austrian Committee" at Court, reacted strongly to this report. They gave themselves over to all kinds of speculation. Could not this outrageous incursion

31 Blanning, *The French Revolutionary Wars*, pp. 48–49.
32 Evans, "The Nootka Sound Controversy," pp. 634–35.
33 Hampson, *Prelude to Terror*, p. 128.
34 Ibid., p. 132.

be the prelude to all the horrors of counterrevolution in France as well as in Belgium? Were there not alarming stories that the French military forces in the northern and northeastern provinces were stretched thin? Were not counterrevolutionary troops, according to all reports, mustering in Savoy and the Rhineland? Was not Prussia verging upon rapprochement with Austria? Such suspicions may have been (somewhat) exaggerated; furthermore, France and Austria were still supposedly allies, and consequently pledged to accommodate each other's strategic needs. Still, accusations relating in any way to Vienna seem to have touched such a raw nerve in the psychology of the revolutionaries that they quickly generated an outburst of Austrophobic paranoia.[35] And from this near-hysteria issued a call for tighter legislative control over the crown in foreign affairs, control to be exercised in part through the creation of a committee charged with reviewing all pacts between France and other powers.[36]

During the final fifteen months of the Constituent Assembly, Franco-Austrian relations were continually roiled by issues we have already reviewed: the grievances of the German princes relating to Alsace; the complaints of French émigrés now congregating in the cities of the empire; the resentments of foreign refugees now lobbying the legislators at Paris; and the legislators' fears about the queen and the so-called Austrian Committee. In connection with this last point, it is relevant to note that Marie-Antoinette's growing conviction that only foreign intervention could stem the tide of revolution had already been attributed to her in advance by the most extreme Patriots. Attitudes of the old France and the new France seemed to be converging in the ever more belligerent stance of the Assembly. An assertion of French superiority and a distrust toward foreign states that harkened back to earlier times were now inspiring a novel kind of nationalism and making old attitudes ideologically respectable. If this was not yet a full-blown development, surely the seeds of it "were in the wind, and if they germinated they would bear poisonous fruit."[37]

To sum up, it is clear, on the one hand, that European and global realities challenged the French even in the radiant early days of their revolution, and, on the other hand, that they were determined eventually to rise to that challenge. That the undying fires of Anglophobia and Austrophobia cast their lurid glow over the otherwise benign landscape of reconstructive French politics in 1789–91 reminds us how closely the Constituent Assemblymen were tied into the old world of politics abroad even as they

---

35 Blanning, *Origins of the French Revolutionary Wars*, p. 76. On the question of Marie-Antoinette and the rumored "Austrian Committee," see also Thomas E. Kaiser, "Who's Afraid of Marie-Antoinette? Diplomacy, Austrophobia, and the Queen," *French History* 14 (2000): 241–71.
36 Blanning, *The French Revolutionary Wars*, p. 49.
37 Hampson, *Prelude to Terror*, p. 138.

strove to fashion a new world at home. Furthermore, as seems particularly obvious in the light of hindsight, some of the legislature's more audacious members in 1791 were already looking much farther afield than the traditional battlefields of western and central Europe. They were presaging new partitions of Poland, and even a dismemberment of the Ottoman Empire, with strategic Turkish possessions in the eastern Mediterranean – including, perhaps, Egypt – to be ceded to a rejuvenated imperial France.[38] What have we here, if not an initial premonition of Napoleon's Eastern Adventure, and of a Gallic challenge to Britain's empire in the Far East?

Of course, all of this lay in the future; moreover, the ability to project French power abroad was contingent from the start upon the restructuring of public authority at home. And achievement of this latter goal required the realization of reforms that would toughen the sinews of this warlike West-Eurasian state even as they furnished new civic and socioeconomic opportunities to "bourgeois" and other French citizens. It is time to reappraise some of these reforms, so central to the foundation of the modern France.

STATE AND SOCIETY AND THE CONSTITUENT ASSEMBLY

The distinguished British historian J. M. Thompson, summarizing the accomplishments of the Constituent Assembly, lauded "the legislative action of deputies drawn from the whole hierarchy of the middle classes, who for a while forgot their class interests and enmities in a genuine zeal for national regeneration."[39] Thompson, who penned these words in the early 1940s against the harsh backdrop of French geopolitical humiliation, and in reaction to Marxist depictions of class conflict in the French Revolution, quite understandably sought to accentuate the larger "national" agenda of the deputies in 1789–91. We can endorse this assessment readily enough, provided that we can construe the term "national" to include matters affecting the state. Frenchmen sensitive as ever to international realities could no more afford to overlook their country's statist requirements than they could afford to neglect their own (and others') "class" interests.

Indeed, a global-historical interpretation of some of the most basic reforms enacted by the Constituent Assembly forcefully underscores the extent to which they strengthened the French state and the collective "national" consciousness of the French in the competitive West-Eurasian context – and this, in a phase of the Revolution customarily noted for its decentralized and pacific aspects. We shall drive this point home by

38 Consult, on this vein of speculation, Sorel, *L'Europe et la Révolution française*, 2:201–3.
39 Cited in James M. Thompson, *The French Revolution* (Oxford: Basil Blackwell, 1943), pp. 226–27.

reconsidering seven specific and crucial areas of legislation: the restructuring of administrative authority, the establishment of electoral procedures, financial and bureaucratic reform, ecclesiastical changes, the curtailment of seigneurialism and transference of properties, the dissolution of all corporate bodies, and the overhaul of the armed forces.

Restructuring administration in revolutionary France entailed the replacement of the old patchwork of conflicting administrative jurisdictions with a rational and simple system of 83 departments, subdivisions known as districts and cantons, and (at the local level) approximately 44,000 communes (or parishes). In discussing this truly fundamental innovation, which has essentially survived down to the present day, George Rudé maintained that "not only absolute monarchy but the whole old system of centralized government was dismantled; and France, at this stage of the Revolution, became virtually a federation of ... departments and municipalities, enjoying a wide measure of local autonomy."[40] Rudé's conclusion is, in substantial measure, valid: after all, the drawing of local administrative boundaries was entrusted to the deputies from the regions concerned; the departments were to derive their names from natural features such as mountains, rivers, and seas; and all the new jurisdictions were henceforth to be administered, not by royal appointees, but by committees of citizens elected from below. To this extent, 1789–91 in France (much like March–November 1917 in Russia) constituted a significant interlude between periods of pronounced centralization of government.

Yet, even so, the situation was not quite that simple. Several recent inquiries into the Constituent Assembly's work enable us to detect behind this apparent break in French administrative history a persisting deference to principles of national unity, administrative efficiency, and hierarchical distribution of power. For most of the representatives, it has been pointed out, creating departments, districts, cantons, and communes of roughly uniform size was one way to keep major provinces like Dauphiné, Burgundy, and Brittany or (at the other extreme) entities as small as Aunis and the Basque *pays* from rejecting – or simply ignoring – the Assembly's directives. Such "uncivic" behavior could prove contagious and could jeopardize the integrity of the new France. This seems to have been the point that delegates from Clermont-Ferrand were conveying when they addressed their watchful compatriots at home: "All the operations of the National Assembly are founded on the metaphysical and moral principle that France, to be regenerated, must necessarily experience a total revolution."[41]

---

40 Cited in George Rudé, *Revolutionary Europe, 1783–1815* (New York: Harper Torchbooks, 1964), p. 111.
41 Ted W. Margadant, *Urban Rivalries in the French Revolution* (Princeton, N.J.: Princeton University Press, 1992), pp. 237–38.

The underlying insistence upon preserving the integrity of this "regenerated" France meant retaining, among other distinguishing features of the old regime, the centralized hierarchy of the administrative structure. What did this signify in terms of the allotment of public functions? Municipal authorities managed town affairs. Each council on the district level distributed the tax burden among the communes in the district, drew up lists of voters, directed public works, and supervised the sale of coveted *biens nationaux*. Councils in each department took over most of the roles previously in the domain of the intendant or provincial assembly. They apportioned taxes among the districts, maintained bridges and roads, watched over the national lands (formerly the jurisdiction of the *maîtrise des eaux et forêts*), controlled the regional police, and administered hospitals, prisons, public welfare projects, and public instruction.[42] Centralizing and decentralizing tendencies, it seems clear, existed side by side in the new administrative structures of the state. Yet the stress lay on the former rather than the latter. For example, the towns in this new polity were certainly emancipated from the "despotic" tutelage of the intendants; yet they found themselves anchored in a hierarchy of authority that clearly linked towns, districts, and departments with the national government. Again, the legislators wanted to protect the departments from any revival of "ministerial despotism"; but they also saw the departments as instrumental in neutralizing provincial opposition to national policies and in curbing the independence of the towns. Yet again, the new administrators at all levels, answerable to the electorate, would presumably shun the old ways of despotism; still, the systematizing and standardizing of administrative structures, and the rationalization and bureaucratization of procedures, could not help but expand the purlieu and prerogatives of government. All in all, it was the officialdom and procedure of departments, districts, and municipalities, rather than spontaneous popular mobilization, that was destined in 1790–91 to fill the vacuum left by the collapse or abolition of the old institutions.[43]

Moreover, these reforms – like so many other revolutionary innovations – were mediated both by contemporary political culture and by the state's geostrategic needs. On the one hand, the move toward ever more hierarchical administrative procedures reinforced a traditional political culture that stressed the benefits accruing (locally as well as nationally) from government service. And administrative and political-cultural tendencies alike received a powerful impetus from the revolutionary leaders' international concerns. The French state, in an ever-competitive Europe, had

---

42 Lynn Hunt, *Revolution and Urban Politics in Provincial France: Troyes and Reims, 1786–1790* (Stanford, Calif.: Stanford University Press, 1978), p. 131.

43 Ibid., pp. 129–32. Refer also to Hunt's seminal article, "Committees and Communes: Local Politics and National Revolution in 1789," pp. 321–46, for some related remarks on these matters.

to concentrate its authority and rationalize its procedures. It also had to enhance its revenues. In the years prior to 1789 it had been notoriously inclined to achieve the latter goal (in part) by selling offices. But this practice, implemented on a massive scale, indelibly affected French society. In one aspect of this process, royal ministers attempting to raise money (above all, of course, for reasons of war and diplomacy) had knowingly tolerated a proliferation of law courts. In doing so, they had created an urban milieu that had a strong interest in cultivating its links with the central government. Come the Revolution, that element in local urban society looked with undiminished interest to Paris for the benison of new tribunals to administer the new justice. On hearing that the Assembly was going to turn the old system of law courts inside out, towns all over France showered the legislators with declarations of support and – more to the point – with requests for new tribunals in their own precincts.

In the narrowest sense, such appeals signified that the power to create and suppress courts of law, which had formerly been an attribute of royal sovereignty, was now passing into the hands of the Assembly, and was doing so under the radical aegis of popular sovereignty.[44] However, taking a broader view, one can see that the often bitter contention among towns for the new tribunals was but one aspect of the larger phenomenon of territorial conflicts over institutions and resources in the revolutionary period. In this sense, Tocqueville's "political-cultural" instincts did not fail him: he perceived that the Revolution only strengthened the French tendency to see the state as a crucial source of local as well as national power. Townspeople struggling to adjust to new realities during 1789–99 believed more than ever that their communities' fortunes depended upon institutions established by the central government. Hence, political-cultural and institutional realities together helped to bridge any gap existing between old and new regimes in France. "The egalitarian rhetoric and civic consciousness of Republican political culture remained consistent with an institutional hierarchy that redistributed resources from the government in Paris to local communities."[45] But beyond even this, the political culture, conditioned by the growing presence of the war-prone state in people's lives, bore witness, as did the revitalized "institutional hierarchy" itself, to the heavy hand of foreign policy upon domestic affairs in France.

Electoral procedures in the new France, although they might mitigate somewhat the centralizing impulses in the rejuvenated hierarchy of administration, worked at the same time to reinforce a very traditional "public consciousness" easily manipulated by French statesmen in times of national crisis. Plainly, there were some significant realities here common to local elections in the old regime and to the updated procedures of revolutionary

44 Margadant, *Urban Rivalries in the French Revolution*, p. 447.
45 Ibid., p. 455.

times. "Traditional electoral practice did not necessarily require the presence of the whole community, simply a token number to authenticate the conduct of business. The choice of personnel might well be informally agreed beforehand, so the assembly itself was merely a ratification of the communal will." What Malcolm Crook has called "this collective rather than individualised approach to the selection of representatives" was "deeply embedded in the popular consciousness and, like so many other aspects of electoral behavior, it endured into the Revolution and even beyond."[46]

This is not to say that meetings held for electoral purposes during the 1790s were not occasionally marred by displays of hostility and even outbreaks of violence. Such contretemps could, and did, result from tensions between rival parishes, clienteles, and political factions. Yet such localized unpleasantness notwithstanding, the revolutionaries by and large seem to have been extremely reluctant to tolerate in their electoral practices anything resembling *formal* party differences and *formalized* competition for votes. Given a prevalent political culture emphasizing communal, collective, and public values, divisiveness in politics could be seen as an attack upon the "general will" of society.[47] This seeming adherence of all or most politicians to a vision of politics in which factional pressures were condemned a priori as subverting the voters' ability to discover their common interests may have made it easier for the French to accept extreme centralization of government – namely, Terror – in 1793–94.[48]

The very ways in which the new electoral regime adopted in the 1790s broke through old privileged and corporate barriers and brought citizens together may have fortified this predisposition. Procedural guidelines adopted by the Constituent Assembly facilitated the emergence of a polity new to the French experience: they brought citizens together in the spring of 1790 by neighborhood or arrondissement rather than by trade, profession, or corps – this, for the purpose of choosing electors for the assemblies of the departments. When, for instance, in the old Breton parlementary city of Rennes, François and Louis Biard, tanners by profession, Laurent, a fish seller, Le Prieur, a carpenter, and Sauvé, a baker, could collaborate with Defrieux, Fournel, and Reslon, magistrates in the presidial court, and with

---

46 Malcolm Crook, *Elections in the French Revolution: An Apprenticeship in Democracy, 1789–1799* (Cambridge: Cambridge University Press, 1996), pp. 193–94.

47 Ibid., pp. 192–93, 194–95. Crook's interpretation here owes something to Patrice Guennifey, *Le Nombre et la raison: La Révolution française et les élections* (Paris: Ecole des Hautes Etudes en Sciences Sociales, 1993).

48 A theme especially prominent in the writings of François Furet; see *Interpreting the French Revolution*, passim. See also the relevant articles by Furet – and others – in François Furet and Mona Ozouf, eds., *A Critical Dictionary of the French Revolution*; and Guennifey, *Le Nombre et la raison*, passim.

Lesguern, formerly a parlementary justice, to have a voice in their common future, it was clear that new patterns of political sociability were being created. And it certainly seems that this transformation of civic life was beginning – slowly, no doubt – to take hold in rural as well as in urban France. That, for example, the Breton village of Sel could bring 650 active citizens together to choose five electors, or that the village of Saint-Servan could assemble 800 active citizens to choose eight electors, certified the creation of political forums that were more accessible and equitable by far than the remote and aloof Estates of Brittany, which had lorded it over such villages since time out of mind.[49]

The reference to "active" citizens brings to mind the Assembly's decision (reflecting in part the counsel of Siéyès and other deputies) to distinguish between citizens to whom the vote was to be given and citizens not to be so enfranchised. The Assemblymen decreed that only those males aged twenty-five or over, domiciled for at least a year, not engaged in domestic service, and paying a direct tax equivalent to three days of unskilled labor, could vote in the primary assemblies. Among these electors, only those whose direct taxation was worth ten days of unskilled labor could vote at the secondary stage for citizens fully qualified (through payment of a "silver mark" of 50 livres in annual taxation) to serve at various levels in the new administrative system.

Precisely how inclusive (or exclusive) these provisions were intended to be or indeed turned out to be is, from our viewpoint, of less than paramount importance. They demonstrably brought many previously unenfranchised Frenchmen into politics and in doing so created a reservoir of citizens upon which the government could draw in time of national emergency. In fact, however, scholars commenting most recently on electoral issues have emphasized the inclusiveness rather than the exclusiveness of France's new voting procedures. "Over the country as a whole," Malcolm Crook has determined, "some 3 million citizens were at least occasionally involved in voting." The "electoral apprenticeship" in revolutionary France was "extremely intensive... especially for the minority (perhaps 500,000 Frenchmen) who attended regularly."[50] Michael P. Fitzsimmons, endorsing the old estimate of roughly 50 percent of males over twenty-five participating at some point in the electoral process in 1790–91, has observed that the Assembly did not require active citizens to be literate, and furthermore "reformed taxation in such a way that liability to direct taxation extended far down the social scale." The deputies, "basing the electorate on taxes rather than property and freeing it of any religious

49 Michael P. Fitzsimmons, *The Remaking of France: The National Assembly, the Constitution of 1791 and the Reorganization of the French Polity, 1789–1791* (New York: Cambridge University Press, 1994), pp. 187–91.
50 Crook, *Elections in the French Revolution*, p. 192.

affiliation, brought into being one of the most participatory and democratic national political structures in the world."[51]

And so the electoral procedures developed by the Assemblymen were – like so many of their other reforms – a double-edged weapon. They were devised in part as a curb upon officeholders in the new France, as a reassurance that the "despotism" of benighted times of old could never return. Yet by helping to break down old barriers of corporate organization and privilege while simultaneously permitting the survival of established patterns of collective and communal political culture, and by mobilizing unprecedented numbers of Frenchmen on public occasions, these procedures indirectly contributed in the course of the 1790s to the reconsolidation of state power.

But whereas local and national elections (like the new hierarchy of departments, districts, and communes) became in time a double-edged weapon, financial-bureaucratic changes seemed to cut in one direction only: toward an enlargement of the public domain, and, hence, of state authority. The whole point of fiscal reform in the 1790s, John Bosher has explained, was to remove all budgetary and related matters from the purview of private individuals – the invidious "capitalists" (bankers, *traitants*, venal officers) – and place them under the watchful eye of the "nation." Those who dared to speak up for the old system – Calonne and Dupont de Nemours, for example – were ignored from the start. "The parliamentary forces imbued with the new principles of nationalism were composed of provincial representatives brought into the Assembly in the elections of 1789. They were only too anxious, once Mirabeau, Custine and others had made the issues clear, to exert the crushing weight of their numbers to thwart the ambitions of Parisian financial interests, whether of bankers or financiers."[52] Accordingly, the Assemblymen, all the more to consolidate the "honest" part of the royal debt – those payments owed to *rentiers* – moved to liquidate the king's obligations to "capitalists" such as venal bureaucrats. They created a national agency, the *Caisse de l'extraordinaire*, to issue notes, the famous *assignats*, which would be used to facilitate the transfer of nationalized properties – clerical and crown estates and buildings – to venal officers, thus extinguishing the offices (and associated national debt) in question. Needless to add, the Assembly insisted on keeping the sale of *biens nationaux* under public control, and the *assignats* themselves, for better or worse, were to be securely tied to the state's fortunes.

To be sure, the deputies had additional reasons in 1790 to expedite this vast transfer of wealth. As Philip Dawson, among others, has noted, some

---

51 Fitzsimmons, *The Remaking of France*, pp. 187–91.
52 John Bosher, *French Finances, 1770–1795: From Business to Bureaucracy* (Cambridge: Cambridge University Press, 1970), pp. 309–10.

of the parlements were still attempting to foment opposition to judicial (and other) reforms in the Assembly; how better to defeat such efforts than to encourage owners of the old judicial posts to accept reimbursement in the form of *biens nationaux*? Moreover, the sooner the liquid capital released by the abolition of venal offices could be absorbed in purchases of ecclesiastical and royal properties, the greater the chances of avoiding a monetary instability that could sap the credibility of the new regime. Hence, in part, the determination of the revolutionaries to finalize plans for a *Caisse de l'extraordinaire* and for another special agency, the General Directory of Liquidation: these two agencies in collaboration would carry out the envisaged operation.[53]

But, in the end, it all came back to the same purpose: legitimizing a transference of fiscal influence and functions from private hands to those of the "nation" – that is, the revolutionized and revivifed state. Inevitably, when France resumed its ways of war, enterprising individuals would still finds ways to profit from the state's military needs; yet never would they be able to worm their way as deeply into the administration as had the accountants and tax farmers of the old regime.[54] This was because liquidating that part of the crown's debt owing to the *financiers* of the past was only the prelude to the main task at hand: creation of a modern bureaucracy to safeguard the nation's finances. Inspired by the vision of a state functioning with mechanical efficiency, the men of the Constituent Assembly hoped to marshal the forces of organization to banish all forms of malversation in office. In France, they decreed, the multitudinous separate treasuries in the hands of free-wheeling, profiteering tax farmers and accountants would have to go. In their place a consolidated, bureaucratic Treasury would emerge whose salaried officials would operate in a rational, prescribed fashion. As the Revolution wore on, bureaus from the old regime's Department of Finance and funds formerly administered by tax farmers and receivers-general were assimilated into the new Treasury and the new ministries of Interior and Public Contributions. The Assembly assumed supervision of employees, salaries, and operating expenses in the new financial system and required the annual submission of unprecedentedly detailed accounts. It seems that most common clerks functioning in the old departments moved over successfully into the new agencies; most of the noble and "venal" accountants, on the other hand, did not. What these latter had known as "an aristocratic system, based on personal position in a social hierarchy, became a bureaucracy with an administrative

---

53 Philip Dawson, *Provincial Magistrates and Revolutionary Politics in France, 1789–1795* (Cambridge, Mass.: Harvard University Press, 1972), pp. 255–59. The liquidation of venal posts thus undertaken would in the end "free up" around 600 million *livres* in capital.
54 Bosher, *French Finances*, pp. 310–11.

hierarchy in which the organization of public functions took precedence over the claims of individual officials."[55]

Admittedly, these were fundamental changes that could not occur overnight; they were part of a process, the ongoing process of revolution. We can now state fairly confidently that at least until 1792 – that pivotal year marked by the reversion to war – the "new" fiscal system retained many if not all of its traditional characteristics. It managed to preserve a degree of its erstwhile autonomy within the state apparatus; it still lacked general operational rules and a precise definition of its place within French constitutional arrangements; its ministries remained somewhat uncoordinated and only partially modernized; and its functionaries, veterans and neophytes alike, retained some of the prejudices and habits of old regime officialdom. Nonetheless, it is clear by the same token that state employees now were no longer hangers-on from Court. They were state servants, subordinate to the directorate of the state and expected to defend the national interest. They worked within a system purged of its ruinous venality and subject increasingly to legislative oversight, a system already taking the first steps toward a major rationalization of routines.[56] It is hard to resist the conclusion that the new financial bureaucracy, "with its flexible hierarchy of command, its division of labor, its central records, its double-entry book-keeping systems, and its mechanical efficiency . . . was capable of mobilizing the . . . resources of the nation to a degree . . . necessary for 20 years of war against nearly the whole of Europe."[57] The geopolitical implications of the Constituent Assembly's reforms in the domain of state finance were, consequently, fairly evident.

This does not mean that, in this particular field of public policy, we cannot find any tensions between individual rights and "public" (i.e., statist) powers. Jean-Pierre Gross has noted that the Declaration of the Rights of Man of 1789 called property "an inviolable and sacred right of which no one can be deprived" and yet simultaneously proclaimed that tax obligations "should be equally distributed among all citizens in proportion to their faculties." The former statement seemed to privilege "possessive individualism," the autonomy of the citizen; the latter assertion appeared to posit "the promise of a fair society" to be realized in the final analysis by state intervention to ensure progressive taxation. Tax reform would navigate tentatively, uneasily, between "these two poles of liberty and equality," between the individual and the state, as the *taille, capitation,* and *vingtièmes,* and the *gabelle, aides,* and *traites* of the old regime gave way by 1791 to the new *contribution foncière* (land tax), *contribution mobilière* (poll tax),

55 Ibid., pp. 310–11.
56 Clive H. Church, *Revolution and Red Tape: The French Ministerial Bureaucracy 1770–1850* (Oxford: Clarendon Press, 1981), pp. 64–68.
57 Bosher, *French Finances,* p. 313.

and *patente* (commercial tax).[58] For a time, in this area at least, "liberty" prevailed over "equality," in part due to the very incompleteness of bureaucratization. How could new taxes be imposed when a fiscal bureaucracy still in its formative stages was not yet able to reevaluate the lands and properties slated for taxation? The authorities, moreover, had to reckon with the intoxicating sense of liberation, of new beginnings among the citizens of the country – an attitude that for some years was all too readily translatable into a refusal to pay taxes.[59] This would mean in practice that the French, still burdened with debts from past wars, and soon needful as ever of funds with which to finance new wars, would have to resort to discredited old methods to raise those funds. In the long run, however, the "bureaucratic revolution" would help to realize a more equitable assessment (and collection) of taxes. The permanent needs of the state, geostrategic and other, would see to that.

As we have already noted, those needs figured as well in the deputies' decision, taken (tentatively) as early as October 1789, to nationalize and sell off ecclesiastical properties. "Sold to meet the deficit incurred by the French contribution to American independence, the alienated patrimony of the Gallican Church was to unite the active and successful groups in French society in their resistance to the kings of Europe."[60] Granted, there was more to it than that: the Assemblymen, after all, had to beard a legion of special interests in their country as they pursued their reforms, and they hoped to generate public support for their controversial policies by transferring church properties to bourgeois and enterprising peasants who had long coveted them. In addition, the concurrent abolition of venal offices, by releasing so much liquid capital, facilitated such a transference of wealth. What was more, the Constituent Assembly's actions in this realm seemed to be entirely compatible, ideologically and economically, with its other initial ecclesiastical reforms – the abolition of tithes, annates, and pluralism in office, and the suppression or consolidation of the contemplative orders of "regular" clergy.

Nonetheless, what especially strikes us about the Assembly's seizure of church properties is the extent to which it pointed up the revolutionaries' sense of the supremacy of the "nation" – and, prospectively, of statist needs. Henceforth, only the rights of individuals (assuming that they were, in real-life situations, defensible) were to impose any limitations upon the new national sovereignty. Ecclesiastical property, along with much else,

58 See Jean-Pierre Gross, "Progressive Taxation and Social Justice in Eighteenth-Century France," *Past and Present* 140 (1993): 79–126.
59 On these issues, see ibid., esp. pp. 107–8. See also Peter M. Jones, *The Peasantry in the French Revolution* (Cambridge: Cambridge University Press, 1988), pp. 185–88, 190–91.
60 John McManners, *The French Revolution and the Church* (Westport, Conn.: Greenwood Press, 1982), p. 30.

now fell into the lap of the nation – and the nation-state. If the crown in olden times had turned to its own (warlike) uses the incomes from church benefices, the Assembly now was basically doing the same thing, if on a larger scale. In the revolutionary nation no privileged corps should frustrate the national will; hence, for legislators like Le Chapelier and Robespierre, the importance of expropriating the clergy so that they could no longer portray the Gallican Church as an eternally separate order in France.[61]

The central importance of this "national" (and statist) theme emerges even more arrestingly in connection with the Civil Constitution of the Clergy, decreed by the Assembly in July 1790. It is especially revealing here to distinguish between what most clerics were prepared to accept in the new "Constitution" and what many of them could not in good conscience approve. Most parish clergy, at least, had good reason to cheer the abolition of chapters and benefices "without cure of souls" and the assimilation of dioceses and parishes into the new framework of departments and communes. Parish priests, after all, were henceforth to benefit from state-guaranteed annual salaries ranging from 1,200 to 6,000 *livres*; bishops, held to proper residence in their dioceses, would receive no more than 12,000 *livres*, and most metropolitan bishops no more than 20,000 *livres*. Thus, the scandalous clerical income inequities of the old regime would be greatly reduced. Again, aristocratic monopolization of churchly promotion would be ended, since bishops, like parish priests, would be elected. Finally, episcopal powers were to be curbed, as bishops in the future were to perform no acts of jurisdiction without the advice of twelve or more vicars episcopal, and *curés* in the parishes were henceforth to select their own assisting *vicaires*.[62]

It is true that such provisions were bound to arouse opposition in some humble curial residences as well as in most episcopal palaces. Even those bishops, *curés*, and *vicaires* whose positions were not to be suppressed might feel that departmental authorities should have no right to take action against nonresident clerics; and some parish priests, inspired by democratic "Richerist" ideas of the past, preferred the notion of election by clerical synod to that of secular election. Furthermore, resistance to the Civil Constitution was only to be expected from those churchmen, high and low, whose livings were to disappear. Even so, as John McManners has noted, the truly "insuperable obstacle" to ecclesiastical acceptance of this reform

61 Ibid., pp. 28–29. Dale Van Kley has recently pointed up the obvious historical precedents for the revolutionaries' neo-Gallican and neo-Jansenist policies. See, in addition to his earlier studies, *The Religious Origins of the French Revolution: From Calvin to the Civil Constitution, 1560–1791* (New Haven, Conn.: Yale University Press, 1996).

62 These specific provisions of the Civil Constitution of the Clergy are discussed in McManners, *The French Revolution*, esp. pp. 38–40. See also André Latreille, *L'Eglise Catholique et la Révolution française*, 2 vols. (Paris: Hachette, 1946–50), esp. 1:99–116.

was the fact that the legislators were imposing changes without consulting Rome. Many canonists rejected the state's claim that it could redraw diocesan borders without the agreement of spiritual authorities, and contested as well the state's right to arrogate to itself the investiture of bishops. But beyond such specific points loomed the larger issue: the problem of finding some way to secure Rome's official approval for the whole reform, taken together.[63]

Yet there could be no doubt as to how most legislators, as laymen, would frame the issue. "When the sovereign believes a reform is necessary," proclaimed one of their number, Treilhard, "no one can oppose it."[64] The revolutionaries were heirs of the kings and of the Gallican traditions of the old regime, and were mindful as well of efforts by "enlightened despots" such as Joseph II of Austria and Catherine II of Russia to remodel church institutions and curb church prerogatives within their dominions. Hence they were not about to be deterred from asserting national-statist control over the Church International. Moreover, by the spring and early summer of 1790 the Assemblymen were receiving encouragement to adhere to this hard line from radical Parisian journalists for whom any defense of churchly rights had become little more than a rationalization of "counterrevolution."[65]

Small wonder, therefore, that the Assembly burned its bridges behind it on this potentially explosive issue, ratifying the Civil Constitution of the Clergy in July and insisting four months later that all clergy take an oath of allegiance to the new religious order. As subsequent research has revealed, following the local fortunes of this oath allows one to distinguish between "citizen priests" amenable to the Revolution's assertion of secular-statist authority and "Tridentine priests" wedded to the older vision of a hierarchy of ecclesiastical institutions in France denying the secular state's supremacist claims. Whether the model of the "citizen priest" who was willing to swear the oath or that of the "Tridentine priest" refusing the oath prevailed in a given region might well decide whether clerical and secular inhabitants would give their allegiance to local patriots and the National Assembly or to local bishop and distant Rome.[66]

Today it is possible to consult a map of France and sketch a rough geography of priestly and popular reactions to the religious oath in 1790–91 (and, by extension, to the Assembly's ecclesiastical reforms in general).

---

63 McManners, *The French Revolution*, pp. 38–41.
64 Cited in ibid., p. 42.
65 See, on this subject, Jack R. Censer, *Prelude to Power: The Parisian Radical Press, 1789–1791* (Baltimore: Johns Hopkins University Press, 1976), esp. pp. 98–99.
66 Timothy Tackett, *Religion, Revolution and Regional Conflict in Eighteenth-Century France: The Ecclesiastical Oath of 1791* (Princeton, N.J.: Princeton University Press, 1986), pp. 290–91.

It appears that, in the region centering on the Parisian Basin, much as in a very broad sweep of provinces cutting diagonally across the core of the country from the border of the Netherlands to the mouth of the Gironde River, and in certain other zones (in the southeast and the central Pyrenees), most clerics and lay citizens were inclined to accept the oath. On the other hand, in many outlying reaches of the realm – the far north and northeast, the eastern periphery stretching from Alsace and Lorraine to Franche-Comté, the Massif Central, Languedoc, and both ends of the Pyrenees in the far south, and the Atlantic provinces extending from Lower Poitou through Anjou and Maine into Brittany and Normandy – clerics and lay citizens tended to reject the oath. Such patterns of response to ecclesiastical reform may not necessarily be reliable predictors of popular reactions to other kinds of revolutionary change, but they do help to place the Constituent Assembly's assertion of "national sovereignty" (and reassertion of statist authority) in religious affairs in a broader national and social context.[67] And by doing so they make it easier for us to understand why the deputies' assault upon the venerable Gallican Church would resonate so powerfully throughout France.

That such an assault inevitably raised issues of property and corporate privilege serves to anticipate the fifth and sixth areas of reform we need to discuss for the early Revolution: namely, the entwined questions of seigneurialism and transference of property, and the fate of *all* privileged corporate bodies in the realm. In both of these areas we again discern, behind the complex interplay of tangible social interests, the central question of the French state's geostrategic and other requirements.

There is no doubt that the revolutionaries' decision to confiscate and sell off crown and church properties and to curtail the rights of all seigneurs reflected powerful social pressures in post-absolutist France. Most citizens with any capital to spare wished to invest it in land, and the peasants ached to be relieved of their seigneurial dues and associated obligations. Yet the men of the Constituent Assembly, as they came to inherit the burden of ruling France, had to have more than socioeconomic interests in mind. John Markoff has in this connection cited the *political* as well as the social calculations behind the deputies' decision to allow the redemption (in cash or in kind) of all seigneurial dues and services supposedly grounded in past "legitimate" transferrals of property. The legislators, many of whom were landed seigneurs themselves, may have viewed indemnification as a reasonable social compromise both for rebellious peasants wishing to have done with seigneurialism altogether and for lords insisting on the retention of all their property rights. But they were also uneasily aware that to go beyond indemnification – that is, to abolish seigneurial obligations outright – would adversely affect state finances. The unconditional abolition

67 Ibid., pp. 291–98.

of seigneurial rights would not only eliminate that minor but heretofore assured state revenue which the king received as "lord" of royal domains; it would also lower the market value of crown and ecclesiastical lands and buildings whose prospective purchasers could no longer look forward to acquiring seigneurial rights. And declining proceeds from such purchases would, naturally, translate into a diminished financial windfall for the (less competitive?) French state.[68]

Thus, the Assembly's adoption of the principle of indemnification for the heaviest of the old seigneurial dues was dictated as much by statist requirements as by social interests. Peter M. Jones has underscored this reality by recalling its harsh implications for some humble Frenchmen toiling in the countryside. Peasants who until 1789 had paid a "wide range of monetary and harvest dues" to ecclesiastical landlords were "henceforth expected to pay to the government" everything they had formerly remitted to their clerical seigneurs. These dues would be collected until November 1791 by district authorities in each department, and thereafter by an agency called the Régie National de l'Enregistrement. It seems that these payments were bringing in around 900,000 *livres* a month and were still rising in May 1792. This suggests a state revenue of about 12 million *livres* a year. Only the onset of a war crisis in the summer of 1792 would cut off this source of income to the state, along with all other remittances to Paris deriving from the by now thoroughly discredited seigneurial regime.[69]

The actual conditions offered by the Assembly for the purchase of *biens nationaux* also disclosed tensions between citizens and the state that were probably unavoidable. A number of the deputies – Thouret, Delley d'Agier, and the duc de La Rochefoucauld among them – spoke of the need to seize the opportunity to spread the ownership of land by selling church estates in small lots for low prices and on deferred terms. Others, however, reminded their colleagues that the whole object of the sale was to rescue state finances from the bankruptcy of the old regime; and this implied getting the highest price possible and enforcing prompt payments. The initial decree on the subject, that of 14 May 1790, provided a "compromise" that probably subordinated the interests of small landowners to those of the state (and, incidentally, to those of wealthier proprietors). Although only 12 percent of the purchase price was immediately due, with the remainder (at 5 percent interest) payable over twelve years, lands were obtainable only in large blocks, and sales were to be by auction (which would drive prices up) and limited to the administrative centers of districts, to which few peasants would have the time to travel.[70] In a sense, the buyers of

68 See John Markoff, "Violence, Emancipation, and Democracy: The Countryside and the French Revolution," *American Historical Review* 100 (1995): esp. 365–66.

69 See Jones, *The Peasantry in the French Revolution*, pp. 109–10.

70 Norman Hampson, *A Social History of the French Revolution* (Toronto: University of Toronto Press, 1963), pp. 124–26.

these properties, whatever their socioeconomic status, had the last laugh, since in subsequent years the government found itself receiving payments sharply reduced in value by runaway inflation. Still, Necker's sobering projection in 1790 of a state deficit rising to at least 294 million *livres* had given the legislators an urgent financial cue, and larger political considerations would continue in ensuing years to lie behind the brisk transactions in *biens nationaux*.[71]

Larger political considerations also profoundly informed the Constituent Assembly's decision in 1791 (embodied in the famous "Le Chapelier law") to dissolve all corporate bodies in the kingdom. Historians addressing this contentious issue have as a rule stressed the *social* motivations behind, and consequences of, the Le Chapelier legislation. And it is incontrovertible that, even if the law's formal prohibitions and penalties were supposed to apply equally to employers and employees, in practice they fell almost exclusively upon workers. It is hard to see how, over the next century or so, this could *not* have been the case: abolition of guilds and other producers' associations and the prohibition of unions and other workers' coalitions, in effect deregulating the marketplace of capital and labor, could only hand the latter over to the "tender" mercies of the former. But the really germane point here is that the chief motive behind the legislation was constitutional (or political) rather than social. Passage of the Le Chapelier law signaled the revolutionary credo that "corporations" as such could not be reconciled with the founding principles of the new, regenerated state. No intermediary body could be allowed to exist between the individual citizen and the nation – and the nation was henceforth to be the sole guardian of civic rights and the sole venue for the exercise of the general will.[72] This, of course, had also been the revolutionary gospel in whose light that venerable "intermediary body" the Gallican Church had stood condemned the preceding summer.

This primarily political reading of the Le Chapelier decree is supported by the fact that the Constitution of 1791 in its final draft began by explicitly abolishing "the institutions that have injured liberty and the equality of rights." In this connection, corporate bodies were dispatched to infamy along with nobility, peerage, hereditary distinctions, all orders of chivalry, the sale and inheritance of public office, religious vows, and the privileges of provinces and cities. "Loyalties to provinces, estates, orders, communities, corporations, all were to vanish before the interests of individual citizens

71 See, on these further details, ibid., and Jones, *The Peasantry in the French Revolution*, pp. 154–55. It is also true, as Hampson has noted, that many deputies were "sceptical of the economic wisdom of splitting large holdings into a number of small plots." Hampson, *A Social History*, pp. 124–26.

72 William H. Sewell, Jr., *Work and Revolution in France: The Language of Labor from the Old Regime to 1848* (Cambridge: Cambridge University Press, 1980), pp. 90–91.

and the supreme loyalty of every citizen to the nation."[73] Here, then, was yet another instance of a reform enacted by the Constituent Assembly that, while catering to real socioeconomic interests, responded as well to larger issues of the polity. Moreover, events in the world beyond France would soon require that the "interests of individual citizens" trumpeted by the early Revolution take a far back seat to that other championed concept, the "supreme loyalty of every citizen to the nation."

For many French citizens, that paramount civic fidelity would soon be demonstrated (voluntarily or not) through service in the armed forces of the revived state. A brief review of the initial stages of the overhaul of the army and navy discloses, in this as in so many other areas of the Constituent Assembly's work, a mix of political and social concerns. Given the martial purposes of these great institutions, such a reassessment also recalls for us the larger connection between geopolitical and sociopolitical issues in Revolutionary France.

Reforms in the army during 1789–91 testified in several ways to the paramount statist concerns of the revolutionaries. For one thing, the deputies' sensitivity to international pressures drove them to contest and eventually deny the crown's traditional role in military affairs. "Whether peace would ever be established in Europe was doubtful," Jean-Paul Bertaud has realistically written. "For all their yearning for universal peace, many bourgeois were well aware that war was not about to disappear from the continent. . . . An army would therefore be necessary in future years. To prevent its becoming an instrument of despotism, it must become national."[74] "National," at the very least, meant in this context "responsive to the Assembly's will." Louis XVI remained in theory chief of the army, working through a war ministry, until his overthrow in August 1792. In fact, however, "by a decree of February 28, 1790, the Assembly reserved to itself the possibility of encroaching on the executive domain. It provided that, at each session of the legislature, the Assembly should determine the funds needed to maintain the army and assure its pay."[75] Alan Forrest has stressed that the Assembly "dramatically" increased its influence over the military in other ways as well: for instance, "by sending to the various armies deputies who had instructions to report on the political loyalty of their generals" and to take up "more routine questions of supply, morale, and general readiness for war." Also important was "the administrative device of . . . a special military committee of the Assembly that could provide the deputies with expert advice."[76]

73 Ibid., pp. 90–91 and 88–89.
74 Bertaud, *The Army of the French Revolution*, p. 40.
75 Ibid., pp. 44–45.
76 Alan Forrest, *The Soldiers of the French Revolution* (Durham, N.C.: Duke University Press, 1990), pp. 42–45.

The Constituent Assembly also bore witness to its dominant political concerns when (by legislation of 7 and 9 March 1791) it transformed the terms of military enlistment. Joining the army no longer was to involve "a contract between one man and another; it became a contract between the individual and the State, represented by the municipalities and the directories of the departments." The reconsolidated state thereby decreed that enlistment be for eight years, that the recruit be between eighteen and forty years old, and that he display "good moral character and physical aptitude." In addition, foreigners were excluded by these criteria; and soon the state (through its legislature) would be insisting that all preexisting foreign regiments "form part of the French infantry, wear the same uniform, and be under the same discipline."[77]

In matters of recruitment of officers and promotion in the ranks, the revolutionaries plainly subordinated social (that is, "new" noble and "bourgeois") aspirations to immediate pragmatic concerns. "Although they might have serious reservations about the aristocratic profile of the officer corps," Forrest has noted, "few in the Assembly saw any alternative to a gradual transfer of authority. Army officers did, above all, need to possess expertise, and the possibility of an army without a clear structure of authority was attractive to no one." In effect, those revolutionaries who above all else sought to inculcate professionalism in the soldiery so as to create an army capable of waging full-scale aggressive war as well as handling defensive operations won out (at least for the time being) over those who viewed the army in ideological terms as helping to fashion the "new man."[78]

This meant, in practice, that the Assembly, hoping to recruit officers on the basis of technical merit, left the nominating process more or less to officers in place. A decree of 20 September 1790 gave noncommissioned officers one out of every four vacancies for the rank of sublieutenant, to be filled either by seniority or by selection. In the latter case, officers of the unit would do the nominating. The same procedure held for the choosing of noncoms. NCOs prepared lists of candidates from which the company commander drew three names to present to the colonel; he actually made the appointment. For promotion to higher ranks, seniority in grade remained the sole criterion, except that, in peacetime, the executive power could fill half of the most senior posts. Military scholars can justifiably conclude that, at this relatively early point in the Revolution, the screening of talent was still in aristocratic hands.[79] This arrangement may have owed something to the fact that the "executive power," (i.e., the king and his advisers) had its own reasons for wishing to put a brake upon social change.

77 Bertaud, *The Army of the French Revolution*, pp. 44–46.
78 Forrest, *The Soldiers of the French Revolution*, pp. 42–45.
79 Bertaud, *The Army of the French Revolution*, pp. 44–49.

Come the summer of 1791, and the advent of a new crisis with international overtones, the conditions of recruitment into and advancement within military ranks would perforce loosen up. Till then, however, the Constituent Assembly's definition of statist needs would favor aristocrats long in place over noncoms, "officers of fortune," and commoners in general.

This certainly does not signify a blanket indifference among France's new rulers to the needs of all those willing to serve under the colors. The Assembly, rejecting Dubois-Crancé's call for universal conscription, abolished the hated militia and replaced it with 100,000 "auxiliaries" to be recruited by voluntary enlistment. Those so enlisting would earn 3 *sous* a day in peacetime; in the event of war they would be incorporated into existing units of the army. The Assembly also made some efforts to ameliorate the living conditions of common soldiers, codify their legal status as "active citizens," guarantee their rights in criminal proceedings, abolish degrading punishments, and provide pensions for widows of those who died in active service.[80] But despite such actions, what Samuel Scott has called "the single greatest problem in the Royal Army, the alienation between soldiers and officers," continued to fester.[81] Indeed, incidents pitting officers against their men occurred with a new frequency during the summer of 1790: in July and August, mutinies broke out at Saint-Servan, Epinal, Stenay, Longwy, Metz, Compiègne, Nancy, and elsewhere. Professional and social differences between officers and soldiers, Scott has noted, were coming to be defined in political terms. "Aristocratic" officers and "patriotic" soldiers were starting to come to blows over questions involving the exercise of power in France, and this would have profound implications within the army's own ranks. In fact, in the spring of 1791, military insubordination reared its head again, and the most striking features of the mutinies of the preceding year – the bellicosity and politicization of the soldiery – were now even more pronounced.[82] The Assembly's reluctance to abandon the principle of aristocratic leadership in the army hence turned out to be problematic and would soon be overtaken by events.

The initial stages of naval reform similarly betrayed the priority of the revolutionaries' statist concerns. Here, again, royal and ministerial control gave way at a fairly early point to legislative oversight. Not that Castries's successor, César-Henri, comte de La Luzerne, spared any effort to prepare French naval forces for a resumption of war upon the seas. During his tenure, the quality of French ships – which, paradoxically, had long been considered superior to those built on the other side of the Channel – improved with the standardization and perfection of classes of warships.

80 Ibid.
81 Samuel F. Scott, *The Response of the Royal Army to the French Revolution* (Oxford: Oxford University Press, 1979), p. 82.
82 Ibid., pp. 82–98.

Ships of the line and frigates were built according to uniform designs, and the naval architects made sure to adopt British technical innovations: copper-sheathed hulls, which provided greater speed capabilities and protection from parasites, and carronades, weapons of short range but lethal effect.[83] Yet La Luzerne incurred the hostility of powerful legislators late in 1790. His resignation, on 23 October, meant that modernization of the navy would henceforth proceed under the aegis of the Constituent Assembly's increasingly influential Marine Committee.[84]

Aristocratic spokesmen on that committee proved as successful as their counterparts on the War Committee at blocking significant changes in recruitment and promotion of personnel. Many of the deputies, as civilian bourgeois, deferred to aristocratic opinions expressed on technical subjects that they considered beyond their competence. Hence, it was fairly easy to persuade them that the interests of the aristocratic corps of naval officers did not diverge significantly from those of the nation, and that the "new" navy's organization did not have to differ radically from that of the old regime's fleet. As a result, the navy emerged in 1789–91 relatively unchanged by the reformist statutes of the Constituent Assembly.[85] In the face of constant warnings from aristocratic naval officers that merging their institution with the upstart and much despised merchant marine would jeopardize French strength on the seas, the representatives decided to maintain the navy and merchant marine as separate entities. True, the navy was now able to recruit merchant officers directly via the rank of *enseigne*, and these men could hope eventually to rise to lieutenancies in the new fleet. Still, young men seeking a permanent naval career were counseled to begin as *aspirants* "and opt for the fighting service as quickly as possible." *Enseignes* serving aboard merchantmen constituted a reserve of officers for time of war, but the navy would continue to rely primarily upon full-time professionals. Furthermore, there was no purge of the aristocratic Grand Corps at this point in the Revolution, and ironically the exclusion of most (non-noble) *sous-lieutenants* from reappointment as lieutenants or as *enseignes* on account of advanced age left the fleet for the time being with a higher proportion of blue-blooded officers than it had had before![86] Thus, in overhauling the navy as in revamping the army, the members of

83 William S. Cormack, *Revolution and Political Conflict in the French Navy, 1789–1794* (New York: Cambridge University Press, 1995), pp. 22–23.

84 Ibid., pp. 97–98. La Luzerne was, at the very least, "an honest administrator and a sincere proponent of opening the service to talent and diminishing the role of privilege."

85 Norman Hampson, "The 'Comité de Marine' of the Constituent Assembly," *The Historical Journal* 2 (1959): 148.

86 Cormack, *Revolution and Political Conflict*, pp. 82–83 and 102–3. See also, on these issues, Norman Hampson, *La Marine de l'An II: Mobilisation de la Flotte de l'Océan, 1793–94* (Paris: Librairie Marcel Rivière et Cie., 1959).

the Constituent Assembly emphatically favored "pragmatic" and strategic considerations over any specifically "bourgeois" or other class aspirations.

The foregoing analysis of seven especially pivotal kinds of reform undertaken by the Constituent Assembly confirms the observation of J. M. Thompson cited earlier. The revolutionaries in 1789–91 were indeed quite capable of favoring the cause of "national regeneration" over their sundry "class interests and enmities." Many of the new arrangements would, of course, open political and professional careers and make new proprietary rights available to enterprising Frenchmen; but (as we have seen) this was not uniformly true. It was, however, invariably true that the representatives were determined to sweep away all "corporations," all interests intervening between the individual citizen and the state, and to supply that state with updated institutions through which it could turn the individual citizen's wealth and energies to national purposes. In all of this there was also a dynamic of domestic politics. The Assembly tended over time to arrogate more and more of the king's policy-making role to itself. This propensity correlated generally with the Patriots' growing distrust of Louis XVI (and his elitist partisans) and thus marked a shift of influence from the Right to the Left within the Assembly. Such a process could only work to consolidate the reforms analyzed here and thereby to provide a more revolutionary direction for the country as a whole.

THE DYNAMIC OF RADICALIZATION: TOWARD VARENNES

Careful scholarship of recent years has enlightened us about the shifting factional alignments within the Constituent Assembly and therefore left us with a somewhat clearer sense of the overall evolution of politics within that body. It is becoming easier for us to see that, even in this relatively "moderate" and "peaceful" phase of the Revolution, the pressures to which France continued to be subjected generated divisive issues and polarized the deputies by forcing them to take sides on those issues. By late 1790 and early 1791, the conspicuous failure of many clerics and nobles (both in and outside the Assembly) to accept the emerging new order, and the even more crucial failure of Louis XVI to identify with what was being wrought, sapped the efforts of "centrists" to control the legislature and played directly into the hands of the Left. This process in many ways culminated in the king's fateful attempt, on 20 June 1791, to escape from a country whose political and social changes he could no longer tolerate. The so-called Flight to Varennes, by raising anew the fundamental question of French security in Europe, foreshadowed the "revolutionizing of the Revolution" that was so soon to follow.

The work of Timothy Tackett, Harriet Applewhite, and Norman Hampson, among others, enables us to follow the general evolution of factional politics and thus to speak of a gradual leftist tendency in France's legislature during 1789–91.[87] Although the October Days did not automatically put an end to the political influence of the deputies on the Right in the National Assembly, they helped to shift the initiative on the Right toward its most extreme partisans – and, over the long haul, this could further legitimize the Left. Four of the "Monarchist" leaders abandoned Versailles in October 1789; those of their persuasion who remained behind participated with decreasing frequency in the debates (and, perhaps, the committee labors?) of the Assembly as France moved into 1790. In these same weeks and months, intransigent deputies on the Far Right took the place of their more moderate colleagues and consequently became chief spokesmen for the conservative wing of the Constituent Assembly down to its last days. Deputies like abbé Maury, Cazalès, and Duval d'Eprémesnil, associated from the start with inflexible resistance to sociopolitical reforms, were now overshadowing Jean-Joseph Mounier's successors on the right side of the Assembly hall in the Tuileries Palace. As a result, opinions on the Left could only harden, and the center of gravity in the legislature in time would shift in that direction.[88]

Perhaps even more crucial to the recovery of the Left, however, was the emergence late in 1789 of the Jacobin Club and its rapid development as a tightly organized political faction. Some of the Jacobins had formerly been members of the radical Breton Club, others had not; what they had in common was a determination to respond to the organizational and ideological initiative of the Right and thus to recapture the direction of revolutionary events. "Organization" and "mobilization" were to be the key words in the Jacobin political lexicon. In addition to holding public meetings in the Dominican convent on the Right Bank from which their society derived its name, the Jacobins invested a "central committee" with the main responsibility to set the overall direction of the club and devised a more efficient machinery for disciplining members' voting in the legislature. Yet the Jacobins went beyond even this – and sowed many of the seeds of their future success – by acting to mobilize public opinion in favor of their policies. They did this in part by creating a correspondence committee to link the Parisian club with affiliated clubs in the provinces.[89]

It is true that the Jacobins' rise to power in the National Assembly was not a smooth, untroubled process. The first half of 1790 witnessed a split in Patriot ranks between those like Barnave and the Lameth brothers, Pétion,

---

87 See again Tackett, "Nobles and Third Estate in the Revolutionary Dynamic of the National Assembly," and *Becoming a Revolutionary*; Harriet B. Applewhite, *Political Alignment in the French National Assembly, 1789–1791* (Baton Rouge: Louisiana State University Press, 1993); and Hampson, *Prelude to Terror*, passim.

88 Tackett, "Nobles and Third Estate," pp. 289–93.

89 Ibid., pp. 293–95.

and Robespierre, united at that point in backing the popular promises of the Revolution and ever wary of the king's intentions, and those like Lafayette, Siéyès and Talleyrand, Thouret and Démeunier, and even erstwhile radical Le Chapelier, who were increasingly concerned about "law and order" issues and consequently favored a closer working relationship with Louis XVI. Most of those in the latter group eventually came together in a rival, "centrist" association, the "Club of 1789," and though some of them for a time maintained a foot in both camps, divisive issues arising in the course of 1790 led most of them finally to sever connections with the Jacobins. As the first year of revolution officially drew to a close with commemorative celebrations at Paris and in the provinces, "a majority of the deputies seemed ready to follow the Society of 1789."[90]

In the end, however, those on the Left like Robespierre and Pétion, Barnave and the Lameth brothers, Lanjuinais and Creuzé-Latouche and Merlin de Douai – those, in other words, who were steadfastly suspicious of the king and most faithful to the promises of the Revolution – inherited the roles of policy-making and reacting to events in the Constituent Assembly. Two points are immediately germane here. By the late summer of 1790, the coalition of former "Monarchists" and ultraconservatives that for some time had been wielding influence on the Right was "rapidly dissolving through the lassitude and departures of its adherents, disillusioned by their failure to achieve their objectives through parliamentary methods." At the same time, the "triumph of the Society of 1789" in hindsight "appears as only a brief hiatus in a moving reality, an alignment soon swept away, almost out of memory, by ... evolving events." Lafayette, Siéyès, Talleyrand, Le Chapelier, and their allies, "already beset by internal rivalries, would find that the center position they had sought to occupy was progressively isolated and perceived as a de facto right." With the advent of autumn, "a revitalized Jacobin contingent would take definitive control of the elections of Assembly officers, both the presidents and secretaries."[91] Never altogether out of the running even during the months of "centrist" supremacy, always active in the Assembly's crucial committee work and eloquent in legislative deliberations, the deputies most radicalized by the iniquitous old regime – and by machinations in the new era to resurrect something of it – came into their own by late 1790 and 1791.

If punctilious research has provided us with this thumbnail sketch of political trends in the National Assembly, it has also spoken – if somewhat more tentatively – of the combination of factors determining those trends. Clearly those factors included the deputies' past estate affiliations and civic experiences, their personality traits, and tendencies in the political culture

90 The emergence of the "Society" or "Club" of 1789 is especially well covered by Tackett in *Becoming a Revolutionary*, pp. 277–88.
91 Ibid., p. 312.

inherited from the ancien régime. To begin with, there is some evidence to suggest that legislators' social origins helped to condition their attitudes toward political and constitutional issues once they became members of the Assembly. After all, membership in estate in the old France had strongly influenced delegates' opportunities and experiences in public life prior to 1789, and distinctions between the orders had had much to say as well about the organization and management of elections to the Estates General. Here, then, was one variable that may have helped to determine deputy alignment in the National Assembly. If so, this turned out to be unfortunate for the centrist deputies of 1790: their past membership in estate and career opportunities had led them to become bureaucrats and professionals much more accustomed to administrative routine in government offices than to political infighting in elected bodies. This left them ill-prepared to hold the Assembly's political center together, thus contributing to the ascendancy of the Left.[92]

Attitudes in the political culture inherited from the past may have also contributed to this state of affairs. There were times when the debates in the Constituent Assembly seemed to indicate an absence of mutual trust among its members and an unwillingness on the part of many of them to accept the basic legitimacy of a political opposition on controversial issues. The heavy hand of the past was particularly evident here: the judicial procedures of the old regime and the long period without a national deliberative assembly had worked against the development of any precedent for sanctioning adversarial debate or legitimate opposition. Come 1789, the mix of deputies' social origins and civic background and current revolutionary roles aborted any chance of developing new values and habits that might have helped to usher in a consensual brand of politics. This, then, was another reason for the polarization within the Constituent Assembly in 1790–91, and – in time – for the success of the Left.[93]

Yet, whatever the importance of past membership in estate, prerevolutionary civic experience, and anticonsensual political culture in affecting the behavior of the Assemblymen during 1789–91, the inescapable, inevitably divisive issues of the Revolution-in-progress played the decisive role in laying the foundations for the Jacobins' eventual triumph. Some of these issues were of a socioeconomic or ideological nature having little

---

92 See Applewhite, *Political Alignment in the French National Assembly*, pp. 193–94, 197, 200–201. Tackett, on the other hand, has portrayed the "centrists" more as "enlightened" Parisian aristocrats and entrepreneurs than as former government officials and divers other professionals. See *Becoming a Revolutionary*, pp. 285–86.

93 Applewhite, *Political Alignment in the French National Assembly*, pp. 201–3. It is only fair to note that Tackett, in his most recent book, also takes into account what for many of the Assemblymen was (in Applewhite's words) the "fundamental unacceptability of the idea of opposition."

or nothing to do with external pressures bearing upon France. Thus, one historian has noted how differences on the Left over suppressing peasant revolts in the southwestern provinces and over judicial matters – the proposed extension of juries to civil suits and the king's right to confirm voters' choices of judges – prefigured the split between the Jacobins and the Club of 1789 in the early months of 1790.[94] And he has plausibly portrayed the Assembly's historic decision, taken on 19 June 1790, to suppress the hereditary nobility and its associated insignia of honor as helping to confirm, at least temporarily, the ascendancy of the legislative centrists and, more permanently, as demoralizing and alienating conservative nobles both within and outside legislative chambers. Considerable truth may, indeed, attach to Rabaut Saint-Etienne's claim that the law of 19 June "aroused the fury of the privileged classes more than any other which had been passed to date" and moved the "majority of the nobles of the kingdom" to become "the irreconcilable enemies of the Constitution."[95]

But the wrath of nobles wounded in their self-esteem, like the quarrels of politicians over domestic issues of social order and judicial reform, could only assume major importance if France were at some point to become dangerously divided between masses of citizens hostile to the Revolution and masses of citizens resolved to defend it. And the most potent fuel for such a division could only be furnished by those issues which, directly affecting the survival of the state, ultimately involved *all* of the citizens of that state. The three most critical of those issues in the period of the Constituent Assembly were the remodeling of the Gallican Church, the debate over the war powers of the executive and legislature, and – most portentous of all – the king's definitive acceptance or rejection of the Revolution.

What gave the controversy over ecclesiastical reform explosive import in the end was its ability to generate popular support in much of the kingdom for a counterrevolutionary movement that might otherwise have been limited to disgruntled aristocrats and squires nursing their grievances over the curtailment of seigneurialism and the abolition of noble status. And, whatever the ideological, idiosyncratic, and social factors favoring the deputies' confiscation of church properties and their "Civil Constitution," there can be no doubt – as we noted in an earlier context – that the imperious needs of the war-prone government of France supplied the critical impetus for those policies.

The ongoing financial crisis, that legacy of France's foreign policy, cast a long shadow over the Assembly and all its projects. "The need for money," declared the marquis de Ferrières, "has halted our progress. We are like the

94 Tackett, *Becoming a Revolutionary*, pp. 281–82.
95 Ibid., pp. 292–95, for a discussion of this decree and, in particular, the comments of Rabaut Saint-Etienne and others. See also, on this subject, Patrice Higonnet, *Class, Ideology, and the Rights of Nobles during the French Revolution* (Oxford: Clarendon Press, 1981).

man whose brilliant plans for the day are disrupted in the morning by the inopportune appearance of his creditors." Whatever difficulty the Assemblymen may have had in coming to grips with the mysterious and complex technicalities of state finance, they had no difficulty at all in arriving at the fundamental conclusion that the administrative and financial crisis which had toppled the ancien régime could now do the same to the Revolutionary regime.[96] Any compunction that the majority of delegates might have felt about offering all, and not merely a selected portion, of the Church's properties for sale was periodically checked by Necker's dire warnings about the possibility – perhaps imminence – of state bankruptcy. An especially gloomy message from the finance minister on 6 March 1790 ensured that "deputy anxiety over the financial stability of the Revolution continued to grow.... In their letters and speeches not only the Jacobins, but many of the more moderate representatives as well seemed obsessed by the threat of bankruptcy." That many of the legislators, recoiling from the technical complexities of budgetary matters, chose to ascribe the state's penury to a counterrevolutionary plot to foment chaos in the countryside and choke off the payment of taxes, only magnified in their eyes the importance of this issue.[97] This in turn made it all the easier for the Patriots and a substantial number of deputies unaffiliated with any specific faction to evaluate the broader ecclesiastical questions raised by the proposed Civil Constitution against the damning backdrop of myopic clerical attempts to frustrate *all* of the Assembly's work. The upshot was the legislature's enactment of the final version of the Civil Constitution on 12 July.

To identify the principal winners and losers emerging from these church-related controversies is to follow the gradual but inexorable shift of influence from Right to Left in the Assembly. On the one hand, the assault upon the Gallican Church undeniably tended to unite delegates of all Patriot persuasions. From the very beginning, prominent Jacobins were closely associated with the anticlerical cause. In the closing weeks of 1789, the "push for the complete seizure of church property was spearheaded ... by a 'phalanx' of radicals, mobilized by the nascent Jacobin group." Later, in the climactic debates of June–July 1790, when "a small group of patriot curés and lay specialists in theology and canon law" constituting a sort of "Jansenist contingent" waxed eloquent on behalf of the Civil Constitution, they did so with the assent of Patriots both inside and outside Jacobin circles.[98] On the other hand, the enactment of the Civil Constitution of the Clergy "marked a harsh turn of events for the conservative clergy and especially for the bishops.... From July 1790 through the end of the year the bishops' participation in Assembly debates dropped to less

96 Tackett, *Becoming a Revolutionary*, p. 261.
97 Ibid., p. 265.
98 Ibid., pp. 261, 290–91.

than one-fourth its previous level."[99] There can be little doubt that the law of 12 July 1790 did for conservatives in the erstwhile First Estate what the antinoble act of 19 June did for the Right in the former Second Estate: namely, spelt defeat and profound demoralization. But this was crucial to the revolutionary process precisely because the resulting clerical alienation from (and eventual resistance to) sociopolitical change in the country only reenergized the Patriots on the Left – particularly the most stalwart Jacobin partisans of the new France.

If the reorganization of the Gallican Church was ultimately driven by the geopolitically induced crisis of state finances, and played to the ultimate benefit of the Jacobins, the great Assembly debate of May 1790 over the constitutional powers of war and peace treated even more directly with issues of European high politics – and it, too, would serve in the end to profit those on the Left. "For many observers," the Assembly's most recent historian has written, "the debate was one of the most important of the entire first year of the Revolution."[100] "Never," exclaimed one of the Assemblymen prophetically, "has a greater question been debated in any political assembly, nor examined by any legislature."[101] In fact, the attempt of the deputies to apportion those most awesome of powers, the powers of war and peace, between the king and the legislature became, in time, something of a domestic and international cause célèbre. As the final rhetoric on the subject rolled through the Assembly hall in the Tuileries Palace on the Right Bank on 22 May, throngs "estimated at between twenty-five and fifty thousand people," and counting among their number European ambassadors as well as plain Parisian folk, reportedly surrounded the building.[102]

Their interest was not misplaced. The terse announcement by Foreign Minister Montmorin that Louis XVI had taken precautionary naval measures in reaction to the Anglo-Spanish imbroglio over Nootka Sound evoked three separate responses – from Right, Center, and Left – in the Constituent Assembly. Predictably, deputies on the extreme Right – Cazalès, Maury, Montlosier, Virieu – demanded that the monarch be conceded a veritable monopoly of powers pertaining to warmaking and peacemaking, and warned that anything less would intolerably diminish both king and country. Just as predictably, the most militant Jacobins – Pétion, Robespierre, Barnave, Gaultier de Biauzat – spoke up for a preponderant legislative role in such weighty affairs. In the Center, those associated with the Club of 1789 – the comte de Crillon and, decisively, Mirabeau and Le Chapelier – advocated a compromise solution. Their call

---

99 Ibid., pp. 291–92.
100 Ibid., p. 283. See also, on these deliberations, Hampson, *Prelude to Terror*, pp. 130–34.
101 Tackett, *Becoming a Revolutionary*, p. 283.
102 Ibid. Also, refer again to Rothaus, "The Emergence of Legislative Control over Foreign Policy in the Constituent Assembly," passim.

for a shared executive-legislative control over war and peace easily carried the day in the Assembly.

Analysts may be correct to see in this celebrated debate a defeat – in the short term, at least – for perfervid Patriots on the Left and a victory for those centrist Assemblymen rallying beneath the banners of political moderation and limited monarchy.[103] It certainly helped to consummate the split in Patriot ranks between radicals and moderates that marked the first half of 1790. Soon, a number of the most noted legislators would be severing all ties to the Jacobin Club and casting their lot with the centrist "89" faction; and for some time that faction would predominate in the Assembly. Yet the centrists' success was ever precarious. It was predicated from the start upon the willingness of the sovereign to play the constitutional role that was now being worked out for him. Should he refuse that role, and thus call the security of France and its revolution into question, all bets would be off in the political arena.

"In the end," one writer has tersely concluded, "everything turned on that irresolute and vacillating man."[104] As we saw in the preceding chapter, Louis XVI's acceptance of the Revolution was problematic even before the end of 1789. He had forthrightly denounced the decrees of 4 August in domestic correspondence, and – perhaps even more revealingly – had informed his royal Spanish cousin and his imperial Austrian brother-in-law of his absolute rejection of every reform associated with the October Days.[105] Although those deputies who *should* have been his natural centrist allies in the Constituent Assembly were eager – pathetically eager – to detect in his every gesture toward that body a sign of royal acquiescence in fundamental sociopolitical change, retrospective inquiry does little to justify their optimism. When, for example, Louis appeared before the Assembly on 4 February 1790 ostensibly to call for unity in the face of peasant insurrections in southwestern France, he also took advantage of the situation to argue for a reinforcement of "executive authority" and for the preservation of religion, property, and the titles of the "honored race" of the nobility. True, both king and queen on this occasion paid a certain homage to the emerging principles of constitutionalism; however, disquieting rumors had Marie-Antoinette viewing the royal address to the deputies primarily as affording an opportunity to foment discord among the Patriots.[106] When, five months later, Louis presided in the Champ de Mars on the Left Bank over what had originally been intended as a festive commemoration of the events of 14 July 1789, he must have been gratified to see the event take on a "fundamentally conservative" nature, "rallying the

103 Tackett, *Becoming a Revolutionary*, p. 284.
104 Hampson, *Prelude to Terror*, p. 169.
105 See, on this subject, Hardman, *Louis XVI*, p. 174.
106 On this incident, refer to Tackett, *Becoming a Revolutionary*, pp. 274–77.

country toward the consolidation of the Revolution under a strengthened constitutional monarchy." Indeed, some orators on the Left fearfully divined behind preparations for this "Federation of 1790" a military plot to stifle any further work of revolution.[107] Such suspicions may have overshot the mark; yet developments involving the king were soon to justify nagging doubts on the Left about his fidelity to France's revolutionary course.

Perhaps Norman Hampson has come closest to defining, sympathetically yet honestly, Louis XVI's dilemma: "He was a conventional man with old-fashioned ideas of his rights and obligations, adrift in a new world that he did not understand.... His tone was that of a benevolent and paternal ruler, always ready to sacrifice himself for the welfare of his subjects – but on his own terms." Hampson has trenchantly noted that one of Louis's most keenly felt grievances "was the Assembly's divorce of the idea of the state from the person of the king. If he was not prepared to accept that, which, in a sense, was what the revolution was all about, there was perhaps no ground for any agreement at all."[108] Our whole analysis in this chapter is keyed precisely on this issue: that is, the emergence of the modernized secular state in its international and domestic contexts. In so many of its important reforms, we have seen, the Constituent Assembly was essentially working to remove the shackles of old tradition from the revived state, and it was to that aspect of this process which affected him most closely that this "traditional" monarch could never agree. Alas, there was, indeed, "no ground for any agreement at all."

The consequences of this impasse played themselves out in a chronology of events in the spring and summer of 1791 familiar to all who have studied the Revolution. In passing, we need only refer to two of the more dramatic incidents: the refusal of a Parisian crowd to allow the royal carriage to leave the Tuileries on 18 April for the annual Easter trip to Saint-Cloud, and – especially traumatic – the royal family's attempt to flee France on 20 June. Marie-Antoinette, in particular, seems to have been spurred by the former contretemps to redouble efforts already under way to secure foreign help for an exit from the kingdom that she (and, increasingly, her husband) were coming to regard as essential.[109] As all the world knows, the royal family was stopped at Varennes in far northeastern France and brought back to a capital grown ominously silent and watchful. Louis would be temporarily "suspended" from his regal duties, and then reinstated upon the understanding that he would definitively endorse the constitution soon to emerge from the Assembly's labors. Yet his "endorsement" of the completed Constitution of 1791 in September rang hollow in the incriminating

---

107 Ibid., pp. 296–301.
108 Hampson, *Prelude to Terror*, pp. 160–61 and 169.
109 For the latest insights on all of this, refer again to Hardman, *Louis XVI*, esp. chaps. 13 and 14.

aftermath of the proclamation he had left behind him at the time of Varennes, castigating his "rebellious" subjects and their subversive works of innovation. The newly elected Legislative Assembly would have to deal as best it could with this ticklish situation in the fall of 1791 and beyond.

Thus for the bare bones of chronology. Our task, as always, is to analyze rather than narrate – in this case, to show how the king's course of action in 1790–91, even more than the clash of opinions in the Constituent Assembly over church reforms and the powers of war and peace, played to the ultimate advantage of the Jacobins, and did so in a political context invoking urgent questions of French security. The radical Jacobins had already been conspicuously opposed to vesting too much military power in royal hands at the time of the Assembly's debate over foreign-policy issues in May 1790 and had raised like concerns on the subsequent occasion of the "Federation of 1790." By the following spring and summer, surging anxieties in the kingdom over the international situation and the potential threat it posed to France conferred a major political opportunity upon the Jacobins – both at Paris and in the provinces.

In the capital, it was apparently popular concern over the possibility of foreign intervention that lay behind the incident at the Tuileries involving the royal family on 18 April 1791.[110] Then, just a few days later, Louis XVI was forced to involve the Constituent Assembly in an attempt to defuse what was becoming a full-blown war scare in many parts of the realm. Having received "several requests to clarify the situation," the king "finally responded clearly and forcefully through a communication that the Minister of Foreign Affairs revealed to the National Assembly during the evening session of April 23. In a letter that was to be sent to all ambassadors and ministers of France in foreign countries, who in turn were to communicate it to their host governments, Louis ... stated that he accepted, without hesitation, an auspicious constitution."[111]

But the Assembly, whose key offices and committees had been increasingly dominated by Jacobin deputies since late in the preceding year, had already for some time been taking concrete steps on its own initiative to ensure the security of a kingdom whose king seemed increasingly unreliable. As early as January 1791, the deputies "on the recommendation of Alexandre de Lameth ... initiated a program of active recruitment" for the army and voted for creation of a volunteer force of 100,000 "auxiliaries" to be drawn from all departments. (Lameth even envisaged as a third line of national defense "a reserve of 250,000 to 300,000 National Guard volunteers, prepared to march to the frontiers at a moment's notice.") The Assembly on 12 June "finalized regulations for the 100,000-man auxiliary force,"

---

110 On this point, see Fitzsimmons, *The Remaking of France*, pp. 223–24.
111 Ibid., pp. 111–12.

and then, in the emergency attending Varennes, "it took an even more popular step, decreeing...the immediate formation of a 300,000–400,000-man volunteer force." In order to energize the new recruits, the legislature permitted them to elect their own officers, waived the usual size and age specifications, promised daily wages in proportion to rank, and eventually directed the departments to provide the soldiers with all needed equipment.[112]

Thus, Louis XVI's reaction to revolutionary developments in 1790–91, even more than the Assembly's pronouncements about church reforms and the "constitutionality" of warmaking and peacemaking, drove politics in the Constituent Assembly toward the (Jacobin) Left. It could not help but do so, since it revived, as nothing else could have, the revolutionaries' first and lasting nightmare, that concerning the possibility of foreign intervention, and hence played naturally into the hands of those radical Jacobins who were utterly determined from the start to defend the Revolution. This does not mean that the Jacobin contingent in the Assembly emerged unscathed from the traumatizing events of the summer of 1791 – the Flight to Varennes, the "suspension" and subsequent reinstatement of the king, the brutal repression of Parisian demonstrators calling for a republic on the Champ-de-Mars on 17 July, and the appearance of a "war scare" in many places. Under the impact of these events, Jacobin unity in the Assembly shattered: longtime tribunes of the Society such as Duport, Barnave, and Alexandre de Lameth withdrew to form their own, more moderate "club," the Feuillants, leaving radical stalwarts like Robespierre, Pétion, and Buzot temporarily in a state of near isolation.

Yet it is crucial to note that the dynamics of the situation, destined to carry these last-named deputies successfully through their season of defeat, had already been established in the months *before* Varennes. Those on the Far Right in the Constituent Assembly had been abandoning that body in increasing numbers ever since the start of 1791, in effect giving up on parliamentary debate and raising the possibility of civil war and foreign intervention. In response to such a drastic course of action, centrist politicians had only been able to suggest lamely that Louis XVI's government be allowed to take back some of its former authority so as to seek to "stabilize" affairs. Yet to the Jacobins on the Left – still precariously unified in the months leading up to Varennes – such talk had smacked of lunacy. With good reason, they had accused delegates in the Center of being ready to jeopardize all that had been gained so far in the Revolution in the foolish hope of working with a king who had yet to demonstrate convincingly

112 Michael L. Kennedy, *The Jacobin Clubs in the French Revolution: The First Years* (Princeton, N.J.: Princeton University Press, 1982), pp. 194, 196–98. See also, on these military developments in 1791: Bertaud, *The Army of the French Revolution*, pp. 49–57; and Scott, *The Response of the Royal Army to the French Revolution*, p. 106.

his acceptance of anything the Assembly had done.[113] What was ironic, of course, was that after Varennes and the Champ-de-Mars "massacre," and the splintering of Jacobin unity, the same critique applied with equal force to those deserting the Jacobin Club to form the Feuillant Club. When one of their number, Barnave, persisted in depicting Louis XVI as uniquely positioned to unify the nation against both "powerful neighbors" abroad and scheming "demagogues" at home, Robespierre could have replied with unimpeachable insight that this king was simply no longer willing to play such a statesmanlike role.[114]

And what was true of the Jacobins at Paris was equally true of their brethren in the provinces: they came grandly into their own with the rumors of international crisis in the summer of 1791. After the flight of the king, rumors that an English naval force was poised to descend on Brittany touched off scenes of panic in the clubs of the west and southwest. Bordeaux's Jacobins railed hysterically against the reported buildup of English arms, while those at Ste.-Foy drafted a call to the English people to overthrow the detestable Pitt. Clubs all over the kingdom reacted to the news of the royal family's flight by convening emergency sessions. Permanent committees in some communities sat through the nights, and as the crisis heated up, huge crowds began to assemble at the halls reserved for the Jacobins just after dawn. The clubs were so overwhelmed by numbers that many of them were forced to convene in public squares. Dark rumors of invasions by Spanish, British, Imperial, and émigré forces placed a premium upon civil defense. Couriers were dispatched to nearby towns to obtain the latest information. Deputations rushed off to the authorities "to demand the mobilization of the National Guards, the placement of beacon fires on the heights, the seizure of the papers of émigrés, and the surveillance of suspects." Clubs in a number of regions – notably on France's threatened frontiers – transformed themselves overnight into recruitment bureaus, took newly formed companies of "volunteers" under their wing, and demanded that all officers in the armies be subjected to rigorous "patriotic" oversight. Needless to add, the provincial Jacobin societies corresponded ceaselessly among themselves and deluged the Parisian mother club and the Constituent Assembly with messages of encouragement.[115]

In all these ways, then, the Jacobins of Paris and the provinces, running the gamut from Assemblymen of national reputation to unheralded local activists, began to harvest the benefits of their long and inflexible adherence to the revolutionary cause. That they were very well positioned to orchestrate a national response to threats from abroad, to lead a mobilization

---

113 Hampson, *Prelude to Terror*, pp. 162–64.
114 Barnave quoted in Applewhite, *Political Alignment in the French National Assembly*, pp. 174–75.
115 See, on all of this, Kennedy, *The Jacobin Clubs*, esp. pp. 194, 196–98, 241, and 269.

of citizens in defense of the Revolution, was of course not yet fully apparent. In retrospect, however, the Jacobins' fundamental strengths seem evident. In this connection, it might be especially useful to enlarge upon a point made earlier, regarding the social origins of those who composed this political faction.

In differentiating the Jacobins in the Constituent Assembly from their fellow deputies of the Center and Right, scholars have underscored their provenance in the professional milieus of urban and small-town France. Whereas the most active and outspoken members of the Center tended disproportionately to be rich entrepreneurs and young "enlightened" Parisian aristocrats of illustrious lineage, and whereas activists of the Right were especially likely to be somewhat older, more traditionally minded nobles and clerics of rural France, Jacobin militants were overwhelmingly of the former Third Estate. Most of the Jacobin representatives in the Constituent Assembly seem originally to have been practitioners of the law or *officiers* of various types in the small towns of provincial France. They were much less affluent than the celebrated nobles, bankers, and merchants of the Club of 1789, and indeed many were among the humbler members of the Third Estate. One scholar has ascertained that nine of the eleven leading Jacobin orators were of the legal vocation. In the legislature as in the country in general, "it was often the men of law who represented the most important bastion of radicalism."[116] We can add to these findings a natural counterpoint: that Jacobin clubs in provincial communities drew their membership from much the same professional strata of middle-class society.[117]

This last observation is important, because in the crises that lay ahead the Jacobins would have to be active *nationally*, and not just at the capital. And here the most relevant fact is that the social elements most faithfully represented among the Parisian and provincial Jacobins were – in a more general sense – assuming the direction of civic affairs all over France. The individuals involved were prospering in various bourgeois callings, if not yet endowed with major political experience. Whether urban entrepreneurs or professionals skilled in the law, they had in the past been denied positions of real power by royal officials, nobles, and clergymen who monopolized the highest social status in the old regime. They were now, nonetheless "the men best prepared by their style of life, reading habits, professional skills,

---

116 Refer again to Tackett, *Becoming a Revolutionary*, pp. 285–87. See also, once again, Applewhite, *Political Alignment in the French National Assembly*, esp. pp. 193–201. Note again that Applewhite sees old-regime bureaucrats rather than young, enlightened aristocrats of Parisian origin as especially prominent among the "centrists" in the Assembly.

117 "During the Constituent Assembly the leaders of the clubs came almost exclusively from the middle and upper strata of the bourgeoisie. The rank-and-file was also overwhelmingly middle class." Michael Kennedy, *The Jacobin Clubs in the French Revolution: The Middle Years* (Princeton, N.J.: Princeton University Press, 1988), pp. 34–35.

economic positions, in short, by their sociopolitical organization, to take power."[118]

Local studies have confirmed this general characterization of sociopolitical change offered by Lynn Hunt. In the capital city, research suggests that the 407 electors who selected the Parisian deputies to the Estates General and helped set the tone for municipal politics in the early Revolution hailed largely from the wealthier strata of the middle class. Among their number present at the Hôtel de Ville on 14 July 1789 were 4 bankers, 26 merchants, 154 lawyers, and 13 doctors and surgeons.[119] At Toulouse, it seems, the individuals emerging as revolutionary leaders in 1790 were businessmen and barristers; and in 1791 the administration was still the preserve of comfortable, educated bourgeois citizens.[120] At Marseilles, so dominated by commercial connections and interests, the municipal government in the early stages of the Revolution was headed by a merchant; trading types also ranked prominently in the administration, as did manufacturers and nonentrepreneurial bourgeois.[121] At Bordeaux, another city in southern France sensitive at all times to issues of profit and trade, those outstanding in commerce and the law now acquired the status recognition that they had so long coveted, and it was they who, in the wake of the municipal upheaval of 1790, controlled the deliberative assemblies in both the city and the department.[122] At Toulon, too, in the far southeast, the Revolution, at least at first, conferred power upon the moneyed elite of *rentiers*, lawyers, and merchants.[123] And in most of the Midi departments one can (unsurprisingly) point to moderate notables, primarily bourgeois, as the "men of 1789" who successfully established the new departmental and municipal governing bodies.[124] These examples could be multiplied ad infinitum, and they further document the transference of power in revolutionary France from the old elites to entrepreneurs and members of the legal and other "bourgeois" professions. *Notabilité* was everywhere coming into its own.

---

118 See Lynn Hunt, "Committees and Communes: Local Politics and National Revolution in 1789," *Comparative Studies in Society and History* 18 (1976): esp. 336–42.

119 Hampson, *A Social History of the French Revolution*, p. 72.

120 Martyn Lyons, *Revolution in Toulouse: An Essay on Provincial Terrorism* (Berne: Peter Lang, 1978), p. 35.

121 William Scott, *Terror and Repression in Revolutionary Marseilles* (London: Macmillan, 1973), pp. 25–26.

122 Alan Forrest, *Society and Politics in Revolutionary Bordeaux* (New York: Oxford University Press, 1975), p. 253.

123 Malcolm H. Crook, "Federalism and the French Revolution: The Revolt of Toulon in 1793," *History* 65 (1980): 384.

124 Hubert C. Johnson, *The Midi in Revolution: A Study of Regional Political Diversity, 1789–1793* (Princeton, N.J.: Princeton University Press, 1986), p. 258.

It was perfectly natural that, in quite a few of these localities, many of the citizens most active in the newly opened arena of governmental-administrative affairs should also have been conspicuous in Jacobin and other "patriotic" societies. This does not of course allow us to posit a tight "fit" between Parisian and provincial policymakers, on the one hand, and Parisian and provincial Jacobin militants, on the other. It does, however, seem fair to speculate that those bourgeois Frenchmen now wielding influence both in public office and in Jacobin clubs would be better prepared by their past experiences and social connections than more "elitist" revolutionaries would be to mobilize masses of newly enfranchised citizens in defense of the Revolution, should it ever become truly imperiled. Beyond this generalization we cannot at this point in our analysis go, though we know that, in times soon to come, the Revolution's middle-class Jacobin leaders would themselves splinter into factions more or less determined to defend France and to pursue the Revolution's domestic agenda.

Of course, in differentiating between "bourgeois" Jacobins on the Left and more "elitist" protagonists of the Center in the tense summer of 1791, we cannot afford to forget those on the Far Right who were now abandoning the Revolution (if they had not already deserted it) altogether. And this reminds us that the old regime had bequeathed to it what Hampson has called a "profound social division" which the Revolution could only politicize and "inflame into bitter and bloody conflict in some parts of the country." Frenchmen were divided into "those who understood and shared the enthusiasm for ... a new kind of society" and "those to whom the whole business was an incomprehensible threat to their traditional values and way of life." On one side of the ever-widening divide was the so-called revolutionary bourgeoisie – a smattering of "liberal" nobles, "members of the professional classes and some of the more politically conscious artisans." On the other side appeared "about half the clergy, many conservative gentry and large sections of the peasantry."[125] Social conflict among the "notables" and their followers in revolutionary France was not quite as it has been pictured by either Marxists or revisionists of later times – but it was real nonetheless. Discernible even in the relatively irenic period of the Constituent Assembly, it was fated to take on a tremendously enlarged significance in subsequent years.

Reevaluating the revolutionary process in France from the October Days of 1789 through the summer of 1791 confirms our working hypothesis that continuities in this period mattered as much as discontinuities. Europe remained a world bristling with challenges to international stability; and

125 Hampson, *Prelude to Terror*, p. 85.

the men of the Constituent Assembly, however busy with the work of re-constructing France, gave frequent signs that they had not forgotten their country's grandiose past role as self-styled "arbiter" of that dangerous world. In their labors for domestic reform, the legislators at Paris showed themselves to be inspired primarily by the need to reconsolidate the French state's power in a war-prone Europe, if also – secondarily – by the need to serve the interests of citizens on the home front. Finally, the thrusts and counterthrusts of political factions in the National Assembly gradually brought to the fore precisely those Frenchmen – activist Jacobins – who would prove in the end most adamant about resurrecting the international might of the old France even while pursuing the most progressive sociopolitical dreams of the revolutionary new France.

Thus, one finds continuity with the past as well as celebration of the present – and anticipation of the future. To mull over this last point is, in part, to recognize anew that, even in this relatively "moderate" and "peaceful" phase of the Revolution, signs abounded of crises lying in wait for the French in the near future. It was as though the greatness of their past required a similar greatness to come – a greatness whose violent realization would eventually sweep away the king, clerics, and aristocrats of the old order and install in their place the citizens and perspectives of a new, modernized, and more competitive commonwealth.

4

The "revolutionizing" of the
Revolution: from 1791 to 1794

A "self-denying ordinance" passed by the Constituent Assembly prior to its dissolution ensured a complete turnover of personnel when the Legislative Assembly first convened at Paris on 1 October 1791. The new legislature included fewer clerics and nobles and boasted more provincial bourgeois than had its predecessor; its members tended on average to be somewhat younger. Moreover, these neophyte deputies, having been elected in the anxious aftermath of the Flight to Varennes, betrayed from the start a radical bent not heretofore encountered in the Revolution's leaders.[1] That radical proclivity manifested itself above all in a foreign policy which before long plunged France into a war that was destined, with only brief interruptions, to last for a generation. The resumption of a significant French role in Great Power politics in turn further radicalized domestic politics and policy-making. It doomed both king and Legislative Assembly, led to a "reign of Terror," and forced a basic legislative review of this society's obligations to its people.

This chapter, after summarizing the events of the period from October 1791 to July 1794, will begin its analysis by reappraising the revolutionaries' foreign policy. It will present that policy as reflecting France's strategic needs quite as much as its internal interests and politics. It will then reassess some of the most important administrative, social, and cultural reforms enacted by the men of the short-lived Legislative Assembly and its storied successor, the National Convention. Those policies, like the reforms instituted by the Constituent Assembly, speak to us of revolutionaries who were forced at times to place state-security considerations above the satisfaction of specific political and social interests on the home front. Finally, this chapter will reconsider the increasingly desperate struggle of politicians and factions for power during 1791–94 and show how this hard political infighting,

---

1 The personnel and policies of the Legislative Assembly have been examined in some detail in C. J. Mitchell, *The French Legislative Assembly of 1791* (New York: E. J. Brill, 1988).

like the substantive reform legislation of the period, was inextricably bound up with the reassertion of French influence in the world's affairs.

PROLOGUE: NARRATIVE OF EVENTS

The Legislative Assembly called for in the Constitution of 1791 first met at Paris on 1 October of that year. Its turbulent one-year history was dominated by a struggle between "Feuillants" and other moderates, who hoped to preserve the monarchy and peaceful foreign relations, and the "Brissotin" adherents of Jacques-Pierre Brissot, who were determined to achieve executive and legislative power by manipulating controversial foreign and domestic issues. In November, the Brissotin deputies secured passage of draconian decrees against émigrés and clergy who refused to take the oath to the Civil Constitution of the Clergy; the king's decision to veto these (and subsequent) punitive measures gradually undermined his political position. At the same time, Brissot and his cronies took up the cudgels for war against Austria (and, possibly, other states) both in the Assembly and at the Paris Jacobin Club. As 1791 ended and 1792 began, other forces also contributed to a deterioration in Franco-Austrian relations: the counterrevolutionary scheming of the Court and its diplomatic agents abroad, Lafayette's desire to use war to impose a political compromise on both Left and Right, and the Austrian government's eventual decision to attempt to reverse the Revolution by intervening militarily in France. In March, a Brissotin ministry was forced upon the king. On 20 April, France declared war on Austria; soon, the French would be at war with the Prussians as well.

The war powerfully contributed to the toppling of the monarchy in France. In June, Louis XVI's dismissal of his Brissotin ministers and vetoes of measures pursuing "non-juring" clerics and setting up a military camp at Paris provoked an ugly antiroyalist demonstration at the Tuileries Palace. In July, the country was declared to be "in danger," and Paris soon learned of a manifesto in which Prussia's duke of Brunswick threatened dire consequences should Parisians not submit to Louis's authority. By early August, forty-seven of the capital's forty-eight sections were demanding deposition of the king; a "revolutionary commune" usurped the Parisian municipality; and on 10 August forces storming the Tuileries overthrew Louis XVI and reinstated the Brissotin ministry dismissed two months before. Over the next month, French voters nervously aware of Lafayette's desertion to the Austrians, of Prussian victories at Longwy and Verdun, and of a massacre of prisoners at Paris still managed to elect delegates to a radical National Convention.

At its first public session (21 September 1792), the Convention unanimously voted to abolish the monarchy. Louis XVI was put on trial by year's end, and executed on 21 January 1793. The international situation at the outset of the Convention's existence seemed favorable to France: the Prussians were stopped at Valmy on 20 September 1792, and the defeat of Austrian forces at Jemappes (6 November) opened the way for a French advance into Belgium. On 19 November and 15 December, Convention decrees offered aid to all peoples desiring to "recover" their freedom and laid out ground rules for French control over and conduct in conquered or "liberated" lands. The Republic soon annexed Savoy and Monaco, and its troops poured into the German Rhineland.

It was in these – momentarily – favorable times that Brissot's faction of Jacobin deputies (the "Girondists"), profiting from their identification with the war, decided to do battle with those Jacobins associated with Robespierre (soon to be referred to as "Montagnards" in the Convention). Unfortunately for Brissot and his allies, the resulting struggle for power unfolded in the first half of 1793 against a backdrop of newly deteriorating conditions both abroad and at home. On 1 February, France declared war on the English and the Dutch; this was followed up with a declaration of war against Spain on 7 March. General Dumouriez, a Girondist protégé, lost the battle of Neerwinden on 18 March and on 6 April defected to the Austrians. The French had to withdraw from the Netherlands and were increasingly besieged on other fronts, too. Meanwhile, inflation and food scarcities were sapping popular support for the government at home, and antigovernment revolt flared in the Vendée (western France) and other regions. The authorities implemented emergency measures – the creation of a Revolutionary Tribunal and Committee of Public Safety at Paris and of "surveillance committees" in the communes, imposition of price controls on grain, and so on – but this was not enough to avert a showdown between Girondists and Montagnards in the Convention. The Parisian insurrection of 31 May–2 June led to the arrest of Brissot and a number of his "Girondist" allies and to a purge of all government committees save for the Committee of Public Safety.

It fell now to the "Robespierrist" Jacobins (Montagnards) to manage what was becoming an ever more perilous situation. "Federalist" insurgents were active at Marseilles, Lyon, Bordeaux, and elsewhere; Valenciennes was lost to the Austrians on 28 July 1793; Toulon went over to the British on 27 August; and on 5 September a popular insurrection at Paris posed a new threat to the government. Its reponse to all these developments was to implement the "Terror." Robespierre had joined the Committee of Public Safety in late July; he and like-minded members of the executive committees and Convention spearheaded a national defense of the Revolution. Over the ensuing months, general price (and wage) controls were enacted; hoarders and speculators were brought to heel; the armies were enlarged, reequipped, and retrained; the queen and other "counterrevolutionaries" were eliminated; and all available national resources were mobilized. As a result, the "federalist" revolts (and rural insurrections in the Vendée and elsewhere) were crushed before year's end; the British had to evacuate Toulon in December; and by June–July 1794 France's armies had resumed the offensive on most fronts. This, of course, made it safe for the leading Montagnard politicians to quarrel among themselves. When Robespierre and several of his confederates insisted upon intensifying rather than relaxing the official Terror, they were overthrown and executed in Thermidor, Year II – that is, late July 1794. In effect, the Revolution's most lethal days were over.

FROM NATIONAL DEFENSE TO NATIONAL AGGRESSION

As part of his attempt to situate French Revolutionary issues within a "revisionist" framework of political and cultural change, François Furet presented France's declaration of war on Austria in April 1792 as largely a consequence of domestic politics.[2] There is something to be said for this point of view; nevertheless, it underestimates the tenacious hold of grandiose geopolitical tradition upon Frenchmen of *all* political factions in the revolutionary era, and moreover it underrates the actual threat posed to French security in the early 1790s. The men who had somehow to govern this country, as deputies to the Legislative Assembly in 1791–92 and then as delegates to the Convention, found themselves shifting gradually from a defensive to an offensive stance in international affairs, and did so in the final analysis at the behest of diplomatic tradition and in response to concrete challenges to France from the other European powers.

Admittedly, it would appear, superficially, that the drift of France toward war with Austria (and eventually Prussia as well) during the first six months of the Legislative Assembly resulted directly from that body's splintered and irresponsible politics. It has long been a commonplace of French Revolutionary historiography that Duport, Barnave, Alexandre de Lameth, and other Feuillants initially very influential in the new legislature could not maintain their colleagues' support for a "centrist" policy of peaceable constitutional monarchism. However much such a policy was sabotaged from the start by the equivocation of the king and queen, and by the obstructionism of delegates on the Far Right in the Assembly, it was also seriously weakened by splits among the Feuillants themselves. Most notably, some of the Feuillant deputies were determined to follow the flamboyant lead of Lafayette. There is little doubt that the "Hero of Two Worlds" wanted to see Louis XVI's authority maintained and, if possible,

---

2 Refer to Furet's rejoinder to Isser Woloch and Donald Sutherland in "François Furet's Interpretation of the French Revolution," *French Historical Studies* 16 (1990): 777–802.

reinforced. On the other hand, Lafayette appears also to have been casting about for ways to augment his own political authority alongside that of the king – and that, fatefully, involved jettisoning the Austrian alliance of 1756 and, indeed, going to war with Vienna.[3]

And so the Feuillants could not even reach a consensus among themselves, let alone garner support for pacific and conciliatory policies on the Far Right. But perhaps the most dangerous threat to Feuillant moderation – and hence to the maintenance of a peaceful foreign policy – emanated from the partisans of Jacques-Pierre Brissot on the Left. The "Brissotin" deputies at this point in the Revolution dominated a Jacobin parliamentary faction already on the rebound from its lean days of the post-Varennes Constituent Assembly. For Brissot and his cronies, consummating what they saw as an incomplete revolution neatly involved their own assumption of power, and achieving both of these goals required overthrowing the Feuillant ministers by raising a national demand for war with Austria. And, in this, the "Brissotins" and "Fayettistes" found some common grounds for a tactical alliance.[4] Hence, the foundation was already being laid for the strangely assorted coalition of politicians – including, in the end, some of the crown's own misguided parliamentary adherents – that would stampede king and Assembly into a declaration of war on Austria in April 1792.

In analyzing the reasons for the Brissotins' stunning success in orchestrating this campaign, one must concentrate upon substantive issues rather than upon the oratorical prowess of Brissot himself, Isnard, Vergniaud, Gensonné, Condorcet, and others. From the very start, the Brissotins based their strategy on the well-founded suspicion that the king's acceptance of the new constitution was utterly insincere. To drive this point home, they began quickly to challenge Louis XVI on issues which left him no room for compromise. Hence, the increasingly acrimonious exchanges between Assembly and sovereign on such questions as the political loyalties of the king's brothers, Provence and Artois, the status of the émigrés, and the fate of the "refractory" clergy.[5]

But the very fact that Brissotin political calculations centered upon the king's growing hostility to the Revolution ensured a discussion of the larger matter of French security – and greatness – in Europe. And it was

3 Blanning, *Origins of the French Revolutionary Wars*, p. 97.

4 Ibid., p. 98. Timothy Tackett has pointed out how markedly the ratio of Jacobins to Feuillants had shifted in favor of the former group since the last days of the Constituent Assembly. By October 1791, the two factions were about even in the Legislative Assembly. (Tackett, "Conspiracy Obsession in a Time of Revolution," p. 709.) See also, on the Feuillant dilemma in all this, Georges Michon, *Essai sur l'histoire du parti feuillant: Adrien Duport* (Paris: Payot, 1924); and Kennedy, *The Jacobin Clubs in the French Revolution: The First Years*, chap. 15.

5 Blanning, *Origins of the French Revolutionary Wars*, pp. 98–99.

precisely their obsession with this geopolitical question that won for the Brissotins their greatest plaudits in the Legislative Assembly. In his first major speech on foreign affairs, delivered to his fellow deputies on 20 October 1791, Brissot denounced the "gigantic international conspiracy" supposedly "designed to restore the old regime" and "then listed the repeated snubs, slurs and insults inflicted on the Revolution by the other European powers." Tellingly, he went on to appeal to age-old sentiments of French honor. "I tell you," exclaimed Brissot, "that you must avenge your glory, or condemn yourselves to eternal dishonor." His confederates similarly appealed to Gallic pride, as witness Isnard: "The French have become the foremost people of the universe, so their conduct must correspond to their new destiny. As slaves, they were bold and great; are they to be feeble and timid now that they are free?"[6] Speaker after speaker descanted upon this congenial theme over the following weeks, all the while denouncing a "plot" against French interests involving princes and émigrés abroad and nobles and clerics at home.

Brissot and his allies took this compelling argument to the Parisian Jacobin Society as well, where their invocations of traditional French greatness prevailed against the less inflammatory analyses of the situation offered by Robespierre and several other members.[7] The climactic debates in the Assembly came in January 1792, when Brissot's faction, abetted by the Fayettistes (and, ironically, by some of the king's supporters) utilized a variety of arguments to secure passage of a decree that was virtually an ultimatum threatening war against Vienna.

But while Brissotin oratory at this fateful juncture of the Revolution touched upon a number of tangible and politically popular issues ranging from the need to secure the credibility of the *assignats* to the need to suppress counterrevolutionary strife in the provinces, this was not in itself enough. The Brissotins had to arouse some deeper impulse in the French psyche to allow emotion to reinforce calculation. And that impulse, unsurprisingly, was the French citizenry's undying Austrophobia and its more positive side, French nationalism; hence, on the one hand, the Brissotins' indictment of the bellwether Franco-Austrian alliance. It was this ill-begotten agreement, they claimed, which had hurled France from its pedestal of greatness into the dust of nullity in European and global affairs. It had resulted almost immediately in Versailles's losing the majority of its overseas colonies in the Seven Years' War. It had frozen the French in a position of impotence as their oldest confederates – Sweden, Poland, and Turkey – were bullied into silence or actual partition. Clearly, Brissot and

6 Cited in ibid., pp. 99–101.
7 The debate between Brissot and Robespierre on this question at the Jacobins is documented in Alphonse Aulard, ed., *La Société des Jacobins*, 6 vols. (Paris: Jouaust, Cerf et al., 1889–1897), 3:292–303.

his friends charged, the Austrians had drawn every imaginable advantage from the alliance of 1756, while the overly trusting French had been left with nothing.

On the other hand, these deputies unfailingly conjured up the positive force of French nationalism. Speaker after speaker dwelt upon the need for a reassertion of traditional French greatness in the world's affairs. They expatiated lovingly upon the unique virtues of *la grande nation*, and they insisted that the best way to restore respect for that "nation" was to go to war against the Austrian authors of so much recent French humiliation. At the same time, the Brissotins could also turn to their uses the revolutionary discourse of national sovereignty – and in doing so, they were joined by speakers across the political spectrum. French affairs could be handled only by Frenchmen. Every time someone made this point, one historian has commented, "he was rewarded by a storm of vocal approval from all sides of the chamber."[8]

What was most striking here, however, was the deadly effectiveness of the leftist deputies' invocation of the past. When one of them recalled on the floor of the Assembly that "Louis XIV, with 400,000 slaves, knew how to defy all the powers of Europe" – and when other Legislative Assemblymen packed their speeches with uncritical invocations of the "golden age" of the Sun King – it was dramatically obvious to what extent the Revolution was merely old wine in the old bottle of French geopolitical pride. Indeed, it is intriguing to see in how many ways the revolutionaries, in pondering issues of foreign policy, knowingly or unknowingly revealed their kinship with their supposedly "benighted" past. When they complacently underrated the war-making capabilities of Austria, Great Britain, and Spain, they were unwittingly reviving the old miscalculations of Louis XIV, whom they could not help but admire. When they talked naively of crafting an alliance with the Prussia of Frederick William II, they were betraying an equally candid admiration of Frederick the Great and acknowledging that to regain the sure footing of an alliance with Berlin would be to resurrect the French preeminence that had been thrown away in 1756.[9] And when the Brissotin candidate for the Ministry of Foreign Affars, Charles-François Dumouriez, actually came to power in the spring of 1792, he found himself shedding his Enlightenment-revolutionary faith in democratic, peaceful relations among states and embracing the unregenerate diplomatic ways of the old regime. As Patricia Chastain Howe has remarked: "It is somewhat disconcerting that Dumouriez ... conspired to produce a war, persuaded the ministers and the diplomatic committee of the Legislative Assembly to approve his plans, and instructed his agents in

8 Blanning, *Origins of the French Revolutionary Wars*, pp. 105–8.
9 On these points, refer again to ibid., pp. 108–11, 121.

the ministries and chancelleries of Europe to intrigue to procure pledges of neutrality from other states in order to isolate the Hapsburg government for the duration of the war." The "democratic foreign policy" Dumouriez had originally advocated "remained a dream"; the new foreign minister and his allies in the legislature convinced their countrymen to return to the realpolitik of the old regime.[10]

It is, of course, undeniable that genuine idealism helped motivate the French to go to war in April 1792. Brissot and his cronies from early on indulged in the fantasy, avidly promoted by the swarm of foreign refugees in Paris, that the oppressed masses of Europe awaited their liberators from revolutionary France; and they were not the only politicians in these heady months who spoke of an imminent international revolutionary upheaval. Again, the Brissotin argument for war served a variety of domestic social, economic, and political interests. Most patently, there was the primal desire to acquire political power – which actuated both the Brissotin and the Fayettiste factions – or to hang onto it – which moved the king and his legislative adherents.[11] Still, after all is said and done, it is clear that a hundred or so Leftist deputies could only have won over a huge majority in the 750-man Assembly, and so translated their ideas into state policy, by vesting their arguments in the splendid raiment of Gallic diplomatic tradition. It is in this crucial sense that the French reversion to war in 1792, arguably the most momentous policy decision of the entire Revolution, was as much a function of *European* affairs as it was a reflex of French "politicking."

This conclusion is only reinforced when we recall that, by early 1792 if not sooner, the French were reacting to, and not merely precipitating, European developments. Although measures adopted by Austria's government along the path toward war were (in Blanning's words) "in large measure responses to events in Paris,"[12] this was by no means entirely the case. As affected as Leopold II and Chancellor Kaunitz were by Marie-Antoinette's entreaties for Habsburg intervention in French affairs, by the related insecurities of Austrians in Belgium, and by the plaints of German princes dispossessed by the French in Alsace, they had also (as always) to worry about developments in eastern Europe. As of 9 January 1792, the signing of the Peace of Jassy between Russia and Turkey left Catherine II free to unleash her victorious troops against the Poles.

---

10 Patricia Chastain Howe, "Charles-François Dumouriez and the Revolutionizing of French Foreign Affairs in 1792," *French Historical Studies* 14 (1986): 367–90.

11 On the ideological, socioeconomic, and political arguments employed by the Brissotins and others favoring a policy of war, refer again to Blanning, *Origins of the French Revolutionary Wars*, esp. pp. 116–19, 210–11.

12 Ibid., p. 118.

"The Russians," as Geoffrey Bruun has accurately commented, "were unwilling to permit a Polish revival. In 1792 Russian armies assailed the truncated Polish state and the need to limit the Russian advance became a matter of urgent concern, not only in Vienna and Berlin, but in London, Stockholm, and Constantinople."[13] But it was Austria, caught as usual between worries about French initiatives to the west and fears about Russian and Prussian machinations to the north, east, and southeast, that had to worry the most about Catherine's insatiate ambitions; for those ambitions threatened the very existence of a sovereign Polish state that had long helped to insulate Austria against the avaricious Russians and Prussians. If Catherine should prevail militarily against the authors of the 1791 reforms in Poland, the Prussians would likely follow in the Russian wake and annex the long-desired regions of Danzig and Thorn. That Austria faced the prospect of a new degree of strategic isolation in central Europe was ever more obvious; and this prospect was no less powerful than the deteriorating situation in the west in pushing Vienna toward a new alliance with Berlin.[14]

The Austrian posture toward France, meanwhile, had been stiffening markedly as early as December 1791. In both public statements and private correspondence, Leopold II and Kaunitz renewed their condemnation of developments within France prejudicial to Louis XVI and Marie-Antoinette, accused Paris of fomenting disorders in Germany, and threatened military action should France "aggress" against the Elector of Trier over his protection of the French émigrés. Then, on 17 January 1792, the Habsburg Council of State "decided that the concert of European powers should be formally reactivated and the following demands put to the French: the armies...being formed on the frontiers of the Holy Roman Empire should be disbanded; all the rights of the German princes in Alsace should be restored; Avignon and the Comtat Venaissin should be returned to the Pope; complete security, liberty, and respect should be granted to the French royal family; the monarchical form of government should be upheld in France and everything contrary to it should be abolished; [and] all treaties between France and the other powers should be confirmed."[15] This was followed up by the signatures, on 7 February, to an Austro-Prussian pact which, albeit "formally a defensive alliance,...was clearly intended to lay the basis for a concert to intervene in France."

13 Geoffrey Bruun, "The Balance of Power during the Wars, 1793–1814," in *The New Cambridge Modern History, Vol. 9: War and Peace in an Age of Upheaval, 1793–1830* (Cambridge: Cambridge University Press, 1965), pp. 250–74.
14 On the Austrian dilemma in 1791–92, see, among other studies, Karl A. Roider, Jr., *Baron Thugut and Austria's Response to the French Revolution* (Princeton, N.J.: Princeton University Press, 1987).
15 Blanning, *Origins of the French Revolutionary Wars*, p. 113.

It is significant that, even before the exchange of declarations of war between Paris and Vienna in April 1792, old acquisitive instincts were powerfully reinforcing security concerns in *all* quarters. We have already seen this, in considerable detail, for the French. At the same time, Prussian ambitions were extending to Polish lands but also included the principalities of Jülich and Berg in Germany, acquisition of which would presumably entitle both the Elector of Bavaria and the Habsburg emperor to compensation (at French expense) in Alsace and Lorraine! Even at Vienna, where Leopold and Kaunitz had long resisted the drift toward war, "acquisitive ambition was beginning to rear its head. In part this was due to the growing assertiveness of a younger generation of ministers.... Trained in the abrasive diplomacy of Joseph II, they put Austria first, and were indifferent to the interests of the Holy Roman Empire." Leopold's sudden death on 1 March left his youthful and inexperienced successor, Francis II, exposed to the rising clamor for war from this direction.[16] And of course at St. Petersburg the appetite for aggressive warfare needed even less in the way of encouragement. Having scored spectacular gains at the expense of the Turks in the eastern Balkans and in the northern Caucasus, the Romanov colossus was now proceeding on toward new annexations in Poland. The growing influence of Catherine's Russia reinforced anxieties at Vienna regarding Austrian security, and this in turn weakened whatever inhibitions there might still have been at Vienna about "buying off" Berlin with the promised spoils of an Austro-Prussian campaign against France.

Thus the historic declaration of war that rang through the Legislative Assembly in the thronged Tuileries Palace on 20 April 1792 was more – *much* more – than a consequence of Brissotin, Fayettiste, and royalist factions jockeying for power in revolutionary France. It was, first and most fundamentally, a function of the inevitable clash of Great Power ambitions and insecurities in the late-eighteenth-century arena of continental geopolitics. Ironically, the two states quickest to take up arms in 1792 would find themselves deceived in many of their early expectations regarding the war's outcome. For France, the conflict would not only prove to be of an unimagined duration; it would also spell the political doom of the Brissotins, Fayettistes, and Rightists whose momentarily converging designs had helped to bring it about. For Austria, the campaign against revolutionary France would not only prove unexpectedly difficult; it would also proceed against the backdrop of a new partition of hapless Poland benefiting St. Petersburg primarily, Berlin secondarily, and Vienna not at all. Catherine the Great, ignoring the Habsburgs altogether, "bought Prussian assistance by offering a share of the spoils. The Second Partition of Poland, arranged by the two powers in January 1793, left [only] one-third of the

16 Ibid., pp. 114–18.

realm independent."[17] The Austrians from early on had shouldered the main burden of the campaign in the west; their Prussian confederates, despite their professed outrage over developments in France, were more attentive to events in the east, and gained handsomely thereby.

But if, at Paris, the unanticipated difficulties of the war swept aside its initial sponsors of Left, Center, and Right, and installed in their place revolutionaries determined to marshal all national resources in the pursuit of victory, the *nature* of the French military commitment remained unchanged – that is, it was still more one of continental realpolitik than one of revolutionary idealism. As of late September 1792, both the king and the Legislative Assembly were irretrievably gone, while the surviving ministers were subordinated tightly to the committees of the popularly elected Convention. Politically, the next nine months were to be marked – and marred – by the struggle between the Brissotins or "Girondists" and the Robespierrist Jacobins; and this struggle will require careful analysis later on. For the moment, however, we need to stay with the geopolitics of the Revolution and witness once again, in the *motivation* of France's statesmen, the triumph of historical continuity over historical discontinuity.

"In two easy stages," Blanning has written, "the revolutionaries progressed from a war of prudence to a war of propaganda to a war of imperial expansion." On 19 November 1792, the Convention marked the former transition by enacting a famous decree that, purportedly speaking for the French nation, promised all needed assistance to those "enslaved" peoples struggling to liberate themselves. Orders were to be conveyed to generals on campaign to ensure that those so aided would suffer no retaliation from their erstwhile oppressors. Yet it was all but inevitable that, over the long haul, propaganda-as-policy would give way to territorial annexation-as-policy. Even before one-time foreign minister and now general Dumouriez stunned the Austrian forces at Jemappes and thus gained easy access to all of Belgium, he was writing, "the Rhine should be the sole limit to our country, from Geneva to the sea." And with this, revealingly, Brissot concurred, writing to Dumouriez from Paris on 27 November: "I can tell you that there is one opinion here which is spreading: namely, that the French Republic must have the Rhine as its frontier."[18] Already, the Revolution was taking on an aggressive coloration, a territorial-mindedness reminiscent of past eras of Bourbon expansion.

Not surprisingly, the "idealistic" decree of 19 November was followed by more pragmatic legislation of 15 December spelling out the implications of French military conquests. This latter decree was (in Blanning's words) a "masterly combination of universalist ideology and nationalist

17 Bruun, "The Balance of Power during the Wars," pp. 253–54.
18 Blanning, *Origins of the French Revolutionary Wars*, pp. 136–38.

raison d'état." On the one hand, it condemned the old regime wherever it might still exist; on the other hand, it enumerated ways in which local resources were to be used to provision France's armies. On the one hand, it insisted that elections be held in "liberated" areas so that the popular will could freely express itself; on the other hand, it tried to ensure that the results of such elections would be compatible with French interests.[19] As time went on, the natural workings of European politics would lead to the triumph of "nationalist *raison d'état*" over "universalist ideology" in the motives and policies of the revolutionaries.

Indeed, the Convention's first year saw this process at work on a number of occasions. On 14 February 1793, for example, Carnot reported to the Convention on deliberations of the diplomatic committee concerning French annexation of Monaco and certain other territories. The Convention accepted Carnot's opinion that France could indeed expand in this fashion if such expansion did not contravene local people's desires or (and this became an increasingly critical "or") such aggrandizement buttressed the greatness and security of the Republic; thus, the gospel in whose light Paris over these months annexed Savoy, the county of Nice, Belgium, and well-nigh a hundred communities in the Rhineland.[20]

By the same token, the decision at Paris to expand the war in the northeast from Belgium to the United Provinces assumed French readiness to reengage the old Britannic enemy in combat. Anglophobia reared its grizzled head in the Convention. All too predictably, Brissot and his intimates – as well as others not of his faction – recited the old strictures against the haughty British and demanded a new indulgence of historic national pride. Dumouriez went so far as to argue that French seizure of the Dutch navy, by enlarging the Republic's fleet, might facilitate French incursions into London's overseas empire.[21] The embers of French nationalism flamed up again on 13 April 1793, when Danton convinced the Convention to disown what most now regarded as its embarrassingly altruistic decree of 19 November 1792: "Above all," cried out Danton, "we need to look to the preservation of our own body politic and to lay the foundations of French greatness."[22] Fluffy talk of international revolution thus gave way – we suspect, *had* to give way – to the more reliable discourse of French national interest.

19 Cited in ibid.
20 T. C. W. Blanning, *The French Revolution in Germany* (New York: Oxford University Press, 1983), pp. 68–69.
21 Blanning, *Origins of the French Revolutionary Wars*, pp. 153, 155.
22 Blanning, *The French Revolution in Germany*, pp. 70–71. See also, on Danton's speech and the Convention's reaction to it, Sydney S. Biro, *The German Policy of Revolutionary France: A Study in French Diplomacy during the War of the First Coalition, 1792–1797*, 2 vols. (Cambridge, Mass.: Harvard University Press, 1957), 1:156–58.

Of course, the "nationalizing" of the Republic's war effort, like the original decision to go to war, not only recalled a venerable French tradition; it also responded to the hardheaded calculations of the other Great Powers. Certainly for Baron Thugut, Kaunitz's successor as Austrian foreign minister, warring in 1793 against revolutionary France meant coldly pursuing Habsburg state interests. For Thugut just as surely as for his predecessor, talk about "balance of power" politics meant dealing in the currency of territorial borders, subject populations, and state resources and revenues. The eighteenth century's diplomatic wisdom still seemed to apply: one state's inordinately large acquisition of lands and/or resources required that other major states be similarly compensated. Hence, Thugut's efforts, in prolonged talks with British diplomats, to "rectify" the imbalance created by the Second Partition of Poland by designating territories (in eastern France, just possibly, or, more likely, in Poland) that might go to Austria in the event of victory in the west. And victory seemed definitely within Vienna's grasp in 1793. On 7 August 1793, as a matter of fact, Austria's seasoned diplomatist Mercy-Argenteau indicated that, in his opinion, the time had come for a final assault upon France, as the Republic's economy, government, and armies had recently been so gravely weakened. In hindsight, Karl Roider has held, August 1793 was the month in which "Austria was closer to defeating revolutionary France than it would ever be again during Thugut's tenure as foreign minister."[23]

If true, this was in part because Vienna now was concerting its efforts not only with Prussia but also with Britain. In August 1793 Toulon fell to the British; and the British now were also threatening the Republic's other coasts. At London, as at Vienna, war was a policy grounded in hard-nosed considerations of national interest. It is important to stress that it was the decision at Paris to "revolutionize" the Low Countries, rather than the overthrow of the monarchy or atrocities like the September Massacres, that had moved Pitt's government from a neutral stance to advocacy of military intervention. The British regarded the Low Countries as the key to their security, not only on the Continent but also on the sea routes to India – for did the Dutch not have a foothold at the Cape of Good Hope and in Ceylon?[24] Yet one can also situate these issues in an even larger context. The British obsession with Belgium and the United Provinces may have been embedded in a more general fear – both rational and ideological – of the dynamism of revolutionary France. A minister like Grenville never tired of insisting that it was the *overall* thrust of French policy that was especially worrying. "The willingness of the French to sponsor or encourage discontent and sedition was not separable from this," it has been

23 Roider, *Baron Thugut and Austria's Response*, pp. 131–35.
24 Blanning, *Origins of the French Revolutionary Wars*, p. 138.

argued, "not a distraction from the vital question of the Low Countries, but an indication both of the essential objectives of French policy and of the means by which they sought to effect them."[25] Obviously, there is more than one way to describe the French threat as viewed from London. Yet, at the very least, it is clear that British intervention on the Continent stemmed from a conviction that her national interests were in jeopardy.

It was perfectly natural, then, that France's National Convention, no less a champion of national interest, and seared by its brush with disaster in 1792–93, should have adopted in its second year of existence an ever more blatantly nationalistic attitude toward the rest of Europe. Even a chastened politician like Charles Jean-Marie Barbaroux, sympathizing with the defeated Girondists and vociferously critical of the Jacobins through much of 1793, was enthralled by the vision of a French economy become, eventually, unchallengeable in a ferociously competitive Europe. In a letter of 18 June to constituents at Marseilles, Barbaroux roundly rejected any notion of "federalist" insurrection precisely because of what it would do to France's power in Europe, in particular to its ability to compete in commercial affairs with the hateful English.[26] After the ultraleftist Parisian uprising of 5 September, R. R. Palmer has written: "Negotiation with the enemy was abandoned. Even diplomatic relations virtually ceased. Ministers and ambassadors were recalled from their posts, except those in Switzerland and the United States." In other countries only chargés d'affaires were left to handle unavoidable details, along with "secret agents to maintain contact with the underground revolutionary societies of Europe."[27] Thus, the French girded themselves for a war *à outrance* against all the powers of Europe.

The French attitude hardened further in the wake of the revolutionary victory at Hondschoote in September. In the Convention, Jeanbon St.-André coolly ascribed the defeats sustained earlier in the year to an excess of well-intended but misguided "philanthropy." The Convention endorsed this analysis and, ominously, decreed "that the generals commanding the forces of the Republic on land and sea, renouncing from henceforth every philanthropic idea previously adopted by the French people with the intention of making foreign nations appreciate the value and benefits of liberty, will behave towards the enemies of France in just the same way that the powers of the coalition have behaved towards them;

---

25 Jeremy Black, *British Foreign Policy in an Age of Revolutions, 1783–1793* (New York: Cambridge University Press, 1994), esp. pp. 461–63. Also, the "conflation of the threat posed by the traditional enemy with a sense that British society and religion were under challenge was potent" (ibid., p. 470).

26 Cited in William Scott, *Terror and Repression in Revolutionary Marseilles*, pp. 96–97.

27 R. R. Palmer, *Twelve Who Ruled: The Year of the Terror in the French Revolution* (Princeton, N.J.: Princeton University Press, 1941), p. 59.

and they [i.e., the French generals] will exercise with regard to the countries and individuals conquered by their armies the customary rights of war."[28] The "customary rights of war" – this, from a nation that, just three years before, in the early bloom of revolutionary enthusiasm, had solemnly renounced the iniquitous ways of the war-scarred ancien régime, and that, just one year before, had offered fraternity to the oppressed peoples of Europe! Alas, the Revolution was taking on more and more of the spirit of the old France, and of the unredeemed Europe that was now threatening the Republic with extinction.

It is instructive to see how, even during the Terror, when revolutionary "idealism" or "ideology" was supposedly at its peak in foreign as in domestic affairs, *raison d'état* maintained its hold over politicians' minds. This was so even though Brissot's "ideological" commitment to a crusade against the crowned heads of Europe had in some respects been replaced by Robespierre's "ideological" adherence to a Rousseauist vision of civic righteousness.

When it came to foreign policy, as to so much else, the Incorruptible himself seems to have been a study in contradictions. On the one hand, there can be little doubt that idealism helped to inform the Robespierrist vision of the world beyond France. R. R. Palmer has observed that Robespierre's refusal to support Danton's diplomatic overtures in the summer of 1793 was partially rooted in a reluctance to see the "prestige of a peacemaker" go to a man he regarded as "a danger to the true republican ideal, a devotee of pleasure, a mere tactician and compromiser, a man without steady principles or real faith in liberty and equality." Moreover, if Palmer is right, Robespierre in spite of himself could not altogether reject the internationalist outlook so recently associated with his Brissotin enemies. While he "did not exactly believe in an expansionist war," he did view the peoples of other countries as "groaning masses" and their rulers as "wicked men," and as such "could be easily brought, with a little impulsion, to favor a general ideological crusade."[29]

Perhaps. Yet the victories of French arms over the forces arrayed against them, and the consequent shift of France from a defensive to an offensive posture, inevitably affected Robespierre as it did all the other revolutionaries. Addressing the deputies on behalf of his fellows of the Committee of Public Safety on 17 November 1793, Robespierre "betrayed his adherence to Soulavie's expulsion-of-all-foreigners idea; he presented a picture of France as the guarantor of the minor states and free cities of Germany against the encroachments of Austria and Prussia; and he argued that since events had proved the Republic to be unconquerable...common sense

28 Cited in Blanning, *The French Revolution in Germany*, p. 72.
29 Palmer, *Twelve Who Ruled*, p. 58.

dictated the end of attempts to conquer it." These were the hallmarks of Gallic nationalism and geostrategic calculation, not of perfervid revolutionary cosmopolitanism. Moreover, Sydney Biro has pointed out, this Jacobin protagonist explicitly renounced on this and subsequent occasions "all desire to convert the world to revolutionary principles by force of arms."[30] In addition, if Robespierre was not friendly to the notion of conquests in the Rhineland, he did believe that Belgium desired unification with France, and therefore accepted the argument that the "annexation of Belgian territory would constitute no conquest" but instead would represent "a natural flowing together of elements that it would require violence to hold apart."[31] Robespierre, it appears, was quite capable of endorsing tangible strategic goals in 1793–94 whose pursuit could keep France at war indefinitely with what was now the "First Coalition."

And what was true for the Terror's most notorious politician was, it seems, even more the case for the Revolutionary Government as a whole: ideology and pragmatism could coexist harmoniously enough – at least in the domain of foreign relations. Granted, it is true, as more than one historian of the Terror has noted, that the revolutionary regime of 1793–94 existed both for geopolitical *and* domestic-political purposes. And this led to a situation in which the waging of war, tightly joined with a Jacobin drive toward (male) democracy and social reform, became the prerequisite for achieving those latter goals. For the Jacobins, prolonging the war meant that factionalism, so dangerous to their Republic, might be kept at bay; whereas peace, by removing the need for an emergency regime, would scuttle all chances for realizing their (utopian?) dreams. Here, then, was a huge paradox from which the Robespierrists could never escape: the war, which many of them had fiercely opposed in 1792, had by 1794 become indispensable for the implementation of their visionary domestic program![32]

All of this rings true; it is undeniable *as far as it goes*. Yet there are signs aplenty that, at a deeper level, the French revolutionaries waging war against virtually all of Europe were Frenchmen before they were revolutionaries. At the Jacobin Club of Lorient, Prieur of the Marne castigated the English in terms strikingly redolent of old times: "London must be destroyed, and London shall be destroyed! Let us rid the globe of this new Carthage.... We shall chase from the Indies and from Bengal these ferocious English, so insatiable for gold.... Soon, next spring I hope, we shall go to visit the banks of the Thames."[33] Again, the Committee of Public Safety, in a letter of January 1794 to one of its members "on mission," alluded to France, "which alone of all European states can and should be a power on both

30 Biro, *The German Policy of Revolutionary France*, pp. 196–97.
31 Ibid., p. 234.
32 Palmer, *Twelve Who Ruled*, pp. 277–78.
33 Ibid., pp. 211–12.

land and sea." In doing so, and in pursuing its plan for an invasion of England, the revolutionary government was but citing chapter and verse from all French geopoliticians since the most auspicious years of the Sun King.[34] Even in the mundane details of French naval strategy in 1793–94, the ambitions and fears and practical concerns of the Bourbons' naval planners seem to cry out once again. The decision to maintain a battle fleet at Brest in hopes that it could one day engage Britain's Channel fleet; designs for the logistics of the envisioned descent upon the Anglo-Norman Islands and the British mainland itself; the defense of the French coasts against London's privateers – these and other considerations, taken together, made up a naval strategy that (one naval authority has noted) "was in large measure the continuation of that of the Ancien Régime."[35] For the Terror's zealots, war abroad and (male) democracy at home may have been two sides of the same republican coin; yet for most French leaders, even in 1793–94, making war was first and foremost the way to preserve their country and, beyond that, to reaffirm its prestige in the brutally competitive politics of Europe.

This is not to deny – and indeed, our argument presupposes – that there were interactions between foreign and domestic affairs throughout this most dangerous period of the Revolution. Still, the evolution of French foreign policy during the years of intensifying revolution reflected geostrategic dynamics and perceptions quite as much as it reflected domestic political and socioeconomic forces. Having reiterated this point, we can now proceed to reappraise some of the most important domestic policies of the years 1791–94, and to weigh the specific considerations that lay behind the enactment of those policies.

STATE RECONSTRUCTION AND RADICAL REFORM

That the "revolutionizing of the Revolution" was closely tied up with France's competitive fortunes in the global arena becomes plain when we review the domestic policies and factional struggles of the 1791–94 period. On the actual politics of those years, more later. For the moment, we may usefully focus upon how the Legislative Assembly and Convention handled five pivotal issues: governmental powers and finance, the status of émigrés and clergy, seigneurialism and the peasantry, the economic and social welfare of the country's urban masses, and recruitment into (and promotion within) the armed forces. To reassess the legislators' primary accomplishments in these areas is to understand that, even at the high

---

34 Ibid., p. 218. Interestingly, Palmer cites the influential naval historian Lévy-Schneider as arguing that France's determination to take the offensive at sea "was a main reason why the Committee of Public Safety, at the beginning of 1794, made its fateful decision not to mitigate the Terror."

35 Hampson, *La Marine de l'An II*, pp. 91–92. My translation from the author's (very literate) French.

tide of radical revolution, considerations of French state security cast a long shadow over a landscape otherwise illuminated fitfully by hopes for improvements in ordinary people's lives.

It has long been a truism that the Terror of 1793–94 brought about an unprecedented centralization of government functions and powers in France. What remains to be emphasized is, first, the way in which developments in this area followed the fortunes of war, and, second, how the war-related process of *bureaucratization* underlay (and would survive) the temporary accumulation of powers in the hands of Robespierre and his colleagues of the Committee of Public Safety.

Even in the last weeks of the abbreviated Legislative Assembly, Hampson has noted, a deterioration in the military situation brought home to Parisians by the issuance of the Allies' menacing Brunswick Manifesto spurred the Council of Ministers and the Paris Commune to send out commissioners to coordinate local measures of national defense. It was during these days, as well, that "the Government and the Assembly took the first steps along the road to economic controls." Efforts to requisition food and transport for the army, ensure the provisioning of civilian markets, and establish a census of grain supplies were no doubt premature at this time: in the first months of the Convention the deputies repealed such measures, "perhaps because of the improvement in the military situation." Such decrees, nonetheless, looked forward to the more drastic government actions of a later day.[36]

Sure enough, the next major downturn in French geopolitical fortunes, at the start of the campaigning season in the spring of 1793, produced "a number of emergency measures aimed at reinforcing the power of the Central Government and destroying the counter-revolutionaries within France." On 9 March, the Convention decided to dispatch eighty-two of its members throughout the country to spur the recruitment of young men into the armies. The very next day saw the creation of the soon-to-be-notorious Revolutionary Tribunal "to judge political offenders and forestall popular 'justice.'" On 21 March, the deputies voted to establish surveillance committees in the sections of the major towns and in all the communes. Initially confined to keeping tabs on foreigners, these committees soon assumed another role as well: controlling issuance of the *certificats de civisme* that allowed access to public jobs. On 6 April, the Convention broke critical new ground by establishing a nine-member Committee of Public Safety to oversee and coordinate all executive agencies of government; and on 9 April, it voted to send deputies entrusted with wide powers to serve as political commissars attached to the Republic's field armies.[37]

---

36 Hampson, *A Social History of the French Revolution*, pp. 158–59.
37 Ibid., pp. 168–69.

In these and other ways, the lawmakers reacted to ominous international developments – the addition of Britain, the United Provinces, and Spain to the Coalition, the treason of Dumouriez in Belgium – by gathering more and more authority unto themselves.

Then came the Revolution's most perilous days, in the late summer and autumn of 1793. It was then, it appears, that Austria felt most confident about vanquishing the French; it was then that the British were handed Toulon, the gateway to the southeastern French provinces, and seemed on the verge of landing in the rebellious western hinterland as well. The logical response at Paris was to invest new powers in the government.[38] In September, the Committee of Public Safety assumed the role of appointing members of all the other executive committees, systematized the detention of all political "suspects," and moved to transform local surveillance committees ("revolutionary committees") into agencies of the central government. On 10 October, the Convention endorsed a proposal from the Committee of Public Safety that gave this committee control over the ministers and all officially "constituted" authorities, all generals in the armies, and all domestic "paramilitary" forces. The Convention also authorized the committee to seize and reallocate foodstuffs and other essential commodities everywhere in the Republic, and formally declared the "provisional government of France" to be "revolutionary until the peace." On 25 November, the legislature decreed that whenever its members were functioning as "representatives on mission," they must strictly obey all mandates of the Committee of Public Safety. Finally came the law of 14 Frimaire (4 December) which was in effect the "constitution" of the governmental Terror. Under its auspices, all officials were now subject to the rigorous oversight of the Committee of Public Safety and the hardly less powerful Committee of General Security. A myriad of locally elected administrators, or those of them who survived the purge for which the new law provided, became "national agents" who could be removed at the whim of the Convention. In addition: local officials were warned not to sponsor unauthorized assemblies; *comités de surveillance* were absorbed into sanctioned governmental agencies; and all raising of troops and moneys was to be authorized at Paris. Logically enough, all of these provisions were to be enforced by the Committee of Public Safety.

The Spartan decree of 4 December 1793, we have already held, was the "constitution" of the Terror. But some have viewed it as even more than that: "Setting up a strong central power, providing channels for the quick flow of authority from Paris to the remotest village, sweeping away all

---

38 On the following points, refer to Palmer, *Twelve Who Ruled*, esp. pp. 66–67, 74–75, and 124–27. See also Jacques Godechot, "The Internal History of France during the Wars, 1793–1814," in *The New Cambridge Modern History, Vol. 9: War and Peace in an Age of Upheaval, 1793–1830* (Cambridge: Cambridge University Press, 1965), pp. 275–306.

intermediate agencies that could obstruct or twist the policies of government, it recalled the age-old efforts of kings and ministers to bring order out of feudalism, and anticipated the means by which Napoleon organized modern France."[39] To this we can only add, from our explanatory perspective, that the continuity binding the Revolution to both past and future, a continuity that appeared so strikingly in the "law of 14 Frimaire," fused the most pressing international and domestic concerns of the historic French state.

If the war emergency of 1792–94 led to a drastic if ephemeral concentration of government powers at Paris, it also forced the legislators to weigh the possibilities for that natural financial device of so much modern governance: progressive taxation. On 18 March 1793, on the motion of Ramel-Nogaret, the revolutionaries decreed that "in order to attain a more accurate proportion in the distribution of the burden each citizen has to bear according to his abilities, there shall be established a graduated and progressive tax on luxury and both landed and transferable wealth."[40] True, the Convention paired this decree with another one, proposed by Barère and Levasseur de La Sarthe, threatening with death anyone who should advocate a division of lands or "any other measure subversive of territorial, commercial and industrial property." Even in the throes of a military emergency, the French would exorcise the ghosts of "communism." Furthermore, progressive taxation itself remained more of a threat than a reality at this time: even the forced loan passed by the legislature on 19 August–3 September was intended more to encourage "bourgeois" investment in a voluntary loan than to tax affluent citizens at confiscatory rates. A certain association between war and "social" taxation nonetheless emerged, both at Paris and in the provinces. In arguing for progressive taxation, Danton reminded the rich that keeping France's enemies at bay would safeguard their investments by securing their lands and other assets. The deputies charged with working out the details of a "progressive contribution" often referred to it as a "war subsidy." And away from Paris, "representatives on mission," who were unhampered by legislative oversight, often took advantage of their freedom of maneuver to levy all manner of imposts, in currency and in kind, upon moneyed citizens. Jean-Pierre Gross has pertinently remarked that the "unprecedented taxes raised all over France were only justified by ... exceptional circumstances [and were raised] in order to provide urgently needed funds in a time of war." That such imposts were frequently labeled *"taxes de guerre"* tells us something

39 Palmer, *Twelve Who Ruled*, p. 127.
40 Jean-Pierre Gross, "Progressive Taxation and Social Justice in Eighteenth-Century France," *Past and Present* 140 (1993): 79–126, for the paragraphs that follow. See also the more recent monograph by the same author: *Fair Shares for All: Jacobin Egalitarianism in Practice* (New York: Cambridge University Press, 1997).

about the way the military campaign was associated with financial issues in many Frenchmen's minds.[41]

But to dwell exclusively on the administrative and financial excesses of the Terror would be to miss the more fundamental fact that the intensification of the Revolution ensured the triumph of bureaucracy in France. Clive Church has stressed the connections between the massive war mobilization and the size, internal organization, and esprit de corps of the state bureaucracy in 1792–94. On the issue of size: "Certainly there must have been at least 13,000 officials and employees in Paris alone, and probably more than 15,000." Outside the capital, "there could have been 250,000 or perhaps even 300,000 if one includes elected officials, field, local, and military employees."[42] Insofar as its internal organization was concerned, the new bureaucracy observed rules of hierarchical distribution of power. The Convention's committees presided over state agencies situated in specific echelons of public authority. The machinery of state was also highly *centralized*, not only because of the political oversight of the Committee of Public Safety but also because of the imposition of new administrative controls on state services.[43]

Finally, there is the matter of the origins, experience, and esprit of these new "bureaucrats." On the one hand, the unremitting pressures under which the youthful republic was attempting to work did not permit it to inquire closely into the motivation and qualifications of those it hired: excessive delay in recruitment, after all, could adversely affect the war effort. Ideologically motivated "patriots" were probably outnumbered greatly in the new ranks of officialdom by opportunists driven into state service by the economic and social dislocations of war. On the other hand, once in office, these apprenticed administrators were all laboring for the same master, the state. "They all worked within much the same structural pattern of divisions and bureaux, and more importantly, they were part of bodies which in the case of the commissions were very much an amalgam of varying services and recruits." They were salaried; they had to satisfy unprecedented standards of discipline; and they had to work through written records as never before. There can be little doubt that, by this time, bureaucratization in wartime France was well under way. Henceforward, the main challenge would be to consolidate the new administration.[44]

So what might be called the "constitutional" aspect of deepening revolution up to 1794 – that is, the centralization and bureaucratization of

41 Gross, "Progressive Taxation and Social Justice," p. 119. A good example of "representatives on mission" levying heavy taxation, in currency and in kind, on affluent *provinçiaux* is that of Saint-Just and Le Bas in Alsace. See again Palmer, *Twelve Who Ruled*, pp. 177–201.
42 Church, *Revolution and Red Tape*, pp. 94–95.
43 Ibid., p. 95.
44 Ibid., pp. 96–100.

governance – was inextricably associated with France's deepening involvement in European high politics. A similar conclusion would seem to hold for the various "social" aspects of the radicalization process. This was, for instance, true when it came to the deputies' treatment of émigrés and clergymen: once again, revolutionary behavior was, if not dictated, then at least heavily influenced by revolutionary perceptions of the evolving international situation.

As a number of historians have observed, this was a tendency adumbrated in the early days of the Revolution. If, for example, fears of émigré conspiracies against France were exercising many in the population by 1792, this was a circumstance reminiscent of recurrent anxieties in the 1789–91 period. At times, patriots had espied émigrés "under every bed" and muttered about "imminent invasions by Swedes, Russians, and their noble native allies." When journals like the *Révolutions de Paris* and the *Gazette de Leyde* in 1789 spoke casually of huge numbers of émigrés securing passports and fleeing the country, and when in October 1791 Marat published a story alleging the presence of fifty thousand émigrés in Flanders alone, patriotic Frenchmen could only darkly assume an unholy collusion between errant nobles and the adversaries of France.[45]

Clergy, too, fell afoul of revolutionary xenophobia. Even in the days of the Constituent Assembly, Jacobins – and some non-Jacobins as well – saw non-juring priests as traitors to the Revolution. Moreover, the Assembly's own actions helped to place such a stigma even on clergy who had accepted the Civil Constitution. Insisting that clerical Assemblymen swear the oath to the Civil Constitution in the highly politicized atmosphere of Paris and decreeing that all lawsuits involving ecclesiastical reforms be entrusted to the administrators in the municipalities, districts, and departments were strategies bound to politicize religious issues in the eyes of citizens increasingly obsessed by the "political" possibility of invasion. Even before Varennes, Parisians increasingly saw religious issues as jeopardizing national unity, and in the wake of that crisis, with fears of domestic counterrevolution and of an Austrian attack sweeping the country, some local authorities interned "refractory" clergy as part of a campaign for security.[46]

As a result, the ground was well prepared in public opinion for the Girondists' attempt – in their march toward war – to associate émigrés and non-juring priests with France's potential enemies. Brissot and his fire-breathing confederates reaped a rich harvest in the Legislative Assembly.

45 Higonnet, *Class, Ideology, and the Rights of Nobles*, p. 96. Still very useful on the subject of the émigrés is Donald Greer, *The Incidence of the Emigration during the French Revolution* (Cambridge, Mass.: Harvard University Press, 1951). On conspiracy fears in the early 1790s, refer again to Tackett, "Conspiracy Obsession in a Time of Revolution," esp. pp. 691–700.
46 McManners, *The French Revolution and the Church*, pp. 61–62.

They gleefully set upon émigrés, for instance, aiming to penalize them as a group. They promulgated an act (which the king, predictably, vetoed) sentencing to death all émigrés who did not return to France by 1 January 1792, as well as all errant nobles inside France advocating military desertion. In December 1791, émigrés were denied the right to garner salaries abroad; and as of February 1792, they once again needed passports for travel outside of France. Over the next several months, the legislature also moved to sequester émigré possessions. At this point, it is true, émigrés were neither unconditionally "deprived of their civil rights nor excluded forever from the bosom of the nation." Nevertheless, in the furies of "patriotic" war to come, things were likely to go hard for them. Some indication of this came on 28–29 July 1792, when legislation forbidding the issuance of new passports that would have allowed new emigrations justified doing so by citing each citizen's "sacred duty to march to the aid of the country."[47]

A like fate befell "non-juring" clergy as France lurched into war – and bid fair to engulf oath-taking churchmen as well. What was more, it became harder to keep ecclesiastical issues separate in patriotic minds from inflammatory suspicions regarding émigrés. "In so far as the wealthy had invested in the spoils of the Church they tended to prefer the hazards of the Revolution to the risk of expropriation by the victorious émigrés," one specialist has aptly noted, "and for that … the war was responsible."[48] From the very beginning, it has also been pointed out, the Legislative Assembly, which would vote for war in April 1792, tended to assimilate religious questions to larger civic matters, and of course the latter came increasingly to be dominated by military and strategic concerns. Ominously, the "religious schism" engendered by the Civil Constitution and its associated oath "came to be spoken of in crudely political terms, 'patriots' on one side, 'aristocrats' on the other." Continued opposition to ecclesiastical reforms in the provinces led the Assembly to decree on 29 November 1791 that non-juring priests be considered "suspects," and as such "liable to expulsion from communes where troubles occurred." That the king chose to veto this act along with decrees aimed at "treasonous" émigrés only cast further "civic" discredit upon clerical doubts about revolutionary change that were, however, deeply felt. It was all too predictable that, in the event of war and its unavoidable reverses, the status of the clergy, like that of the émigrés, would further deteriorate. As early as 26 May 1792, in fact, with the specter of defeat already in the air, the legislature decreed that every refractory priest denounced by twenty "active" citizens would be deported. Meanwhile, local officials who had been satisfied simply with interning some non-juring clerics the year before in the wake of Varennes now acted more aggressively, arresting priests indiscriminately in some

47 Higonnet, *Class, Ideology, and the Rights of Nobles*, pp. 77–78.
48 Hampson, *A Social History of the French Revolution*, p. 145.

cases and restricting their domiciliary options and freedom of movement in others.[49]

As the Revolution sank more deeply into the morass of total war, and as part of the "social leveling" inherent in national mobilization for such a struggle, émigrés and refractory clergy were treated with mounting severity. Emigré property, put under state control as early as April 1792, and formally alienated from its noble possessors on 27 July, was subsequently offered to prospective purchasers under terms that became increasingly generous. In August 1792, the representatives, having been reminded that "the sale of émigré property offers a means of binding the country people to the Revolution," decreed that buyers of such property were to have priority over tenants and that local officials were to ensure that these holdings were "divided as usefully as possible into small lots."[50] These provisions were amended by a law of 3 June 1793, which reiterated that émigré lands were to be divided up "as far as possible, without damaging each farm or estate, into lots or portions" but also made special provision for landless farmers in communes containing émigré lands but no partible common lands. In such villages, rural proletarians were to rent plots of one *arpent* apiece directly from the state.[51] Such initiatives were followed up during the Terror by new laws that not only anathematized noble emigrants in language by now become familiar but also hedged in the inheritance rights of emigrants' relatives still resident in the country.

For clerics, too, this was a time of tribulations. With the toppling of the monarchy, and an "invasion panic" justified for Parisians by the threatening terms of the Brunswick Manifesto, all stays were lifted on deportations of non-juring clergy already ordered, and the number of denunciations by active citizens required for new deportations was reduced from twenty to six. ("This was tantamount," John McManners has commented, "to a universal proscription.") Perhaps even more revealing of the revolutionary attitude toward the clergy was the fact that *all* churchmen were now ordered "on penalty of loss of place or pension" to take a new oath binding them to all-out support of the embattled Republic. That 3 bishops and 220 priests (on McManners's reckoning) were killed in the September Massacres in Paris serves as another dramatic indication of the clergy's worsening situation. Anticlerical violence flared up in the provinces as well, and often in such incidents the distinction between "juring" and "refractory" priests was blurred.[52] In the course of 1793, with the Republic combatting virtually all of Europe, the treatment of clerics and churchly interests became yet harsher. After 23 March, for instance, deportations of non-jurors followed

49 McManners, *The French Revolution and the Church*, pp. 63–67.
50 Hampson, *A Social History of the French Revolution*, p. 149.
51 Jones, *The Peasantry in the French Revolution*, p. 155.
52 McManners, *The French Revolution and the Church*, pp. 63–67.

automatically upon their identification. And after 22 November, the injunction to split up émigré estates wherever possible "was extended to the remaining ecclesiastical property coming up for sale."[53]

There were, admittedly, limits to the Revolution's campaign against former members of the first two Estates. Despite the ferocity of attacks upon the émigrés, most erstwhile nobles survived the hecatombs of the Terror simply by lying low upon their rustic lands.[54] The French nobility was not, like the Russian gentry of 1917–18, swallowed up in the deluge of revolution. By the same token, the Gallican Church survived "institutionally" throughout this period, retaining the grudging support of the state-at-war. (Only in 1795 would it be disestablished.) It is nevertheless suggestive – from our global-historical viewpoint – that, as Revolutionary France became ever more engulfed in war, it should have increasingly envisioned the émigrés and "refractory" clergy in *political* terms as "traitors" to the besieged fatherland and condemned them in that capacity. But beyond that, the "ex-nobility" and Church *as a whole* were, like all other interest groups in the country, searingly affected by the war crisis. Only a regime desperately reliant upon popular support for its survival would have countenanced progressive taxation and mass arrests of "suspect" nobles; and only such an embattled regime would have tolerated even temporarily the "de-Christianizing" excesses of many of its middle-echelon officials and provincial partisans.

To reconsider émigrés and the Church in connection with the revolutionary land settlement is to return naturally enough to the old question of seigneurialism and the peasantry. The outstanding development in this area was, of course, the abolition – at first conditional but then absolute – of the entire seigneurial regime. And in no area of social policy was the correlation between intensification of revolution at home and growing geopolitical engagement abroad more palpable. Yet here, too, in the revolutionaries' conception of peasant needs and rights, limitations upon change would ultimately assert themselves.

Tellingly, scholars at the forefront of research in this area have been at pains to stress the motif of war in connection with the epochal legislation of August 1792 and July 1793. Until the actual approach of war, they have pointed out, lawmaking on major seigneurial questions did not in any fundamental way affect what had been wrought in this area by the declarations of 4–11 August 1789 and by the somewhat more detailed legislation

---

53 Jones, *The Peasants in the French Revolution*, p. 155. See also McManners, *The Church in the French Revolution*, pp. 63–67, on these matters.

54 On this point, consult Donald Greer, *The Incidence of the Terror during the French Revolution* (Cambridge, Mass.: Harvard University Press, 1935). Higonnet, in *Class, Ideology, and the Rights of Nobles*, pp. 277–98, updates and reassesses the pertinent scholarly literature.

of March and May 1790. However, as "interstate tensions became more ominous, peasant insurrection began to suggest a dangerous failure of the existing scheme." Not altogether coincidentally, peasant insurrection-ism attained its second highest peak of the entire revolutionary era in April 1792 – the month of the initial French declaration of war. Over the following months, a spate of legislative attacks on the compromise decrees of August 1789 would culminate in laws of late August 1792 that all but destroyed the immemorial system of "feudal" dues and services.[55]

Of course, more was involved here than the pressures of high continental politics upon the French. At the start of 1792, for instance, a disappointing harvest and an initial outbreak of inflation were cruelly afflicting many peasants. The legislators' stubborn adherence to freedom of the grain trade only compounded problems for rural – and some urban – citizens. Even Paris suffered price-fixing riots in January and February. In addition to all this, however, war was in the wind. It was, revealingly, on 18 June – a day on which Parisians first heard of threatening military moves by Lafayette – that the Legislative Assembly voted *lods et ventes* and other "casual rights" out of existence unless they were certified to come from a formal conces-sion of land. On 20 August, the delegates chipped away further at "casual" and harvest rights, while all dues levied collectively were abolished uncon-ditionally. Still, with foreign troops now occupying French soil and a rad-ical Paris Commune challenging the political status quo, such concessions seemed glaringly inadequate. On 25 August, the critical act was rammed through the Assembly: essentially, it declared all dues and services defunct unless the affected lords could somehow document their legitimacy. The "burden of proof," in other words, now shifted decisively from peasant communities to the seigneurs. The deputies reconfirmed their work with an additional measure three days later, but the decisive blow had been dealt to seigneurialism on 25 August 1792.[56]

Particularly fascinating – and pertinent – in all of this was the way the war transformed the revolutionaries' view of seigneurialism. The more Brissot and his confederates associated "feudalism" as a benighted legacy of the past with the national Austrian foe, and presented the French mil-itary effort as aimed at delivering Europe's groaning masses from their "feudal" chains, the more they were compelled to acknowledge – and con-demn – vestiges of feudalism/seigneurialism within France. After all, could Frenchmen risking all to destroy "feudalism" abroad be expected to brook its continuation in any form at home? Hence – in part – the historic decrees

---

55 John Markoff, "Violence, Emancipation, and Democracy: The Countryside and the French Revolution," *American Historical Review* 100 (1995): 360–86. Markoff has explored all these issues in greater depth in *The Abolition of Feudalism*, passim.

56 Jones, *The Peasantry in the French Revolution*, pp. 90–94. See also Markoff, "Violence, Emancipation, and Democracy," esp. pp. 378–80.

of August 1792. And this war-assisted process would reach its logical conclusion – the unconditional abolition of *all* seigneurial dues and services, documented or not documented – with the enactment of the famous decree of 17 July 1793.[57]

Indeed, as the French marched triumphantly into "feudal" territories beyond their borders, the old questions resurfaced insistently. On 15 December 1792, the Convention proclaimed the unconditional abrogation of all seigneurial prerogatives in those areas of Belgium and Germany controlled by its forces. Peasants everywhere, it seemed, could look to Paris to support their revolutionary demands. In the meantime, the warring deputies could scarcely afford to ignore rural uprisings at home. In March 1793, Bertrand Barère recommended to his colleagues a package of rural policies combining repression with conciliation; but this plainly was not enough. Again, the linkage between affairs foreign and affairs domestic asserted itself. If French peasants were to hazard life and limb for German or Piedmontese farmers, could France's lawmakers spare *any* aspect of "feudalism" in their own country? If the Convention really wanted to encourage antiseigneurial revolt abroad, how could it fail to countenance antifeudal movements at home? And what about French peasants expected to do battle with compatriots involved in *domestic* campaigns against the Revolution? Could there be for them any incentive less compelling than the total, unequivocal abolition of seigneurialism? The response to all such queries came with the decree of 17 July 1793. "It took years of rural violence," one expert has concluded, "to push the revolutionary legislatures to make of the dismantling of feudalism a reality recognizable in the villages. And it is far from obvious that they would have done so without the wartime stresses."[58]

What is more, the revolutionary state-at-war continued in months to come to seek the support of rural plebeians. No doubt, expediency here was leavened with the yeast of altruistic concern. "The idealism of the Revolution," R. R. Palmer has argued, "helped the peasants, removing their feudal burdens, granting them land on instalment payments, promising them education, taking steps to relieve their poverty, endowing them with rights of citizenship." Yet Palmer himself has conceded and, in fact, expatiated upon the limitations of revolutionary *bienfaisance* as applied to French peasants. Rural Frenchmen asked in vain that price and wage controls (the famous *Maximum général*) be extended to their payments of rent. They "objected to the share-cropping system of *métayage*; they were still objecting in 1913. They wished the right to join in collective purchase of confiscated land, and to buy it without competitive auction.

No one supported these requests." Many farmers "wished to keep their old communal methods of agriculture," but these were "officially frowned upon," deemed "feudal" and even "counter-revolutionary." Moreover, the same government that refused to place a ceiling on peasants' rental obligations was willing enough, in the spring of 1794, to apply the *Maximum* to wages of harvesters. On 30 May, the Committee of Public Safety "requisitioned agricultural workers, proclaimed a uniform wage, and threatened recalcitrants with the Revolutionary Tribunal." Even the so-called Ventôse Decrees of March–April 1794, long applauded by certain Marxist scholars as foreshadowing rural communism, did "not in fact state that real property was to be divided. They stated that it was to be confiscated from suspects, and an indemnity paid from the proceeds to the poor." Landed wealth appropriated from "suspects," like that already taken from émigrés and the Church, was to be used above all "to uphold the financial structure of the Revolutionary state." The rural poor would have to be content with receiving an "indemnity" in paper money.[59]

It would be unfair to conclude from all of this that the men ruling France in its years of deepening revolution were crassly indifferent to the needs of their humble rural countrymen. As urbanites, as lawyers, administrators, and entrepreneurs, they were, perhaps, not so much indifferent to as largely ignorant of rural problems. But in a sense this is beside the point. The revolutionary leaders of 1791–94 became overwhelmingly preoccupied with waging war on an unprecedented scale. This forced them into some dramatic accommodations of peasant demands; yet it never compelled them to jettison "bourgeois" economic interests anchored in existing relations of property holding and production.

In framing urban subsistence policies and mooting projects of general welfare, the legislators of these years, again, revealed an inescapable preoccupation with their country's security needs and geopolitical goals. Whether acting to provide food for the masses, sketching out plans for a "national" education, or struggling to define a permanent government responsibility to assist those in need, the revolutionaries were both energized and inhibited by their unconditional commitment to the war effort.

Take the primal necessity of food. In the late summer and autumn of 1792, we have seen, deputies galvanized by the presence of Austrian and Prussian troops on French soil "took the first steps along the road to economic controls." Government agents were authorized to "requisition food and transport for the army at prices fixed by the local authorities"; municipalities were given the green light to employ similar methods to supply local

59 Palmer, *Twelve Who Ruled*, pp. 312–15. Even in this attenuated form, the Ventôse Decrees did not survive. They were absorbed into a general program of charity. On the conversion of land "grants" into payments or vouchers to the poor, see also P. M. Jones, *The Peasantry in the French Revolution*, p. 155.

markets; and a census of all stocks of grain in the country was ordered. Yet if, at this point, "all shades of revolutionary opinion seemed to be inclined towards the control of the grain trade," the deputies of the Convention would soon revert to a philosophy of laissez-faire economics – probably because of the (momentary) improvement in French military fortunes.[60]

With the war crisis of 1793, however, the Convention's free marketeers were constrained to meet popular demands halfway. In a spring overshadowed by Dumouriez's treason and by British entry into the conflict, the legislators endorsed two popular measures that, earlier, would have drawn their censure: the *cours forcé* of the *assignat* (compelling acceptance of this paper currency at face value) and a *maximum* or ceiling to be imposed by the departments on the price of grain. On 27 July, acceding again to popular demand, the delegates decreed the death penalty for the hoarding of necessities and appointed sectional "hoarding commissioners" to apply the new law. In perilous August, the Convention voted for the establishment of public granaries, granted one hundred million *livres* to the Committee of Public Safety for grain purchases, and authorized all "representatives on mission" to requisition grain for Paris, and for all departments lacking it.[61] Crowning all of this legislation was the *Maximum général* of 29 September. Prices were set for a host of commodities judged to be "of prime necessity," ranging from meat and salted fish to butter and oil to coal, candles, and soap. "For most of these items the highest lawful price was fixed at a figure one-third higher than the current local price in 1790. The level of wages was also determined – the maximum wage was to be one-half more than the corresponding wage in 1790. An advantage was thus offered to wage earners, who might earn a half more than in 1790 while paying only a third more for commodities."[62]

Thus, the late summer and early fall of 1793 – marking the low point of French geopolitical fortunes – logically enough marked the all-time *high* point of this "bourgeois" government's willingness to accommodate the subsistence needs of urban plebeians. By the same logic, the government's gradually solidifying military (and domestic) situation in subsequent months permitted a scaling back of official efforts to alleviate popular distress. Just a month after the promulgation of wage and price controls, the Convention voted to relax the latter by allowing prices to reflect costs of transportation and a 5 percent wholesaler's and a 10 percent

60 Hampson, *A Social History of the French Revolution*, pp. 158–59.
61 Ibid., pp. 176 and 192–94, for a succinct discussion of these measures. On popular attitudes toward subsistence issues at Paris, and popular pressures on the Convention in 1792–94, see also Richard Cobb, "The Revolutionary Mentality in France, 1793–1794," *History* 52 (1957): 181–96; and George Rudé, *The Crowd in the French Revolution* (New York: Oxford University Press, 1959).
62 The *Maximum général* is thoroughly discussed in Palmer, *Twelve Who Ruled*, p. 239.

retailer's profit. It took until the following spring to implement this policy; by then, the authorities were ready to modify their economic policy on a number of fronts. The *Maximum* itself was weakened by authorized exceptions, and indeed became largely "an instrument of discipline, available on occasion to check profiteering or counter the demands of labor." The government granted premiums and subsidies to businessmen, privatized some state-controlled munitions plants, dismantled what remained of the preceding summer's antihoarding legislation, encouraged a certain amount of export trade, requisitioned labor for various employers, and (after suppressing radicals in the Paris municipality) applied wage controls to workers in the capital previously unaffected by them.[63] There is no reason to doubt that Robespierre and some of his colleagues, both of Public Safety and of the Convention as a whole, felt a genuine compassion for working and necessitous Frenchmen and Frenchwomen. However, there is also no reason to doubt that the government felt less obliged to intervene in matters of popular subsistence as its sense of security grew in 1794.

In the area of education, the social benevolence accompanying the Revolution ran up even more brutally against the limitations imposed by war. Certainly, progressive plans were not lacking for a national system of education that might fill the vacuum created by the revolutionary assault upon ancien régime institutions.[64] Even before the Constituent Assembly dissolved itself in September 1791, Talleyrand had offered a draft proposal for an extensively revamped system of education in France. Condorcet presented an even more visionary scheme to the Legislative Assembly, one that spoke of equal education for women and of the systematic training of teachers, even if it rejected the notion of compulsory and completely secularized instruction. In the Convention, projects like that of Lepeletier de St.-Fargeau went yet further, insisting that the priesthood be denied any pedagogical role, and that education in France henceforward be compulsory, free, Republican, and common to all. In no area of public policy was the Revolution at this stage more fertile and forward-looking than in that of education.

Alas, it was not to be. "While the revolutionaries agreed that the establishment of a new, national educational system was of fundamental

---

63 Ibid., pp. 239–40, 311–12, 316. On popular economic issues in Paris under the Terror, see also the essays in Jeffrey Kaplow, ed., *New Perspectives on the French Revolution* (New York: John Wiley, 1965).

64 For what follows here, see: Isser Woloch, *The New Regime: Transformations of the French Civic Order, 1789–1820s* (New York: W. W. Norton, 1994), pp. 177–78; Martyn Lyons, *France under the Directory* (Cambridge: Cambridge University Press, 1975), pp. 86–87; and R. R. Palmer, *The Improvement of Humanity: Education and the French Revolution* (Princeton, N.J.: Princeton University Press, 1985). The Revolution most notably disrupted the educational mission of the Church.

importance," Martyn Lyons has sadly noted, "they were preoccupied with other matters, like winning the war, and uniting the country. Until the military security of France was assured, long-term projects were shelved." Condorcet – tellingly – found his reading of a report on education on 20 April 1792 interrupted by the Legislative Assembly's declaration of war against Austria. Eight months later, Marat ridiculed Girondists promoting educational schemes in the Convention by likening them to a general who diverted himself with plans to grow fruit trees while his soldiers were dying of hunger. The choice of analogy was significant: France was a country engaged in total war.[65] Other factors, it is true, also contributed to the frustration of these humanitarian efforts to "revolutionize" education in France. The Convention's Committee on Public Instruction found itself mired in debates over the precise degree of state control of education to be established and over the roles to be assigned to faculties of higher learning. Again, many parents of prospective students objected to the notion of a politicized, propagandistic education in republican schools, or to the idea of sending their children to any school at all. Moreover, the logistical difficulties involved in setting up a new, national system of education would have been daunting even in the best of circumstances. Still, revolutionary *bienveillance* in this (as in every) area was thwarted above all by war. Even in the first half of 1794, as it meditated and launched its boldest social and cultural experiments, the Revolutionary government was "primarily concerned with mobilization.... Questions of education were subordinated to military requirements." Not that war worked altogether against educational purposes in France, at least in the long run. Palmer's wry comment here is apt: "It is probable that the army, over the whole period of the wars from 1792 to 1814, through providing travel to young men in France and foreign countries and through its lessons in camp hygiene, care of weapons, group living, and the general raising of political consciousness, had more effect on popular education than all the laws of the Revolution and Empire."[66]

When it came to the government's general obligation to assist those in need, the Revolution's noblest promises again foundered on the shoals of war. The Convention might declare grandly that "every man has a right to subsistence through work, if he is well; through free assistance, if he cannot work." It might also sanctify provisioning the poor as "a national debt."[67] Yet, all too predictably, war made the implementation of any really visionary program of public welfare impossible. That the scarce funds

65 Lyons, *France under the Directory*, pp. 86–87.
66 Quotes here are from Palmer, *The Improvement of Humanity*, pp. 181–82, 185, and 197–98. See also Woloch, *The New Regime*, pp. 177–78, on the sparring over education in the Convention's Committee on Public Instruction.
67 Citations (my translation) are taken from Lyons, *France under the Directory*, pp. 95–96.

earmarked for this purpose went chiefly to the relatives of deceased soldiers was in itself another striking commentary on the priority assigned by the representatives to the war effort.[68] So were the expensive war's draining of desperately needed tax and charitable revenue away from hospitals and the government's need to confiscate hospital properties as *biens nationaux*. Frenchmen, Frenchwomen, and their children could only be fed, educated, and cared for insofar as these beneficent functions did not impede the engines of war.

Reference to the "engines of war" brings us finally to a reappraisal of army and naval issues in the years of intensifying revolution in France. The resumption of war making on a massive scale was bound to have an especially dramatic impact on those institutions charged most directly with defending the country and projecting its interests and ideals abroad. We can ascertain the nature of that impact during 1791–94 by revisiting questions of officer promotion, recruitment of fighting personnel, and what we might call "motivation and mentality."

The shock of Varennes, one specialist on the French army has written, "greatly accelerated the process of change which had been going on since 1789." Many officers, whether because of growing politicization and insubordination in the ranks, or due to pressures brought to bear by embittered émigrés, or out of genuine loyalty to the king's imperiled cause – or for all these reasons – resigned their commands and left France altogether. Small wonder, then, that, on one calculation, 2,160 army officers emigrated between 15 September and 1 December 1791, and that, from 15 September 1791 to 1 December 1792, "one third of the units in the line army lost one third or more of their authorized officer strength as a result of resignations, illegal absences, and emigrations."[69]

The Revolution's imperative need to replace these officers – many of whom, as well-connected aristocrats, had blocked channels of upward mobility in the old regime officer corps – generated new opportunities for frustrated NCOs, soldiers of fortune, ambitious provincial nobles, and commoners with limited military experience. NCOs and officers of fortune, Samuel Scott has said, "came to form an essential element in the officer corps of the Revolution. They brought to their new positions a practical skill, a knowledge of their troops, a commitment to their career, and a devotion to the Revolution that only a minority of the pre-revolutionary officer corps possessed." Ambitious and professionally minded provincial squires who remained in the army after the emigrations of 1791–92 could also expect from the Revolution promotional chances unavailable to most

---

68 Ibid. See also Isser Woloch, *The French Veteran from the Revolution to the Restoration* (Chapel Hill: University of North Carolina Press, 1979).

69 Scott, *The Response of the Royal Army to the French Revolution*, pp. 109–10.

of them prior to 1789. Few of them in olden times could have attained even the grade of lieutenant-colonel; by 1792, with the country plunging headlong into war, "many commanded regiments, and the rank of general was not beyond reach." Those of them who were willing to place pursuit of career and loyalty to France before any lingering fealty to the crown, and were able to retain the support of their troops, could continue to rise in their profession throughout the Revolution.[70] As for commoners who had not been NCOs or officers of fortune as of 1789, they, too, could make successful careers in the Revolution. Take, for example, company-level officers – captains, lieutenants, sublieutenants – in the battle infantry. Jean-Paul Bertaud has given the social origins of captains in 1793–94 as: 44.2 percent bourgeois, 25.8 percent artisan, and 22.3 percent peasant (with a smattering of nobles, clerics, and foreigners). For lieutenants, the figures were: 36.5 percent bourgeois, 33.6 percent artisan, and 24.4 percent peasant. (For sublieutenants, the percentages were similar.) About half of these company-level officers had known something of the trade of arms before 1789, but they largely owed their promotions to the Revolution: for instance, "only 4.6 percent of the captains had been officers in 1789, and most of them... had been only corporals."[71]

If war more than any other factor modernized the army's officer corps, it just as deeply affected its overall social makeup. Inevitably, France's exploding manpower needs meant that voluntary enlistment (the Volunteers of 1791 and 1792) would be followed by conscription. The turning point here came in 1793. The vestiges of voluntary enlistment were maintained even as the Convention decreed a levy of 300,000 men on 24 February 1793 to bring the army up to full strength. Yet, Bertaud has argued, the legislators on this occasion were introducing the principle of conscription, for "all men of ages 18 to 40, unmarried or widowers without children, were put in a state of permanent requisition."[72] With the famous *levée en masse* of 23 August, conscription would become a more massive (if not yet permanently institutionalized) reality.

"We have only fragmentary information on the social origin of the draftees," Bertaud has written. Nonetheless, what he has unearthed suggests to us an army increasingly reflective of French civil society. Even with the February 1793 "levy of the 300,000," fewer lawyers, teachers, students, and state bureaucrats appeared than had among the Volunteers of 1792; most of the new enrolees were "farm laborers and workers in the

---

70 Ibid., esp. pp. 111–20.
71 Bertaud, *The Army of the French Revolution*, pp. 178–79, 182–87, and 189. Research on the army officer corps in this period is also summarized in John A. Lynn, *The Bayonets of the Republic: Motivation and Tactics in the Army of Revolutionary France, 1791–1794* (Urbana: University of Illinois Press, 1984), pp. 67–96.
72 Bertaud, *The Army of the French Revolution*, pp. 90–96.

most ordinary trades." The "leveling" tendency was only confirmed with the *levée en masse*. Perhaps 16 percent of the draftees had urban origins, corresponding more or less to the proportion of the French population reckoned then as urban. Some of these individuals continued as before to hail from the "respectable" middle class – merchants, teachers, notaries, and so forth – but increasingly they tended to be artisans and workers. Moreover, the artisans now serving under the colors represented an unprecedented variety of occupations. Nonetheless, the army of the early Republic, however much it might style itself as the "patriotic" nation in miniature, was heavily peasant in its composition, differing markedly in this respect from the institution of 1789–91. Rural plebeians thus dominated in military as in civil society. We should also note here that the levies of 1793 brought in young men from *all* departments in the country, even if those rallying most enthusiastically to France's martial standards came disproportionately from the Parisian basin and from regions (in the northeast and the west) menaced most directly by invasion and/or domestic rebellion.[73]

Thus the war crucially affected both the command structure and the overall composition of the Revolution's armies. It also profoundly influenced the mentality of the *militaires*, producing in the long run a professional outlook that would leave Jacobin idealism far behind. Even Bertaud, for all his republican sympathies, has seen signs of this evolution predating Robespierre's final days. He has pointed, for example, to Carnot's decision in July 1794 to launch a new journal, the *Soirée du camp*, for mass consumption in the ranks. Carnot apparently intended thereby to popularize the notion of the army as an institution distinct in its ways of thinking and managing problems from the "nation." For Carnot – as, later, for the Thermidorians – the men serving in the camps were to see themselves no longer as political militants, as bearers of an ideological message, but rather as professional soldiers who had mastered the technical aspects of a vocation they could now proudly exercise in common.[74]

Other historians have corroborated Bertaud's findings. Some of them, generalizing from studies of motivation and morale in the Republic's field armies, have detected in the weeks preceding the drama of Thermidor, Year II, a gradual weakening of the emotional ties that, hitherto, had bound civilians and *militaires* together in a common defense of the Revolution. Henceforth, army and civil society would begin to diverge.[75] Other scholars, tracing the relationship between the Jacobins and the military, have noted that, even at the height of the Terror, the Jacobins subordinated democratic/participatory ideals to the requirements of discipline.

73 On all these points, see ibid., pp. 66–74, 90–96, 130–32. Refer also to Lynn, *The Bayonets of the Republic*, pp. 43–66.
74 Bertaud, *The Army of the French Revolution*, pp. 217–19.
75 Lynn, *The Bayonets of the Republic*, p. 285.

Officers during this period were increasingly selected for their professional merit – that is, for their grasp of strategic issues, their technical knowledge, their discipline and efficiency – and the men in the ranks, if encouraged to involve themselves in the politics prescribed from Paris, were expected above all to obey those in authority.[76] Already, then, we can see in the making the army that would stand by quietly as the Robespierrists were marched to their doom in late July 1794, and that would be instrumental later on in the cynical coups d'état of the Directory.

Available documentation may never enable naval historians to character-ize the social origins and motivation of French sailors in analogous fashion, but it does permit conclusions regarding the Revolution's impact upon the officers of the French fleet. Clearly, resignations, desertions, and emigra-tion by noble officers had by 1792 left the navy as dangerously weakened as was the army. In May 1791, the Constituent Assembly had envisioned a naval officer corps of 9 vice-admirals, 18 counter-admirals, 170 captains, and 530 lieutenants. The Legislative Assembly determined, the following March, that of the officers accounted for in May 1791, only 2 vice-admirals, 3 counter-admirals, 42 captains, and 356 lieutenants remained. By the autumn of 1792, it now appears, the navy could not even provide one captain per warship or two lieutenants per warship or frigate.[77]

The French, haunted once again by the specter (and, soon, the reality) of war, reacted to the crisis in the navy as they did to that in the army: by greasing the tracks of upward mobility and favoring selective criteria of professionalism over those of ideological purity. As one of its final actions in September 1792, the Legislative Assembly passed emergency decrees to deal with the situation. The government recalled some retired officers to duty, accelerated the promotion of lieutenants, and invited officers of the merchant marine to compete for places as *enseignes* who could one day earn further promotion. There would also be an unlimited number of *aspirants* (roughly equivalent to British midshipmen) entitled to compete for further promotion, and this grade was opened to all. The Convention, pressed by the same military exigencies, legislated in a similar vein. It expedited the elevation to lieutenancies of both "military" and "merchant marine" officers, and authorized the naval minister to choose for the *Grands Corps* deserving officers of any of the lower grades. True, at the height of the Terror, Jeanbon St.-André, naval "specialist" for the Committee of Public Safety, came under tremendous pressure to promote individuals on the basis of ideological considerations. Yet those most knowledgeable on the subject insist that Jeanbon's promotion to the highest grades of such men as

76 Alan Forrest, *The Soldiers of the French Revolution* (Durham, N.C.: Duke University Press, 1990), pp. 55–56, 76, and 123–24.
77 Hampson, *La Marine de l'An II*, pp. 43–45. See also Cormack, *Revolution and Political Conflict in the French Navy*, pp. 117–22, 145–47.

Villaret-Joyeuse, Van Stabel, Cornic-Dumoulin, and Pierre Martin shows the Jacobin government's paramount concern for talent, initiative, and discipline in the naval officer corps.[78]

Unfortunately, all the government's efforts to fill the gaps in the naval officer corps left by the desertions of aristocratic officers could not give the French, in 1793–94, a fleet capable of realistically challenging British supremacy on the seas. Manpower deficiencies on shipboard and in the arsenals, and failures in administrative discipline in the Naval Ministry and in the ports, were among the many problems that dogged French naval strategists throughout the Revolution.[79] We can see nonetheless that, in the case of the navy as in that of the army, France's reversion to war created new opportunities for professional advancement even as it reconfirmed the importance of old professional standards. The two phenomena were complementary parts of the same process.

To sum up, in weighing the need for domestic changes, the men governing France in its years of intensifying revolution showed themselves to be driven as much by geostrategic concerns as by the tug-and-pull of domestic interests and ideals. As we shall see in the following pages, foreign and internal pressures also asserted themselves in the increasingly radical politics of that period.

GEOPOLITICS, DOMESTIC POLITICS, AND "TERROR"

In seeking to explain the radicalization of French politics from the summer of 1791 into Thermidor, Year II (July 1794), some historians, abandoning notions of dialectical class conflict, have posited a competition of discourses stressing the virtues of popular sovereignty. For these scholars, ideology, rather than socioeconomic interest, drove revolutionary politics ever leftward.[80] We shall argue, instead, that a mix of international and domestic factors (with the accent on the former) led, first, to the triumph of militant Brissotins over moderate Feuillants in the Legislative Assembly and, then, to the more decisive victory of Robespierrist Jacobins (Montagnards) over Brissotins (Girondists) in the Convention. We shall also see that, in the critical year 1793, war, more than any other issue, dictated the terms of a contentious political dialogue between Paris and the provinces.

Truth to tell, there is no need to expand greatly upon what we have already said regarding a struggle for power in the Legislative Assembly

---

78 See again, on all of this, Hampson, *La Marine de l'An II*, pp. 188–201; and Cormack, *Revolution and Political Conflict in the French Navy*, pp. 145–47, 269–71.

79 On the sorry overall state of the French navy in this period, see again Hampson, *La Marine de l'An II*, pp. 64–65.

80 Again, see Furet, *Interpreting the French Revolution*, for the most stimulating articulation of this thesis.

so obviously dominated by the war question. C. J. Mitchell, certainly, has usefully reminded us of the problems inherent in assigning deputies of that period to factions identified too readily as the "Feuillants" and the "Brissotins."[81] His cautionary insight notwithstanding, there can be little doubt that a clique of politicians associated with Jacques-Pierre Brissot, employing a variety of arguments but relying above all on the chauvinistic instincts of the majority of Assemblymen, ran roughshod over the attempts of a few delegates (whether "Feuillants" or not) to preserve pacific Franco-Austrian and Franco-Prussian relations. In this parliamentary confrontation, of course, key diplomatic and domestic issues were – as always – tightly joined. The indefinite maintenance of peace might have meant the indefinite prolongation of constitutional arrangements apportioning state power between a monarch and an elected national assembly. But a reversion to the hallowed ways of war would (and did) discredit irredeemably a sovereign whose flight to Varennes had already exposed his rejection of revolutionary changes. Significantly, the downfall of the monarchy in August 1792 was precipitated by the intervention of Parisians moved in part by economic distress but especially maddened by the news of Prussian and Austrian incursions into France. In subsequent months, Louis XVI's fate would be sealed by the discovery, at the Tuileries, of royal correspondence with other European heads of state; and, for a time, the politicians seemingly poised to derive maximum advantage from that circumstance were Brissot's coterie of warmongers.[82]

To make this last point is another way of saying that geopolitical issues, which had favored all "Jacobins" indiscriminately in the final year of the Constituent Assembly, advantaged Brissot's circle of "Jacobins" in the last months of the succeeding Legislative Assembly and gave some prospect of benefiting them as well in the radical Convention to come. But if Brissot had been shrewd enough to play upon the patriotic heartstrings of his fellow legislators in furthering his own political agenda in 1791–92, he was not sufficiently prescient to see in the war a phenomenon whose unprecedented manpower and matériel needs would require ever more centralization of governmental powers and a concomitant democratization of politics at Paris and in the provinces. In the end, the question of war, which had come to dominate all other matters in the Legislative Assembly, would do so as well in the Convention – and it would swallow up the Brissotins, the "Girondists," in 1793 as it had engulfed the Feuillants the year before.

81 See C. J. Mitchell, "Political Divisions within the Legislative Assembly of 1791," *French Historical Studies* 13 (1984): 356–89; and *The French Legislative Assembly of 1791*, passim.
82 Refer, on these issues, to Hardman, *Louis XVI*, passim; Rudé, *The Crowd in the French Revolution*, passim; and Mitchell, "Political Divisions within the Legislative Assembly," pp. 356–89.

Clearly, the war was on the minds of most citizens who, in augmented numbers,[83] convened in departmental assemblies in September 1792 to elect delegates to the recently decreed National Convention. This preoccupation manifested itself in several ways. For one thing, nearly half of the electoral bodies went beyond their official duties to lend support to the war effort. These supportive efforts included: mounting subscription campaigns to help finance the cost of outfitting and equipping volunteers and maintaining their families while they were on military duty; furnishing horses, provisions, and transport services to the army; conducting inventories of local reserves of ammunition for the artillery; and even assisting emissaries from Paris in coordinating strategies of military defense for entire departments.[84] That, in addition, so many of the electors unhesitatingly rejected openly royalist candidates for Convention seats, and in some cases insisted as well upon purging royalists from local administrative and judicial posts, testified indirectly to the widespread anxiety and indignation over the danger to which the king's duplicity had exposed his subjects.[85] Finally, it is revealing in this connection that most electors were disinclined to condemn the Parisians for the killings which had occurred in the capital's jails just a few days before. Five of the six electoral assemblies that, we know, had heard of this event had also just learned of the fall of Verdun to the Prussians; significantly, not one of them bothered at this time to discuss the September massacres. Attitudes might change later on as the fear of invasion faded, and as the extent of the carnage at Paris was fully revealed; for the time being, however, a "sympathetic understanding of the situation which had produced the massacres" was more in evidence.[86]

Initially, Brissot and his allies from the Gironde appeared well positioned to profit in the Convention from such patriotic concerns, shared as they were by electors and elected alike. Had they not been among the first to clamor in the preceding legislature for war against the historic Habsburg foe? Had not their man Dumouriez, first in the ministry of foreign affairs and then in an army command, promised laurels for revolutionary France? And in fact did not the victories at Valmy and Jemappes, however incomplete they might be in some technical respects, reverse the tide of military fortune in France's favor as the campaigning season of 1792 wound down? The Girondists, buoyed by these events, felt sufficiently secure in late 1792

83 The *absolute* number of voters nationwide probably registered an increase over 1789–91, although, given the recent increase in the pool of eligible voters, the *percentage* of the latter exercising the franchise was on the decrease. This matter is closely reviewed in Crook, *Elections in the French Revolution*, pp. 79–101.

84 Alison Patrick, *The Men of the First French Republic* (Baltimore: Johns Hopkins University Press, 1972), p. 173.

85 Ibid., pp. 172–75.

86 Ibid., p. 169.

and early 1793 to battle the emergent "Montagnard" faction of Jacobins in the Convention on a number of fronts, ranging from responsibility for the September massacres to the king's trial and punishment to the respective roles to be assigned to Parisians and to provincials in the affairs of the new Republic.

All of this might have gone on inconclusively, and certainly never have acquired a new pitch of murderous intensity, had it not been for the dramatic reversal in military fortunes that (we have already seen) placed the entire Revolution in jeopardy the following spring and summer. The addition of the Dutch, the Spanish, and above all the British to the list of France's enemies surely had not been foreseen by Brissot and his partisans in 1792. Even less anticipated, and more immediately dangerous to them, was the treason in April 1793 of their champion Dumouriez. In the harsh light of these developments, the political infighting between the Girondists and "Montagnard" Jacobins in the Convention gradually took on the characteristics of mortal combat.

Whether or not the traditional scholarly division of the Convention into leftist "Jacobins" (the "Mountain"), a centrist "Plain" or "Marsh," and rightist "Girondists" or "Girondins" still serves useful analytical purposes has recently occasioned much debate.[87] Yet even in questioning some aspects of the traditional schema, a trio of Americans recently reaffirmed the notion of a "factional struggle that began in the Legislative Assembly in 1792 and would end with the liquidation of the Jacobins' enemies after June 1793 and with the persecution of Jacobins by the surviving Girondists after July 1794."[88] Indeed, it would seem difficult now to deny that representatives in the Convention identified *at that time* as "Jacobins" combatted deputies labeled "Girondists." Moreover, the Jacobins appear to have gradually won over enough deputies to have constituted a fairly reliable majority in France's ruling assembly during 1793–94. And retrospective analysis suggests that it was above all their concentration upon the country's imperative need for security that opened the way for the Jacobins' ascendancy in the Convention.

Leading Jacobins were quick to grasp the gravity of the situation – and to sense that mastering it would require an embrace of truly "popular" politics. In March 1793, Jeanbon St.-André, on mission in Lot and Dordogne, had written: "If we expect the multitude to help us to safeguard the Revolution it is very necessary indeed to keep them alive." In recollections

---

87 See, along with Patrick's study: M. J. Sydenham, *The Girondins* (London: Athlone Press, 1961); Gary Kates, *The Cercle Social, the Girondins, and the French Revolution* (Princeton, N.J.: Princeton University Press, 1985); and Michael S. Lewis-Beck, Anne Hildreth, and Alan B. Spitzer, "Was There a Girondist Faction in the National Convention, 1792–1793?" *French Historical Studies* 15 (1988): 519–36.

88 Lewis-Beck, Hildreth, and Spitzer, p. 536.

penned after the event, Baudot was even more direct: "Only the masses could hurl back the foreign horde. Therefore we had to inspire them to support us by giving them a real interest in our success."[89] And in fact the Jacobins' ability to woo centrists away from any affiliation with Brissot's coterie of politicians in the spring of 1793 was rooted in the realism of such insights, which on all occasions assumed the interrelatedness of domestic and geostrategic issues. The Jacobins perceived, for instance, that both the British naval blockade and the outbreak of civil war in the West had jeopardized the distribution of food. They understood by the same token that, if Dumouriez's treason had shaken public confidence in the paper currency, so had the hoarding of food, by aggravating shortages and thereby inflating prices expressed in *assignats*. Apart from worrying about their immediate political status in the Convention, the Jacobins had also to worry about saving revolutionary France; and they realized that achieving the latter objective meant addressing the many causes of domestic discontent.[90] Hence, apparently, the Jacobin deputies' accelerated campaign in April and May 1793 to reach an understanding with popular Parisian interests on economic and political matters, even as they were battling their Girondist foes and seeking new alliances with uncommitted representatives in the legislature.

Analyzing the terms of parliamentary debate during these decisive months ultimately enables us to understand why the Jacobins prevailed over their Girondist opponents in the struggle for paramount influence in the Convention, and thus in the revolutionary state-at-war. In those debates, two questions – one purely domestic and the other transcending domestic considerations – interacted continually. The first question was: how to maintain the Convention's independence from radical pressure groups in Paris? The second question was: how to go about the main business of securing the Republic? The Girondists, to their ruin, placed too much emphasis upon the first question and not enough upon the second. They could not see, as the Jacobins and their allies could, that first the Republic must be salvaged by winning the war, and that doing so required that the provinces (at least temporarily) be subordinated to the capital – including, crucially, its patriotic male and female artisans and shopkeepers (*sans-culottes* and *sans-jupons*). To identify with *provinçiaux* at Lyon and Marseilles and Bordeaux who opposed the encroachment of national upon local government, and to condemn accordingly the "anarchy" of the Parisians, was to undercut the war effort upon which all else depended, and yet this was what Brissot and his confederates did in the spring of 1793. The inevitable response of the more pragmatic Jacobin deputies came with the

89 Citations from Sydenham, *The Girondins*, pp. 167–68.
90 Ibid.

journées of 31 May–2 June: the mass demonstrations by means of which a tactical alliance of Jacobin politicians and Parisian *sans-culottes* secured the expulsion of twenty-nine prominent Girondists from the Convention.[91] The events of 31 May–2 June 1793, however reluctantly endorsed by many of the lawmakers, had the desired and essential effect of purging from the legislature a faction of politicians no longer able to govern but still capable of making governing well-nigh impossible for others. The Parisian insurrection, it has been fairly concluded, "broke the parliamentary deadlock in favor of a group of men who not only had better claims to govern than the Girondins, but had in fact been doing most of the work of government for some time."[92]

Painstaking research into the origins of the members of the Convention has done much to invalidate whatever remained of the old Marxist postulation of major socioeconomic differences between Girondists and Jacobins. Experience of public life and the assumption of responsibility in the Revolution, rather than wealth or social standing, provided the key to variations in political attitudes in this body; and the Jacobins, it turns out, had "experience" and "assumption of responsibility" to burn. They comprised a large proportion of ex-Legislative Assemblymen in the Convention; indeed, their record of participation in debates, committee work, and administrative/political labors in the provinces during 1791–92 made that period (in one historian's words) "a nursery of the politicians of the Terror."[93] Then, again, while the debate over the king's fate in December 1792–January 1793 was characterized in part by Girondist arguments for clemency that revealed scant political (or geopolitical) realism, Robespierre and his allies knew that they had to appeal to the revolutionary idealism of plebeian citizens whose activism was fueling the Republic's efforts to survive.[94] Jacobin sensitivity to the needs of the *sans-culottes* – activists already spurned by the Girondist orators – made such a strategy as logical as it was necessary.[95]

Moreover, it is clear in hindsight that even some legislators not closely leagued with Robespierre endorsed the execution of Louis XVI in January 1793, and the willingness of some of them to collaborate on committees like that of Public Safety paralleled the more general willingness of deputies

91 On these critical *journées*, see Rudé, *The Crowd in the French Revolution*, pp. 120–25; and Morris Slavin, *The Making of an Insurrection: Parisian Sections and the Gironde* (Cambridge, Mass.: Harvard University Press, 1986).

92 Patrick, *The Men of the First French Republic*, p. 135.

93 Ibid., pp. 299–300.

94 Ibid., p. 72.

95 On the debate over the king's fate, see also David P. Jordan, *The King's Trial* (Berkeley: University of California Press, 1979); and Michael Walzer, ed., *Regicide and Revolution: Speeches at the Trial of Louis XVI* (New York: Columbia University Press, 1992).

to share the burdens of the Terror in the Convention's sessions.[96] The absence from Paris of some Jacobins toiling as *représentants en mission* in the provinces prior to 31 May–2 June may have temporarily allowed the Girondists to prevail on some nonessential issues until then. But the Jacobins would be in charge after 2 June 1793, and would continue to do a disproportionate share of the state's administrative work in committees and "on mission" even as they participated (as their other duties allowed) in parliamentary deliberations.

Any doubts we might harbor about the centrality of French security needs to the downfall of the Girondists and to the success of their Jacobin antagonists necessarily dissolve in light of the subsequent arraignment of the former by the latter. An official, Jacobin-inspired "Address to the French People" proclaimed that the vanquished Girondists had "neglected the public welfare and exposed the state to the danger of foreign conquest."[97] Then came the formal indictment of the proscribed Girondist leaders, read out by Amar on the floor of the Convention on 3 October 1793, and it faithfully mirrored the revolutionaries' preoccupation with the threat posed to France. Brissot and his cronies, so Amar charged, had plotted to deliver France to the Prussians in the summer of 1792, conspired at the end of 1792 to conceal proofs of the king's "treachery," deliberately expanded the war and thus courted disaster the following spring even as they anticipated Dumouriez's treason in Belgium and the revolt in the Vendée, and – finally – advocated "federalism" and incited rebellion throughout the imperiled country.[98] In all of this, it is fairly obvious, we see, not so much the spokesmen for a set of "class" interests or for one specific discourse of "popular sovereignty," but rather the angry and frightened avatars of the French sense of national security – and national greatness.

It is important, too, to stress that Jacobins all over France were as eager as the "Montagnard" politicians in the Convention to fuse international and domestic issues, take on the many duties of governance, and broaden their bases of popular support. In fact, most of the provincial Jacobin clubs were clamoring for war well in advance of some of the politicians in the capital: Michael Kennedy, for example, has found that 141 of 154 clubs he sampled over the period from 1 December 1791 to 20 April 1792 "demanded offensive war" prior to the latter date.[99] More significant, however, was their conscious fusing of geostrategic and internal issues. Examples of this are rife. Bouzonville's Jacobins warned Louis XVI, "Either quit the throne or sustain the independence and sovereignty of the nation." Montauban's Jacobins advised the Legislative Assembly in June 1792 to use

96 Patrick, *The Men of the First French Republic*, p. 302.
97 As cited in Sydenham, *The Girondins*, p. 22.
98 Ibid., pp. 26–27.
99 Michael L. Kennedy, *The Jacobin Clubs in the French Revolution: The Middle Years* (Princeton, N.J.: Princeton University Press, 1988), pp. 129–31.

"all constitutional powers available to it" to combat the enemies of the fatherland. "If these are not enough...indicate to the country how to form a new representative assembly with great powers and short duration." From Le Mans came a pronunciamento to the "Patriots of the Empire" adjuring them to "rise up and teach Louis XVI that it is up to the nation to provide for its defense and demand reparations for anything that strikes at the social compact." Queried the militants at Besançon: "What is to be done when the king, to recover his despotism, arms all the powers of the earth against the nation?" Again and again, we see in the pronouncements of the provincial societies a foretaste of what was to come in the Jacobin rhetoric of the Convention: the automatic conjoining of international and domestic – especially constitutional – affairs.[100]

And these Jacobins, too, like their more famous counterparts at Paris, made some effort at "social outreach" even as war-related circumstances forced them to take on more and more of the daily tasks of governance. Although, it seems, respectable bourgeois continued to wield the greatest amount of influence in the clubs even under the Terror, there is also some reason to believe that this influence was shifting downward *within* the middle class. The "moyenne" and "haute" bourgeoisie – doctors, lawyers, teachers, priests, wholesale merchants, investors, government officials – accounted for somewhat less of the membership after September 1791; shopkeepers more or less held their own; but craftsmen and small tradesmen and even urban wage earners registered noticeable gains in the overall membership, if not in leadership positions. And with somewhat greater social inclusiveness came the assumption of greater local power. On the one hand, the number of Jacobins ensconced in local office had reached a new high by early 1793. On the other hand, the clubs themselves were being transformed, by gradual stages, into agencies of the government.[101] The former process owed something to the fact that representatives on mission in 1793–94, irritated by the lethargy or open hostility of departmental and district authorities and other local notables who had often embraced the Girondist cause, reacted by purging local officials and replacing them with Jacobins and *sans-culottes* outside the clubs.[102] Thus, the key to the Jacobin ascendancy, in provincial France as in the country's ruling assembly, lay in a willingness to subordinate all other objectives to that of securing victory in foreign and civil warfare.

Foreign and civil warfare – and, where the latter phenomenon threatened or actually broke out in 1793, pitting *chouans* in the West or "federalist"

---

100 Ibid., pp. 252–63, for these (and other) pronouncements by Jacobins in the provinces.
101 Ibid., pp. 34–42, for changes in the personnel and functions of the provincial Jacobin societies.
102 Many examples are furnished in Hampson, *A Social History of the French Revolution*, pp. 209–10. On the situation in the Parisian municipality, see Marc Bouloiseau, *The Jacobin Republic, 1792–1794* (New York: Cambridge University Press, 1984), esp. p. 113.

insurgents in the South against Paris, it was most often touched off by the central government's war-compelled intrusions into local society. The war on Europe, that is to say, did much to set the basic terms of the political relationship between Paris and provincial France in this most dangerous phase of the Revolution.

We should first point out in this connection that even as the hurly-burly of combat between Feuillants and Brissotins, and then between Girondists and Montagnards, gripped political observers in the country's capital, sociopolitical evolution was progressing – sometimes smoothly, sometimes by fits and starts – in provincial communities. (We have, for that matter, just seen something of it reflected in the changing composition of local Jacobin clubs.) At Toulouse, the moderate lawyers and entrepreneurs who had wrested control of civic affairs from the old elitists of sword, robe, and miter had by 1793 compassed a thoroughgoing overhaul of old regime institutions.[103] At Bordeaux, the citizens securely established in the hierarchies of trade and the law were now enjoying the full status recognition and political clout that they had so coveted in prerevolutionary times. As of the mid-1790s, their middle-class values prescribed the preservation of the revolutionary status quo as reflected in political stability, flourishing local businesses, and vigorous international trade.[104] At Lyon, a certain nascent bourgeois class-consciousness emerged in 1792 and 1793. Affluent and "respectable" Lyonnais, no longer divided among themselves by juridical status distinctions, and facing the perceived challenge of democratic demands from silk weavers and other "proletarians," came together in a concerted defense of the political powers now officially reserved to bourgeois of property, the professions, and commerce.[105] Both at Caen in coastal Normandy and at Limoges in the west-central province of Limousin, merchants and craftsmen dominated local politics from 1791 on, and there are some signs that political evolution was favoring a shift of influence within the commercial bourgeoisie toward its less affluent members.[106] Meanwhile, Marseilles seems to have witnessed the ascendancy, by 1793, of bourgeois of various kinds, merchants of moderate income, school instructors, members of the legal professions – of, that is, "the middle-ranking group of articulate and educated individuals" solidly installed in the sectional organizations of the municipal regime.[107] And so it went, all over France. However the process might vary from community to community, the general impression we derive from the pertinent local research is of the "down-shifting" of influence from the noble-dominated elites of the

103 Lyons, *Revolution in Toulouse*, p. 39.
104 Forrest, *Society and Politics in Revolutionary Bordeaux*, pp. 253, 159–60.
105 Edmonds, *Jacobinism and the Revolt of Lyon*, pp. 134–35.
106 Hanson, *Provincial Politics in the French Revolution*, p. 212.
107 Scott, *Terror and Repression in Revolutionary Marseilles*, pp. 101–4.

ancien régime to more middling strata of professionals and entrepreneurs. (In smaller towns and villages, an analogous process transferred power from seigneurs to affluent peasants and their advocates in law and administration.)

The news of an all-out French commitment to European war exploded upon all these local urban and rural scenes early in 1793. This posed, for all localities, a painful choice between accepting (however reluctantly) or rejecting the taxes, conscription, and other demands of a government at Paris grown ever more bureaucratic, impersonal, and intrusive. In the end, most communities fell in line with Jacobin wishes at Paris; but for many of them it must have been the lesser of two evils. Patently, something more basic than the purging of twenty-nine leading Girondists from the Convention was involved here, however much consternation the news of the Parisian uprising of 31 May–2 June and its aftermath may have caused across the nation. The insurrection in the capital did not so much cause outrage in the provinces, Bill Edmonds has written, as serve "as a convenient justification for resistance to Jacobin centralism which was gathering force anyway." But, as Edmonds has suggested perceptively in an article on the "federalist" movements of 1793, most cities and towns knew where to draw the line when it came to opposing the will of Paris, and could even make their endorsement of the Jacobins' war pay local dividends. The "shape of the emerging Montagnard dictatorship" may have been "abhorrent to those who had embraced (and profited by) the system of government established between 1789 and 1791." And the federalist threat was extensive precisely because this "abhorrence" was itself widespread. "But in the final analysis, faced with the risks of civil war, invasion, and counterrevolution, the provincial bourgeoisie abandoned its political principles. Acquiescence in Montagnard centralism at least offered the possibility that direct Parisian intervention in local affairs could be avoided and the local predominance of the *notables* maintained largely intact."[108] By choosing the politic path of cooperation with Paris, most communities in 1793 avoided the horrors of repression visited by wrathful government emissaries upon rebellious cities like Marseilles, Lyon, and Toulon.[109]

What, then, drove some citizens – most notably, those of the three last-named communities – to take the fatal step of open military revolt against Paris? Again, Edmonds has provided a valuable insight by suggesting that "only where 'federalism' appeared in a context of deep-rooted local political violence and instability did serious revolts follow." Where prolonged

---

108 See Edmonds, "Federalism and Urban Revolt in France in 1793," *Journal of Modern History* 55 (1983): pp. 22–53.

109 For a different explanation of the "federalist" phenomenon of 1793, see Hanson, *Provincial Politics in the French Revolution*, pp. 235–38, 246–47. Hanson's explanation keys more upon local "environmental" (social and cultural) factors.

periods of conflict and agitation had left plebeian loyalties significantly divided between local Jacobins and their less radical opponents, and left the "men of property" with but a tenuous grip on power, the impact of the central government's war taxation and conscription could be translated into an anti-Jacobin fervor that temporarily united moderate bourgeois and *menu peuple* against local militants and their allies from Paris. "Federalist" revolt, in such situations, was a result of insecure notables fending off Jacobin opponents and finding at least some support for doing so from skilled artisans, shopkeepers, and manual laborers who were alienated by adverse local conditions from the Jacobin-dominated government at Paris. Hence the antigovernment uprisings – occurring at a time of maximum national peril – at Lyon, Marseilles, and Toulon. At Bordeaux, things very nearly came to the same pass.[110]

In all citadels of urban France, whether of "federalist" inclination or not, the war was unmistakably *the* preeminent issue in 1793–94. As early as May 1793, those Bordelais who were still thinking of resisting the desires of Paris heard unnerving reports of Spanish troops crossing into France and menacing the town of Bayonne. And panic spread in the department of the Gironde, for instance, over rumors "that 40,000 English troops had disembarked at La Teste on the Bassin d'Arcachon."[111] Small wonder, perhaps, that Bordeaux in the end remained "patriotic." At Marseilles, we learn unequivocally, the Terror "was principally a means of national defense – the immense military effort of a city which was decidedly anti-militaristic." The "rich egoists" there had willy-nilly to adopt "a more realistic assessment of their interests than they had shown in their involvement in the federalist revolt – interests which hardly would be served by the English at Toulon or the Prussians at Paris."[112] The Committee of Public Safety's draconian treatment of formerly "federalist" Lyon during the period from October 1793 to July 1794 reflected in part Parisian perceptions of pervasive Lyonnais corruption; but the committee's paramount concern "was to deter further revolt at a time of continuing military crisis."[113] At Toulouse, the progress of the Revolution through the Terror "followed the progress of French arms in the Pyrenees." The city's "revolutionary surveillance committee" was set up "to spur on the recruiting drive in March 1793." The guillotine was first erected permanently there "after the anti-conscription

110 Refer again to Edmonds, "Federalism and Urban Revolt in France," esp. pp. 52–53. In addition to the works cited above, see M. H. Crook, "Federalism and the French Revolution: The Revolt of Toulon in 1793," *History* 65 (1980): 383–97; and Colin Lucas, *The Structure of the Terror: The Example of Javogues and the Loire* (New York: Oxford University Press, 1973).
111 Forrest, *Society and Politics in Revolutionary Bordeaux*, pp. 113–14.
112 Scott, *Terror and Repression in Revolutionary Marseilles*, pp. 344–45.
113 Edmonds, *Jacobinism and the Revolt of Lyon*, pp. 282–83.

riots of September 1793 had frightened the municipal authorities into repressive action." Harsh treatment meted out to the local clergy mirrored in part a "popular identification of the enemy with the most superstitious beliefs of traditional Catholicism." And the relaxation of the Terror at Toulouse – as elsewhere – responded directly to the improved military situation.[114] The evidence, again and again, points to an urban experience of government-orchestrated "terror" whose undeniable social, economic, and cultural aspects were necessarily subordinated to the requirements of diplomacy and war.

In rural France, too, the Terror above all meant an unheard-of assertion of central government concerns – concerns ineluctably centered around the war. In this connection, it is significant to find two specialists concluding, in a general fashion, that the antigovernment violence in rural Brittany known as *chouannerie* resulted from "traumatic" disruptions in the "balance of power" inside individual communities caused by intrusive Parisian revolutionaries and their local allies. The *chouans* could perceive all too clearly that the Revolution spelled an end to the old regime's tolerance of self-government in most local affairs and naturally tried to turn the "moral unity of the community" against all proponents of integration into national revolutionary politics.[115] In a very real sense, this kind of "political/ sociological" interpretation of antigovernment, counterrevolutionary agitation could be extended to the Vendée region on Brittany's southern flank, as well as to the Massif Central and other areas in the South.[116] "It hardly needs repeating," one historian has remarked, that "the Revolution was ... chiefly a centralizing and modernizing phenomenon centred in the towns; its consequences were most traumatic in the countryside."[117]

But, again, if the general question in rural France was one of rallying to or against the disputed banner of novel government interference in people's daily lives, the specific issue providing the sharp edge to the debate was the issue of war. "In practical terms," P. M. Jones has written, "it was the war emergency consequent upon the formation of the First Coalition during the spring of 1793 that brought the Terror to every peasant's doorstep." The ordinance of 24 February summoning three hundred thousand men to the colors was followed up by the *levée en masse* of August: one recruitment drive gave way to another, and parliamentary *commissaires*

---

114 Lyons, *Revolution in Toulouse*, pp. 131–33.
115 See T. J. A. Le Goff and D. M. G. Sutherland, "The Revolution and the Rural Community in Eighteenth-Century Brittany," *Past and Present* 62 (1974): 96–119.
116 The literature (up to 1968) on the uprisings in the Vendée is reviewed in Harvey Mitchell, "The Vendée and Counterrevolution: A Review Essay," *French Historical Studies* 5 (1968): 405–29.
117 Harvey Mitchell, "Resistance to the Revolution in Western France," *Past and Present* 63 (1974): 122.

and (eventually) "representatives on mission" used the opportunity presented to "give provincials an elementary lesson in republican politics." This turned out in many cases to be too much for rustic Frenchmen, whose accumulating grievances against Paris overflowed when they had to face the hateful prospect of being dragooned into combat against other Europeans. "In Burgundy, in the Massif Central, in parts of the South West, in Brittany, and more generally throughout the West," Jones has observed, "a mood of exasperation prevailed. It was as though the issue of whether or not to fight for the republic had brought to the boil a host of simmering discontents." When the youths of Beaune and Arnay-sur-Arroux, of Autun and Dijon, and of hundreds of other communities cried out that those benefiting most handsomely from the Revolution – Jacobin clubbists, public officials, buyers of *biens nationaux* – should be the first to march to the frontiers, they were forcefully personalizing the cutting geopolitical issue that had impelled the revolutionary process forward from the start.[118]

And so the massive war effort of these years was pivotal in defining the nature of political relations between Paris and the provinces – which is to say in forging (at least for the time being) new chains of dependency linking the outlying regions of the nation to the revolutionary center. Once successful, however, that same military effort, which had imposed unprecedented demands upon Frenchmen (and Frenchwomen) of all walks of life and in all places, was just as likely to lead to an unraveling of the extraordinary coalition of middle- and working-class citizens that it had called into being in the first place. To put it somewhat simplistically: the great French victory at Fleurus in Belgium on 26 June 1794 opened the way for Robespierre's overthrow a month later and for the more gradual but also more comprehensive relaxation of wartime controls known conventionally as the "Thermidorian Reaction."

There are, essentially, two points we should underscore here: one deals with the erosion of "bourgeois" support for Maximilien Robespierre and his closest confidants in the Committee of Public Safety and the Convention; the other deals with the breakdown of the alliance between the revolutionary leaders and the Parisian *sans-culottes*. To revisit each issue even briefly is to reaffirm the inescapable centrality of the war.

Too much has probably been made of the role played in this critical phase of the Revolution by Robespierre.[119] Outstanding spokesman though he

---

118 For these citations, see Jones, *The Peasantry in the French Revolution*, pp. 207, 223–24.

119 The literature on the "Incorruptible" is, of course, vast. For the American reader, these English-language works should prove especially helpful: J. M. Thompson, *Robespierre and the French Revolution* (New York: Collier Books, 1962); Norman Hampson, *The Life and Opinions of Maximilien Robespierre* (London: Duckworth, 1974); George Rudé, *Robespierre: Portrait of a Revolutionary Democrat* (New York: Viking Press, 1976); and David P. Jordan, *The Revolutionary Career of Maximilien Robespierre* (New York: Free Press, 1985).

undoubtedly was for one early experiment in political democracy in the Western world, Robespierre was only one member of an executive committee (and of a much larger Convention) whose collective effort staunched the military bleeding of 1793 and made the victories of the following year possible. When, in the spring and summer of 1794, the assertion of French arms abroad (and the suppression of the last vestiges of counterrevolutionary insurrection at home) made it safe to quarrel in the governing committees and in the Convention over the excesses of the Terror, there was really no philosophy or argument that could justify sustaining those sanguinary excesses – or the politicians most persistently identified with them. There was certainly nothing in the nature of a "personality cult" that could have indefinitely focused Jacobin loyalties upon, say, a clique of "Robespierrists." Nor could even so terrifyingly idealistic a Jacobin as Saint-Just have seen in dictatorship a permanent solution to constitutional problems in France. Even after Ventôse, the Robespierrists (if we can even assume the temporary existence of such a group) did not regard themselves as "absolute" in any lasting *legal* sense. Of course, Robespierre may have wanted the Terror to last until democracy was securely founded; but "most people considered its usefulness over when the Allies were defeated."[120] Now that France appeared to be safely on the offensive on all military fronts, the former bureaucrats, lawyers, and entrepreneurs of the Convention wished to get back to legislative and economic business-as-usual. Not for them Robespierre's moralistic and democratic dreams; and his attempt to threaten them over the realization of those dreams only hastened his downfall.

The war was also critical in first requiring and then undercutting the collaboration between the "bourgeois" revolutionaries and the artisans and shopkeepers of the capital. The contradictions built into that collaboration were, in part, economic, involving tensions between the propertied and propertyless, between capital and labor, between producers and consumers. The contradictions were also gendered: activist *sans-jupons* could find themselves at odds with their male counterparts as well as (more and more) with bourgeois politicians. Most telling, however, were the *political* strains in this alliance. The *sans-culottes* recognized up to a point that to prosecute the war and crush "federalism" and *chouannerie* required centralized and authoritarian governance. Simultaneously, however, they tended to favor precisely what the government-at-war could not tolerate: a "popular," decentralized, direct politics. The *sans-culottes*, prepared for a government that would wage war on foreign and domestic foes, were not adequately prepared for a belligerent government that, in the end, would also oblige *them* to "toe the line."[121]

120 Palmer, *Twelve Who Ruled*, pp. 361–62.
121 For the classic scholarly account of economic and political contradictions within the *sans-culotte* movement at Paris, see Albert Soboul, *The Sans-Culottes: The Popular Movement and Revolutionary Government 1793–94*, trans. Rémy Inglis Hall (Princeton,

The prosecution of the war weakened the *sans-culottes* in more insidious ways as well, thus helping to deprive the radical Jacobins of crucial popular support in the first half of 1794. For one thing, plebeian militants given jobs in the swelling ranks of officialdom became little more than docile instruments of authority, while the activism of their sectional organizations was curtailed by the burgeoning demands of national defense. Thus, the spontaneity and militant mentality of the masses atrophied; the energy and enthusiasm of the sections and streets were transferred to the state's bureaux and armies, and were applied to duties discharged at the behest of the authoritarian government. Then, again, the waging of the war deprived the leading militants of many of their natural adherents: young apprentices and shop workers who were inclined to action in domestic politics, but who also saw defending the nation as their most pressing civic duty. Conscription thereby depleted the ranks and attenuated the revolutionary ardor of the popular movement.[122] These dynamics were presumably at work in other major cities as well during this period; but it was naturally in Paris that they operated most directly to undermine the popular basis of the Revolutionary Government of the Year II.

And so the "international mission" of the French, rooted in three centuries of the ancien régime and at the same time instrumental in its collapse, had by 1794 (and by a similar historical logic) both contributed to and set limits upon the succeeding era of revolution. The reversion to the historic ways of war thrust state power into the hands of men who dreamed bold dreams of cultural and social innovation, of public welfare as well as of private enrichment. In the long run, however, the insatiate demands of war engulfed the humanitarian aspirations and the very lives of these men, exhausted their humble supporters in the ranks of the *sans-culotterie*, and (in Thermidor, Year II) placed the victorious state in the hands of middle-class Frenchmen with a less visionary agenda. In the period extending from 1794 to 1799, these last-named citizens would endeavor to stabilize the Revolution on a basis of sociopolitical compromise; but would they prove any more successful than their royalist and revolutionary predecessors at managing the furies unleashed by war?

N.J.: Princeton University Press, 1980). On the question of gendered tensions within the movement – and, more generally, on women's participation in popular politics in revolutionary Paris, refer (initially) to Harriet B. Applewhite and Darline G. Levy, eds., *Women and Politics in the Age of the Democratic Revolution* (Ann Arbor: University of Michigan Press, 1990).

122 On all of this, refer again to Soboul, *The Sans-Culottes*, esp. pp. 260–62.

5

The second attempt to stabilize the
Revolution: from 1794 to 1799

If the impact of the October Days of 1789 upon the revolutionary process in France has sometimes been exaggerated, much the same may be said of 9 Thermidor, Year II (27 July 1794). Granted, Robespierre's downfall was important in that it signaled the start of a drastic turnabout in the government's policy of political and economic "terror." It is also safe to conclude in hindsight that the execution of the "Robespierrists" dashed any prospects for the realization of the most millenarian social, economic, and cultural reforms envisioned by the Jacobins and their *sans-culotte* allies. Still, when we contemplate the Revolution in its larger, global-historical setting, Thermidor seems to be but a halting place on a road marked from beginning to end by the crushing continuity of *war* and all its attending circumstances. And in fact an analysis of the five years or so running from the end of the Terror to the Bonapartist coup d'état of November 1799 drives this point home with added force by showing us a revolution ultimately consumed in the blaze of an unprecedented international conflict.

The following pages commence with a brief synopsis of events. Turning then to analysis, the chapter will first reappraise the interactions between an ever more aggressive and globally oriented France and the other European Powers. The discussion will then take up the most important domestic policies of the French government in this period and show how those policies at times exposed enduring tensions between the state's ambitions and the idealism and socioeconomic interests of the Revolution. Finally, Chapter 5 will reassess the attempt by the revolutionaries of 1794–99 to institutionalize "liberal" or contestatory politics and show how that enterprise foundered in the end on the shoals of international war and discredited domestic governance.

With the executions of Robespierre and over one hundred other "terrorists" in late July 1794, politics in France lurched back toward the Center (the "Thermidorian Reaction"). The powers of the Committee of Public Safety, the Revolutionary Tribunal, the "surveillance committees" in the communes and sections, and other institutions of the Terror were curtailed. Before year's end, the Paris Jacobin Club had been shut down and its sister societies in the provinces hobbled or silenced; some Girondists had been readmitted to the Convention; thousands of prisoners had been released from detention; and wage and price controls (the *Maximum*) had been rescinded. (Interestingly, the government also moved at this time to separate Church and State: complete freedom of worship was decreed on 21 February 1795.) A general deterioration of economic conditions helped set off the huge but disorganized *sans-culotte* uprisings of April and May 1795 (the "days" of *Germinal-Prairial*) in the capital; they led to a systematic disarming of the Paris sections by the authorities.

But the Thermidorian leaders soon had to face an even more dangerous challenge on the Far Right. The problem, at least for the time being, did not involve foreign affairs: by making peace in 1795 with Prussia (in March), the Dutch (in May), and Spain (in July), the Republic dislocated the Allied war effort and won a new prominence in Europe. At home, however, a murderous "White Terror" broke out in the South; royalists assassinated ex-terrorists in other regions as well; and the death in captivity of the child-king "Louis XVII" in June 1795 enabled the comte de Provence to proclaim himself Louis XVIII and serve henceforth as rallying point for the counterrevolution. At Paris, the Convention enacted the Constitution of the Year III on 22 August; but its insistence upon ensuring its own members at least two-thirds of the seats in the projected new (bicameral) legislature touched off a royalist insurrection in the capital. The uprising of *Vendémiaire* (October 1795) was, however, dispersed (with Bonaparte's "whiff of grapeshot"), and the Convention was able to give way peacefully to the new regime (Directory) on 26 October 1795.

Over the next four years, the Directory tried to stabilize conditions within a republican France. Yet, at least into 1798, it probably scored its most signal successes beyond the country's borders. The Directory sent armies into central Europe, set up a chain of sister republics stretching from Holland to the Italian peninsula, made peace temporarily with Austria at Campo Formio in October 1797, and by 1798 would be sending Bonaparte and an armada of soldiers and scientists to Egypt. Nevertheless, at home political and economic problems persisted. Playing a *jeu de bascule* that would characterize French politics to the end of the decade, the government struck out at "Gracchus" Babeuf and his far leftist "Conspiracy of Equals" in the spring of 1796, then purged nearly two hundred rightist deputies and two Directors in Fructidor, Year V (September 1797), and then in Floréal, Year VI (May 1798) purged leftist deputies and locally elected officials. Revolutionary decrees against émigrés and "non-juring" clergy remained in force, though the vigor with which they were applied depended upon the pendulum swings of French politics. Meanwhile, the government by 1797 was forced to replace its depreciated and discredited paper currency with metallic currency, and attempted with its "two-thirds bankruptcy" and with a revamped system of taxation to reconstruct its finances upon a sounder basis.

In the end, however, the Directory fell victim to a conjuncture of international and domestic crises. French aggression in Europe and the Near East led to the creation, in 1798–99, of a Second Coalition whose members included Great Britain, Austria, Russia, and Turkey. By the summer of 1799, the Republic's armies had been driven out of most of Italy, and France itself faced the prospect of invasion. A logical domestic corollary of these developments was a revival of patriotic Jacobinism. In the coup of Prairial, Year VII (June 1799), the newly elected Director abbé Siéyès collaborated with the legislative councils to replace the other four Directors with men who were determined to preserve the Revolution. Siéyès's desire to "stabilize" the Revolution upon the basis of a strengthened executive was one of the key antecedents to the coup d'état of 18–19 Brumaire (9–10 November 1799). Masséna's defeat of the Russians at the Second Battle of Zurich (25–27 September), however important in relieving the pressures upon France, and in fact in presaging the collapse of the Second Coalition, came too late to save the Directory. Bonaparte, who managed to slip back into France from Egypt, conspired with Siéyès and several other politicians to make the coup of Brumaire and, using it to seize power for himself, proved to be its ultimate beneficiary. Revolutionary France thus gave way to Napoleonic France.

"LA GRANDE NATION" ON THE MARCH

European affairs in the middle and late 1790s were, arguably, dominated by three interlocking realities: the dynamism of an ever less "idealistic" and ever more predatory France, the undiminished centrality of Russia to eastern continental politics, and Great Britain's ongoing pursuit of a balance of power on the Continent and of preeminence in the world beyond it. The renascent dynamism of France in part contributed to, and in part profited from, the breakup of the First Coalition. But the continuing advance of the French into the heart of Europe eventually prompted the formation of the Second Coalition of opposing European states. It was in the midst of the resulting international struggle, vaster than any war Europe had heretofore witnessed, that General Bonaparte seized power in France, effectively ending the Revolution.

In the National Convention's final year (1794–95), the revolutionaries dropped all thoughts of defensive strategy and moved unabashedly onto the offensive. Fleurus (26 June 1794) was an especially crucial battlefield triumph in that it definitively removed long-standing enemy pressure on the northeastern borders and heralded a reversion to historic French aggression in the Low Countries. Scarcely less significant, however, were victories in late 1794 on other fronts: those successes allowed the Republic's armies to carry the war eastward into the German Rhineland, south-eastward against Piedmont-Sardinia in Italy, and south across the Pyrenees into Spain.[1]

Savoring the intoxicating wine of such successes, France's Thermidorian leaders unsurprisingly seized the opportunity to proclaim to the world that their country "was back." Rumors of peace prompted government spokesman Merlin de Douai to outline in the Convention on 4 December a foreign policy boding trouble for the rest of Europe. Yes, said Merlin, his compatriots wanted peace, "but we want [a peace] guaranteed by our own power and the powerlessness of our enemies ever to harm us." Clearly, the time had not yet come to beat swords back into plowshares.

No, Frenchmen, no! You...have not advanced so rapidly in this glorious career to halt at the moment when the goal is in sight....Soon we will prove, by new efforts and new triumphs, that we also desire peace, but a peace worthy of our intrepid defenders....When the French people no longer regard the war as necessary either to appease their wounded dignity or to guarantee themselves against new perfidies, then only will they rein in the steeds of victory, then only will they command peace.

The day after these words had rung out in a wildly applauding Convention, the deputies ordered that Merlin's speech be translated into "every tongue" and relayed to all the armies and all communes. Equally revealing was the fact that the rumors of imminent peace were slightingly ascribed (by delegate André Dumont) to surviving "Robespierrists."[2]

Additional signs of waxing French ambitions were not lacking. A German diplomatic agent, reporting back to his home government in the Rhineland after a stay of several months at Paris, warned in December that a majority in the Convention favored continuation of the war and stated that French war aims "were of such a nature that France's enemies could not possibly subscribe thereto." Even more telling (because more specific) were remarks made in the Convention at the end of January 1795. Speaking in the name of the Thermidorian Committee of Public Safety, Boissy d'Anglas declared that the Republic's imperative need for

---

1 For a useful review of all these issues, see Steven T. Ross, *Quest for Victory: French Military Strategy, 1792–1799* (New York: A. S. Barnes, 1973).
2 Biro, *The German Policy of Revolutionary France*, 2:262–63.

indemnities and for a durable peace securing it from "all invasion...for a long series of centuries" would compel it to wage war to attain French boundaries designated by "Nature." Another deputy, Léonard Bourdon, reacting to this rodomontade, praised Boissy as courageous for having said, "in the midst of the prosperity of our arms...that we have fought only for our liberty, that we will confine ourselves within the limits that Nature has prescribed." Sydney Biro is probably correct to infer from these speeches that there were already legislators who envisioned the extension of French power *beyond* the supposedly "natural" boundaries of the Rhine, the Alps, and the Pyrenees.[3] Soon, French cavalry would be riding into Amsterdam on the ice; French administrators would be following victorious soldiers into the wonderland of petty principalities in the Rhineland; and a youthful Bonaparte, at the behest of the government at Paris, would be poring over topographical maps of a yet-to-be-invaded Italy. Realpolitik would drown out the "new diplomacy," and the men of the "new" France, even as their country became ever more predatory, would find themselves irretrievably "enmeshed in the diplomatic imbroglios of old."[4]

Not all of this was immediately apparent in the year or so after the French breakthrough at Fleurus. What did become increasingly obvious by 1795, nonetheless, was that the Republic's multiplying victories were subjecting the First Coalition to severe strains. Before the year was out, in fact, three key players – Prussia, Spain, and the United Provinces – had dropped out of the anti-French alliance, leaving Great Britain and Austria more or less to "go it alone" against the strategists at Paris.

Yet more was involved here than the martial accomplishments of the French, however impressive they might be. Paris could take much comfort – and, in the end, would benefit mightily – from the inability of the countries in the First Coalition to subordinate their own selfish interests to the common cause of defeating revolutionary France. In the eastern marches of Europe, Catherine's Russia was positioned as always to play the feuding "Teutonic" states of Prussia and Austria off each other even as it dutifully paid lip service to the ideological crusade against the barbarous regicides of France. To the west there was, as ever, the other "flanking state" of

---

3 For these incidents, refer again to ibid. For a vigorous critique of the "natural frontiers" concept as a motivating force in French foreign policy, consult Gaston Zeller, "La Monarchie d'Ancien Régime et les frontières naturelles," *Revue d'histoire moderne* 8 (1933): 305–33. The concept has been partially rehabilitated by Peter Sahlins, "Natural Frontiers Revisited: France's Boundaries since the Seventeenth Century," *American Historical Review* 95 (1990): 1423–51.

4 Linda Frey and Marsha Frey, " 'The Reign of the Charlatans Is Over': The French Revolutionary Attack on Diplomatic Practice,'" *Journal of Modern History* 65 (1993): esp. 742–43. Or, as Biro has put it: "The enlightened propaganda that once aspired to introduce a better world became the instrument of a lust for conquest as insatiable as that which ever emerged from a royal chancellery." Biro, *The German Policy of Revolutionary France*, 2:479–80.

Europe, Great Britain, and the British would find their calls for a sustained Coalition unity falling upon deaf continental ears even as they themselves were distracted at times from continental affairs by developments in the vast world beyond Europe. The French, needless to add, would be more than happy to rush into the geopolitical vacuum created by the unraveling of the First Coalition.

From the start, Catherine's transparent designs upon what was left of Poland after the Second Partition of 1793 functioned as a "wedge issue" between the Austrians and the Prussians. It distracted them from their concerted military campaign against the French and induced Berlin in particular to redeploy a significant portion of its striking forces from West to East after the 1792–93 campaigns. (This largely explains why there was no effective Prussian effort against the French through most of 1794.) By March 1795, Prussia would be abandoning its Austrian confederate altogether, making peace at Basle with the regicide Republic. Even before that came to pass, however, the Third Partition of Poland (in January 1795) had effected a final division of that hapless country among its three rapacious neighbors. At the same time, secret conversations dealt with the ulterior ambitions of two of those "neighbors." St. Petersburg and Vienna agreed that, should Austria not recover its Belgian provinces from France, it might be compensated with Bavaria, or with Venetian territories. Moreover, the Russians and Austrians once again pledged, when the time should prove right, to partition Turkey's European holdings along lines proposed thirteen years earlier by Catherine and Joseph II. In other words, such arrangements "tacitly conceded the aggrandisement of France while envisaging a restoration of equilibrium by reciprocal compensations for the other continental powers."[5] Yet behind all talk of a "restoration of equilibrium" and "reciprocal compensations" to be realized on the Continent at this time lay the fundamental ascendancy of Russia in the East, paralleling that of France in the West. And these realities do much to explain both the final demise of the First Coalition and the determination of the British and the Austrians to fight on, with or without their erstwhile allies, against the French.

Historians have often contended that the secret provisions attached to the Third Polish Partition by Vienna and St. Petersburg were defective. They *were* defective – in a way that suggested Austria's continuing vulnerability in central Europe and weakness vis-à-vis Russia. The nub of the matter was that any ulterior gains for Vienna envisioned at this juncture – whether in the Low Countries, southern Germany, or northeastern Italy – were bound to antagonize one or more of the other major powers. Habsburg recovery of Belgium would be at French expense, given Fleurus and its aftermath, and so would likely prove costly in military terms.

5 Bruun, "The Balance of Power during the Wars," pp. 255–56.

On the other hand, any decision at Vienna to cede Belgium to the French in return for Bavaria would not only alienate the British, permanently opposed as they were to any growth of French influence in the Low Countries, but would also alarm the small German states suspicious of Habsburg designs in south Germany. (And, naturally, Prussia would be only too eager to profit from the latter circumstance!) Finally, any Austrian attempt to annex Venetian territories could lead to a new confrontation with the French in Italy. (As we have seen, by 1795 Thermidorian geopoliticians were already mooting plans to invade Italy.) It was all very well, then, for Catherine II to pledge to use "all means in her power" to help the Austrians win additional compensation "at the expense of France, of the Venetian Republic, or elsewhere." Such compensation – if obtainable at all – would be primarily an Austrian rather than a Russian problem; and in the meantime, Catherine's largely meaningless verbal commitment was bought at the cost of continued Habsburg adherence to the tsarina's pet project, the "Greek Project" in the Turkish Balkans.[6]

That Catherine held the whip hand in the Austro-Russian relationship was due in considerable measure, as it always had been, to the secular Austro-Prussian rivalry in Germany. Significantly, in this connection, the Russian ministers handling the negotiations associated with the Third Polish Partition could bluntly warn their Austrian counterpart, Cobenzl, that any hesitation on his part to deal forthrightly with them would speedily result in new Russo-Prussian conversations.[7] Thus, even while helping to work out a final division of Polish territories that awarded the Habsburg monarchy West Galicia, an area almost as large as Bohemia, the Russians reaffirmed their paramount influence in the harsh affairs of interior Europe. They knew all too well that for the Austrians, concerned as they must ever be with Prussian moves in central Europe as well as with French aggression to the west and south, freedom of diplomatic maneuver was limited. Russia could therefore logically relish the prospect of dragging Vienna into yet one more war with Turkey and, as a result, carving out an expanded sphere of influence in the Balkans. Pending that major development, in 1796 "Catherine and her latest lover, Platon Zubov, embarked on an even more grandiose scheme – the 'Oriental Project,' designed to give Russia political and commercial domination of the entire region between Turkey and Tibet."[8] The tsarina's death put an end to that project, even as a Russian force was being assembled in the Caucasus for an invasion of Persia; yet Catherine's demise would not noticeably diminish Russia's ability to manipulate affairs in eastern Europe.

6 On all of this, see again Roider, *Baron Thugut and Austria's Response to the French Revolution*, esp. pp. 170–71.
7 Ibid., p. 172.
8 Blanning, *The Origins of the French Revolutionary Wars*, p. 187.

Although Russia's undiminished ability to play Vienna and Berlin off against each other was evident in the brutal partition politics of 1795, it figured as well in related developments to the west. We have already seen that Prussia's flagging enthusiasm for the campaign against revolutionary France was directly linked to its growing anxiety over Russian (and, possibly, Austrian?) designs on Poland. The upshot of this in the West was that France was able to detach Prussia (and then, in short order, the Spanish and Dutch) from the First Coalition. The Treaty of Basle, concluded between Barthélémy and Hardenburg in March 1795, established Prussian neutrality, created a "neutral zone" in northern Germany in which the Hohenzollern state might eventually make territorial gains, and solidified France's hold upon the Left Bank of the Rhine. This last provision in turn assured French mastery over the Dutch. French cavalry had already marched into Amsterdam; only the diplomatic niceties required completion, and that came later in 1795. "At the Hague, Reubell and Siéyès negotiated an offensive and defensive alliance with the Dutch, which condemned them to pay an indemnity of one hundred million florins. . . . Holland was further asked to support a French army of 25,000 men, and to yield all her territory south of the Meuse. Dutch naval strength was now at the disposal of Britain's enemies." Spain, too, would soon be compelled to drop out of the war; indeed, the Treaty of San Ildefonso would revive the old Franco-Spanish alliance and (at least in theory) add Spanish naval forces to those of the French and Dutch.[9]

Before the end of 1795, consequently, Austria was left practically alone on the Continent to face the rising power of revolutionary France. The Habsburgs received verbal support (but little else) from a Russia increasingly beguiled by extra-European aspirations, and financial support (but little else) from a Britain similarly distracted by interests beyond Europe.[10] Why, then, did Vienna continue to deploy armies against Paris? Austrian resolve to persist in the war was stiffened in part by what Vienna saw as the unsatisfactory aftermath of the Polish Partition talks. As we noted above, those talks pointed to the Low Countries, southern Germany, or Italy as areas for future Austrian military activity, and in two of those three regions, French interests would have to be confronted. But it is only fair to observe that, for Habsburg statesmen, greater issues were also involved. Austrian Chancellor Thugut "would not seek peace," a recent

9 The French negotiations with Prussia, the United Provinces, and Spain are usefully recapitulated in Martyn Lyons, *France under the Directory* (Cambridge: Cambridge University Press, 1975), pp. 192–94. Refer also to Bruun, "The Balance of Power during the Wars," pp. 255–56.

10 The limited and selfish nature of British support for Vienna is a major theme in Paul W. Schroeder, *The Transformation of European Politics 1763–1848* (Oxford: Oxford University Press, 1994).

biographer has aptly written, "because ... he had changed none of his views of revolutionary France. It was still a dangerous force that threatened to destroy the social and political fabric of Europe. In fact, it mystified him that the Prussians, regardless of their feelings toward Austria or toward him, still did not comprehend the true danger of revolutionary France." Reacting to intelligence from Berlin that the Prussians no longer feared the Revolution, Thugut "expressed bewilderment that they could be so blind."[11] None of this, it is true, should lead us to overlook the very real statist ambitions at Vienna that served at all times as accompaniment to Austrian concerns about "balance of power" and sociopolitical stability in Europe. Even so, Thugut's larger vision of the geostrategic and sociopolitical threat posed to Europe by a French Revolution triumphantly on the march displayed considerable realism; it was not grounded solely in Austria's specific strategic interests.

If the shift in geopolitical fortunes in 1794 and 1795 left the Austrians determined to stay in the field against the French, the British were left similarly disposed, although for somewhat different reasons. London's European and global situation in the 1790s was paradoxical. On the one hand, the British, who even before 1789 had scored stunning successes in the world of commerce and colonies and had left the "defeat" of the American War far behind, found conditions in the extra-European theater even more propitious in the years after 1789. We have already seen this to have been the case in the early 1790s; and nothing in this regard would change fundamentally during the remainder of the decade. Pitt's government, for example, reacted to the latest Franco-Spanish-Dutch alliance by smashing the Spanish navy off Cape St. Vincent and blockading what remained of it in Cadiz, and by virtually destroying the Dutch naval forces at Camperdown. Naturally enough, London followed up these resounding victories by seizing vital Dutch and Spanish colonies in the West and East Indies, at Africa's Cape of Good Hope, off India (Dutch Ceylon), and elsewhere. The English were also poised to deprive the French of their most valuable West Indian colonies, and thus to disrupt the colonial-domestic trade exchanges through France's western ports.[12] Moreover, losses of colonies and of commerce could have broader economic implications. The most percipient observers could see that England, by using its supremacy at sea to dislocate continental commerce, could thereby damage key continental industries as well. Significantly, French industrial output collapsed during these years, and as late as 1800, according to one set of calculations, amounted to only 60 percent of what it had been before 1789. The roots of this disaster were

11 Roider, *Baron Thugut and Austria's Response to the French Revolution*, pp. 181–82.
12 On all of this, see Kennedy, *The Rise and Fall of the Great Powers*, pp. 123–24; and Lyons, *France under the Directory*, pp. 192–94.

complex, but the interruptions of French foreign trade (owing not only to London's blockade but also to the closing of continental markets inimical to France) were a pivotal factor.[13] Meanwhile, out in India, "only . . . French military adventurers survived to trouble the English," and they could do little to disrupt Indian markets for the goods being produced in a rapidly industrializing England.[14]

This, then, was assuredly one side of the strategic-economic coin for the British. Profiting from the preoccupation of France and its allies with continental affairs, London could tap into the markets and raw materials of the extra-European world and thus further develop its own economic (and strategic) resources. On the other hand, there is reason to question whether Britain's preeminent role in regions *beyond* Europe, however impressive in itself, could adequately compensate for France's growing power *within* Europe.[15] This was, of course, the paramount issue – and must have been for *any* government at London. The British were still facing their permanent strategic nightmare: the prospect of an adversary's achieving hegemony on the Continent and then threatening to marshal all continental resources to defeat them in their own (maritime) element. In this case, the collapse of the First Coalition in 1795 seemed to leave Pitt's ministry with little choice but to continue subsidizing Austria and hope for some dramatic turn of events in Europe. "There was no consistent 'right' policy for a British government to pursue," Piers Mackesy has put it. "Only coalition warfare in Europe could lead to a decisive victory and the checking of France's overweening power; and only during a coalition war could Britain hope to maintain a military front in western Europe. Without major allies she could pursue no independent strategy of her own in the European heartland." For the foreseeable future, the British could do little but react in opportunistic fashion to the "shifting continental situation" and hope for new developments that could somehow produce a new combination of European powers to fight the French.[16]

As it turned out, those "new" developments were not long in coming, and they derived from a traditional quarter: unremitting French aggression that appeared to portend a Gallic domination of much of Europe. There was, in fact, no real letup in the message of expansionism emanating from Paris. Even in the waning days of the Convention in October 1795, Merlin de Douai was insisting that "there is no one among us who does not hold steadfastly to this one great truth . . . namely, that the consolidation of the

---

13 François Crouzet, "Wars, Blockade, and Economic Change in Europe, 1792–1815," *Journal of Economic History* 24 (1964): 567–88.
14 See again K. A. Ballhatchet, "European Relations with Asia and Africa," pp. 229–30.
15 Kennedy, *The Rise and Fall of the Great Powers*, p. 123.
16 Piers Mackesy, *War without Victory: The Downfall of Pitt, 1799–1802* (Oxford: Clarendon Press, 1984), pp. 228–30.

Republic and the peace of Europe are linked essentially to the extension of our territory to the Rhine." French soldiers, Merlin declared, were not currently risking all "beyond that river . . . for the sake of a shameful return to our old frontiers."[17] This continued to be the guiding spirit in ruling circles after the inauguration in France of the new constitutional regime known as the Directory. True, several of the country's new executive Directors – Carnot, Barthélémy, Letourneur – courageously advocated a quick peace on the basis of France's return to its *anciennes limites*; but they were opposed stubbornly by their colleague Jean-François Reubell. As a Director throughout this period, "and through his control of the various diplomatic agencies, he served as a stable pole around which all the other forces pushing for the *grandes limites* could cluster."[18] The coup d'état of 18 Fructidor, Year V (or 4 September 1797) "put an end to [the Directory's] vacillation by expelling Carnot and Barthélémy, the strongest opponents of annexation, and by introducing Merlin de Douai and François de Neufchâteau, both supporters of Reubell's line."[19]

There were, at this point as at every juncture in the revolutionary period, powerful interests arguing for French aggrandizement. Some of these interests were of a domestic nature. Domestic considerations in part involved the implications of revolutionary war for French industry, commerce, and finance. No doubt there were those industrialists, merchants, and financiers who advocated an aggressive foreign policy for the new markets, raw materials, and speculative opportunities it might afford in interior Europe. (Many of these entrepreneurs were, we recall, being shut out of overseas and peripheral European activities by the English blockade.) But the most critical domestic considerations probably were the Directory's need to retain the support of its armies and its perpetually strained finances. On the former matter, it has been noted,

the penniless Directory could not feed its soldiers, but it could not disband them [either], because they were needed to keep the ruling clique in power, and because it was feared that they would enter the pay of the government's political opponents unless work were found for them. . . . The only solution was to continue the war, and order the troops to "live off" the invaded countries.[20]

War, then, was needed to keep the generals and their men happy and amenable to Directorial wishes – and, belike, to keep them out of France altogether. But the financial side of this dilemma was also all-devouring. To begin with, scholars have cited the Directory's increasing tendency to

17 Blanning, *The French Revolution in Germany*, p. 74.
18 Ibid., pp. 74–75. On Reubell and his co-Directors, see also Albert Goodwin, "The French Executive Directory: A Revaluation," *History* 22 (1937): 201–18.
19 Blanning, *The French Revolution in Germany*, p. 79.
20 For this discussion of the domestic roots of the Directory's foreign policy, see Biro, *The German Policy of Revolutionary France*, esp. 1:963–66.

see its conquests as financing not only the armies in the field but also the government's *entire* war effort. Yet, beyond even this, "there was a further development, from making war finance itself, to waging war *for the purposes of finance*" in general.[21] As one official put it to the Venetian ambassador in August 1796, the Directory could not afford to wage war, but it could not afford to stop either.

There can be little doubt, then, that the Directory's aggressive foreign policy was responding in part to domestic pressures. But, as always, Frenchmen in positions of power were also mesmerized by the possibilities of *gloire* to be achieved in a Europe that seemed almost to be inviting such adventurism. For all his accentuation of economic arguments for French expansion, Sydney Biro has also made a point of listing additional motives: "bounds of Gaul, territorial ambition, military glory," and "national prestige."[22] Sorel, we may feel, came closest to the heart of the matter in writing that "The feeling of the 'purged' Directory was arrogance. It believed itself to be the master of Europe, just as it was the master of Paris."[23] It is also important to stress once again the disunity prevailing at this time among France's natural adversaries. The collapse of the First Coalition, opening as it did a power vacuum into which French statesmen were tempted to expand, left the strategic situation much as it had been a century before, when Louis XIV had been lured down the primrose path of aggression. Once again, it seems fair to conclude, a powerful confluence of international and domestic forces was drawing French forces outward. But this time, French ambitions would take on a "global" dimension that the Sun King himself might have found breathtaking.

Even before the *coup d'état* of 18 Fructidor strengthened the hand of Reubell and his expansion-minded colleagues in the government, the French war effort had received a dramatic boost from the heroics of Bonaparte on battlefields in northern Italy. Yet, as one specialist has correctly noted, the Directory had been projecting French power beyond the so-called natural boundaries even *before* the Italian campaign of 1796, converting conquered Holland into a "Batavian Republic" subservient to French wishes and covetously eyeing lands east of the Rhine. The Directors "still mouthed, for a time, the natural-boundary theory, it is true, but they did it out of one side of the mouth while the other side told a different story." Bonaparte "introduced a new era only from the point of view of degree": the political regime at home was already strongly committed to expansion.[24] What Bonaparte's Italian triumphs over the Austrians permitted Paris to do was to reiterate its demand for historic gains in western

21 Blanning, *The French Revolution in Germany*, pp. 76–77.
22 Biro, *The German Policy of Revolutionary France*, 1:966.
23 Cited in Blanning, *Origins of the French Revolutionary Wars*, p. 176.
24 Biro, *The German Policy of Revolutionary France*, 1:958.

Germany even as it carved out a new sphere of influence in Italy. The purging of Reubell's opponents from both the executive and the legislature in Fructidor (that is, September 1797) cleared the way for ratification of the Treaty of Campo Formio (October 1797). Under its terms, Austria acquired Venice, Istria, and Dalmatia from the partitioned Venetian Republic, as well as a promise of French support for Habsburg annexation of Salzburg and part of Bavaria. On the other hand, Vienna had to abandon Belgium and the Left Bank of the Rhine to France and recognize new, French-dominated entities in northern Italy, the "Cisalpine" and "Ligurian" republics. Moreover, Campo Formio not only legitimized the new French presence in the Low Countries, Germany, and Italy; it also presaged the collapse of the Habsburg-led Holy Roman Empire. It did so by stipulating that those German princes who lost possessions west of the Rhine to France could be compensated for those losses at the expense of the ecclesiastical states of the empire.[25] The Habsburgs' most venerable – and validating – links with Europe's mythic past were being jeopardized, even as Habsburg Austria's current Great Power status was being reduced, in the struggle with the regicides at Paris.

These developments, arresting as they were, only whetted the appetite of the French, who now moved inexorably back into a mode of aggression on high seas and Continent alike. Desultory talks with the British, under way at Lille since early in July, were cut off abruptly in the wake of 18 Fructidor; before the end of October, preparations were on foot for an invasion of England. At the same time, "if the reluctant acceptance of Campo Formio meant an end to the war with Austria for the time being, it did not prevent further expansion on the Continent. In fact, French influence spread further and faster during the year of 'peace' than it had done during wartime."[26]

That Paris was developing a larger strategic vision could clearly be seen from the attention it now began to devote to Swiss affairs: after all, control of the Swiss Confederation meant control of crucial mountain passes connecting northern Italy with theaters of action in eastern France, western Germany, and the Low Countries. In late 1797 and early 1798, French military intervention helped to secure the foundation of a "Helvetic Republic," and Paris would soon annex outright two erstwhile members of the Confederation, Mulhouse and Geneva. That a Franco-Swiss pact of 2 August 1798 ceded to the French in perpetuity free access to the Alpine passes disclosed something of the revolutionaries' strategic thinking here. However, truth to tell, events transpiring several hundred miles to the south had for some time been paralleling the Republic's moves against the Swiss. In February 1798, French forces invaded the Papal States,

25 Bruun, "The Balance of Power during the Wars," pp. 255–56.
26 Blanning, *Origins of the French Revolutionary Wars*, p. 176.

exiled the pope, and declared a "Roman republic" at Italy's ancient capital. Later, a "Parthenopian" or "Neapolitan" republic was established – on the authority of French bayonets – at the foot of the peninsula. In the meantime, Paris tightened its control over the strategic northwest Italian state of Piedmont with a military occupation foreshadowing Piedmont's annexation to France and intensified its exploitation of the other "sister republics" – the Batavian, Cisalpine, and Ligurian republics. The French now possessed an unbroken belt of territories extending from the North Sea to the central Mediterranean.[27]

At the same time, French influence was spilling over irresistibly into Germany. Campo Formio had made French acquisition of the Left Bank of the Rhine contingent in part upon French diplomatic support for Vienna's annexation of Salzburg and a portion of Bavaria. Yet the Republic's strategists were in fact not at all inclined to abide by the terms of Campo Formio. They wanted both to claim the Left Bank of the Rhine *and* to deny Vienna any compensation in Germany.[28] When the French negotiators opened talks with their counterparts from the Holy Roman Empire at a Congress convened at Rastatt, they sensed that the split between Prussia and Austria, and the willingness of the temporal German princes to discard the empire and swallow up the small ecclesiastical states, might play directly into their hands. Events bore out their predictions. On 11 March 1798 the Congress agreed to hand the Left Bank over to France; on 4 April it accepted in principle the idea that the secular princes could be compensated for territorial losses on the Left Bank with laicized ecclesiastical lands. The Directory seemed to have mastered German affairs as thoroughly as it had those of Italy.[29] And Austria remained thwarted in its own acquisitive designs.

All these events were sufficiently troubling to advocates of a balance of power in European affairs: already, France had attained a greatness on the Continent to which even Louis XIV could not have aspired. But when the Directory's soaring ambitions began to extend to areas far to the east, thereby threatening Russia and Turkey as well as Great Britain and Austria, the possibilities for renewed coalition warfare increased commensurately. The centerpiece of the French thrust to the east was, of course, the "Egyptian adventure" of 1798–99. The actual decision to authorize an expedition to conquer Egypt came on 5 March 1798. As far back as July 1797, however, Talleyrand had presaged such a grandiose initiative in an address

27 Ibid., pp. 176–78. For classic syntheses of the historical literature on France's "sister republics" in the 1790s, consult R. R. Palmer, *The Age of the Democratic Revolution: The Response* (Princeton, N.J.: Princeton University Press, 1964); and Jacques Godechot, *France and the Atlantic Revolution of the Eighteenth Century*, trans. Herbert H. Rowen (New York: Free Press, 1965).
28 Blanning, *Origins of the French Revolutionary Wars*, pp. 176–78.
29 Ibid., p. 178.

delivered at the Institute at Paris. Talleyrand, soon to be named foreign minister, had reminded his auditors of Choiseul's suggestion after the Seven Years' War that France seize Egypt as compensation for colonies lost to London. And he had continued in this audacious vein: "Nothing is more important than to establish ourselves on a sound footing in Albania, Greece, Macedonia and the other provinces of the Turkish Empire in Europe, especially those with a Mediterranean coastline, and most notably Egypt, which one day could prove immensely useful for us."[30]

But there were also opportunities beckoning to the French in the far northeast. As the Directors moved toward their decision to invade Egypt, rumors were rising in Europe about renewed French interest in Poland! In January 1798, a Russian spy in the French embassy at Berlin sent back disturbing reports to St. Petersburg about a possible French attempt to fashion a resurrected Polish state from the Partition spoils of the three eastern autocracies. That a seven-thousand-man Polish Legion was currently serving under French colors in the West, and that military units of Polish exiles were also being formed in the Danubian basin in the Southeast, appeared to lend credence to these stories.[31]

The challenge that the French Revolution posed to the equilibrium of political forces in Europe by 1798 was starkly "modern": that is, it looked forward to Napoleon and to the threat presented by Germany in the two "world wars" of the twentieth century even more than it recalled the earlier aggrandizement of Charles V and Louis XIV. For the very first time, a European power was menacing the vital interests of *both* "flanking powers" (Great Britain and Russia) even as it ran roughshod over the more traditional battlefields of west-central Europe. Even as the Directory repeatedly struck at Britain directly through the partially opened "back door" of Ireland, it called the entire British Empire into question through an occupation of Egypt that might in turn provide a base for a descent upon India (via the Red Sea or the "overland route").[32] At the same time, by challenging the status quo in a Germany frozen for centuries within the framework of the Holy Roman Empire, by working to undo the massive changes wrought in the three Polish partitions, and by appearing in force in the eastern Mediterranean and upon its strategic littoral, the French not only infuriated the Russians but also reconciled them with their inveterate foes, the Ottoman Turks. In addition, Paris wanted to block any effort by Austria to parlay its new Adriatic possessions into a major Mediterranean presence – and this, naturally, could only reinforce Vienna's conviction

---

30 Ibid., p. 180.
31 Ibid., p. 190.
32 On the Irish situation in the 1790s, see Thomas Pakenham, *The Year of Liberty: The Great Irish Rebellion of 1798* (New York: Random House, 1998). On the threat posed to British India by the French presence in Egypt, see Edward Ingram, *Commitment to Empire: Prophecies of the Great Game in Asia, 1797–1800* (Oxford: Clarendon Press, 1981).

that a resumption of coalition warfare against the overbearing French was imperative.

The revolutionaries, then, did much to prepare the way for a conflict of even greater international scope than that of 1792–97. And, truth to tell, the principal members of the Second Coalition – Britain, Russia, Austria, Turkey – were shocked into a substantial measure of cooperative planning by the perceived magnitude of the challenge emanating from Paris. When Pitt invited the new tsar, Paul I, to take the lead in organizing the Second Coalition, he suggested a program of diplomatic goals strikingly anticipatory of the settlement later to be hammered out at the Congress of Vienna. France should be reduced to its prerevolutionary borders, and renewed French expansionism might be barred by, among other things, the creation of a Dutch/Belgian state in the Low Countries and the restoration of the Kingdom of Piedmont-Sardinia-Savoy in Italy. The Swiss would regain their territories and sovereignty; Austria could receive Italian possessions as compensation for losing Belgium; and Prussia might be lured into the coalition with the promise of German acquisitions.[33] Austria's Chancellor Thugut, too, was "seeking a new kind of coalition," hinting, at least, "at the concert that would later emerge under Metternich's auspices in 1814." Painfully aware that the First Coalition had been hobbled by "the lack of joint planning among the allies," Thugut insisted that, this time, "comprehensive plans must be laid, the right objectives chosen, and the proper timing selected so that the coalition would achieve victory."[34] That St. Petersburg and Constantinople were prepared to bury the swords of their historic rivalry and join in the common effort against the French similarly boded well for the prospects of the new alliance. True, Prussia's adamant refusal to relinquish its neutral status was a major disappointment to the allies; but this in itself did not necessarily doom their enterprise.

The members of the Second Coalition, moreover, were able to agree upon a common set of war plans whose successful implementation would presumably lead to the overthrow of the Directory, the restoration of the Bourbons, and the curbing of French power. In general terms, an Austro-Russian force was to drive the Republican armies out of Italy; Russian troops would then "liberate" Switzerland and move into eastern France; and an Anglo-Russian army would simultaneously "liberate" the Low Countries and then advance into northern France. In the summer of 1799, this military strategy seemed well on the way to achieving complete success: the "sister republics" in Italy collapsed as the Directory's forces were expelled from the Italian peninsula; the French were initially defeated in Switzerland and driven back west of the Rhine; and the northeastern

33 Bruun, "The Balance of Power during the Wars," pp. 256–57.
34 Roider, *Baron Thugut and Austria's Response to the French Revolution*, pp. 287–88.

French provinces seemed perilously vulnerable to the projected Anglo-Russian invasion through the Netherlands.

The coalition's successes, it is true, owed something to the faulty military planning of the Directory. Deciding to adopt an offensive *military* posture in the spring of 1799 to accomplish the *political* objective of preserving the satellite republics and the integrity of France itself, the Directory threw undermanned and inadequately supplied armies against superior enemy forces "along a line stretching from Alsace to the Adriatic Sea." Launching simultaneous and ill-coordinated attacks along such a broad front rather than concentrating decisive forces upon a few vital points was to court disaster. French problems were only compounded by Spain's failure to coordinate its naval forces with those of the Republic. The French, it appeared, had sowed too aggressively in Europe; were they about to reap the whirlwind?[35]

However, the French were saved in 1799, as they had been earlier in the decade, by a combination of the underlying abilities (and good luck) of their generals, the military advantages always to be derived from defending interior positions, and – most critically – discord among the allies. Some scholarly controversy has arisen in connection with this last point. Historians agree, to be sure, that the joint Austro-Russian campaign in Italy soon became mired in dispute: the Habsburgs had acquisitive designs in the peninsula that Paul I's government and generals could not endorse. Again, the revival of tension between London and Vienna over the ultimate status of Belgium, and over certain German issues, has been well documented. What remains sharply disputed is the importance of (and reasoning behind) Thugut's insistence that most of Archduke Charles's Austrians move north from Switzerland into the Rhineland, rather than remaining in place to cover the Russian troops as they entered France. Lacking adequate protection on their right flank, the Russian troops in Switzerland were isolated, and their rout by Masséna's army at the Second Battle of Zurich in September dislocated the entire allied war effort. Some scholars have taken the Austrian chancellor to task for his tactics, which they depict as disastrous and as having been motivated by Habsburg territorial ambitions in Belgium and Italy.[36] For other specialists, Thugut's initiative bespoke legitimate diplomatic and military concerns,[37] and in any case was but one of many factors contributing to the allied defeat at Zurich.

35 On the details of the military campaigns of 1799, see Steven T. Ross, "The Military Strategy of the Directory: The Campaigns of 1799," *French Historical Studies* 5 (1967): 170–87; and A. B. Rodger, *The War of the Second Coalition, 1798–1801* (Oxford: Clarendon Press, 1964).

36 See, for example, Ross, "The Military Strategy of the Directory," pp. 183–84.

37 See Paul W. Schroeder, "The Collapse of the Second Coalition," *Journal of Modern History* 59 (1987): esp. 285.

There may be considerable truth to Karl Roider's contention that the defeat "was largely a result of the many handicaps characteristic of coalition warfare," and that, indeed, the plan lying behind it may have been "utterly impractical to begin with."[38]

Be that as it may, the reverses of the Russians in Switzerland, their defeat (along with that of their British confederates) at the hands of General Brune in Holland, and the exacerbation of the tensions among the allies prompted a disgusted Tsar Paul I to withdraw from the coalition (22 October 1799). It would be only a matter of time before the French, negotiating separately with the Russians, Austrians, and British, achieved the official demise of yet another coalition aimed against them. Bonaparte, soon to hold power in France, would (briefly) be leagued with Paul I in a fantastic scheme to invade India by way of central Asia; eventually, pacts concluded with Austria and Britain at Lunéville and Amiens, respectively, would seem to herald a durable French preponderance in the affairs of western and central Europe.[39]

To review the geopolitics of the 1794–99 period, then, is to see the "revolutionary" French coming back full circle – back, that is, to a glorious season in their country's prerevolutionary past. "However much change the Revolution may have brought to the domestic structures of France, in international terms a better description than revolution would be 'revival': the revival of French power after three-quarters of a century of feeble leadership, misconceived policies and demoralizing failure."[40] The France that could cynically join its ancient Austrian foe in a partition of the even more "ancient" Venetian Republic had, indeed, traveled far back along the road from heady revolutionary cosmopolitanism to the *raison d'état* of the supposedly rejected past. That, it turned out, was the price to be paid in the "real" European world for France's full recovery of its international stature.[41] Yet, as the shrewdest observers of Europe were also aware, Gallic success on the international front assumed the continuing implementation of significant reforms at home. Austria's Baron Thugut, for example, knew his country's foe "to be a France that had somehow harnessed great new energy" and thus been able to conjure up "armed forces of enormous size" and "commanders of remarkable ability."[42] This insight takes us on to a reappraisal of critical domestic policies in the last five years of France's revolution.

38 Roider, *Baron Thugut and Austria's Response to the French Revolution*, pp. 326–27.
39 On these diplomatic developments, refer again to Bruun, "The Balance of Power during the Wars," pp. 256–60.
40 Blanning, *Origins of the French Revolutionary Wars*, p. 207.
41 On this point, see again Linda and Marsha Frey, "'The Reign of the Charlatans is Over,'" esp. pp. 742–43.
42 Roider, *Baron Thugut and Austria's Response to the French Revolution*, pp. 384–85.

THE RESTRUCTURING OF FRENCH INSTITUTIONS TO 1799

In the years intervening between the overthrow of Robespierre and the accession of Bonaparte, public policy in France continued to reflect realities and priorities characteristic of the entire Revolution. Whether the matters at issue involved the modernizing of government (administration, civil service, finance), education, schemes of *bienfaisance*, or military reforms, one recurring theme consisted of the insatiable needs of a state locked in an enduring pattern of large-scale warfare. As they developed or further elaborated policies in these areas, the men guiding French affairs in 1794–99 (like those in earlier years of the Revolution) showed themselves ready to accommodate or to deny the tangible interests of their constituents insofar as those interests sorted well or ill with the requirements of the bellicose French state.

It is a commonplace of French Revolutionary historiography that the months following 9 Thermidor witnessed a relaxation of emergency government controls in the Republic.[43] Still, however true this may have been, it should not blind us to the fundamental reality of centralized, bureaucratized governance that came ever more fully into its own in the later years of the Revolution. Within reasonable limits, the Thermidorians retrospectively endorsed the Committee of Public Safety's utilization in the Year II of *agents nationaux* to assert the authority of Paris in the provinces. To be sure, elected local governments were reinstated; nonetheless, they had henceforth to cooperate with officials dispatched from the capital. The five-man Executive Directory which gave its name to the overall constitutional regime of 1795–99 appointed a salaried "commissioner" to all administrative bodies in the departments and cantons. These *commissaires* made sure that officials elected in the localities enforced the laws and decrees promulgated by the central government. Cantonal commissioners had to report to their departmental superiors, who in turn owed a regular accounting to the Interior Ministry about conditions in their departments. The *commissaires* could recommend disciplinary action against recalcitrant local officials, and even assume their functions in times of emergency.[44] Thus, the hierarchical administrative arrangements put in place a few years earlier by the Constituent Assembly, preserving the concentration of state power at the center, survived the dismantling of the governmental "terror" of the Year II.

True, the new system of "commissioners to the departments and cantons" was not without its weaknesses. The *commissaires* for the most part were local political figures selected for the Directors by legislators

43 Consult, on this issue, Bronislaw Baczko, *Ending the Terror: The French Revolution after Robespierre* (New York: Cambridge University Press, 1994).
44 Woloch, *The New Regime*, p. 53.

representing the regions in question, rather than apolitical functionaries; as a result, they were vulnerable at all times to the shifting winds of French politics. Furthermore, they found themselves frequently at odds with the elected administrators in the departments and cantons who were charged on a day-to-day basis with such crucial matters as supervising the raising of taxes, maintaining public order, and supplying local markets. Yet the apparent fact that the locally elected officials did not carry out their assigned duties altogether satisfactorily made the oversight of the government's agents all the more necessary.

The commissioners, for all their problems, did not fail the authorities. A leading scholar on the subject has concluded that the *commissaires* performed their tasks well enough to ensure the continuity of government in the provinces.[45] Also, the Directory made an innovative attempt to integrate rural France – as represented in the village communes – into the structures of state authority and civic life. The rural communes were grouped into a kind of administrative "super commune" under the eye of a commissioner at the cantonal level; cantonal municipalities thus were links in a chain of command and communication extending from Paris down to the humblest peasant communities.[46] For the first time, the villages were expected to hire constables and maintain local roads, and to do so at their own expense. Admittedly, this arrangement was somewhat reminiscent of the old regime's subordination of villages to the state. But it also foreshadowed the future. When the state intervened in rural communal affairs in this fashion, it was prefiguring the integration of the countryside into an increasingly well-ordered polity. This process may not have been consummated until late in the nineteenth century; yet it was surely under way in the revolutionary era.[47]

As state power continued to grow in an *administrative* sense, ever more tightly subordinating rural France to urban France and outlying regions to the capital, it continued to grow in a purely *bureaucratic* sense as well. Clive Church's research has established this point, showing the Revolution's later years to have been crucial to the "coming of age" of the French civil service. We can see this basic development reflected in the professional experience, social differentiation, and geographical origins of the civil servants at Paris, as well as in the bureaucratized routines to which they were increasingly subjected.

Church has pointed out that, of the 4,340 civil servants he has identified as staffing the Directory's ministries, "2 in 7 at least ... had held administrative appointments before 1789," and as such "provided the ministries

45 Denis Woronoff, *The Thermidorian Regime and the Directory, 1794–1799* (New York: Cambridge University Press, 1984), esp. pp. 37–38, 40–42.
46 Ibid., pp. 40–42.
47 Woloch, *The New Regime*, pp. 427–28.

and other bodies with a hard core of fairly senior clerks well versed in the responsibilities, traditions and expertise of the old civil service." Yet an even higher proportion of these 4,340 functionaries had also held significant posts in the burgeoning bureaucracy of the early years of revolution. Thus, as Church has trenchantly remarked, there was a certain analogy between patterns of recruitment to the state bureaucracy and those to the armies that were currently carrying out the state's strategic assignments. "The Directory completed the assimilation of the hordes of bureaucrats thrown up by the exigencies and social chaos of the Revolution and married this new corps with the cadres inherited from the *Ancien Régime*, rather in the same way as the amalgam operated in the revolutionary army."[48]

At the same time, however, the ongoing professionalization of the bureaucracy meant less rather than more "democracy." Greater subordination and deference inside the civil service went hand-in-hand with its internal division along social lines under the new regime. Very few of those in senior positions came from the army or navy, from the "public sector" administration of such services as the *postes* or the *assignats*, or from trading or "menial" service occupations. They came instead from more elitist quarters: for instance, from the liberal professions, the diplomatic corps, the *monde* of justice and old royal officialdom, or even the ranks of religion. They hailed, in other words, "from a higher social category and from a more restricted range of professions and administrations than their inferiors in the hierarchy."[49] Even at the height of the Terror, Jacobin egalitarian tendencies, which had run toward conferring bureaucratic posts upon revolutionary activists and other "unprofessional" types, had had to defer to a more pragmatic philosophy stressing the war-related need for an efficient (and thus hierarchical) civil service. With the waning of Jacobin idealism, social differentiation and a corresponding stress upon hierarchy within the world of state officialdom were bound to become – and did become – paramount realities.

Other characteristics stamping the Directory's civil servants as increasingly "modern" and oriented to the purposes of the state included their geographical origins and daily work routines. "The vast majority of all the employees," Church has observed, "were drawn from the north-east of France. 40% of the departments produced 85% of the clerks, and most came from the triangle – Rennes, Lilles and Besançon. Within this area, the Parisian region dominated, supplying 48.5% of the total."[50] Given that, in general, the Parisian basin and northeastern regions of France were most

48 Clive H. Church, "The Social Basis of the French Central Bureaucracy under the Directory, 1795–1799," *Past and Present* 36 (1967): 64–67, 72.
49 Ibid., pp. 68–69. Church has of course enlarged upon these themes in *Revolution and Red Tape*, passim.
50 Church, "The Social Basis of the French Central Bureaucracy," p. 62.

closely attuned to the purposes of the Revolutionary Government and/or most directly vulnerable to attack by the British, Austrians, and Prussians, it is significant that these "hotbeds" of Gallic patriotism supplied a disproportionate number of functionaries to the state. Granted, citizens were driven into government service in part by expediential considerations – for instance, the desperate need for security in a time of economic upheaval and the traditional and unquenchable French taste for office. Still, it would be unwise to take no account of the "idealism released by the Revolution among the young who saw in the civil service a chance...of serving the Republic."[51] Such officials, many of them in their forties, thirties, and twenties, were most likely predisposed to internalize the state's expansionist values. As the 1790s wore on, moreover, this process must have been helped along by the integration of these state servants into the increasingly precise routines, punctilious work schedules, and voluminous paperwork of government bureaucracy.

The revolutionary state, then, continued under the Directory to assimilate the French nation into its administrative framework and to "fine-tune" its bureaucratic procedures. But what of its finances? Here, obviously, was the acid test for the government – especially in light of its unprecedentedly costly foreign policy. What becomes very clear, in reviewing this question, is that the war, in this as in some other revolutionary connections, was both a stimulating and an inhibiting factor. It spurred the country's leaders to initiate or continue significant fiscal reforms yet simultaneously raised insuperable barriers to the full realization of those reforms.

Certainly there were ongoing and new success stories in this period. It is first of all important to acknowledge that, whatever problems the revamped Treasury and Finance Department encountered, they remained vastly more efficient than their predecessor agencies of prerevolutionary times. The budgetary and accounting reforms so dearly achieved earlier in the decade were preserved, and slippery financial operatives like Gabriel-Julien Ouvrard never secured the kind of stranglehold upon state finances that the venal accountants and the tax farmers of the old France had enjoyed.[52] More specifically attributable to the period of the Directory, however, and equally important for the future, was the comprehensive overhaul of the country's system of taxation. To begin with, the allocation and collection of direct impositions, together with any appeals to which they might give rise, were now to be transferred from local elected functionaries to committees of appointed officials working in the departments under the vigilant eyes of central government *commissaires*. The direct taxes themselves were also being taken thoroughly in hand. Legislation

51 Ibid., p. 68.
52 Bosher, *French Finances, 1770–1795*, pp. 251, 317.

established a system of four basic imposts (on trade licenses, on land, on "doors and windows," and on citizens and their movable property) that was destined in essence to last down to the start of World War I. Again, the Directory invented or revived a host of indirect taxes: they ranged from highway tolls to powder and saltpeter and tobacco imposts to mortgage, registration, and stamp duties.[53]

Thus the revolutionaries labored in the late 1790s to resuscitate state finances. Tragically, however, they were floundering in a bottomless ocean of war making – their own state's ever more ambitious war making – and thus they never could find a way to stave off national bankruptcy. For one thing, all their attempts to rescue the revolutionary concept of a paper currency – first in the guise of the *assignats*, then in a form of the *mandats territoriaux* – were fated to fail.[54] The French were never able to confiscate and sell enough *biens nationaux*, whether in France itself, in Belgium, or elsewhere, to cover the immense gap in governmental accounts between revenue and (war-dominated) expenditure. That taxpayers had in effect been on strike since the earliest days of the Revolution, and that expenditure for war simply could not be contained, only made the situation worse. So, for that matter, did the decision in 1796 to make the *assignats* convertible into the newer *mandats* at one-thirtieth of their nominal value. Both paper currencies were hopelessly discredited, and the *mandats* were withdrawn from circulation in February 1797. A state bankruptcy no longer avoidable by any means was then adumbrated in a law of 30 September 1797. Under its terms, only one-third of the public debt was "consolidated" – that is, declared a "sacred" charge on which full interest would continue to be paid – while redemption of the remaining two-thirds of state indebtedness was indefinitely put off. (In March 1801, the state "legally" finalized what became known as the "bankruptcy of the two-thirds.") "The consequent shock to public credit may be imagined," Albert Goodwin has written. "The spectre of national bankruptcy which had haunted Mirabeau in the early days of the revolution had at last materialized."[55]

The all-consuming war cast a dark shadow over every aspect of revolutionary finance. It imposed a regime of forced loans during 1795–99 deliberately shorn of any "progressive" traits that could revive memories of Jacobin "terrorism"; the loans wound up fattening the purses of contractors and bankers indispensable to the government's survival.[56] It helped to

---

53 Albert Goodwin, "The French Executive Directory – A Revaluation," *History* 22 (1937): 201–18.

54 Refer to Seymour E. Harris, *The Assignats* (Cambridge, Mass.: Harvard University Press, 1930); and Goodwin, "The French Executive Directory," pp. 322–23.

55 Ibid., pp. 323–25.

56 On this point, see Gross, "Progressive Taxation and Social Justice," p. 121; and Woronoff, *The Thermidorian Regime and the Directory*, p. 97.

stymie the authorities' effort to draw all fiscal operations into the public domain: thus, Ouvrard was allowed after 1797 to take naval supplies out of a government *régie* and to manage them as a private enterprise "in the manner of the ancien régime."[57] It worked directly against the government's goal of generating more taxable revenue through economic development, not only by cutting French entrepreneurs out of international trade exchanges, but also by drafting young men away from "neglected arts, agriculture, and commerce" at home.[58] And, most fatefully perhaps, the war's crushing financial burden forced the state into an ever-greater reliance upon booty from the conquered territories. During 1797–99, Denis Woronoff has suggested, the revenues extorted from that source "brought in ... about a quarter of the annual budget."[59] This (along with all other fiscal devices associated with the war) could only divert French leaders from tackling and resolving their country's financial and underlying economic problems.

Military adventurism, then, both stimulated and retarded the modernization of French governance during 1794–99. But it had a more consistently negative impact upon projects of cultural and social amelioration. Whether we review the educational reforms launched by the Thermidorian Convention and the Directory or ponder some of their projects of charity and other forms of *bienfaisance*, we can see how the ever more massive commitment to war (in combination, to be sure, with other factors) exerted a baleful influence upon the Revolution's final efforts to "improve" French humanity.

This was notably the case when it came to primary education. Under the auspices of the so-called Lakanal Law of 17 November 1794, the Republic was supposed to furnish a primary school with a schoolmaster (*instituteur*) and schoolmistress (*institutrice*) in every commune with at least one thousand souls. The teachers, endowed with the dignity of public functionaries, were expected to teach such subjects as arithmetic, writing, reading, the Constitution, the Declaration of the Rights of Man, "republican" morals, geography, basic principles of the French language, the history of "free peoples," and some elements of "natural science." *Instituteurs* and *institutrices* were to receive from the central government annual salaries of 1,200 *livres* and 1,000 *livres*, respectively (and supplements would go to teachers in larger cities). They were also promised state pensions upon retirement. Initially, the districts (which at this point in the Revolution still functioned as administrative units) played a central role in the competitive selection of primary-school instructors; in the long run, however, that role would fall (at least in part) to students' parents. The districts, on the other hand, were

57 Bosher, *French Finances, 1770–1795*, p. 314.
58 See, on these issues: Crouzet, "Wars, Blockade, and Economic Change in Europe, 1792–1815," pp. 567–88; and Woloch, *The New Regime*, p. 388.
59 Woronoff, *The Thermidorian Regime and the Directory*, p. 97.

supposed to retain a permanent function of oversight in matters relating to the schools.[60]

Unfortunately, implementing the Lakanal Law proved to be impossible. Even in the best (i.e., most peaceful) of circumstances, the legislation might have failed. Instructors in primary education were expressly forbidden to accept supplementary compensation from parents for boarding or tutoring their children and never received a legal mandate to enhance their incomes by engaging in secondary occupations. Moreover, local authorities endeavoring to apply the new legislation encountered a legion of problems. They were pressured to set up additional schools in small rural communities; they had difficulties separating boys and girls in the classroom owing to the shortage of *institutrices*; and they became enmeshed in bitter controversies over the utilization of nationalized rectories supposedly earmarked for the purposes of primary education.

But the inescapable factor of war was also telling here, as it was in virtually every other area of revolutionary beneficence. As Isser Woloch has put it, "military mobilization had claimed an entire cohort of young men for the army, leaving civil society bereft of potential new recruits for public school teaching." Local boards of education were reduced to the desperate ploy of petitioning the War Ministry for the discharge of soldiers with "very weak physical conditions" who could be more useful in schoolrooms than on European battlefields. Such military discharges assumed some sort of working relationship between the Executive Commission on Public Instruction and the manpower bureau in the War Ministry; unfortunately, that collaboration never materialized, and as a result the primary schools never could acquire the requisite *instituteurs*. The war effort sabotaged the Lakanal Law in a more indirect way as well – through its disastrous impact upon the French economy. By undermining the paper currency, the war made it all the more unthinkable for *rentiers*, urban workers, and government employees dependent upon the shrinking asset of salaries paid in *assignats* to enroll their children in public schooling. Just as obviously, inflation turned the fixed salaries of *instituteurs* and *institutrices* into derisory compensation – and we recall that these individuals had no other legally allowed sources of income. Finally, the war-related economic crisis, leading as it did to popular unrest in the spring of 1795, hardened the social attitudes of the Thermidorian deputies, making it easier for them to countenance a fundamental retreat in the area of primary education.[61]

That retreat took the form of the so-called Daunou Law of 25 October 1795.[62] The Daunou Law provided for the creation in the departments of

---

60 Woloch, *The New Regime*, pp. 181–82.

61 Ibid., pp. 189–91.

62 On this legislation, especially as concerned its establishment of Central Schools in the departments, refer to Palmer, *The Improvement of Humanity*, pp. 230–32, 242–45, and 252–57.

secondary-level "Central Schools." Yet it gave little in the way of assurances that there would continue to be a mission in elementary education, stating only that public primary schools would somehow be instituted in the Republic's cantons but neglecting to specify any curricular or other connections between these projected institutions and the Central Schools. As one historian has all too justifiably concluded: "The Daunou Law – which lasted well into the Napoleonic Era – abandoned the principle of universal and free primary education. It also left the *instituteurs publics* on their own (save for free lodging or an indemnity)... with no salary from the state and no distinctive status to go along with their titles." Hence, the legislators left in place "a kind of shell – a thin network of ostensibly state-sponsored schools."[63] In effect, elementary schooling in France became an arena of unregulated competition between "public" institutions, hampered as they were by all the problems enumerated above, and religious and other private schools to which those parents able to defray educational expenses usually preferred to send their sons and daughters.

The antiroyalist coup of Fructidor, Year V (September 1797) and its political aftermath seemed to augur new initiatives in the area of education. Woloch has even spoken of a sort of coalition of government officials, educators, and deputies trying in late 1798 and 1799 to place educational issues once again back on the Republic's legislative agenda. Alas, it was not to be – and, in large measure, for the same old reasons. In the summer of 1799, the "military and political crisis touched off by the war of the Second Coalition overwhelmed the legislature. Debates on such matters as education had to be suspended.... A passionate republican commitment to free public schools – forged in the ideological zeal of 1793 but tempered in subsequent experience – came to a dead end."[64] Once again, the revolutionary state's commitment to war had taken priority over its commitment to education.[65]

Military pressures similarly limited the government's ability to alleviate the misery and enhance the living standards of its citizens. To be sure, war initially bid fair to play a positive role in this area, insofar as it helped in 1793 to bring to power Jacobin politicians who entertained relatively generous ideas on the subject of government-sponsored *bienfaisance*. In March 1793, the Convention presented a blueprint for a national system of poor relief, and then in truly ground-breaking legislation over the next

63 Woloch, *The New Regime*, pp. 192–95.
64 Ibid., p. 206. As Palmer has shown, things did not go quite so badly in the late 1790s for the new Central Schools in the departments. Still, they, too, were adversely affected by the insatiable manpower and financial demands of the war. Palmer, *The Improvement of Humanity*, pp. 230–32, 242–45.
65 See also, on this general issue, H. C. Barnard, *Education and the French Revolution* (Cambridge: Cambridge University Press, 1969).

year or so it endowed this blueprint with some meaningful details. The Jacobin-dominated legislature proclaimed a specific national responsibility for those falling into certain categories of need and made provisions to allocate moneys from the Treasury to the enumerated individuals via the district administrations. Those declared to be deserving of the state's beneficence included old and infirm indigents; "mothers and fathers who have no resources other than the product of their labor, whenever the product of their labor is no longer commensurate with the needs of their family"; widows with young children; orphans living as foster children with necessitous families; and aged agricultural workers, rural artisans, and rural widows. The Convention, with an eye to its indispensable *militaires*, also came up with a package offering "patriotic assistance" in the form of subsistence pensions to the impecunious dependents of volunteers and draftees, as well as more substantial stipends to wounded veterans.[66]

This was all very impressive on paper, and really visionary in that it looked forward to a much later era in which governments would generally view the provision of such public assistance as one of their primary responsibilities. In the France of the late 1790s, however, it was only a matter of time before state projects of *bienfaisance* encountered multifarious constraints imposed by state-engendered war. For one thing, the revolutionaries were driven by the financial burden of war to reverse the cautionary stipulation of March 1793 that charitable properties should be nationalized only "after the complete and definitive organization of public assistance" had been placed "in full activity." On 11 July 1794, the legislators decided that such properties and their attached endowments (with the sole exception of actual hospital buildings) should be confiscated and sold off as soon as possible. Because the authorities did not reverse this policy until October 1796, and did not return unsold properties to the affected institutions until 1797, institutional charity over that period became almost totally reliant upon government funding.

This was bad enough in that it recalled how the Constituent Assembly, pressed by war-dominated state indebtedness earlier in the Revolution, had confiscated and sold off Church buildings, lands, and endowments, thus drastically undercutting the charitable and other social functions of ecclesiastics in France.[67] What made the new rounds of confiscations of charitable institutions and endowments so baneful to the purposes of revolutionary *bienfaisance*, however, was their *timing* – right in the midst of an economic crisis that itself reflected the immense strains imposed upon the country by its ever-widening military commitments.

---

66 See, on all of this, Woloch, *The French Veteran from the Revolution to the Restoration* (Chapel Hill: University of North Carolina Press, 1979); and Woloch, *The New Regime*, pp. 247–50, 293–95.

67 On this matter, refer again to McManners, *The French Revolution and the Church*, passim.

The hyperinflation and widespread crop failures of this period worked together to reduce the financial aid pledged by the government to charitable institutions and to pensioners inscribed by name on the *Grand Livre de Bienfaisance Nationale*. Funds originally earmarked for hospitals, orphanages, and workshops all too often were diverted toward emergency purchases of grains and other foodstuffs. At the same time, the collapse of the currency virtually nullified the value of pensions paid out to aged farm workers, necessitous parents, artisans, and widows. As one example: installments of 207,000 *livres* in *assignats* allocated to twenty departments for September 1795 were in real terms worth only a few thousand *livres* by that time. Hence, the related burdens of war and a weakened economy radically diminished the promised benison of state assistance to needy citizens and to institutions caring for the truly indigent.[68]

It is revealing that the government's humanitarianism in the late 1790s was always curbed by its prior concern for *militaires* and military issues. Take, for instance, what one historian has uncovered regarding disbursements by the Commission on Public Assistance:

About 62% of its total funding between floréal Year II and the end of... Year III paid for medical services to *militaires*...in France. Moreover, one third of the Commission's non-hospital expenditures went for "patriotic assistance" to the needy dependents of *militaires*. Obviously plans to make the national government responsible for *bienfaisance* were being diverted and distorted by the side effects of military mobilization in a democratic society.[69]

Wounded and ailing soldiers occupying hospital beds in swelling numbers meant that facilities were effectively unavailable to noncombatants in French society. This turn of events bespoke a set of military-patriotic values that had prevailed even at the height of the "idealistic" Terror. Bertrand Barère, in setting forth a bold new plan for state assistance to incapacitated farm workers, had stressed their moral equivalency to the Republic's most celebrated citizens, its men in arms: "Let the public treasury open at once to the defender and the nourisher of the fatherland."[70] Is it at all surprising that, with the decline of Jacobin idealism later on, the state should have abandoned any notion of such a moral equivalency and frankly favored *militaires* and their dependents and survivors in the dispensation of assistance? Pensions to the deserving (but noncombatant) poor were terminated in legislation of late 1796; military pensions managed to survive until 1799, when even they were scaled back due to the monstrous financial burden of the War of the Second Coalition.

68 Woloch, *The New Regime*, pp. 259–63. On the interplay of these issues in the provinces see Alan Forrest, *The French Revolution and the Poor* (Oxford: Oxford University Press, 1981); and Robert M. Schwartz, *Policing the Poor in Eighteenth-Century France* (Chapel Hill: University of North Carolina Press, 1988).
69 Woloch, *The New Regime*, p. 254.
70 Barère is cited in ibid., pp. 250–51.

Here was a telling paradox: the more broadly conceived and "modern" (and therefore more costly) France's military ambitions became, the more restrictive and less "modern" became its efforts at home relief. "Out of this debacle," as one historian has expressed it, "the foremost casualty was the belief that the State could actually organize and support such services as ... *bienfaisance*. Where the nation's resources had once seemed abundant (thanks to nationalized church lands and printing presses), the treasury was now bare, revenues uncertain, and budgets swollen by military priorities." Accordingly, the period of the Directory witnessed a melancholy but probably unavoidable retreat from the modern concept of nationally administered pensions and poor relief to a more traditional philosophy stressing the primary charitable responsibility of municipalities and other local entities. This had the further unhappy effect of contravening the Revolution's drive toward greater national unity by setting cities and rural communities against each other. Urban imposts provided funds for poor relief in cities and towns but could do nothing for rural indigents. "Urban *bienfaisance* had a chance to recover, but in the bourgs and villages public assistance scarcely existed."[71] The Revolution may have started to integrate rural areas into a national system of administration; it could not, however, bring them into a nationally funded system of public assistance, or even assure them the minimal assistance available in the country's more densely populated precincts.

It is important in reevaluating revolutionary *bienfaisance* to stress how very dependent it had to be upon a government able to devote time and money to charitable undertakings in an economy enjoying a reasonable amount of prosperity. Yet it was precisely these conditions that were ruled out in the 1790s as French geopoliticians cast covetous glances farther and farther abroad. The more discerning officials of the Directory were cognizant of the fundamental developmental dilemma posed for their country by its international ambitions. As one of them commented in June 1796: "The more the Directory steps up its efforts to come to the aid of neglected arts, agriculture, and commerce, as well as families without support, by letting them keep the soldiers they claim when the public interest permits it, the more it fears sowing discouragement in the armies and disorganizing their ranks by permitting soldiers on active duty to return to their families."[72] How, then, to define the "public interest"? Did it lie, as the first revolutionary idealists had enthusiastically proclaimed, in the unconditional betterment of "humanity," starting (presumably) with French "humanity"? Or did it lie in securing and, if possible, improving the

71 Ibid., pp. 259–63. Two studies on these issues in provincial France are: Colin Jones, *Charity and Bienfaisance: The Treatment of the Poor in the Montpellier Region, 1740–1815* (Cambridge: Cambridge University Press, 1982); and Kathryn Norberg, *Rich and Poor in Grenoble, 1600–1814* (Berkeley: University of California Press, 1985).
72 Cited in Woloch, *The New Regime*, p. 388.

situation of France (i.e., the French state) in the murderously competitive world of European power politics? The men of the Directory ultimately embraced the latter definition, as indeed had all their predecessors since 1789. They revoked military furloughs and hardship dispensations and eventually devised the system of conscription that has in one form or another lasted down to the present day. They harkened, in other words, to the clamorous advocates of war rather than to the quieter voices calling for long-term economic development and for the dispensation of state assistance to the needy.

So far, we have noted the paradoxical impact of war upon the domestic policies of the Thermidorian and post-Thermidorian revolutionaries in France. The country's military "mission" placed a premium upon a more tightly integrated, hierarchical system of administration, a modernized central bureaucracy, and streamlined financial procedures; and yet it also impeded the completion of desperately needed fiscal reforms and sapped the productivity of the economy undergirding the government. The country's military requirements were crucial in bringing the Jacobins to power, and thus – indirectly – in raising the issues of state-sponsored education and state assistance to necessitous and deserving citizens; yet those same military needs worked in the end to shoulder those meliorist causes off the Republic's agenda. We shall also see much that was para-doxical about the army's ongoing evolution during 1794–99. The effect of interminable war was further to professionalize the Republic's armed forces yet at the same time to throw up some obstacles to the completion of that process. What was more, behind the process of professionaliza-tion lurked the larger phenomenon of *militarization* in both army and society. Symptomatic of this latter development were such factors as the increasingly despotic control exerted by army officers over their troops, the massive conscription of young men into the army from 1798 on, and the insidious erosion of civilian authority over the Republic's military chiefs.

Historians agree that, over the period between 9 Thermidor, Year II, and Bonaparte's accession to power, the French army's officer corps continued to acquire greater professionalism. Howard G. Brown has noted that a list of prospective generals submitted to the post-Robespierrist Convention by military specialist Dubois-Crancé bespoke "the importance of zeal, ac-tivity, and intelligence as well as the specifically military virtues of length of command, expertise in a particular branch of the army, and above all bravery in determining who would remain or become a general." That the deputies did not accept all of Dubois-Crancé's choices did not necessarily rele-gate these criteria to a back burner.[73] We know, for example, of legislation

---

73 Howard G. Brown, "Politics, Professionalism, and the Fate of Army Generals after Thermidor," *French Historical Studies* 19 (1995): 151–52.

of April 1795 that placed a new stress upon experience as a criterion for promotion in the ranks. The new measure discarded the overly vague requirement of seniority in years of service and replaced it with seniority *in existing rank*. By combining this principle with the requirement of four years to be served in the rank just below the one to which promotion was to be made, the deputies hoped to discourage the advancement of men who had entered the army many years before but were lacking in demonstrated ability. The same decree also tentatively suppressed the election of officers by fellow soldiers and suggested instead the nomination of officers by peers, with the final selection to be made by superiors. (Later legislation confirmed this tendency, vesting the final powers of selection in the government.)[74] The authorities also sought to strike a judicious balance in the matter of age, setting up bureaucratic procedures to eliminate incompetent officers who were overage, and yet at the same time using the new requirement of four years in a given rank prior to a promotion to curb the promotion of immature young madcaps (*sabreurs*).

The results of these policies were consequential. Bertaud, for instance, has found that the sublieutenants he sampled for the late 1790s were experienced soldiers; over half of them had served as privates, corporals, or higher NCOs prior to 1789. Volunteers of 1791 and 1792, who had been serving in the ranks for five years or more, shared with them the company-level officer posts. Neither the volunteers of 1793 nor the subsequent draftees could have much chance of promotion among such veterans.[75] In addition, officers of all ranks in these post-Jacobin times were expected to be mindful of their socioprofessional "dignity." Earlier in the Revolution, army officers had been instructed to think of themselves as "magistrates" who must at all times merit the confidence of the citizen-soldiers who were in civic terms their equals. Now, with a more strikingly hierarchical division of labor prevailing at all levels in the army, an officer could be rebuked for "compromising himself with subordinates" or for "being by nature a corporal and not changing with the change of costume." What was more, a stigma fell upon those officers who had made what were deemed "improper" marriages with women "without fortune."[76]

Nonetheless, if many of the attributes soon to characterize Napoleon's officer corps already described the army's commanding personnel under the Directory, the process of professionalization remained somewhat tentative. It has recently been observed, for example, that the Convention's efforts in 1794–95 to institutionalize "impersonal" criteria for the selection of generals were at times directly contravened by unjustified appointments that fostered factionalism, brought civilian supremacy into

74 Bertaud, *The Army of the French Revolution*, p. 280.
75 Ibid., pp. 283–84.
76 Ibid., pp. 284–85.

contempt, and undermined professionalism. But the larger point here is that the Directory's growing dependence upon military success for its very legitimacy – a deadly fruit of its own overextended foreign policy – tempted it into the trap of currying favor among army commanders by authorizing them to promote through the ranks whomever they pleased. This could only have the effect of encouraging clientage and militating against recent decrees that required greater experience and technical proficiency in officer ranks.[77]

In similar fashion, the professionalization of the rank-and-file soldiery continued along a path marked by a host of pitfalls. Through much of the Revolution, it is true, the infantryman could claim the right to be judged by his professional peers and was no longer subjected to degrading punishments meted out by an authoritarian organization. In addition, reformed recruitment procedures made for less discrimination in the ranks and gradually produced a fighting force more representative of the nation. Equally important were the tangible amenities, instruction, compensation, and provisions for the future that came to be associated with military service. The government, for instance, tried to resolve issues of pay and supply so as ensure that the recruit could realistically expect the logistical support he required – support taking the form of adequate food and housing, of serviceable weapons and abundant ammunition, of care when he was wounded, of pensions for his widow and children if he were to be killed.[78] The common soldier, one expert has gone so far as to assert, "became an image of the technicians of war, the NCOs and officers who commanded them."[79] As potentially "enlightened" citizens of the Republic performing a supremely patriotic and honorable task, the soldiers in the camps were to be accorded a professional status and self-respect denied to their forerunners of the ancien régime.

Yet, as we would expect, here too professionalization had its limits. For one thing, the infantryman's right to be "judged by his peers" and (in a more general sense) to assume any terms of equality between himself and his officers was ultimately overridden by the tendency toward hierarchy, subordination, and the specialization of roles within the army – which, to be fair, could itself be seen as indicating "professionalism" in another sense. More to the point is Alan Forrest's allusion to "financial crises which left the army denuded of funds."[80] More than any other factor, the

---

77 Howard G. Brown has recently enlarged upon all these issues in *War, Revolution, and the Bureaucratic State: Politics and Army Administration in France, 1791–1799* (New York: Oxford University Press, 1996).

78 Forrest, *The Soldiers of the French Revolution*, pp. 192–93. See also, once again, Woloch, *The French Veteran from the Revolution to the Restoration*, passim.

79 Bertaud, *The Army of the French Revolution*, p. 272.

80 Forrest, *The Soldiers of the French Revolution*, p. 193.

government's chronic fiscal difficulties crippled its ability to equip, instruct, and care adequately for its soldiers and to ensure decent pensions to their dependents and/or survivors.

We have had several occasions to describe the increasing subservience of soldiers to their officers in the late 1790s as indicative of rising professionalism in the army. Yet, especially in light of what was so soon to come, this subservience can just as easily be cited as betokening (along with other developments) the somewhat broader phenomenon of *militarization* in army and society. Another way of putting this would be to say that the specifically martial values that lay at the heart of the vocation of fighting men helped to inspire generals like Bonaparte and Hoche and Jourdan to extend their domination over their inferiors in the army to French civilians in the larger society as well.

Close attention to the issue of military justice reveals something of this process as it concerned the generals' growing domination of affairs within the armies. It appears that, from 1795 on, judicial procedure in the army came ever more under the generals' control. The Convention enacted a new law addressing this question on 18 September 1795. Heretofore, the courts martial had been composed of civilian judges, with juries made up half of military men and half of civilians; henceforth there were to be "councils" made up exclusively of military men, who would not need to show any special judicial competence. At least these councils or "courts" retained a vestige of democracy in that their military contingents consisted of three common soldiers along with three NCOs and three commissioned officers. In November 1796, however, even this changed. The courts or "councils" established and regulated earlier were replaced by permanent "councils" set up within each division of the army. These were to consist almost wholly of officers, though the division commanders were supposed to add one NCO to their ranks. Nor was this all. Each commander was entitled to change his council's membership however he saw fit, "in the interests of the service." The upshot of all this, plainly, was that soldiers were to be subordinated ever more strictly to their generals.[81] Through these and other measures, the generals came to dominate deliberations in the camps and from this reinforced position of influence could nominate whomever they pleased to inferior posts and so enlarge their personal following in the separate armies.

That the generals also came to wield a broader influence in French society derived in part from the state's expanding manpower needs and the new, permanently institutionalized conscription to which those needs eventually gave rise. Even specialists writing in a republican tradition have not glossed over the fact that the army lost its mass "democratic" basis under the late

81 Bertaud, *The Army of the French Revolution*, pp. 328–31.

Convention and early Directory. This resulted in some measure, of course, from losses sustained on the battlefield, but even more it reflected the endemic problems of military desertion, draft dodging, and soldiers' refusals to return to the ranks upon the expiration of furloughs and "hardship" leaves. As late as August 1794 the government had estimated that 732,474 soldiers were serving under the colors; by 1796 and 1797, however, that number had shrunk to less than 400,000. The manpower requisition originating in the famous levies of 1793 continued to operate perfunctorily, but "it must be admitted that its yield was limited." Bertaud's figures suggest attrition rates in the battalions and demibrigades rising from 4 percent in the Year II to 8 percent by 1796 and 1797. For this, he has conceded, "the scourge of desertion was mainly responsible."[82] Intriguingly, the pattern of geographical recruitment to the army during these lean years rather closely paralleled that of recruitment to the central bureaucracy: the northeastern departments and the Parisian basin were disproportionately represented. French patriotic sentiment – and the heavy hand of the government at Paris – still counted for something. But the overriding challenge for the military (and, thus, for those managing France's foreign policy) remained: how to counter the insidious plagues of draft dodging and desertion?[83]

The answer eventually came with the celebrated "Jourdan Law" of September 1798, the foundation stone of modern state conscription in war-prone France. Under this law, Woloch has explained:

men between the ages of 20 and 25 would thereafter be subject to conscription, but would actually be called to service by legislative decree only as needed. Each annual birth cohort formed a "class" of *conscripts* (a new term designating young men who became subject to conscription in a particular year rather than those actually inducted). Mobilization would begin with the class of 20-year-olds, and would move forward as needed. If they were not called by the end of their 25th year, conscripts would be permanently discharged from the obligation.[84]

Insofar as the Jourdan Law intended to deny conscripts actually called to the colors the old option of hiring replacements, it seemed to exemplify the "social leveling" so frequently imposed by state-security needs in the Revolution.

The government, which, as we know, was about to plunge into the vast War of the Second Coalition, wasted no time in invoking this formidable new instrument to bring its armed forces back up to size. Before September's end, the authorities called up the entire first "class" of twenty-year-olds, ostensibly for a maximum of five years' service, and

---

82 Ibid., esp. pp. 272–73, 275.
83 This issue is thoroughly discussed in Forrest, *Conscripts and Deserters: The Army and French Society during the Revolution and Empire* (New York: Oxford University Press, 1989).
84 Woloch, *The New Regime*, p. 390.

conscription became the key priority for officials – and the most agitated topic of conversation – all over France. But, as experts on the period have been quick to remark, the fact that the Directors soon had to ask the legislature to mobilize men as needed from the "classes" of twenty-one- and twenty-two-year-olds and by June 1799 to call *all* young men in those categories to the colors shows how bitter and deep-seated was the opposition to conscription in many departments. Young Frenchmen in many regions found the notion of military service repugnant, and – significantly – their families, always needful of their labor on the land, especially at harvesttime, tended to back them strongly.[85] A law of 17 April 1799 attempted to mitigate the societal impact of institutionalized conscription. It permitted "conscripts" to choose (and possibly pay?) volunteers to replace them in advance or to draw lots among themselves; those drawing in bad luck could also purchase replacements. However this act may have militated against the "egalitarian" purposes of the *loi Jourdan*, the main thrust of military legislation in 1798–99 was, it seems, "toward a militarization of society as desired by career soldiers."[86] We may question, however, whether this militarization was an asset or a threat to a political regime too weak to enforce its original legislation on the crucial matter of military requisitions.

But militarization challenged the government most directly when it took the form of insubordinate generals. In this connection, we should underscore the critical importance of the civilian commissioners to the armies. They were only too obviously a bridle to politically ambitious *militaires*; hence the insistence with which generals like Bonaparte and Hoche demanded their suppression. That suppression eventually came in December 1796. It was an action bound to have major consequences. From this time forward, the men in the ranks would be subjected entirely to the authority of the generals; and the latter would be largely free to pillage conquered lands as they saw fit.[87] Unsurprisingly, the civilian authorities later revived the *commissaires aux armées* in a desperate attempt to restore their control over the armies' commanders. But, in the wake of the coup of 18 June 1799, the Directory was forced once again to suppress the *commissaires*. The government thus lost perhaps the only means of reining in the generals, whose increasingly blatant independence in military, administrative, and even diplomatic affairs spoke directly to the weaknesses of a revolutionary government awash in warfare.

Some political regimes "awash in warfare" manage to survive. In fact, they may even draw renewed strength from the (frequently interrelated) developments of heightened military professionalism and militarization of society as a whole. But the Directory, we know, did not survive. It therefore

85 Ibid., pp. 390–91.
86 Bertaud, *The Army of the French Revolution*, p. 344.
87 Ibid., pp. 328–31.

falls to us now to reconsider the evolution of politics in France during the final years of the Revolution and to reassess the relative significance of internal and external factors in preparing the way for General Bonaparte's seizure of state power in November 1799.

On the morrow of the coup that brought Bonaparte to power in November 1799, co-conspirator Joseph Fouché averred that the late government had been "too weak to uphold the glory of the Republic against external enemies and to guarantee citizens' rights against the domestic factions."[88] Fouché's judgment, however colored by self-interest, does speak to a larger fact: that the Directory, like all the regimes preceding it in eighteenth-century France, succumbed to a conjunction of foreign and domestic crises. Historians of recent vintage have tended to stress the Directory's internal weaknesses. They have, in the first instance, pointed to flaws in the "Constitution of the Year III" that made the government founded upon it problematic from the start, but have wisely followed this up with a deeper analysis of contradictions in the political culture and society of those years. Yet any explanation of the Directory's collapse is likely to be incomplete if it fails to place all of these undeniably relevant factors in a larger context of geopolitics. War, we shall argue, aggravated all of the constitutional and sociocultural weaknesses of the regime of 1795–99, sapped its finances, and ensured that it would ultimately be discredited in the eyes of the politically attuned "notables."

It is fair enough to commence with the actual constitutional arrangements of 1795–99 and the problems in day-to-day governance that, to some degree, stemmed from those arrangements. The Constitution drawn up for France by the Thermidorians apportioned power between a legislature (now to be bicameral) and a five-man Directory. The Council of Five Hundred (all of whose members had to be at least thirty years old) would propose laws. The Council of "Elders" or "Ancients" (consisting of 250 deputies aged forty or above) would approve or reject laws proposed by the Five Hundred. Executive power would lie in the five-man Directory. The original Directors were chosen by the Elders from a list of ten candidates for each post prepared by the Five Hundred. One Director was to retire each year, and he would be ineligible for reappointment for five years. Moreover, the Directors were forbidden, without legislative sanction, to position troops within 60 kilometers of the assemblies. Hence, the risk of undue pressure being exerted by the executive upon the legislature would supposedly be curbed. Yet the Directors would control the daily labors of the ministers and the officialdom of government, and were

88 Cited in Lyons, *France under the Directory*, p. 233.

to be represented in the local departments and cantons by *commissaires* overseeing the application of laws by elected administrators at those levels. (The Directors also appointed *commissaires* to the law courts and – intermittently – to the armies.) Finally, all elected officials, from the national deputies to local administrators, were to be chosen during a ten-day cycle of voting in late March and early April. The electoral system of 1795–99 recalled that instituted earlier in the Revolution by the Constituent Assembly in that it was "two-tiered" and indirect, allowing a much broader adult male franchise at the primary stage than at the secondary stage.[89]

Whether or not these arrangements were seriously flawed has been vigorously debated by historians. Back in the 1930s, Albert Goodwin stoutly argued for their essential viability.[90] While some subsequent scholars have concurred in this judgment, others have not been so sure. Martyn Lyons, for example, has seen the Constitution of the Year III as a "creation of abstract theorists, who imagined that the most 'rational' plan would necessarily work best." The government's "executive arm," he has contended, "was fatally and deliberately weakened." For one thing, a five-man executive might easily fall prey to internal squabbling, and blind chance could influence the quality of its personnel, in that lots were ostensibly to be drawn annually to determine which Director would "retire." More crucial, arguably, was the "rigid separation of powers" mandated by the Constitution. The ministers did not sit in the legislature, and the Directors had to communicate with the deputies by official "messages." Moreover, because the Five Hundred controlled the purse strings, it could, if dominated by a hostile majority, paralyze the Directors. "The Directory, which had no power of dissolution, and no veto, could only reply by unconstitutional methods." The way was open, in other words, for the coups, the executive purges of the legislature and (belike) of local government, for which the Directors indeed became notorious. More generally, a certain inflexibility plagued the government's internal workings. Not only were executive and legislative powers rigidly separated; the inability of the Elders to amend the edicts proposed by the Five Hundred made for tensions *within* this bicameral legislature. And the procedure for amending the Constitution itself, Lyons has pertinently noted, "was almost Byzantine in its complexity."[91]

It would be difficult to disagree with the inference Lyons has drawn from all of this: namely, that the frequent Directorial coups and "exceptional laws" of this period reflect unfavorably on the Thermidorians' constitutional handiwork. Yet it is just as certain that a satisfactory explanation of

---

89 These constitutional arrangements are summarized lucidly in Woronoff, *The Thermidorian Regime and the Directory*, pp. 29–42. The electoral system is discussed in detail in Crook, *Elections in the French Revolution*, pp. 131–57.
90 Refer again to Goodwin, "The French Executive Directory," pp. 201–18.
91 Lyons, *France under the Directory*, pp. 18–20.

the Directory's shortcomings must take us beyond a critical reading of the Constitution of the Year III. It must take us into complex issues of political culture and (polarized) social relations, and it requires as well that we reassess the relationship between Paris and the provinces and – ultimately – that obtaining between France's domestic and foreign policies.

On the matter of political culture, we need to recall one of the central legacies of the ancien régime to the Revolution: the preference for political consensus in society, which is to say the distrust of any notion of a pluralistic politics, of a free competition of political factions or parties. We have already seen how this legacy was reflected in the increasingly acrimonious factionalism of earlier phases of the Revolution and in the Jacobin dictatorship of the Year II. But the tendency hardly expired with Robespierre. When Boissy d'Anglas, one of the most prominent survivors of the Terror, insisted that 9 Thermidor, Year II, "was not a party victory, but a national movement which gave back to the people the exercise of its rights and to the Republic its independence," he was giving voice to the persistent resistance in France to the notion of a multiparty, competitive politics.[92]

And indeed, this became one of the hallmarks of the Directory. In theory, it offered representative governance based – at least in part – on electoral politics, but it never fully accepted the need for a contestatory system of organized political parties. "It was better to die with honor defending the republic and its established government," revealingly claimed one of the Directors, La Révellière-Lépeaux, "than to perish or even to live in the muck of parties and the play-things of the factions."[93] There can be little doubt that this deeply rooted consensual political philosophy, this predilection for a "fraternity of citizens" over the divisiveness of "factions," powerfully motivated the Directory to play its *jeu de bascule*, its balancing game of purges and counterpurges during the four years of its existence. Thus its inauguration in late 1795 upon the basis of a legislature two-thirds of whose members were to come from the departing Convention – this, to fend off resurgent royalism. Thus its decision in September 1797 (the famous Fructidor coup d'état) to purge declared or suspected royalists from the legislative assemblies and from the councils of local government as part of an effort to combat a renewed threat from the Right. Thus its decision less than a year later (in the coup of Floréal, Year VI) to round upon the very Jacobins holding national and local office who had been so recently enlisted in its antiroyalist campaign, but who were now viewed as personifying a resurgent threat from the Left. And thus the Directors' entreaties to their *commissaires aux départements* the following spring to

92 Boissy d'Anglas cited in Lynn Hunt, David Lansky, and Paul Hanson, "The Failure of the Liberal Republic in France, 1795–1799: The Road to Brumaire," *Journal of Modern History* 51 (1979): 738.
93 Cited in ibid., pp. 737–38.

find candidates for office who would pledge strict adherence to the government's line in all matters.[94] "In essence," a trio of American historians have concluded, "the republicans of 1795 wanted to establish a liberal republic without accepting the imperatives of liberal politics."[95]

But the republicans' political concerns were powerfully reinforced by their *social* anxieties. Throughout the 1790s, political polarization had invariably betokened the presence of social polarization. Hence, when the Directors in 1796 and 1797 lashed out at the "Philanthropic Institutes" that were enlisting candidates and mobilizing voters on the right, and at the "Constitutional Circles" and other Jacobin groups on the left, they were trying as much to defend a social *via media* against social extremes as to champion a "middle way" (supporting the government) in politics.

On the right, the authorities could always see (and genuinely feared) émigrés and domestic ex-nobles "dug in" upon their rustic estates who were probably of one mind in desiring a return to the good old days of social privilege, deference, and all the services associated with seigneurialism. They were keenly aware as well of the Declaration of Verona issued in 1795 by the comte de Provence ("Louis XVIII") and promising an eventual restoration of the old regime's social structure and prerogatives.[96] But if the French leaders could see the Revolution's social gains being menaced from the right, they were just as quick to perceive a social threat posed to middle-class "respectability" on the left.

Colin Lucas has noted on this last point that the Revolution "was by and large the business of only part of the population," a "political nation" whose members "continued to form the *pays légal* of property owners who voted in national elections and provided the personnel of local government."[97] These were, for the most part, the "solid" Frenchmen to whom the Directory wished to confine the full rights of active citizenship. Hence, the consternation aroused in governing circles by the increasingly aggressive Jacobin campaign – especially in the days after Fructidor, Year V – to broaden the social basis of French politics. As one historian of Jacobin activism in these late days of the Revolution has remarked, the politicians and clubbists on the left did not define their sociopolitical goals with any great precision. Still, they did share "a minimal preference

---

94 A lucid synopsis of these purges and counterpurges staged by the Directors during 1795–99 can be found in Woronoff, *The Thermidorian Regime and the Directory*, esp. pp. 30–36, 55–58, 60–61, and 176–82.
95 Hunt et al., "The Failure of the Liberal Republic in France," p. 736.
96 On the social views of those on the Far Right, see Jacques Godechot, *La Contre-Révolution: Doctrine et Action* (Paris: Presses Universitaires de France, 1961); and D. M. G. Sutherland, *France, 1789–1815: Revolution and Counterrevolution* (New York: Oxford University Press, 1986), passim.
97 Colin Lucas, "The First Directory and the Rule of Law," *French Historical Studies* 10 (1977): 258.

for a republic where political oligarchy and social pretension would be attacked, and where the 'workingman' had a rightful place in civil and political life." The membership of the Jacobin societies during 1795–99 seems to have consisted for the most part of "a conglomerate of intellectuals, white-collar employees, and 'workingmen' or artisans of all varieties with fairly low status and poor education."[98] These last – workingmen or artisans – were precisely the citizens whom officials under the Directory associated most closely with the Terror. It is not at all astonishing, consequently, that Jacobin efforts to involve such laboring Frenchmen in post-Terrorist politics should have raised Directorial hackles and helped to convince the government to strike out at the Left in 1798 and 1799.

It is clear in retrospect that French governance in the late 1790s was caught in a difficult if not necessarily fatal domestic bind. Government at the center was itself internally divided and at times well-nigh paralyzed by an overly strict separation of constitutional powers. Beyond that problem, however, officials in both the executive and the legislative branches found it difficult to observe the letter and the spirit of the competitive system of politics through which they were sworn to govern the country. This was so in part because, Frenchmen that they were, they tended to regard such a system as favoring factionalism and divisiveness in public affairs. But it was also true that those who were ruling France genuinely feared – and had some reason to fear – the impact upon politics of the deep polarization induced in society by the years of revolution. Hence, the Directory's notorious *politique de bascule*, its attempt to strike a sociopolitical "balance" with alternating blows against the Right and the Left. Such a policy, however, guaranteed as it was to alienate those at both ends of the political spectrum, made it absolutely essential for the government to develop a centrist political party and local patronage connections upon which it could, in these agitated times, rely.

Yet this was precisely what did *not* come to pass. As one member of the Council of Five Hundred lamented in Fructidor, Year VII:

I know that people have talked a lot about a neutral and centrist party, equally opposed to all extremists and destined, by its wisdom, ever to hold the balance of affairs in its hand; but this party is without life, without color, without movement; it consists, throughout France, of some disguised Royalists, and many weak individuals ready to compromise themselves; in all times of troubles, the balance falls from their timid hands."[99]

Delivered a few months later, this commentary could have served as an epitaph for a political regime that, for lack of a viable sociopolitical center,

98 Isser Woloch, *Jacobin Legacy: The Democratic Movement under the Directory* (Princeton, N.J.: Princeton University Press, 1970), esp. pp. 92–93, 95–96, and 112.
99 Cited in Lyons, *France under the Directory*, pp. 230–31. My translation from the French.

had to place its powers and responsibilities in the hands of a talented (and lucky) general.

Why, then, did the Directory fail to develop a strong political constituency in revolutionary France? In part, no doubt, this was a matter of inherited political culture, an inflexibility of political outlook already discussed. Just as the Directors could not really brook the existence of competitive parties on the right and the left, viewing contestatory politics as "factionalism" destructive of society's common weal, so they could not conceive of a government "party" in positive terms. But, clearly, we have to deal here with more than a matter of political culture. Socioeconomic interests were (or should have been?) deeply engaged as well. However, recent scholarly commentary does very little to validate the Marxist paradigm of a "bourgeois" Directory solidly anchored in the bedrock of entrepreneurial and other middle-class interests. Indeed, British "bureaucratic" historian Clive Church has gone so far as to declare that "the Directory failed precisely because it was not a bourgeois regime.... The Directors and their supporters were basically a political group, lacking roots in society, and consequently failing to maintain themselves in power." Without "anything but the most grudging support from public opinion and its leaders," the regime had no reason to be surprised if, in the end, businessmen and other notables whose aspirations it had never systematically represented abandoned it, preferring a "leap in the dark" with a political and social outsider like Bonaparte.[100] Church's fellow Briton Martyn Lyons has concurred in this interpretation to the point of allowing that "it may indeed be too simple to describe the Directory as a *bourgeois* Republic, since, in the last resort, the *bourgeoisie* abandoned the regime." On the other hand, Lyons has also seen Church's revisionism as itself simplistic: after all, some of the Directory's policies – preservation of a free economy, protection of property rights, denial of universal male suffrage, and so on – were without doubt policies favored by the "bourgeoisie," however it is defined. To this extent, the Directory, like all its predecessor regimes in the revolutionary era, reflected the social biases of the middle strata in French society.[101]

Martyn Lyons's comments may constitute something of a "middle-of-the-road" approach to the question of the Directory's basis in French society, navigating as they do between the extremes of neo-Marxist analysis on the one hand and bureaucratic reductionism on the other. Yet they scarcely add up to a compelling portrayal of a government courting, and receiving strategic support from, a powerful array of interests in society.

100 Clive Church, "In Search of the Directory," in J. F. Bosher, ed., *French Government and Society, 1500–1850*, esp. pp. 274–76, 279–80, and 288–89.
101 Lyons, *France under the Directory*, pp. 236–37.

This conclusion takes on additional credibility if we return once again to the relationship (problematic throughout the Revolution) between Paris and outlying regions of France. We have already had ample occasion to note, in sundry connections, the indifference (or, in some cases, outright antipathy) displayed by many provincial Frenchmen and Frenchwomen toward revolutionary events in their country's capital.[102] The current scholarly interest in political culture, frequently helping to inform the research conducted in provincial archives, makes it possible to continue to question (if not altogether deny) the Revolution's relevance to most "ordinary" provincial folk during the tumultuous 1790s.

A number of historians working in this mode have maintained, for instance, that there was a widespread tendency on the local level to ignore national politics altogether during the so-called First Directory (1795–97). Unfortunately, they have also found, the Republic's leaders did little in practice to "improve" provincial attitudes in this respect. What they ought to have done, it may appear obvious today, was to try to convince locally prominent citizens that what transpired in Paris *did* affect them directly. Yet to do so would have required demonstrating to the local citizenry that the government was able to deal with *local* problems, perceived as such within a local context. It made little difference what the Directors and deputies viewed as their international and domestic goals if, in the departments and cantons, their *commissaires* and other agents were unable (for example) to maintain order on the highways, apply military conscription fairly, manage urgent issues of subsistence, and find ways to accommodate arguments for and against government intervention in local affairs. Seen in this light, the government's problems were daunting if not insoluble from the start. As early as 1796, the Directory was finding it difficult to persuade the politically conscious in the departments that it could solve local problems in a professional, nonpartisan fashion. The Directors subsequently staged the coup of Fructidor, Year V, to overturn earlier elections that they (rightly) perceived as rejecting their local policies of 1796. But this, in another ironic twist, led the so-called Second Directory (of 1797–99) to adopt illegal political and administrative measures that in turn only further discredited the government in provincial minds.[103]

What deepened the government's isolation in the departments and cantons of the Republic was its ostensibly neutral but really intolerant and even persecutory stance on religious affairs. The Thermidorians and Directors

---

102 In this connection, refer again to the works by Richard Cobb cited specifically in the Introduction.

103 See again Lucas, "The First Directory and the Rule of Law," pp. 231–60; and Hunt et al., "The Failure of the Liberal Republic in France," esp. pp. 736–38. Lynn Hunt also analyzes these issues in *Politics, Culture, and Class*, passim.

have won some scholarly plaudits for attempting to instill a new civil religion in the minds and hearts of the citizenry.[104] Yet there is little evidence to indicate that the new faith, with its patently political overtones, ever caught on in a major way among the traditionally Catholic masses. What is more, the government, even in the relatively tolerant times preceding the leftist Fructidor coup, only grudgingly conceded Catholic liberties. Sunday had to be a working day under the revolutionary calendar, and the customary holidays also fell victim to the new temporal schema. In addition, local officials played an intrusive role of surveillance over religious services: preachers were often dismayed to find police spies attending their sermons. Moreover, priests were subjected to civic "tests" reminiscent of the Civil Constitution and were held answerable, under penalty of arbitrary deportation, for any violations of the myriad rules against bells and "exterior signs." Again, those who opened schools could incur official wrath if they scheduled lessons for the *décadi* or treated Sundays as holidays.[105]

During 1796 and much of 1797, the Directors and their local agents did not pursue these policies with an ironclad consistency; however, in the wake of Fructidor (September 1797), conditions for the clergy and communicants of the disestablished Church worsened. A tough loyalty oath was imposed on all priests determined still to minister to their flocks; at the same time, the government arrogated to itself the power to deport or incarcerate "refractory" priests by simple administrative order. As the geostrategists at Paris overextended themselves ever more perilously in continental high politics, eventually becoming immersed in the war crisis of late 1798 and 1799, they struck out at rumored émigrés and recalcitrant priests in the provinces in a manner all too reminiscent of the deepening war crisis and revolutionary situation of the early 1790s.[106] And, just as earlier, so now, harassing *curés* and *vicaires* only helped to turn the local populace against the government. "Local documents are full of examples of strife and resistance over the religious issue," Church has observed. "In the quiet department of the Haute Marne this was practically the only cause of public disorder, leading on one occasion to a whole village rioting when two luckless gendarmes tried to arrest a refractory priest." While we may assume that most rural communities in this period that were roused at times from political quiescence were not exercised solely about religious

---

104 For some reflections on this fascinating subject, consult Mona Ozouf, *Festivals and the French Revolution*, trans. Alan Sheridan (Cambridge, Mass.: Harvard University Press, 1988); and Ozouf's articles "Revolutionary Calendar" and "Revolutionary Religion" in Furet and Ozouf, eds., *A Critical Dictionary of the French Revolution*, pp. 538–70.
105 McManners, *The French Revolution and the Church*, pp. 120–21.
106 Ibid., pp. 121–27.

questions, we can agree with Church that the government's brutal treatment of priests and their flocks "was a major cause of the alienation of public opinion during the later stages of the Directory's existence."[107]

In summing up this situation, one historian has criticized the Directory for preferring "anticlerical growling and bristling to the genuine neutrality in religious affairs which might have brought about a pacification."[108] In the final analysis, this may be a valid judgment, all the more in that now the Directory's mismanagement of religious affairs can be readily contrasted to Bonaparte's statesmanlike approach to the problem just a few years later. But the Directory's behavior, however counterproductive it may have been, is explicable on several counts. For one thing, the political culture within which the policymakers of the late 1790s were operating tended to blinker their religious perceptions much as it did their political perceptions. Just as the Directors had a difficult time accepting the notion of organized and freely competing political parties, so they could not in the end resist the temptation to police and even persecute a Catholic Church that was supposed to be free to compete with other faiths for the popular favor. More important, however, was the "force of circumstances." The Directory, eventually besieged on the international front by the Second Coalition, and challenged at home by political extremists on both the right and the left, was tempted to confuse apolitical Catholicism with the royalist-counterrevolutionary cause, and to enlist Jacobin anticlericalism in a patriotic if sporadic campaign against these ecclesiastical and secular threats to the Revolution. Hence the continuation under the Directory of revolutionary anticlericalism – and a further means by which the post-Thermidorian regime undercut its own position in France.

What emerges from this analysis of conditions in France in the late 1790s is the fact that the Directory, even if it had not been so hopelessly mired in warfare of ever-expanding scope, would have found the task of establishing its legitimacy to be daunting. But of course there was in reality no way of "getting away" from the war – a war that, as Mirabeau and others had earlier prophesied, was fated to become an integral part of the revolutionary process. Warfare undermined the Directory both directly and indirectly: directly, by crippling its finances and sapping its base of support in society; and indirectly, by militarizing domestic politics to such an extent that only generals and their armies could rescue the civilian government from the consequences of its weaknesses.

To weigh the direct impact of the war upon the Directory is, in large part, to range over points we have already made in other contexts. To begin

---

107 Church, "In Search of the Directory," pp. 286–87.
108 McManners, *The French Revolution and the Church*, p. 129.

with, finances are the "sinews of government," and it was overwhelmingly French foreign policy which prevented the Directory from ending the protracted fiscal crisis that had dogged the revolutionaries since 1789. Moreover, official efforts to deal with that crisis only cost the government support in what should have been its key "middle-class" constituencies. The final agonies of the *assignats*, and their replacement by *mandats territoriaux* that themselves depreciated almost as quickly, may have fattened the purses of certain speculators in currency and allowed some debtors a windfall in paying off their debts, but such a turn of events could only have diminished the Directory in the eyes of creditors, military and civilian pensioners, government employees, and others dependent upon the Revolution's paper currency. Even more damaging was the "bankruptcy of the two-thirds," which, however necessary it may have seemed from a strictly financial point of view, effectively wiped out two-thirds of many *rentiers'* most crucial form of income. Finance ministers of the Bourbon kings in prerevolutionary times had – with good reason – vetoed such wholesale state bankruptcies for fear of antagonizing the influential *rentiers* of Paris and provincial capitals; here, now, was a "revolutionary" government forced into just such a course of action by the monstrous expenses of war. Then, again, there were the shipbuilders, insurance agents, merchants, and refiners of port cities like Le Havre and Nantes, La Rochelle and Bordeaux and Marseilles, whose lucrative earnings from overseas colonies and trade were in the late 1790s stifled by the British blockade. Although, obviously, there existed the counterpoise of currency speculators and military contractors – Gabriel-Julien Ouvrard and others – who knew how to profit from the situation, nevertheless the Directory's expansionist foreign policy (or, rather, the bill for that policy) must have antagonized a veritable army of "bourgeois" citizens: entrepreneurs of all stripes, *rentiers* and pensioners, and many of the government's own functionaries.[109]

The impact the Directory's war had on the masses is naturally more difficult to gauge; still, there are indications aplenty of widespread apathy if not universal resentment in plebeian ranks over the French "descent upon Europe." In the southern department of the Gard, Gwynne Lewis has found, the endless war, "although reviving the revolutionary ardor of some, particularly the urban workers, offered little to the rural Catholic population." The Catholics were, in any case, likelier to be aroused by drastic religious and economic changes than by foreign policy.[110] From the central department of the Seine-et-Oise came this realistic appraisal of the local peasantry by the government's *commissaire*: "The French victories

109 On these economic points, see again Goodwin, "The French Executive Directory," pp. 201–18; and Crouzet, "Wars, Blockade, and Economic Change in Europe," pp. 567–88.
110 Gwynne Lewis, *The Second Vendée: The Continuity of Counter-Revolution in the Department of the Gard, 1789–1815* (Oxford: Clarendon Press, 1978), pp. 134–35.

appeal to a section of them, but do not touch them greatly, because they are purchased at the cost of their sons' blood, and the peasantry are not sufficiently committed to accept such sacrifices. They neglect the exercise of civic rights because exercising these rights has exhausted them." It would only require "peace, tranquility and a certain period of calm," offered this observer wistfully, "to make them feel the advantages of the Revolution and to make them like the Revolution again."[111] If only "peace, tranquility and a certain period of calm" could have been France's lot! But there was, as always, the war ... and as of 1798, that meant a military draft of unprecedented onerousness. And, whatever republican historiography may tell us, nothing was so ideally designed to sow widespread fear and hatred of the Revolution's war making among the French as the conscription that was institutionalized in the *loi Jourdan*.[112]

Hence, the war probably undercut the Directory's legitimacy as much as did any flaws in its constitutional arrangements or in the political culture and social relations of the day. But the war also contributed most decisively to the regime's downfall by militarizing its politics in such a fashion as to make its subversion and eventual overthrow by the generals virtually unavoidable.

To begin with, there was militarization on the radicalized right. On the eve of Fructidor (September 1797), most of the conservative deputies in the legislature found themselves confronting a devil's choice between sanctioning military action by reactionaries – action which, if successful, would likely benefit irreconcilable royalists – and accepting their own (militarily compassed?) defeat by the Directory. In the end, despite last-minute military precautions on the royalist right, the majority of conservatives allowed themselves to be defeated (and, in some cases, purged) by a progovernment coup put through, significantly, by Bonaparte's stand-in general Augereau and troops loyal to the regime. The conservative "Clichyites" were painfully aware of, and for the most part wished to dissociate themselves from, those implacable foes of the Revolution who tended to discredit all of its critics by taking up arms against France. When the comte de Provence issued his inflammatory and reactionary Declaration of Verona in 1795, when irreconcilable émigrés sought to prolong the civil war in the Vendée or to foment military uprisings in the eastern and southern provinces, and when extremists on the right lobbied the other European powers to form a new coalition against Paris, they were contributing to the militarization of conservative (and, by extension, all) politics in the Republic.[113]

111 Cited in Church, "In Search of the Directory," p. 286.
112 On this point, refer once again to Forrest, *Conscripts and Deserters*, passim, and *The Soldiers of the French Revolution*, passim.
113 Harvey Mitchell, *The Underground War against Revolutionary France* (Oxford: Clarendon Press, 1965), esp. pp. 249 and 252.

Indeed, if a militarization of politics manifested itself on the right, it was just as evident on the left. The recrudescence of Jacobinism around the time of Fructidor, and over a subsequent two-year period dominated increasingly by military and security issues, indicates this clearly.

Tellingly, in the preamble to the coup of Fructidor, Year V, a certain sympathetic resonance developed between the armies abroad and progressive activists at home.[114] In the troubling wake of elections in the spring of 1797 energizing the Right, apprehensive "patriots" found themselves looking for political salvation to the victorious republican armies stationed in Italy and Germany. The generals and their men, in fact, had a variety of ways to express their displeasure with the conservative trend of politics at home and to hearten activists on the Left. General Bonaparte used his divisional newspaper to sound the charge against the Right. Petitions and proclamations swearing fealty to the Directory flooded into Paris from the battalions. And toasts ostentatiously drunk by officers and their troops (and publicized back home) trumpeted such messages as: "To the unity of French republicans; may they follow the Army of Italy's example and, supported by it, regain that energy which is fitting for the leading nation on Earth!" For their part, Jacobins and other activists responded eagerly to such expressions of support. Literally thousands of citizens in departments all over the Republic (Puy-de-Dôme, Mont Blanc, Nord, Ille-et-Vilaine, Côte d'Or, Vienne, Saône-et-Loire, and so on) sent petitions back to the *militaires*, declaring that they were inspired by the attestations of support in the camps, were alert to the dangers of political "reaction," and were ready to defend the Republic with their lives. Reporting rapturously on all of this, a leading leftist journalist voiced the hope that "this general explosion of patriotism will inform our brave brothers-in-law that the nation still has in its midst numerous battalions of *enfans fidèles.*"

Small wonder that, in these circumstances, the Directors and several key generals were able in concert to engineer the coup and extensive purges of Fructidor. Small wonder, as well, that in the months to come Jacobin beneficiaries of Fructidor from one end of the Republic to the other would seize every occasion to proclaim solidarity with France's brave *militaires*. Some clubs fraternized ceremoniously with passing detachments of troops. Some even tried to involve army units in local political controversies, pitting the "honest" patriots against citizens suspected of sinister designs against the Republic.[115] But perhaps the issue most calculated to strengthen ties between soldiers and activists on the Left, if it could be adequately exploited, was that involving the veterans' bonus. The Convention had promised such a special compensation to the *défenseurs de la patrie* back in the Year II, but

114 Woloch, *Jacobin Legacy*, pp. 70–76, for this discussion.
115 Ibid., pp. 134–35.

for financial and political reasons nothing had come of this grand gesture. The lawmakers under the Directory, acutely aware of their dependence on the goodwill of the armies, had kept the notion of a veterans' bonus on their agenda but as of 1797–98 had still failed to pass it into law. Yet this was an issue ideally calculated to attract the support of the two most reliably patriotic interests in French society: namely, the Jacobins and the soldiery. Why not mobilize some of the nation's resources in the form of the veterans' bonus so as to succor courageous citizens to whom the Revolution owed so much and yet had hitherto accorded so little?[116] Predictably, therefore, local clubbists bombarded the government with petitions demanding swift establishment of this compensation for the tried and true heroes of the nation.

In these and other ways, Jacobins betrayed a continuing – if problematic – reliance on armed force that paralleled developments at the other end of the political spectrum. But the Directors – at least in 1798, a year of relatively favorable geopolitics – would have none of it. As we know, they struck out at the Left in the spring of 1798, severely curtailing leftist activism in all its forms. Yet, in the following year, with the crisis of the War of the Second Coalition, Jacobinism's identification with French geostrategic security produced – for the last time – an efflorescence of leftist political influence and activism. In the wake of the coup of 30 prairial, Year VII (18 June 1799), power shifted somewhat from the executive to the legislature, and a number of measures bearing a Jacobin imprint and recalling the perilous times of the Year II were enacted. They included a call-up of all classes of conscripts, a forced loan to be assessed on the rich, and a "law of hostages" aimed at relatives of émigrés and ex-nobles in the provinces. Jacobin deputies galvanized by the national crisis hurled accusations of corruption at a number of the Directors, ministers, and *commissaires* to the armies, and coordinated activities with a revitalized Jacobin Club in Paris. Throughout the country, clubs were founded or reinstated; newspapers were established or revived; and an outpouring of petitions calling for a return to the military-patriotic heroics of the Year II reinforced this "classic pattern of resurgent Jacobinism in Directorial France."[117]

Unhappily for the Left, it was too good to last. After all, the Year VII was not the Year II: precisely because the Revolution had succeeded so well at its chief task of rebuilding civilian and military institutions, nothing like the Jacobin idealism (and terrorism) of 1793–94 was now required to safeguard France's place in the world. This was, significantly, the message given by Director Paul Barras to General Jourdan in a confidential interview granted at the time. "We have today an organization, great civil and military organizations," Barras insisted. The way to master the current

116 Ibid., pp. 165–69.
117 See, on these developments: ibid., pp. 367–70; and Lyons, *France under the Directory*, pp. 224–29.

crisis was simply to turn existing resources to account and mobilize all citizens "in a regular way and without any shock." A Jacobin motion to declare *la patrie* once again *en danger* was voted down in the Five Hundred on 14 September; the most prominent pro-Jacobin in the government, War Minister Bernadotte, was cashiered; and leftist deputies, clubbists, and propagandists were once again badgered into silence.[118]

So there would be no repetition of the Terror in France. Yet this in no way signaled the notables' approval of the constitutional status quo. Changes in the personnel of the Directory – above all, the accession to executive power of Siéyès, the Revolution's most celebrated constitutional theorist – pointed toward an important revision of French governance. As Lyons has truthfully remarked, "there were many former supporters of the Directory who now sensed the inadequacy of the Constitution of the Year 3.... A strong government had to be found to defeat the Coalition, eliminate the deficit, and control political extremism." But, given the profound militarization of revolutionary France – of its foreign policy, its leftist, rightist, and even "centrist" politics, its public institutions and its populace – what were the chances that yet another civilian politician or coterie of politicians could furnish that strong, unified leadership in Paris? Siéyès and his co-conspirators may have thought that they could fill the bill – once they had "used" yet another general to overthrow the Directory. But a more permanent solution was likely to lie in another direction. "On 17 vendémiaire VIII, Bonaparte landed at Fréjus. The Directory's nemesis was at hand...."[119]

"Though it was chance that gave power to Bonaparte," Jacques Godechot has written, "the coup d'état of 18 Brumaire was a logical outcome of the revolution." After all, others in their turn – Patriots in the Constituent Assembly, Girondists in the Legislative Assembly, Jacobins in the Convention, Thermidorian politicians and Directors thereafter – had endeavored (and failed) to master the revolutionary process in France. "Why shouldn't a victorious general become the chief of state in turn?"[120] Perhaps. But behind what might initially appear to have been a simple "process of elimination of alternative solutions," deeper forces were at work. Early on in the Revolution, observers as ideologically dissimilar as Edmund Burke in England and Maximilien Robespierre in France had foreseen the possibility of a military finale to this upheaval. In retrospect, they appear to have shared this vital insight: that a country long given over to (and likely for the foreseeable future to embrace) the waging of war, yet striving at the

118 Woloch, *Jacobin Legacy*, pp. 370–71.
119 Lyons, *France under the Directory*, pp. 228–29.
120 Godechot, *France and the Atlantic Revolution of the Eighteenth Century, 1770–1799*, trans. Herbert H. Rowen (New York: Free Press, 1965), pp. 246–47.

same time to renew social institutions at home, would be prone at some point to entrust its international and domestic tasks to some charismatic soldier/statesman. That, by the late 1790s, politics of *all* hues on the spectrum, and society at large, had become so thoroughly militarized by the experience of the Revolution only pointed further to the realization of such a prophecy. Hence, in this more profound sense as well, Godechot was correct. Napoleon Bonaparte himself was not "inevitable"; but someone very much like him was, by this time, scarcely to be avoided.

Conclusion: the Revolution in the French and global context

The French Revolution, one scholar has recently concluded, was a "decisive historical rupture" that placed Louis XVI and his eventual successor, Napoleon I, in "totally different spheres."[1] To adopt this view is to disagree in some measure with those writers, from Alexis de Tocqueville to Georges Lefebvre to François Furet, who over the years have accentuated continuities undergirding historical developments in prerevolutionary, revolutionary, and postrevolutionary France.[2] In completing what we have defined in these pages as a "global-historical" analysis of the upheavals of 1789–99, we may find it possible to accommodate both of these explanatory tendencies. In doing so, however, we shall probably have to conclude that most historians of the Revolution, whether they stress themes of discontinuity or themes of continuity in their work, have failed to situate the drama of 1789–99 in its larger, international/domestic context. This will become increasingly clear in this Conclusion as we do essentially two things: (1) reassess the Revolution against the broad backdrop of early-modern and modern French history; and (2) situate it within a world-historical context of modern sociopolitical upheavals.

On the first point, if there is anything that we have learned from our phase-by-phase analysis of the French Revolution, it is that the men dictating French destinies in this period were driven in their politics and policy-making by a "dialectic" of foreign and domestic concerns. To say this, however, is not to cite something in the French experience that was unique to the revolutionary era. One of the most intriguing findings to emerge in recent years from a growing body of historical works has been that

1 Martyn Lyons, *Napoleon Bonaparte and the Legacy of the French Revolution* (New York: St. Martin's Press, 1994), p. 296.
2 Refer again to any edition of Tocqueville, *The Old Regime and the French Revolution*; Lefebvre, *The Coming of the French Revolution*, esp. chap. 1; and Furet, *Interpreting the French Revolution*, passim.

this dialectic of external and domestic pressures has played a key role in shaping France's public life at various times – that is to say, during certain specific periods – ever since the dawn of the old regime. As a general rule, this phenomenon has been most pronounced when the French have found themselves preoccupied with international issues of security and prestige. Since the Revolution occurred in the midst of one of these foreign-policy-dominated periods, its commingling of external and internal incentives to reform was only to be expected. In this fundamental sense, then, the maelstrom of 1789–99 was but a microcosm – unprecedentedly dramatic and sharply defined as an historical event, to be sure, but nonetheless a microcosm – of the early-modern and modern French experience.

There is no need at this point to review the myriad ways in which the dialectic of external and domestic challenges to French statesmen manifested itself in prerevolutionary times. My earlier synthesis identified the seventeenth and eighteenth centuries as a period during which France gradually shifted from a defensive posture vis-à-vis the Austro-Spanish Habsburgs to an expansionist "mission" both in Europe and on the high seas. Against this background, it presented as exemplary of the dynamic interplay between international and domestic forces such developments as the proliferation of venal offices, the deepening divisions within the army, the gradual reduction of social-status-related tax exemptions, and the growing constitutional confrontation between the crown and the tax-resisting parlements of the realm.[3] All of these phenomena point to one paramount fact: that the old regime's ruling elite, pursuing its vision of a perdurably secure and powerful France, was compelled to sponsor domestic policies that over time became ever more difficult to reconcile with the social and ideological tenets underpinning absolutism and social privilege. The bellicose ancien régime, to put it succinctly, did much to dig its own grave. The end result was the Revolution.

But, again, this is ground we have already explored in manifold detail. What might be more useful at this point would be to suggest cursorily how the dynamic interaction between foreign and domestic affairs reasserted itself in French politics and policy-making in postrevolutionary times. Such an analytical perspective appears in hindsight to apply most fruitfully to the Napoleonic era (1799–1815), when French war making scored its most spectacular achievements, and to the years from 1870 to 1945, when a unified Germany forced French foreign policy back onto the defensive.

In the years immediately after the Revolution, dominated as they were by Napoleon Bonaparte, the international/domestic dialectic is all too easy to discern and need not detain us long. "The Consulate and the Empire,"

---

3 Refer again to Stone, *The Genesis of the French Revolution*, esp. chaps. 2, 4, and 5.

it has been said, "were not simply exercises in domestic political stabilization under authoritarian 'modernizing' rule. Institutionally speaking, Napoleon's regimes furthered the fusion of the political and the military, and the subordination of domestic policy to foreign policy, that had begun under the Jacobins and progressed through the Directory." In the Napoleonic armies that rampaged from the Iberian Peninsula to the Middle East and Moscow, the requirements of "high politics" and of civil society forcefully merged. In putting together his *Grande Armée*, Napoleon artfully realized the democratic and meritocratic potentialities of the Revolution. In marshaling such vast forces on battlefields all over Europe, he demonstrated how effectively the energies of the masses released within France by revolution could be turned to geostrategic purposes far beyond the country's borders.[4] Moreover, in the less tangible but equally important realm of political culture, the first Bonapartist empire actually "democratized" the bureaucratic-military values of the old French society, "giving the people access to a domain once reserved for the aristocracy." Far from having delegitimized these values of the old France, the Napoleonic adventure positively reinforced them.[5] Furthermore, the France of future generations would only solidify the triumph of bureaucratic-military values, values that owed more to the "French absolutism and... state-bureaucratized society of the Ancien Régime" than to the newfangled "Manchester" spirit of capitalism.[6]

Of course, the French could not indefinitely pursue war making on such a grandiose scale: after 1815, domestic policy would never again be so crushingly subordinated to the requirements of such an ambitious foreign policy. In this connection, it is noteworthy that among the clearest "winners" emerging from the revolutionary and Napoleonic eras were Frenchmen not at all implicated, at least directly, in the operations of the modern fiscal-military "establishment." In any inventory of such gainers, holders of property must loom large. Property, above all rural property, would define the elite of notables ruling France, as electors, through most of the nineteenth century. Though, for a long time, restored nobles would continue to predominate in the ranks of the great proprietors, and though, at the other end of the social spectrum, small peasant landholders were the most numerous beneficiaries of the revolutionary land settlement, it was "bourgeois" citizens who would profit most handsomely from the sales

---

4 Theda Skocpol and Meyer Kestnbaum, "Mars Unshackled: The French Revolution in World-Historical Perspective," in Ferenc Fehér, ed., *The French Revolution and the Birth of Modernity* (Berkeley: University of California Press, 1990), pp. 23–24.
5 François Furet, "Transformations in the Historiography of the Revolution," trans. Brian Singer, in ibid., p. 271.
6 Ibid.

of crown and ecclesiastical lands. The *notabilité* of post-1815 France, then, was a reconstituted elite of landholders (and of professionals of various stripes) as well as of politicians, bureaucrats, and soldiers.[7]

But in the years after 1870, even as proprietors and professionals continued to enjoy legacies of wealth, status, and power handed down to them from the revolutionary-Napoleonic era, they would find international affairs once again casting a long shadow across the landscapes of their lives. In the wake of France's resounding defeat in the Franco-Prussian War, geostrategic issues took on an urgency at Paris not experienced for generations. In practical terms, this meant a replay of the old, pre-1815 script: namely, French legislators and policymakers were caught between interacting geopolitical and domestic-political imperatives.

In no area was this more dramatically apparent than that of welfare reform. Particularly relevant to our argument is the fact that the historiography on the rise of the welfare state in this period has, in the words of one leading specialist, "undergone a sea-change in recent years." The prevailing wisdom once had it that the Third Republic established the welfare state by enacting "a battery of social reforms – old-age pensions, accident insurance, and the like – that were aimed at pacifying an expansive and militant working class." This interpretation, however, has yielded much ground to a scholarly vision of pro-family reforms *predating* the turn-of-the-century workers' legislation, reforms driven by anxiety "not so much about social disorder as about a declining birth rate, degeneration of racial stock, and loss of stature vis-à-vis France's competitors on the continent."[8]

A number of feminist scholars, concerned above all to examine the gendered aspects of modern social reform and thus focusing as much upon French mothers and children as upon male workers, have figured prominently in this recent historiographical "sea-change." What is most significant from our "globalist" viewpoint, however, is the fact that these historians have come to view the lawmakers of late-nineteenth-century and early-twentieth-century France much as we have viewed the revolutionaries: namely, as motivated by a mix of geostrategic and domestic concerns. The key dynamic here was demography. Whereas, between 1850 and 1910, the population of France grew by only about 3.4 million to just over 39 million, the German population was forging ahead from 33.4 to 58.4 million. While all of the Western industrializing countries experienced a falling birthrate in this period, France lost out most in terms of absolute – and relative – numbers. The strategic results likely to follow from this trend necessarily obsessed French policymakers from 1870 on. "In the

---

7 See Doyle, *The Oxford History of the French Revolution*, esp. pp. 407–10, for a more detailed discussion of this subject.

8 From a review by Philip Nord in *American Historical Review* 102 (June 1997): 830–31.

wake of France's defeat by Germany and the loss of Alsace-Lorraine, leaders of the Third Republic were painfully aware of the international implications of the decline; the German victory underscored the relationship between population and national might, at least as measured by military strength."[9]

This newly urgent French sense of "losing out" in the endless competition of European states served as one catalyst for the rise of the welfare state in France. Logically enough, the status of women was most immediately at issue. As Rachel Fuchs has put it: "To remedy depopulation, . . . reformers placed reproduction at the center of the cultural crisis and positioned women as mothers, regenerators of a degenerating race. The valorization of maternity translated into legislation, as French bureaucrats and social reformers enacted family reforms before they developed welfare regulations directly affecting men" – hence the laws of the next few decades granting pensions to unmarried as well as married mothers and widows, protecting children, and establishing maternity leave. Yet, as Fuchs and a number of like-minded historians have pointed out, in France (as in the other major states) politicians caught up in strategic anxieties had more than the status of mothers in their sights. They harped upon the "need to improve the physical and productive efficiency of the mass of the population." They subjected issues of "degeneration," illness, and poverty to careful analysis and looked for ways to increase the numbers and enhance the living conditions of the masses. Employers naturally wanted healthy workers and pressured the government to implement welfare measures that, by improving workers' lives, would increase "national efficiency."[10]

Palpably, more was involved here (in the French case) than resentment over the outcome of the Franco-Prussian War and fear of a unified Germany. Historians working in this area have done well to insist on the importance for welfare advocates of new notions of state intervention in citizens' lives, of a republican "solidarist" philosophy perpetuating the revolutionary values of "liberty, equality, and fraternity," of bourgeois anxieties regarding working-class unrest, and of recent advances in medical science bearing upon theories of "racial degeneration." Yet, somehow, it all seemed to come back in the end to the larger concern over France's role in the world. Hence, for example, the ever-present patriotic theme underlying republican worries about public health: France's population had to overcome its physical inferiority to the German people.[11] No more than

9 Karen Offen, "Depopulation, Nationalism, and Feminism in Fin-de-Siècle France," *American Historical Review* 89 (June 1984): 651–52.

10 Cited from Elinor A. Accampo, Rachel G. Fuchs, Mary Lynn Stewart, et al., *Gender and the Politics of Social Reform in France, 1870–1914* (Baltimore: Johns Hopkins University Press, 1995), pp. 166, 174–75.

11 Elinor Accampo, cited in ibid., p. 15.

the policymakers of the old regime and the revolutionary era could the leaders of pre–World War I France insulate themselves from the pressures of the outside world.[12]

And of course, as other historians probing these same issues have been quick to point out, French anxieties about that outside world would only intensify in the years after the 1914–18 conflict. During the 1920s and 1930s, Sarah Fishman has noted, the 1.4 million men killed in the Great War, the continuing fall in the birthrate, and the increasingly isolated diplomatic position of France in a time of German recovery were factors that favored the arguments of those advocating drastic measures to strengthen the family and rebuild the population. After years of lobbying by conservatives, feminists, republicans, pronatalists, Catholics, and others, the Third Republic finally promulgated an extensive Family Code in July 1939 that was designed to bolster traditional gender roles within the family and so encourage Frenchwomen's customary procreative function. In introducing this code, Prime Minister Daladier, in language paraphrased by Fishman, sounded the ineluctable patriotic alarm. "Population decline meant fewer men to serve in the army, fewer people to share the burden of military and social spending, labor shortages, abandoned farms, even colonial contraction; a feeble population also dealt a blow to France's intellectual and artistic prestige."[13] Once again, international and domestic issues were inseparably intertwined; once again, the old dialectic assumed new life against the somber background of a France placed profoundly at risk.

This dialectic persisted through and beyond the bleak years of the Occupation. Some of the most compelling evidence of this – not surprisingly – has come from recent historians of women and the family. In 1980, Michel Chauvière could still arouse controversy by asserting the Occupation-era Vichy regime's concern over "maladjusted children" and other problems symptomatic of dysfunctional family life.[14] Yet an accumulating body of research has robbed that controversy of much of its heat and fire. Now, as a result, Miranda Pollard can without undue commotion characterize Vichy's effort to organize French society along traditional gender lines (and thereby protect women's reproductive role) as having been motivated by a combination of statist and social anxieties that we find

12 For some additional work in this area, see Rachel G. Fuchs, *Abandoned Children: Foundlings and Child Welfare in Nineteenth-Century France* (Albany: SUNY Press, 1984); Sylvia Schafer, *Children in Moral Danger and the Problem of Government in Third Republic France* (Princeton, N.J.: Princeton University Press, 1997); and the contributions in "Forum: Population and the State in the Third Republic," in *French Historical Studies* 19 (Spring 1996): 633–754.

13 Citations from Sarah Fishman, *We Will Wait: Wives of French Prisoners of War, 1940–1945* (New Haven, Conn.: Yale University Press, 1991), pp. 18–19, 21.

14 I owe this reference to my colleague Sarah Fishman. Consult Michel Chauvière, *Enfance inadaptée: L'Héritage de Vichy* (Paris: Les Editions Ouvrières, 1980).

very familiar by now. Vichyite pro-family policies offered "a panacea for the ills of the 1930s" as well as "a direct response to the trauma of Defeat and Occupation."[15]

Politicians during 1940–44 might anathematize the vanquished Third Republic, and their successors just a few years later might scramble to disassociate themselves from the years of Vichyite dishonor; nonetheless, the interplay between foreign and domestic pressures upon French governance remained the controlling reality in public affairs. This is, perhaps, the chief message we should draw from Charles de Gaulle's postwar exhortation: "No matter what way we organize our national work, our social relations, our political regime, even our security,... as long as the French people do not reproduce, France will be nothing more than a bright light that vanishes away."[16] Constitutional and political arrangements could come and go in France – indeed, they have, ever since 1789 – but those entrusted with the management of national affairs, at least in the years after 1870, would continually find themselves beset by interlocking challenges of an international and domestic nature.

In light of all this, is it not perfectly understandable that so much current literature on post–World War II France should also speak of such interlocking challenges? One review of some of this recent work has seen in it an interplay between two principal themes: "first, the experience of the French with 'modernization,' their efforts to promote, cope with, and resist the huge social and cultural changes that accompanied rapid economic growth after the war; and second, 'national identity,' the perennial struggle in France to affirm the distinctiveness of the country and the Frenchness of its people."[17]

It may be true that the destruction of Hitler's war machine in the 1940s and the postwar "baby boom" in France finally put to rest some of the strategic anxieties so prevalent in earlier decades west of the Rhine; nevertheless, it is arguable that the 1950s and 1960s only recast the old dialectic of challenges in different, if somewhat less threatening, terms. French scholars, admittedly, have not been as forward as some of their American colleagues in examining the postwar manifestations of this dialectic. Yet it may be only a matter of time before they will have to make their own contributions to this historiography, as they and their countrymen strive to define the implications for France of even more recent developments such as European unification, the immigration into France of non-Europeans, and the ongoing globalization of economic forces.

15 Miranda Pollard, *Reign of Virtue: Mobilizing Gender in Vichy France* (Chicago: University of Chicago Press, 1998), esp. pp. 201–2.
16 Ibid.
17 See Herrick Chapman, "Review Article: Modernity and National Identity in Postwar France," *French Historical Studies* 22 (Spring 1999): 291–314; citation from pp. 292–93.

Thus, to review the French Revolution against the backdrop of specifically French history is to realize that the sociopolitical cataclysm of 1789–99 was not simply the "decisive historical rupture" that some scholars have depicted. In each successive phase of the Revolution we have discovered and analyzed a dynamic interaction between exogenous and endogenous pressures on those fighting for power and striving to govern. And in this, we now descry fundamentally the same dynamic that characterized (and eventually destroyed) the ancien régime, and that was going to reassume its old vigor in the newly urgent circumstances of post-1870 France.

Emphatically, this is *not* to deny the French Revolution all breathtaking novelty, all historical uniqueness. Lynn Hunt was, after all, right to assert that the Revolution "was the moment in which politics was discovered as an enormously potent activity, as an agent for conscious change, as the mold for character, culture, and social relations." Certainly she can appropriately argue that "democratic republicanism" was one of the defining legacies of the Revolution.[18] In an earlier work I affirmed much the same thing, stating that how "ordinary Frenchmen and Frenchwomen...for a few unforgettable years after 1789...fashioned through rhetoric and ritual and raw human action a new identity for themselves...is assuredly one of the most fascinating and portentous stories of the revolutionary decade in France."[19] There is no reason whatever to reverse these judgments.

Yet the Revolution was pivotal in other ways as well. If, for instance, we situate it within a global-historical context, we cannot help but see it as a "transitional upheaval" in the history of modern sociopolitical revolutions. The transition referred to here was one from revolutions, such as those in mid-seventeenth-century England and late-eighteenth-century British North America, which took place in essentially insular societies under minimal pressure from the outside world, to revolutions of the twentieth century, such as those in Russia and China, which have occurred in societies under extreme exogenous pressures. The cataclysm in France may have differed from both of the earlier revolutions in some of its domestic aspects, but it differed from them most arrestingly in its geographic and derivative geopolitical aspects. True, we noted earlier that international credibility was not a negligible consideration for Charles I in 1640. Nonetheless, the French in 1789, unlike their revolutionary forerunners, were attempting to live up to a very old tradition of greatness in the chief geostrategic theaters of the world; and they were essaying this in the teeth of the armed opposition of much of Europe. Is it at all astonishing, in the light of these realities, that the Terror of 1793–94 had no real equivalent in either of the earlier revolutions? On the other hand, the upheaval in France was less

18 Hunt, *Politics, Culture, and Class*, pp. 224 and 236.
19 Stone, *The Genesis of the French Revolution*, p. 237.

brutal and involved less thoroughgoing sociopolitical change than either the Russian or the Chinese Revolution. This was so for a number of reasons, of course; but foremost among them was the fact that the Russians and the Chinese in the first half of the twentieth century faced, in Germany and Japan respectively, much greater external threats to their existence than the French confronted in the 1790s, and did so, in part, because of greater relative technological and infrastructural backwardness than the French had to overcome in the late eighteenth century.

So the winds of change that gusted across the picturesque French landscape during 1789–99 were pivotal in what we might call the world history of revolution. Although the cataclysm in France has sometimes been regarded as the last and most profound of the "liberal" or presocialist revolutions of the early-modern West, it also looked forward to the socialist or communist upheavals of the twentieth century. The imperative driving the French toward sociopolitical modernization was, for sure, not so much a dire threat to France's continued existence from one or several expansionist and vastly more advanced rival states as it was a vision, "imposed from within," of revived French greatness in the competitive world at large; but it was an imperative, an undeniable challenge, nonetheless. Moreover, once the Revolution in France had gotten under way, it launched a challenge to the monarchical-"feudal" world of its time comparable in many ways to the challenge hurled later at the liberal-"capitalist" world by the revolutions in Russia and China. And, like those upheavals, and others that have taken place in the past century on a less enormous scale, it survived despite the violent efforts of its enemies to destroy it.[20]

Of course, whether we reinterpret the Revolution against the backdrop of specifically French history or set it within a larger context of world history, we can plausibly accentuate either its traditional or its novel aspects – or both, for that matter. Yet, to bring this inquiry to a close, we shall probably do best to reiterate what has been from the start its central contention: that the ultimate significance of the French Revolution transcends the domestic gains or breakthroughs that various interpretations have attributed to it over the years. Yes, the Revolution innovated in the realm of popular political culture and helped to found a new politics of "democratic republicanism." Yes, it foreshadowed – and helped to lay the groundwork for – the

[20] There is, of course, a vast historical and sociological literature analyzing, comparing, and contrasting sociopolitical revolutions in the early modern and modern eras. There is still no better survey of that literature than the one offered in the first section of Skocpol, *States and Social Revolutions.* Of the comparative studies that have appeared since the publication of Skocpol's book, one of the most stimulating is Arno J. Mayer, *The Furies: Violence and Terror in the French and Russian Revolutions* (Princeton, N.J.: Princeton University Press, 2000).

rule of landed "notables" in nineteenth-century France. Yes, it removed or weakened at least some of the obstacles barring the way to a more "class-conscious" and entrepreneurial society. And, yes, it immensely facilitated the triumph of the centralized, bureaucratized state – that quintessentially "modern" creation that was possibly the prime benefi
ciary of the upheaval of 1789–99. The Revolution did all these things, but it also did something of yet greater import, something of genuinely global-historical significance. It pointed unerringly to the overarching international/domestic challenge that confronts all modern leaders of goodwill in an unforgivingly competitive world.

The imperative need of France's revolutionary policymakers to mobilize their country's human and material resources so as to ensure its survival and restore its battered prestige in the world's affairs guaranteed that they would sympathize with the grievances and in fact address the needs of individuals and groups in society – but only insofar as doing so accorded with the demands of French *raison d'état*. And in this the French Revolution anticipated so very much of what was to come, most obviously in the future years of France itself, but also (to a greater or lesser extent) in countries all over Europe, and indeed all over the globe. Even today, and perhaps today more than ever before, what even the most benevolent political leaders can do for their peoples is deeply conditioned by the strategies they must adopt in confronting the competitive forces of their contemporary world. By pointing the way toward this challenging reality, and by doing so in such a dramatic, unforgettable fashion, the French Revolution made its deepest impression upon modern France, and indeed upon the modern world as a whole.

Suggestions for further reading

It would obviously be impossible to provide here a complete inventory of the scholarly literature on the French Revolution. Rather, my intention in this bibliographical essay is to point the interested reader toward a few of the classic studies in the field as well as some carefully selected scholarship of recent years. These works seem to fall most naturally into the following seven categories: General Accounts and Historiography; Origins and Background; Diplomacy and War; Domestic Politics; Administrative and Financial Reforms; Socioeconomic Developments; and Religious and Cultural Issues. Naturally, these are not hard-and-fast categories; consequently, the reader who cannot locate a specific work under one rubric may very well find it under a related heading. Additional sources appear in the footnotes. This is especially true regarding the extensive documentation on the old regime cited in connection with Chapter 1.

GENERAL ACCOUNTS AND HISTORIOGRAPHY

The reader seeking a "Marxist" view of the Revolution should consult either Georges Lefebvre, *The French Revolution*, trans. E. Evanson and J. H. Stewart, 2 vols. (New York: Columbia University Press, 1951), or Albert Soboul, *The French Revolution: 1787–1799*, trans. A. Forrest and C. Jones (New York: Random House, 1962). Important "social revisionist" works include: Alfred Cobban, *The Social Interpretation of the French Revolution*, 2d ed. (New York: Cambridge University Press, 1999); François Furet and Denis Richet, *The French Revolution*, trans. Stephen Hardman (New York: Macmillan, 1970); and, by Furet himself, *Interpreting the French Revolution*, trans. Elborg Forster (New York: Cambridge University Press, 1981). Claude Mazauric has spoken for the Marxist defense in *Sur la Révolution française* (Paris: Editions Sociales, 1970). Two urbane overviews of the debate between Marxist and social-revisionist historians are: Geoffrey Ellis, "The 'Marxist Interpretation' of the French

Revolution," *English Historical Review* 93 (1978): 353–76, and George Comninel, *Rethinking the French Revolution: Marxism and the Revisionist Challenge* (New York: Verso, 1987). See also, in this connection, Furet, *Marx and the French Revolution*, trans. Deborah Kan Furet (Chicago: University of Chicago Press, 1988). A recent valuable insight into Furet's rendering of the Revolution is offered by Michael Christofferson, "An Antitotalitarian History of the French Revolution: François Furet's *Penser la Révolution française* in the Intellectual Politics of the Late 1970s," *French Historical Studies* 22 (1999): 557–611.

Theda Skocpol has advanced a very different exegesis of the Revolution in *States and Social Revolutions: A Comparative Analysis of France, Russia, and China* (Cambridge: Cambridge University Press, 1979). Her explanation has been challenged by William H. Sewell, Jr., in "Ideologies and Social Revolutions: Reflections on the French Case," *Journal of Modern History* 57 (1985): 57–85. But see also Skocpol's reply in the same issue, pp. 86–96: "Cultural Idioms and Political Ideologies in the Revolutionary Reconstruction of State Power: A Rejoinder to Sewell." Similarly critical of Skocpol, and promoting a "political-cultural" reading of the Revolution, is Lynn Hunt, *Politics, Culture, and Class in the French Revolution* (Berkeley: University of California Press, 1984).

Dating from about the time of the Bicentennial are four works on the revolutionary era revealing substantial interpretive depth. They are: D. M. G. Sutherland, *France 1789–1815: Revolution and Counterrevolution* (New York: Oxford University Press, 1986); John F. Bosher, *The French Revolution* (New York: Norton, 1988); William Doyle, *The Oxford History of the French Revolution* (Oxford: Clarendon Press, 1989); and Simon Schama, *Citizens: A Chronicle of the French Revolution* (New York: Knopf, 1989). Jack R. Censer has perceptively evaluated these four surveys in "Commencing the Third Century of Debate," *American Historical Review* 94 (1989): 1309–25.

Since the Bicentennial, yet other scholars have come forth with overviews of the Revolution accentuating specific aspects of historical change. See, for example, Florin Aftalion, *The French Revolution: An Economic Interpretation* (New York: Cambridge University Press, 1990), and David Andress, *French Society in Revolution, 1789–1799* (Manchester: Manchester University Press, 1999). Then again, a number of specialists have placed the revolutionary upheaval within a broader context of "modernization" and other international processes. See, as examples of this, Ferenc Fehér, ed., *The French Revolution and the Birth of Modernity* (Berkeley: University of California Press, 1990), and Joseph Klaits and Michael H. Haltzel, eds., *The Global Ramifications of the French Revolution* (New York: Cambridge University Press, 1994).

As of this writing, clearly, no one interpretation dominates the field. For some of the latest historiographical trends, see: Jack R. Censer, "Social Twists and Linguistic Turns: Revolutionary Historiography a Decade after the Bicentennial," *French Historical Studies* 22 (1999): 139–67; and Suzanne Desan, "What's after Political Culture? Recent French Revolutionary Historiography," *French Historical Studies* 23 (2000): 163–96.

ORIGINS AND BACKGROUND

Books focusing on the specific issue of revolutionary origins have multiplied over the years. The reader here can do no better than commence with Alexis de Tocqueville, *The Old Regime and the French Revolution*, trans. Stuart Gilbert (New York: Doubleday, 1954). The classic neo-Marxist rendering of revolutionary causes remains Georges Lefebvre, *The Coming of the French Revolution*, trans. R. R. Palmer (Princeton, N.J.: Princeton University Press, 1947; reissued 1989). Lefebvre's ideas were vigorously challenged in the 1960s by Elizabeth Eisenstein, "Who Intervened in 1788? A Commentary on *The Coming of the French Revolution*," *American Historical Review* 71 (1965): 77–103, and (in a more general way) by George V. Taylor, "Noncapitalist Wealth and the Origins of the French Revolution," *American Historical Review* 72 (1967): 469–96. The kinds of economic issues emphasized in the Marxist view of revolutionary causation have been updated by David Weir, "Les Crises économiques et les origines de la Révolution française," in *Annales: E. S. C.* 46 (1991): 917–47.

Recently, however, new exegeses of revolutionary origins have emerged. Prominent among them have been those stressing cultural dynamics. Refer to: Keith Baker, *Inventing the French Revolution* (New York: Cambridge University Press, 1990); Roger Chartier, *The Cultural Origins of the French Revolution*, trans. Lydia G. Cochrane (Durham, N.C.: Duke University Press, 1991); and Dale Van Kley, *The Religious Origins of the French Revolution: From Calvin to the Civil Constitution, 1560–1791* (New Haven, Conn.: Yale University Press, 1996). On the other hand, domestic (that is, French) and international politics have also drawn renewed interest. William Doyle has played up domestic political causation (and deemphasized socioeconomic factors) in his *Origins of the French Revolution*, 3d ed. (Oxford: Oxford University Press, 1999). In the meantime, C. B. A. Behrens as far back as 1967 had argued the case for the centrality of foreign-policy concerns to the onset of revolution in *The Ancien Régime* (London: Harcourt, Brace, and World, 1967; reissued by Norton, 1989). That kind of analysis has figured most recently in Bailey Stone, *The Genesis of the French Revolution: A Global-Historical Interpretation* (New York: Cambridge University Press, 1994).

Integral to any discussion of the question of revolutionary origins is a studied reconsideration of the "prerevolutionary crisis" of 1787–88. Here, the standard point of departure remains Jean Egret, *The French Prerevolution, 1787–1788*, trans. Wesley D. Camp (Chicago: University of Chicago Press, 1977). Egret's work in this area has been notably updated by Vivian Gruder's articles. See, for example: "A Mutation in Elite Political Culture: The French Notables and the Defense of Property and Participation, 1787," *Journal of Modern History* 56 (1984): 598–634; "The Society of Orders at Its Demise: The Vision of the Elite at the End of the Ancien Régime," *French History* 1 (1987): 210–37; and "Un Message politique adressé au public: Les pamphlets 'populaires' à la veille de la Révolution," *Revue d'Histoire Moderne et Contemporaine* 39 (1992): 161–97. Michael Fitzsimmons has criticized some of Gruder's notions in "Privilege and the Polity in France, 1786–1791," *American Historical Review* 92 (1987): 269–95. Also helpful in this connection is Kenneth Margerison, "History, Representative Institutions, and Political Rights in the French Pre-Revolution," *French Historical Studies* 15 (1987): 68–98.

Rather than venturing too far into the dense thickets of scholarship on France before 1787, we have to limit ourselves to citing some of the most recent works on selected topics in that area. Jeremy Black has furnished two of the most recent surveys of the geopolitics of that era: *The Rise of the European Powers 1679–1793* (London: Edward Arnold, 1990); and *European Warfare, 1660–1815* (New Haven, Conn.: Yale University Press, 1994). Orville T. Murphy looks at the nexus between French "public opinion" and French foreign policy in *The Diplomatic Retreat of France and Public Opinion on the Eve of the French Revolution, 1783–1789* (Washington, D.C.: Catholic University of America Press, 1997). John Hardman has deepened our knowledge of domestic politics in the late ancien régime: see *Louis XVI* (New Haven, Conn.: Yale University Press, 1993), and *French Politics 1774–1789: From the Accession of Louis XVI to the Fall of the Bastille* (London: Longman, 1995). Two recent studies of the political culture of the high Parisian magistracy under Louis XVI also require mention: Sarah Maza, *Private Lives and Public Affairs: The Causes Célèbres of Prerevolutionary France* (Berkeley: University of California Press, 1993); and David Bell, *Lawyers and Citizens: The Making of a Political Elite in Old Regime France* (New York: Oxford University Press, 1994). Especially revealing on the nature of privilege (social and political) in the twilight of the old regime is Gail Bossenga, *The Politics of Privilege: Old Regime and Revolution in Lille* (New York: Cambridge University Press, 1991). Finally, L. M. Cullen reinterprets the fiscal and economic aspects of the demise of the ancien régime in "History, Economic Crises, and Revolutions: Understanding Eighteenth-Century France," *Economic History Review* 46 (1993): 635–57.

DIPLOMACY AND WAR

A very old but still very useful conspectus on international politics in the revolutionary era is Albert Sorel, *L'Europe et la Révolution française*, 8 vols. (Paris: E. Plon, 1885–1904). Two helpful updates of Sorel were provided in the 1960s by Geoffrey Bruun and Steven T. Ross. Refer to Bruun, "The Balance of Power during the Wars, 1793–1814," in *The New Cambridge Modern History, Vol. 9: War and Peace in an Age of Upheaval, 1793–1830* (Cambridge: Cambridge University Press, 1965), pp. 250–74; and Ross, *France against Europe: European Diplomatic History, 1789–1815* (New York: Doubleday, 1969). Recently, T. C. W. Blanning has revisited the issues involved in the bellicose European diplomacy of the 1790s. See, in particular, *The Origins of the French Revolutionary Wars* (London: Longman, 1986), and *The French Revolutionary Wars 1787–1802* (London: Arnold, 1996).

A number of studies of specific incidents in and aspects of French Revolutionary diplomacy also deserve mention. They are as follows: Barry Rothaus, "The Emergence of Legislative Control over Foreign Policy in the Constituent Assembly, 1789–91" (Ph.D. diss., University of Wisconsin, 1968); H. V. Evans, "The Nootka Sound Controversy in Anglo-French Diplomacy – 1790," *Journal of Modern History* 46 (1974): 609–40; Patricia Chastain Howe, "Charles-François Dumouriez and the Revolutionizing of French Foreign Affairs in 1792," *French Historical Studies* 14 (1986): 367–90; Linda Frey and Marsha Frey, "'The Reign of the Charlatans Is Over': The French Revolutionary Attack on Diplomatic Practice," *Journal of Modern History* 65 (1993): 706–44; and Sydney Biro, *The German Policy of Revolutionary France: A Study in French Diplomacy during the War of the First Coalition, 1792–1797*, 2 vols. (Cambridge, Mass.: Harvard University Press, 1957).

The reader may also wish to consult works delving into the diplomacy of the other European states. Crucial for the Austrian perspective is Karl A. Roider, Jr., *Baron Thugut and Austria's Response to the French Revolution* (Princeton, N.J.: Princeton University Press, 1987). Some information on Russian foreign policy appears in Isabel De Madariaga, *Russia in the Age of Catherine the Great* (New Haven, Conn.: Yale University Press, 1981). Not surprisingly, however, monographs on British diplomacy predominate in this area. For the early years of the revolutionary era, see Jeremy Black, *British Foreign Policy in an Age of Revolutions, 1783–1793* (New York: Cambridge University Press, 1994). Notably useful for the late 1790s are: Edward Ingram, *Commitment to Empire: Prophecies of the Great Game in Asia, 1797–1800* (Oxford: Clarendon Press, 1981); and Piers Mackesy, *War without Victory: The Downfall of Pitt, 1799–1802*

(Oxford: Clarendon Press, 1984). Finally, Paul Schroeder offers a more systemic analysis of developments in the late 1790s in "The Collapse of the Second Coalition," *Journal of Modern History* 59 (1987): 244–90.

War has ever been the handmaiden of diplomacy; and certainly the reader will find no lack of scholarly literature treating the military strategy and institutions of revolutionary France. A good overview of military planning in the 1790s is Steven T. Ross, *Quest for Victory: French Military Strategy, 1792–1799* (New York: A. S. Barnes, 1973). Marcel Reinhard has provided useful "Observations sur le rôle révolutionnaire de l'Armée dans la Révolution française" in the *Annales historiques de la Révolution française* 168 (1962): 169–81. There is now a substantial body of works on the armies of the 1789–99 period. Outstanding among them are the following: Samuel F. Scott, *The Response of the Royal Army to the French Revolution* (Oxford: Oxford University Press, 1978); John A. Lynn, *The Bayonets of the Republic: Motivation and Tactics in the Army of Revolutionary France, 1791–1794* (Urbana: University of Illinois Press, 1984); Alan Forrest, *Conscripts and Deserters: The Army and French Society during the Revolution and Empire* (New York: Oxford University Press, 1989), and *The Soldiers of the French Revolution* (Durham, N.C.: Duke University Press, 1990); Jean-Paul Bertaud, *The Army of the French Revolution: From Citizen-Soldiers to Instrument of Power*, trans. R. R. Palmer (Princeton, N.J.: Princeton University Press, 1989); and Howard G. Brown, *War, Revolution, and the Bureaucratic State: Politics and Army Administration in France, 1791–1799* (New York: Oxford University Press, 1996). The politically sensitive issue of army veterans is addressed by Isser Woloch, *The French Veteran from the Revolution to the Restoration* (Chapel Hill, N.C.: University of North Carolina Press, 1979). Ken Alder situates French military issues in a broader cultural context in *Engineering the Revolution: Arms and Enlightenment in France, 1763–1815* (Princeton, N.J.: Princeton University Press, 1997).

Perhaps understandably, the Revolution's naval forces have drawn less scholarly attention than have its armies. Still, the reader is by no means bereft of resources in this area. Norman Hampson, for example, presented much valuable information in "The 'Comité de Marine' of the Constituent Assembly," *The Historical Journal* 2 (1959): 130–48, and in *La Marine de L'An II: Mobilisation de la Flotte de l'Océan, 1793–94* (Paris: Marcel Rivière et Cie., 1959). Hampson's work, however, is in some respects superseded by William S. Cormack, *Revolution and Political Conflict in the French Navy, 1789–1794* (New York: Cambridge University Press, 1995).

DOMESTIC POLITICS

The domestic politics of the eventful year 1789 have inspired the labors of numerous historians. Jacques Necker's role in 1789 is thoroughly examined in Jean Egret, *Necker: Ministre de Louis XVI, 1776–1790* (Paris: Honoré Champion, 1975), and Robert Harris, *Necker and the Revolution of 1789* (Lanham, Md.: University Press of America, 1986). The crisis touched off in early July by the king's dismissal of Necker is reexamined by Munro Price in "The 'Ministry of the Hundred Hours': A Reappraisal," *French History* 4 (1990): 317–39. Lynn Hunt has very deftly analyzed political developments in the cities and towns of France during the summer months in "Committees and Communes: Local Politics and National Revolution in 1789," *Comparative Studies in Society and History* 18 (1976): 321–46. On the significant split at summer's end between "Patriots" and "Monarchists" in the Constituent Assembly, see, first, Egret, *La Révolution des notables: Mounier et les Monarchiens* (Paris: Armand Colin, 1950), and then Robert H. Griffiths, *Le Centre perdu: Malouet et les "monarchiens" dans la Révolution française* (Grenoble: Presses Universitaires de Grenoble, 1988). Barry M. Shapiro takes early revolutionary politics into 1790 in *Revolutionary Justice in Paris, 1789–1790* (New York: Cambridge University Press, 1993).

The labors of the National Constituent Assembly (1789–91) have in recent years attracted growing scholarly interest. See, especially: Norman Hampson, *The Constituent Assembly and the Failure of Consensus, 1789–1791* (New York: Blackwell, 1988); Harriet B. Applewhite, *Political Alignment in the French National Assembly, 1789–1791* (Baton Rouge: Louisiana State University Press, 1993); Michael P. Fitzsimmons, *The Remaking of France: The National Assembly, the Constitution of 1791 and the Reorganization of the French Polity, 1789–1791* (New York: Cambridge University Press, 1994); and Timothy Tackett, *Becoming a Revolutionary: The Deputies of the French National Assembly and the Emergence of a Revolutionary Culture (1789–1790)* (Princeton, N.J.: Princeton University Press, 1996). The principal (and not altogether satisfactory) work on this assembly's short-lived successor, the Legislative Assembly, is C. J. Mitchell, *The French Legislative Assembly of 1791* (New York: E. J. Brill, 1988).

The storied National Convention of 1792–95 – especially in its faction-ridden first year – has been the subject of extensive research. M. J. Sydenham inaugurated the "modern" phase of this historiography with his controversial monograph *The Girondins* (London: Athlone Press, 1961). Alison Patrick followed this up by reappraising the "Political Divisions in the French National Convention, 1792–93" in the *Journal of Modern History* 41 (1969): 421–74; she then enlarged upon her political analysis in *The Men of the First French Republic* (Baltimore: Johns Hopkins University Press, 1972). Gary Kates has more recently contributed to this controversy with *The Cercle Social, the Girondins, and the French Revolution* (Princeton, N.J.: Princeton University Press, 1985). So have Michael S. Lewis-Beck, Anne Hildreth, and Alan B. Spitzer, in "Was There a Girondist Faction in the National Convention, 1792–1793?" *French Historical Studies* 15 (1988): 519–36. Other historians, too numerous to mention, have helped to keep this particular pot boiling.

There is, of course, a vast literature on the most radical years of the Revolution. The reader can get a good grasp of the politics of this period by consulting Marc Bouloiseau, *The Jacobin Republic, 1792–1794,* trans. Jonathan Mandelbaum (New York: Cambridge University Press, 1984). On the king's trial, the following works are recommended: David P. Jordan, *The King's Trial* (Berkeley: University of California Press, 1979); Michael Walzer, ed., *Regicide and Revolution: Speeches at the Trial of Louis XVI* (New York: Columbia University Press, 1992); and Susan Dunn, *The Deaths of Louis XVI: Regicide and the French Political Imagination* (Princeton, N.J.: Princeton University Press, 1994). Robert R. Palmer has unforgettably analyzed the "great" Committee of Public Safety in *Twelve Who Ruled: The Year of the Terror in the French Revolution* (Princeton, N.J.: Princeton University Press, 1941; reissued 1989). The Committee's most notorious member, Maximilien Robespierre, has attracted countless biographers. James M. Thompson's classic *Robespierre,* 2 vols. (Oxford: Blackwell, 1935) has been supplemented, if not superseded, by Norman Hampson, *The Life and Opinions of Maximilien Robespierre* (London: Duckworth, 1974), and David P. Jordan, *The Revolutionary Career of Maximilien Robespierre* (New York: Free Press, 1985). Morris Slavin has usefully studied aspects of the Parisian Terror in *The French Revolution in Miniature: Section Droits-de-l'Homme, 1789–1795* (Princeton, N.J.: Princeton University Press, 1984) and *The Making of an Insurrection: Parisian Sections and the Gironde* (Cambridge, Mass.: Harvard University Press, 1986). The dismantling of the Terror receives effective coverage in Bronislaw Baczko, *Ending the Terror: The French Revolution after Robespierre* (New York: Cambridge University Press, 1994).

Denis Woronoff discusses both the Thermidorian period and the Directory in *The Thermidorean Regime and the Directory, 1794–1799,* trans. Julian Jackson (New York: Cambridge University Press, 1984). Although very old, Albert Goodwin's stout defense of the Directory is still worth consulting: "The French Executive Directory – A Revaluation," *History* 22 (1937): 201–18. J.-R. Suratteau updates the pertinent historiography considerably in "Le Directoire d'après des travaux récents," *Annales historiques de la Révolution française* 224 (1976): 181–214. Also meriting a reading is Martyn Lyons, *France under the Directory* (Cambridge: Cambridge University Press, 1975). More specifically, there is an ever-growing body of monographs and articles focused upon the politics and political culture of those years. Consult, as examples in point: Isser Woloch, *Jacobin Legacy: The Democratic Movement under the Directory* (Princeton, N.J.: Princeton University Press, 1970); Colin Lucas,

"The First Directory and the Rule of Law," *French Historical Studies* 10 (1977): 231–60, and "The Rules of the Game in Local Politics under the Directory," ibid., 16 (1989): 345–71; and Lynn Hunt, David Lansky, and Paul Hanson, "The Failure of the Liberal Republic in France, 1795–1799: The Road to Brumaire," *Journal of Modern History* 51 (1979): 734–59.

Of course, some of the research on Parisian and "national" politics in the revolutionary epoch shades off inevitably into a reexamination of local politics; and this reminds us that some of the finest recent work has deliberately focused on politics in the provinces. Playing a transitional role here have been studies of electoral procedures and of institutions like the Jacobin Clubs that were pivotal simultaneously in national and local politics. Two books on the Revolution's elections are: Patrice Guennifey, *Le Nombre et la raison: La Révolution française et les élections* (Paris: Ecole des Hautes Etudes en Sciences Sociales, 1993), and Malcolm Crook, *Elections in the French Revolution: An Apprenticeship in Democracy 1789–1799* (Cambridge: Cambridge University Press, 1996). On the Jacobins, Crane Brinton's *The Jacobins: An Essay in the New History* (New York: MacMillan, 1930) is still a useful starting point. But the reader will then want to go on to Michael Kennedy, *The Jacobin Clubs in the French Revolution,* 2 vols. (Princeton, N.J.: Princeton University Press, 1982–88). Most recently, there is Patrice Higonnet, *Goodness beyond Virtue: Jacobins during the French Revolution* (Cambridge, Mass.: Harvard University Press, 1998).

Among the myriad regional studies that have appeared in the last several decades, the following stand out: Philip Dawson, *Provincial Magistrates and Revolutionary Politics in France, 1789–1795* (Cambridge, Mass.: Harvard University Press, 1972); William Scott, *Terror and Repression in Revolutionary Marseilles* (London: Macmillan, 1973); Colin Lucas, *The Structure of the Terror: The Example of Javogues and the Loire* (New York: Oxford University Press, 1973); Alan Forrest, *Society and Politics in Revolutionary Bordeaux* (New York: Oxford University Press, 1975); Lynn Hunt, *Revolution and Urban Politics in Provincial France: Troyes and Reims, 1786–1790* (Stanford, Calif.: Stanford University Press, 1978); Gwynne Lewis, *The Second Vendée: The Continuity of Counterrevolution in the Department of the Gard, 1789–1815* (Oxford: Clarendon Press, 1978); Martyn Lyons, *Revolution in Toulouse: An Essay on Provincial Terrorism* (Berne: Peter Lang, 1978); Hubert C. Johnson, *The Midi in Revolution: A Study of Regional Political Diversity, 1789–1793* (Princeton, N.J.: Princeton University Press, 1986); Paul R. Hanson, *Provincial Politics in the French Revolution: Caen and Limoges, 1789–1794* (Baton Rouge: Louisiana State University Press, 1989); and Bill Edmonds, *Jacobinism and the Revolt of Lyon, 1789–1793* (Oxford: Clarendon Press, 1990).

Historians have also endeavored to fashion broader explanations of political resistance to the will of Paris in provincial France. On the "federalist" revolt of 1793, for example, see in particular M. H. Crook, "Federalism and the French Revolution: The Revolt of Toulon in 1793," *History* 65 (1980): 383–97; and Bill Edmonds, "Federalism and Urban Revolt in France in 1793," *Journal of Modern History* 55 (1983): 22–53. The massive literature on the Vendée (at least up to 1968) is reviewed by Harvey Mitchell, "The Vendée and Counterrevolution: A Review Essay," *French Historical Studies* 5 (1968): 405–29. To this, Mitchell himself has added "Resistance to the Revolution in Western France," *Past and Present* 63 (1974): 94–131. T. J. A. Le Goff and D. M. G. Sutherland have coauthored two valuable articles on peasant resistance in western France: "The Revolution and the Rural Community in Eighteenth-Century Brittany," *Past and Present* 62 (1974): 96–119; and "The Social Origins of Counter-Revolution in Western France," ibid. 99 (1983): 65–87. See also Sutherland, *The Chouans: The Social Origins of Popular Counter-Revolution in Upper Brittany, 1770–1796* (New York: Oxford University Press, 1982). On the international counterrevolution, see (in addition to the older works by Jacques Godechot) Harvey Mitchell, *The Underground War against Revolutionary France* (Oxford: Clarendon Press, 1965).

ADMINISTRATIVE AND FINANCIAL REFORMS

The books and articles that fall under this heading are relatively few in number but, arguably, disproportionately important, treating as they do the specific structures of government and modalities of financing policy-making in revolutionary France.

The reader should start here with Isser Woloch's recent overview of "civic" institutions dating from this era: *The New Regime: Transformations of the French Civic Order, 1789–1820s* (New York: Norton, 1994). The pivotal figure in modern research on the development of bureaucracy in the Revolution is Clive Church. See, first of all, three of his articles: "The Social Basis of the French Central Bureaucracy under the Directory, 1795–1799," *Past and Present* 36 (1967): 59–72; "Bureaucracy, Politics and Revolution," *French Historical Studies* 6 (1970): 492–516; and "In Search of the Directory," in J. F. Bosher, ed., *French Government and Society, 1500–1850* (London: Athlone Press, 1973), pp. 261–94. Church then produced a full-length study of this subject: *Revolution and Red Tape: The French Ministerial Bureaucracy 1770–1850* (Oxford: Clarendon Press, 1981). Although there is nothing quite like this last-named work for the provinces, Ted W. Margadant has written incisively on provincial aspects of the Constituent Assembly's administrative reforms in *Urban Rivalries in the French Revolution* (Princeton, N.J.: Princeton University Press, 1992).

On the somewhat technical but nonetheless crucial subject of government finances, the reader may wish first to consult the old-fashioned but still useful studies by Charles Gomel, René Stourm, and Marcel Marion. J. F. Bosher, however, has signally modernized our views of the subject. See, in particular: "French Administration and Public Finance in Their European Setting," in *The New Cambridge Modern History, Vol. 8: The American and French Revolutions, 1763–1793* (Cambridge: Cambridge University Press, 1965), pp. 565–91; and *French Finances, 1770–1795: From Business to Bureaucracy* (Cambridge: Cambridge University Press, 1970). A stimulating comparison of French and British finances throughout (and beyond) this period is given by Peter Mathias and Patrick O'Brien, "Taxation in Britain and France, 1715–1810. A Comparison of the Social and Economic Incidence of Taxes Collected for the Central Governments," *Journal of European Economic History* 5 (1976): 601–50. More recently, there is the research of Jean-Pierre Gross into the relationship between sociopolitical radicalism and modes of taxation in revolutionary France. See, notably: "Progressive Taxation and Social Justice in Eighteenth-Century France," *Past and Present* 140 (1993): 79–126; and *Fair Shares for All: Jacobin Egalitarianism in Practice* (New York: Cambridge University Press, 1997).

SOCIOECONOMIC DEVELOPMENTS

Under this heading, the reader may usefully begin by reviewing the scholarly literature on the *cahiers de doléances* of 1789. A number of historians have analyzed them to explore the tensions between nobles and bourgeois in the early days of the Revolution. See, notably: George Taylor, "Revolutionary and Nonrevolutionary Content in the Cahiers of 1789: An Interim Report," *French Historical Studies* 7 (1972): 479–502; Guy Chaussinand-Nogaret, *La Noblesse au XVIIIe siècle. De la féodalité aux lumières* (Paris: Hachette, 1976); Roger Chartier, "Culture, lumières, doléances: Les Cahiers de 1789," *Revue d'histoire moderne et contemporaine* 28 (1981): 68–93; and Gilbert Shapiro, John Markoff, et al., eds., *Revolutionary Demands: A Content Analysis of the Cahiers de doléances of 1789* (Stanford, Calif.: Stanford University Press, 1998).

The fate of the nobility in the revolutionary maelstrom has of course attracted much scholarly attention over the years. The reader can still find much useful information in two studies by Donald Greer: *The Incidence of the Terror during the French Revolution* (Cambridge, Mass.: Harvard University Press, 1935), and *The Incidence of the Emigration during the French Revolution* (Cambridge, Mass.: Harvard University Press, 1951). Robert Forster has offered subsequent reflections on the subject in "The Survival of the Nobility during the French Revolution," *Past and*

Present 37 (1967): 71–86. Even more recently there is Patrice Higonnet, *Class, Ideology, and the Rights of Nobles during the French Revolution* (Oxford: Clarendon Press, 1981).

On the "bourgeoisie" (in this supposedly "bourgeois" revolution) there is considerably less scholarship. The reader, still, may wish to consult the following works, among others: Jeffrey Kaplow, ed., *New Perspectives on the French Revolution* (New York: John Wiley, 1965); William Sewell, *A Rhetoric of Bourgeois Revolution: The Abbé Siéyès and "What Is the Third Estate?"* (Durham, N.C.: Duke University Press, 1994); and David Garrioch, *The Formation of the Parisian Bourgeoisie, 1690–1830* (Cambridge, Mass.: Harvard University Press, 1996).

Over the past several decades, without doubt, practitioners of social history have shown a special interest in the urban and rural masses. On the former subject, a classic is Albert Soboul, *The Sans-Culottes: The Popular Movement and Revolutionary Government 1793–1794*, trans. Rémy Inglis Hall (Princeton, N.J.: Princeton University Press, 1980). Several of the articles in Jeffrey Kaplow's anthology *New Perspectives*, cited in the preceding paragraph, are also significant in this connection. George Rudé has studied the great popular insurrections of the Parisian revolution in *The Crowd in the French Revolution* (New York: Oxford University Press, 1959). Rudé has adopted a more comparative approach to the subject in *Paris and London in the Eighteenth Century* (New York: Viking Press, 1973). Colin Lucas offers some updated reflections, at least for the early Revolution, in "The Crowd and Politics between *Ancien Régime* and Revolution in France," *Journal of Modern History* 60 (1988): 421–57. William Sewell analyzes the discourses of Parisian laborers in *Work and Revolution in France: The Language of Labor from the Old Regime to 1848* (New York: Cambridge University Press, 1980).

Georges Lefebvre was indisputably the foremost historian of the peasantry in the French Revolution. His greatest work is *Les Paysans du Nord pendant la Révolution française* (Paris: A. Colin, 1924). But see also, by Lefebvre, *The Great Fear of 1789: Rural Panic in Revolutionary France*, trans. Joan White (New York: Pantheon, 1973). Albert Soboul collected his articles on the French peasants in *Problèmes paysans de la Révolution (1789–1848)* (Paris: Maspero, 1976). P. M. Jones provides a more recent synthesis on the subject in *The Peasantry in the French Revolution* (Cambridge: Cambridge University Press, 1988). Among American specialists in this area, John Markoff clearly stands out. Consult, among his efforts: "Peasant Grievances and Peasant Insurrection: France in 1789," *Journal of Modern History* 62 (1990): 445–76; "Peasants Protest: The Claims of Lord, Church, and State in the *Cahiers de Doléances* of 1789," *Comparative Studies in Society and History* 32 (1990): 413–54; "Violence, Emancipation, and

Democracy: The Countryside and the French Revolution," *American Historical Review* 100 (1995): 360–86; and *The Abolition of Feudalism: Peasants, Lords, and Legislators in the French Revolution* (University Park, Pa.: Pennsylvania State University Press, 1996). Yet Markoff shares his expertise somewhat with fellow American Hilton Root: see, by the latter, "Challenging the Seigneurie: Community and Contention on the Eve of the French Revolution," *Journal of Modern History* 57 (1985): 652–81. For a broader perspective on the issue of peasants in revolution, see J. Craig Jenkins, "Why Do Peasants Rebel? Structural and Historical Theories of Modern Peasant Rebellions," *American Journal of Sociology* 88 (1982): 487–514.

Some historians have preferred to deal with "popular" history in ways that transcend the boundaries between urban and rural plebeians. The exemplar of this approach in recent decades has been Richard Cobb. See, among his works: *The Police and the People: French Popular Protest, 1789–1820* (New York: Oxford University Press, 1970); *Paris and Its Provinces, 1792–1802* (New York: Oxford University Press, 1975); and *The People's Armies: The Armées révolutionnaires*, trans. Marianne Elliott (New Haven, Conn.: Yale University Press, 1987). In a somewhat similar mode are books authored by several of Cobb's countrymen. See, for example: Alan Forrest, *The French Revolution and the Poor* (New York: St. Martin's Press, 1981); and, by Colin Jones, two studies: *Charity and Bienfaisance: The Treatment of the Poor in the Montpellier Region, 1740–1815* (New York: Cambridge University Press, 1982), and *The Charitable Imperative: Hospitals and Nursing in Ancien Régime and Revolutionary France* (London: Routledge, 1989).

There is also an ever-growing body of works on the roles of women in the revolutionary era. These include (but are scarcely limited to) Harriet B. Applewhite and Darline G. Levy, eds., *Women and Politics in the Age of the Democratic Revolution* (Ann Arbor: University of Michigan Press, 1990); Joan Landes, *Women and thePublic Sphere in the Age of the French Revolution* (Ithaca, N.Y.: Cornell University Press, 1988); Olwen Hufton, *Women and the Limits of Citizenship in the French Revolution* (Toronto: University of Toronto Press, 1992); Sara Melzer and Leslie Rabine, eds., *Rebel Daughters: Women and the French Revolution* (New York: Oxford University Press, 1992); Shirley E. Roessler, *Out of the Shadows: Women and Politics in the French Revolution, 1789–1795* (New York: Peter Lang, 1996); and Dominique Godineau, *The Women of Paris and Their French Revolution*, trans. Katherine Streip (Berkeley: University of California Press, 1998). Of related interest are: James F. Traer, *Marriage and the Family in Eighteenth-Century France* (Ithaca, N.Y.: Cornell University Press, 1980); Roderick Phillips, *Family Breakdown in Late*

Eighteenth-Century France: Divorces in Rouen, 1792–1803 (New York: Oxford University Press, 1981); and Suzanne Desan, "'War between Brothers and Sisters': Inheritance Law and Gender Politics in Revolutionary France," *French Historical Studies* 20 (1997): 597–634.

Readers interested in the purely economic dimensions of the Revolution should consult Tom Kemp, *Economic Forces in French History* (London: Dobson, 1971), and (for greater detail) Ernest Labrousse and Fernand Braudel, eds., *Histoire économique et sociale de la France*, 4 vols. (Paris: Presses Universitaires de France, 1970–82). François Crouzet has placed the Revolution in a broader context of international economic developments in two influential articles: "Wars, Blockade, and Economic Change in Europe, 1792–1815," *Journal of Economic History* 24 (1964): 567–88; and "Angleterre et France au XVIIIe siècle: Essai d'analyse comparée de deux croissances économiques," *Annales: E. S. C.* 21 (1966): 254–91. Also meriting consultation are two articles in *The New Cambridge Modern History, Vol. 8: The American and French Revolutions, 1763–93* (Cambridge: Cambridge University Press, 1965): H. J. Habakkuk, "Population, Commerce and Economic Ideas," pp. 25–54; and K. A. Ballhatchet, "European Relations with Asia and Africa," pp. 218–51. Again, see the important article by R. M. Hartwell, "Economic Change in England and Europe, 1780–1830," in *The New Cambridge Modern History, Vol. 9: War and Peace in an Age of Upheaval 1793–1830* (Cambridge: Cambridge University Press, 1965), pp. 31–59.

Much of the work cited in this last paragraph relies heavily upon *Annaliste* assumptions (in the 1960s and 1970s) about cyclical and structural weaknesses in the economy of early modern France. Over the past twenty years, however, a revisionist literature has arisen that paints a much brighter picture of France's economic resiliency in this period. See, in this connection: Rondo Cameron and Charles E. Freedeman, "French Economic Growth: A Radical Revision," *Social Science History* 7 (1983): 3–30; Robert Aldrich, "Late-Comer or Early-Starter? New Views on French Economic History," *Journal of European Economic History* 16 (1987): 89–100; David Weir, "Tontines, Public Finance, and Revolution in France and England, 1688–1789," *Journal of Economic History* 49 (1989): 95–124; Philip T. Hoffman, *Growth in a Traditional Society: The French Countryside, 1450–1815* (Princeton, N.J.: Princeton University Press, 1996); Philip T. Hoffman and Kathryn Norberg, eds., *Fiscal Crises, Liberty, and Representative Government, 1450–1789* (Stanford, Calif.: Stanford University Press, 1994); George Grantham, "The French Cliometric Revolution: A Survey of Cliometric Contributions to French Economic History," *European Review of Economic History* 1 (1997): 353–405; and Philip T. Hoffman and Jean-Laurent Rosenthal, "New Work in French Economic History," *French Historical Studies* 23 (2000): 439–53.

On the possible emergence of a "modern" political economy in this period, see (among other works) Judith A. Miller, *Mastering the Market: The State and the Grain Trade in Northern France, 1700–1860* (New York: Cambridge University Press, 1999); and, by the same author, "Economic Ideologies, 1750–1800: The Creation of the Modern Political Economy?" *French Historical Studies* 23 (2000): 497–511. Finally, the reader should again consult Florin Aftalion's conspectus on the economic history of the Revolution.

RELIGIOUS AND CULTURAL ISSUES

An indispensable starting point for readers interested in religious developments during the Revolution is André Latreille, *L'Eglise catholique et la Révolution française*, 2 vols. (Paris, Hachette, 1946–50). They may wish to follow this up with John McManners, *The French Revolution and the Church* (Westport, Conn.: Greenwood Press, 1982; orig. 1969). Ruth Necheles has examined the crucial role played by clerics at the start of the Revolution in "The Curés in the Estates General of 1789," *Journal of Modern History* 46 (1974): 425–44. For the impact of the Revolution upon French Catholicism in later years, see the following works: Michel Vovelle, *Religion et Révolution: La déchristianisation de l'an II* (Paris: Hachette, 1976); Timothy Tackett, *Religion, Revolution and Regional Conflict in Eighteenth-Century France: The Ecclesiastical Oath of 1791* (Princeton, N.J.: Princeton University Press, 1986); and Suzanne Desan, *Reclaiming the Sacred: Lay Religion and Popular Politics in Revolutionary France* (Ithaca, N.Y.: Cornell University Press, 1990). On the fate of Protestants during these years, refer to Burdette Poland, *French Protestantism and the French Revolution, 1685–1815* (Princeton, N.J.: Princeton University Press, 1957). Jews are discussed by Ruth Necheles in "L'Emancipation des Juifs, 1787–1795," *Annales historiques de la Révolution française* 48 (1976): 71–86, and by David Feuerwerker, *L'Emancipation des Juifs en France* (Paris: A. Michel, 1976).

For an impressive overview of cultural issues in the revolutionary era, see Emmet Kennedy, *A Cultural History of the French Revolution* (New Haven, Conn.: Yale University Press, 1989). Significant controversies involving symbolism and civic rituals during these years are treated in Mona Ozouf, *La Fête révolutionnaire, 1789–1799* (Paris: Gallimard, 1976); Maurice Agulhon, *Marianne into Battle: Republican Imagery and Symbolism in France, 1789–1880* (Cambridge: Cambridge University Press, 1981); Michel Vovelle, *La Mentalité révolutionnaire* (Paris: Messidor-Editions Sociales, 1985); and, more recently, Antoine de Baecque, *The Body Politic: Corporeal Metaphor in Revolutionary France, 1770–1800*, trans. Charlotte Mandell (Stanford, Calif.: Stanford University Press, 1997).

In a somewhat more traditional vein, Robert R. Palmer has traced educational developments through the revolutionary era in *The Improvement of Humanity: Education and the French Revolution* (Princeton, N.J.: Princeton University Press, 1985). Works on journalism in the 1790s include Jack R. Censer, *Prelude to Power: The Parisian Radical Press, 1789–1791* (Baltimore: Johns Hopkins University Press, 1976), and Jeremy Popkin, *The Right Wing Press in France, 1792–1800* (Chapel Hill: University of North Carolina Press, 1980). On science in the Revolution, see Joseph Fayet, *La Révolution française et la science, 1789–1795* (Paris: M. Rivière, 1960). Studies on medical progress in this period include David Vess, *Medical Revolution in France, 1789–1796* (Gainesville: University Press of Florida, 1975), and especially Toby Gelfand, *Professionalizing Modern Medicine* (Westport, Conn.: Greenwood Press, 1980). There are, in addition, a host of books treating literature, theater, and the other arts during the revolutionary era. Last but surely not least, the reader should at some point consult the wide array of essays in Keith Baker, François Furet, and Colin Lucas, eds., *The French Revolution and the Creation of Modern Political Culture*, 4 vols. (Oxford: Pergamon Press, 1987–94); and two important articles by Thomas E. Kaiser: "The Evil Empire? The Debate on Turkish Despotism in Eighteenth-Century French Political Culture," *Journal of Modern History*, 72 (2000): 6–34, and "Who's Afraid of Marie-Antoinette? Diplomacy, Austrophobia and the Queen," *French History* 14 (2000): 241–71.

Index

LaVergne, TN USA
29 December 2009
168335LV00006B/1/P

9 780521 009997